YUVAL MONOGRAPH SERIES
XII

The Hebrew University of Jerusalem • Faculty of Humanities
The Jewish Music Research Centre
In collaboration with the Jewish National and University Library

Academic Board of the Jewish Music Research Centre
Chairperson: Moshe Idel
Yom Tov Assis, Yoram Bilu, Don Harrán, Ruth Hacohen,
Galit Hasan-Rokem, Eliyahu Schleifer, Yoram Tsafrir

Director: Edwin Seroussi

Projects of the Jewish Music Research Centre
are made possible thanks to endowments from

The Szlama Czyzewski Memorial Fund for Liturgical Music;
The Lipman Fund, South Africa;
Dr. Paul Sacher, Basel

contributions from

A group of Friends of the Hebrew University in Italy,
established by the late Dr. Astorre Mayer, Milano;
The Esther Grunwald Memorial Fund;
The Toni and Noah Greenberg Memorial Endowment Fund,
established by the Estate of Jacob Perlow;
The Pinto Family Fund for Jewish Liturgical Music
in memory of Avraham Moses Pinto;
The Chemjo Vinaver Memorial Fund
established with the support of N. Goldman, J. Gruss and other.

and the additional support of

The Cantors Assembly Research and Publication Fund;
The Rabbi Milton Feist Fund Memorial Fund;
The A.Z. Idelsohn Memorial Fund, established by his daughters;
The Yehudi Menuhin Foundation, established by
the Friends of the Hebrew University in Belgium;
Maître Maurice Rheims, Paris;
The Alan and Leslie Rose Memorial Fund;
The Silvio Samamma Fund, The Netherlands;
The Fannie and Max Targ Research and Publication Fund;
The Elyakum Zunser Foundation.

RUTH KATZ

"The Lachmann Problem"
An Unsung Chapter in Comparative Musicology

Including Unpublished Letters and Lectures
of Robert Lachmann

THE HEBREW UNIVERSITY MAGNES PRESS, JERUSALEM

Distributed by The Hebrew University Magnes Press
P.O. Box 39099, Jerusalem 91390, Fax 972–2–5633370
E-mail: magneshl@pob.huji.ac.il

Cover illustration: The photograph of Felix Bonfils
courtesy of the Israeli Museum of Photograpy,
at Tel Hai Industrial Park, from the Museum's collection

©
All rights reserved by
The Hebrew University Magnes Press
Jerusalem 2003

ISSN 0334-3758

Printed in Israel
Typesetting: Art Plus, Jerusalem

CONTENTS

Preface   9

Prologue

Part One
The Protagonist: His Background and Social Milieu

Preliminaries	19
The End of the Republic	20
Post-War Sentiments: Highlights	21
Robert Lachmann: Representative of a Deceptive Ideal	24
Lachmann: A Member of the Berlin School of Comparative Musicology	29
The Uprooted	34

Part Two
"The University of the Jewish People"

The Jews and Higher Education	39
Liberalism, Civic Rights and Higher Education	40
The "Land of Israel": Place of Refuge, Cultural Center, or Both?	43
"The University of the Jewish People"	45
Assorting Commitments	47
Between an Envisaged Future and an Ambiguous Past	50
J. L. Magnes: First Chancellor of The Hebrew University	53

The Docudrama

Act I
Exploring New Hopes

Lachmann Makes Contact with The Hebrew University	56
A Revealing Correspondence	59

Act II
Dreams Confronted by Reality

Early Impressions	101
Getting Established	104
Shifting Concerns	127

Act III
Lachmann and Magnes: The Merging of Two Battles

Lachmann Summarizes his Enterprise	137
The *Zeitschrift* as "Catch 22"	153
The Reopening of the Lachmann Appointment	157
The Highlights of the Struggle	179
Gasping for Life Against the Current	199
Last Blows and their Aftermath	212
"Burial" and "Resurrection"	235

Epilogue

Part Three
Professional Success and Institutional Failure

Lachmann's Unchallenged Scholarly Standing	241
Shared Interests and Mutual Concerns	243
German Scholarship and the Development of American Musicology	253

Part Four
Finding a Genre that Fits

Tragedy, Religious Drama, or History in the Making?	274

Appendices
Documents, Letters and Lectures of Robert Lachmann

Appendix I:	Personal and Professional Documents from Germany	283
Appendix II:	"Liebe Eltern" – Robert Lachmann's Letters to his Parents (March 5–May 1, 1932)	303
Appendix III:	"Oriental Music": A Series of Twelve Talks on the Palestine Broadcasting Station (1936–1937) by Lachmann	328
Appendix IV:	Four Lectures on Eastern Music delivered at The International Association of University Women Palestine Branch	379

Musical Examples Recorded by Lachmann and Incorporated in his Radio Lectures "Oriental Music" (Supplement to Appendix III) 416

CD attached on back cover

PREFACE

The Lachmann Problem tells an unknown story about a well known musicologist. The name Robert Lachmann (1892–1939) is best known among musicologists whose interest centers on Arabic music, but the name is familiar, too, among all who take interest in the history of the discipline and, in particular, in the history of the Berlin School of Comparative Musicology established in the early decades of the last century. Among German musicologists, even those uninterested in the history of the discipline or in the subjects that interested Lachmann, he remains a well entrenched figure to this very day.

Together with his former teachers – Johannes Wolf, Curt Sachs, Georg Schünemann and Erich M. von Hornbostel – Lachmann established the *Gesellschaft zur Erforschung der Musik des Orients* (The Society for the Study of Oriental Music), a society that was deemed a worthy counterpart to Oriental studies in other domains. As one of the founding fathers of Comparative Musicology, and as the first and only editor of the *Zeitschrift für Vergleichende Musikwissenschaft* (The Journal of Comparative Musicology), Lachmann took part in the overall shaping of the scientific study of non-European music and was one of the key figures in charting its course.

Like most of his colleagues, Lachmann was a well rounded musicologist, privy to the major developments and scientific achievements of the discipline up to his time. The discipline was still relatively young in those days and encompassed a much smaller number of scholars than nowadays. The most prominent among these were in close contact and followed each other's work. Moreover, since musicology had not yet been guaranteed a place in institutions of higher learning, alongside other humanistic studies, they were imbued with a joint sense of mission. This relationship, however, was badly hurt with the rise of the Nazis to power. Musicology, like many other scientific endeavors in the early decades of the century, was disproportionately populated by German scholars, and a significant number of its outstanding members were of Jewish origin.

In a recent book with the suggestive title, *Most German of the Arts*, Pamela Potter examines musicology and society in Germany from the Weimar Republic to the end of Hitler's Reich. The author persuasively demonstrates how particular social, economic, and intellectual factors caused some German musicologists to support the ideological aims of the Nazis. In fact, many of the ideas that served the aims of the regime, the author claims, not only predated Hitler's rise to power, but survived the Nazi period to influence the conception of music history. Potter's well researched and exciting book unveils disturbing factors about a goodly number of musicologists who collaborated with the regime in one form or another and to various degrees. The list, unfortunately, also includes some of the key figures who are otherwise known for their outstanding scholarship and for the influence they exerted on the discipline and its development. Indeed, after reading Potter it is difficult to look unperturbed at the shelves in one's library.

Just as German scholarship, no doubt, influenced our conception of music history, the same sort of influence surely affected other scholarly fields as well. Having engaged in scientific study as diligently as the Germans, one can hardly expect them not to have had an influence both on the nature of subsequent investigations and on the scientific agenda, i.e., on what deserves to be investigated and in what order. That some of this influence should be undergoing careful scrutiny nowadays is hardly surprising. The atrocities committed alongside cultural and scientific achievements invites a reassessment not only of the personal behavior of people, but of their achievements as well. Indeed, the German case revealed, unambiguously, an *inverse* relationship between what was generally believed to be positively correlated, i.e., Culture (with a capital C) and culture, i.e., civilized human behavior. Much has already been written, and more will be forthcoming, in the attempt to unravel this paradox.

This incomprehensible phenomenon, no doubt, also contributed a significant share to the growing fear of the unchallenged supremacy of Western culture. Much of what is referred to as "Western ways of thinking" (including that of the Germans) continues, however, to pass unchallenged in the natural sciences, while in the social sciences and the humanities it has raised eyebrows in the past few decades. The natural scientists, in all likelihood, are better able to resist all kinds of corrective trends because the laws of nature are believed to be "there," independent of their descriptions, which in and of themselves *are* subject to change. But now that greater attention is being paid to cultures, populations and groups that have too long been overlooked, much of what was deemed to have universal standing no longer strikes us as such, resulting in all kinds of revisionist writings. The re-examination of German thought and its contribution to culture, while also part of this general trend, remains nonetheless quite unique. Ironically, it is the undeniable events associated with the Germans that reaffirm the limits of historical representation.

Like many other intellectuals of Jewish origin, Robert Lachmann lost his position with the rise of the Nazis to power. He had been employed in the music department of the Prussian State Library, and had no reason to expect "retirement," in the language of the letter of his dismissal. His new predicament, like that of many of his colleagues, entailed more than the loss of a source of livelihood, for it aimed to usurp the individual of his identity and status as a member of the society to which he belonged and with which he felt identified. Being ostracized from a society which one appreciated, trusted in, and believed oneself to have been an integral part, requires not only a reorientation to one's own life, but to all that made it worthwhile. Different people reacted in different ways to this new situation, yet all those who had fully imbibed German culture, all who had embraced its enlightened features, felt betrayed. Lachmann was one of them.

As is well known, a goodly number of German scholars of Jewish descent found their way to America. Compared to most European countries, America seemed like heaven. Moreover, America had by then developed an impressive infrastructure in many research fields, harboring great promise for future developments. Even if musicology was still in its infancy across the ocean, considering the trying times, hope emanated from the New World for all of the disillusioned, regardless of occupation and fields of interest. As we now know, the uprooted musicologists who landed in America contributed greatly to the development of the field in their newly-adopted country, yet the historical unfolding that accompanied this development is rarely discussed, nor has it been thoroughly investigated.

Lachmann's interest in non-European music made the promise of Palestine more alluring than a sheer place of refuge. Given its varied population, Palestine seemed like an ideal laboratory in which he could both continue his inquiries into Arabic music and add the study of other ancient Eastern traditions, some of which might even throw new light on the historical development of Western music. He had a very sound basis for expecting an appointment as a full member of the faculty at the newly-established University in Palestine. Had this materialized, he could have established the music department of his dreams, one that would have met his accustomed high standards, while taking full advantage of the special character of its locale and its unique research potential. The research Lachmann had in mind dictated, among other things, the establishment of a well-documented Sound Archive that would not only serve students and researchers, but would constitute a repository of disappearing musical traditions. Were this the case, he could transfer to Jerusalem the activities of The Journal of Comparative Musicology, of which he was still the editor, and possibly obtain some desired copies of the recordings of the Berlin *Phonogrammarchive* – an archive to which he himself had contributed a sizable amount. "Jerusalem," Lachmann consoled himself, "was after all a more suitable place for the study of Eastern musical traditions!" Taking into account his scholarly standing and his wide-spread professional connections, Lachmann even entertained the thought that diligence and prudence, based on a proper infrastructure and assiduous research training, might draw attention to Jerusalem to the point of turning the historic city into *the* center for the study of non-European music.

These were no idle dreams; it all seemed quite feasible at the time. Despite all the signs given by the new regime in Germany, nobody, but nobody, could clearly and assuredly decode what has become self-evident in retrospect, not even the Nazis, not knowing themselves how far they would go in order to achieve their objectives. But there was plenty of push, even then. On the side of the pull, there was a University, with high academic aspirations, that came into being in no small measure as an answer to the needs of those students and scholars who were rejected by other institutions of higher learning, because of their Jewish origin. Moreover, "The University of the Jewish People" *had* to excel, not only because some outstanding scholars were Jews, but because the University was eager to contribute a significant share to the underpinnings so urgently needed for the establishment of a *viable* Jewish state in the *ancient* homeland. This University, clearly, was no less interested in the "archeology" of the Past than it was concerned with the "structuring" of the Future. In fact, bridging between the two was the order of the day. Though hardly motivated by Zionist ideology, the aims of the institution struck Lachmann as compatible with his own situation as with his scientific interests. Having been forced, only recently, to become more conscious of his Jewish affiliation, Lachmann knew very little about the actual struggles the University was facing, but for reasons that seemed obvious, he was quite confident that he would be welcomed with open arms.

However reasonable the expectations, and however compatible with the aims of the new institution, the Hebrew University was in no position to absorb all of those who in their desperation turned to it, hoping to be invited to join. Moreover, this newly-established institution was eager to follow its own agenda – priorities arrived at after long, strenuous and heated debates. Nevertheless, the University could not be oblivious to scholars who sought refuge in Palestine, many of whom needed the University more than the University needed them. Under disquieting world political circumstances – the full meaning of which was not yet apparent – and endless local financial difficulties, the University made room for some who were highly recommended and, somehow, suited its own overall plans.

Lachmann, of course, was not in want of recommendations. Furthermore, the then Chancellor of the University, J. L. Magnes, was eager to have him. Many University officials and staff members, however, did not share Magnes's enthusiasm. While their lack of enthusiasm was partially due to a misunderstanding of Lachmann's interests, it was primarily based on a conception which regarded the unfamiliar field of musicology as a "luxury" which the University could ill afford at the time. In fact, the negotiations that took place, even before Lachmann set foot in Palestine, tell an interesting story about a pioneering society and an academic institution that was too busy inventing itself to make room for scholars whom, in retrospect, it could hardly have afforded to overlook. Of course, speculations based on hindsight distort the view current at the time, and its very different historical context.

With the tiresome negotiations behind him, Lachmann was pleased finally to land in Palestine. Full of hope and renewed energy, he looked forward to an adventure which seemed to harbor exciting promise. Without suspecting the kinds of struggle he was yet to face, he was caught, from the outset, in an intricate historical web which he was in no position to avoid. Rejected by the culture which he imbibed, Lachmann found himself in a situation which forced him to confront *himself* in ways he had never entertained before. Ironically, Lachmann's personal struggle coincided with the struggle of the man who had invited him, the American reform rabbi, J. L. Magnes – the first Chancellor of the University. While Lachmann was struggling to achieve the identities that Magnes symbolized for him, Magnes himself was reexamining their worth for himself! Both before and after Lachmann's arrival, Magnes had offered his support and encouragement, enlisting the help of donors, from among the American Friends of the Hebrew University, on behalf of "the worthy scholar who failed to be included in the University's regular budget." Unfortunately, the harder he tried to accommodate Lachmann, the more opposition he encountered from his immediate surroundings. Similarly, the more Lachmann adapted himself to the needs of the society which he came to appreciate and genuinely respect, the more he was evaded by the people he was eager to serve. The Promised Land clearly failed him. Having chosen to go to Palestine, Lachmann's predicament there adds a chapter to the predicament of many professionals who were betrayed by their native cultures but failed to be absorbed adequately by the culture to which they turned.

While the Lachmann File (in the University archive), together with his personal files (in The Jewish National and University Library), provide interesting historical documents that concern Lachmann, they also contain much else. In fact, his methodical record keeping, extensive correspondence and elaborate memos provide a comprehensive picture of the early days of Comparative Musicology. Indeed, the files provide an intimate view of the founders of the new enterprise – their aims, assumptions, scientific methods, etc. – and of the social-political milieu in which they labored, from World War I through the Weimar Republic. During this period, contacts were established with scholars in other countries who shared their interests, including the American pioneers in the field. In addition, the files also render a picture of life in Palestine during the thirties, in particular of the Jewish population which was busy striking new/old roots. Though spiritually and intellectually equipped to know better, this population, like many of the German Jews, failed to anticipate the pending catastrophe. All of this, and more, comes to the fore in the voluminous documents which Lachmann preserved, thereby providing us with a solid frame for the present study.

Many of these documents are incorporated in the present volume. They provide new information on the early stages of Comparative Musicology and offer new insights into the thinking of its founding fathers. Others of these documents betray the daily routines, working style and methodology, as well as the unanticipated hardships which Lachmann encountered. These are embedded in letters to parents, correspondence with former colleagues, progress reports and petitions to academic and bureaucratic authorities, and several brilliant attempts to introduce non-European music to Europeans, but also to Orientals – Arabs and Jews alike – who were urged to prize their musical heritage. All of these sources are drawn upon extensively, but it is important to emphasize, however, that the documents were chosen primarily for their relevance to *The Lachmann Problem.* They focus, above all, on the heretofore *unsung* chapter in the history of the field which epitomizes Lachmann's trying times.

Lachmann died in 1939, only four years after his arrival in Palestine. Unsettled by historical circumstances, this brilliant, systematic scholar was trapped at a crossroads of history that wrested his life beyond any choosing. "Fate lurking at the crossroads" well describes the Lachmann case. The case may be read as personal tragedy, or as the pangs of the uprooted, or even as religious drama. History tolerates many layers. Unveiling the forces which were operative *at one and the same time* at a critical moment gives insight into that which eluded the actors performing their parts. Thus, *The Lachmann Problem,* I hope, will tell several of these tales, all of which meet unwarranted punishment on their protagonist.

In a sense, the book bears some resemblance to a docudrama which seeks deeper meaning in documents that might otherwise be expected to speak for themselves. While the documents that relate to his scientific work (including reference to his many-sided publications) provide raw material for the study of the foundations of the field, they also provide deep insight into his painful situation. By organizing and contextualizing these documents – valuable, in themselves, to fellow professionals – this essay will reveal the conflicts inherent in a situation of a lone scholar having to missionize for his profession in an alien culture and in an impossible organizational context. Such a situation requires all sides to spell out their beliefs, or, more often, their competing commitments. But it is thanks to these awkward, almost absurd dialogues that such enlightening material came into existence!

It is for these reasons that the book virtually begs for dramatic form. Accordingly, the central section of the book is divided into Acts so as to allude to the tragic web in which Lachmann was caught. They enact the anxiety that accompanied the redefinition of self that was imposed upon him, as well as the tensions produced by his tenacious adherence to his professed mission. These are preceded by a two-part prologue that sets the stage. The first part discusses the "protagonist's" background and the social milieu from which he was evicted, while the second provides the background of the institution to which he turned in hope. After the curtain is drawn, a two-part epilogue follows: the first celebrates Lachmann's scholarly triumph despite personal afflictions, while the second examines the dynamics of history in terms of theatrical genres.

While the drama draws heavily on documents – including the letters to parents, correspondence with former colleagues, reports and petitions to academic authorities, and the several attempts to valorize indigenous musical traditions – the interested reader is also offered an unmediated impression of the man and the scholar in four appendixes that are attached. The first contains diverse documents, meticulously filed by Lachmann, relating to his personal and professional situation in Germany, including the list of individuals and institutions who subscribed to the journal he edited.

The three remaining appendixes are in Lachmann's own words. One of them contains the telling series of letters Lachmann wrote to his parents from his last (1932) extended field expedition, while the others consist of twelve radio talks on Oriental Music and four lectures on Eastern Music respectively. In these heretofore unpublished talks, Lachmann addresses a lay audience whom he tries to educate and persuade. He would say no less to a contemporary audience, for whom the problem of understanding is no less acute, even if there is a newly-raised consciousness of the "other" (and the "self"). While his cultural-anthropological approach to non-European music no longer strikes us as novel, and much that he tells us is well known by now, his expositions remain unique. Yet, it is the knowledgeable and already convinced who stand to learn most from them, for they masterfully display the inter-relationships between detail and synthesis, between scientific exactitude and the need to understand.

To repeat, although Lachmann occupies center stage in this Life as Theater, he serves us primarily as a pivot that provides insight into the subtle and convoluted ways in which historical circumstances affect personal predicaments that, in turn, harbor implications for the development of cultural and scientific endeavor. While the book covers much of Lachmann's biography and discusses the initial stages of Comparative Musicology – highlighting its aims, objectives and methods of inquiry – it is neither a full-fledged biography of Lachmann nor a comprehensive history of the early stages of the field. Rather, by positioning Lachmann at the cross-roads that affected his life and scientific work, it wishes to re-emphasize the relevance of *particular* junctions, i.e., distinct historical contexts, not ideologies, to the development of scientific work, whether at the individual, organizational, or institutional levels. However strongly one feels about the scholarly proclivities of the Jews, there can be no denying that the specific circumstances that governed their lives in the thirties and forties of the last century bore directly on the paths and nature of their self definition and cultural creativity.

Ruth Katz

The Hebrew University of Jerusalem

Prologue

PART ONE
THE PROTAGONIST: HIS BACKGROUND AND SOCIAL MILIEU

Preliminaries

A letter dated September 19, 1933, reached Robert Lachmann on a regular work day at the Prussian State Library in Berlin. The letter was from the Ministry of Science, Art and National Education informing him of his "retirement."[1] Born November 1892, the letter, on the face of it, seemed somewhat premature. He had no reason to assume that it was one of those elegant ways in which the authorities, whether the director of the library or the ministry, express their dissatisfaction with his professional performance. After all, he had repeatedly enjoyed their goodwill and confidence as a qualified librarian and devoted civil servant. Not so long ago, the ministry even saw fit to appoint him a member of the library's advisory council.[2] Still, he could not for long maintain that the letter he received was some kind of administrative blunder, for he received a subsequent one, a week later, this time from the director of the library himself, repeating the content of the previous one, with an added formal statement promising "forthcoming information" concerning financial arrangements.[3]

Though confounded, he did not challenge the decision to get rid of him; it seemed pretty final. He had formerly dismissed what seemed like distorted stories of other such cases, trusting it could not happen to him. Now, however, he was eagerly awaiting further information, shifting his attention from his position at the library to the basic question of livelihood.

1   See document 1, appendix I
2   Document 2, appendix I
3   Document 3, appendix I

Could the latter be handled as carelessly and irrationally as was his dismissal? Definitely not, not in the Germany he knew, grew up in, and was part of.

As expected, the Construction and Finance Office in Berlin *did* come through and was extremely accurate in its calculations regarding his pension (based on his pension fund and years of service). Yet these two miserable months of waiting seemed endless, marked by a kind of restlessness which he had never experienced before. He felt relieved, therefore, when he finally received the letter from the director of the library, as promised, relaying the information concerning his pension. The letter was dispatched December 30, 1933.[4]

The End of the Republic

The year 1933 was no ordinary year in Germany; it was experienced as such by all who contributed to making it so, and all who bore its consequences. On January 30 that year, Hitler, by entirely legal means, became chancellor of the German republic. The Nationalists, with whom the Nazis still shared power, did not occupy positions in the new cabinet for long, since Hitler, shortly thereafter, called for another election (March 1933) that would yield more decisive results. A week before election day the Nazis set the Reichstag on fire, blaming the Communists for the "tragic" event, raising a terrific scare throughout the land. Though the Nazis won only 44% of the vote, Hitler assumed dictatorial powers as a measure of "national emergency." Thus 1933 marked the end of the Weimar Republic and the beginning of the Third Reich which, unlike the Holy Roman Empire (the First Reich) or the empire founded by Bismarck (the Second Reich), was "prophesied" by Hitler to last a thousand years!

It takes much effort to make prophecies come true. Hitler, certainly, did not mince effort. Grandiose visions are not commonplace, nor were his. After all, the National Socialist German Workers Party, which he

---

[4] Document 4, appendix I

headed, represented a *revolutionary* movement that aimed to cure the ills that befell Germany after her defeat in World War I. In fact, the National Socialists had obtained a considerable following as early as 1919, but the Weimar government, denounced by the Workers Party for its shameful submission to post-war conditions, managed, for a while, to arrest the German loathing of the Treaty of Versailles. It was the Social Democrats, reinforced by the Catholic Center Party and other moderates (who were, by then, more afraid of the Left than of the Right, in light of the stories brought out of Russia), who drew up the constitution for a democratic republic at the city of Weimar, which was to last from 1919 to 1932.

Post-War Sentiments: Highlights

While only a small number of Germans would have voted for a republic in 1914, moderate socialists, agrarians and nationalists, after the war, had to contend with reactionaries and members of the old aristocracy, on the one hand, and deal with real revolutionaries, on the other hand. The air of progressive democracy pervaded almost all of Europe after the war; even the victors had to face demobilized soldiers who found themselves unemployed and restless. Neither Russian communism nor historic Western capitalism seemed to provide respectable answers. A middle course, involving some moderate planning on a national level, seemed to harbor a promise for a modicum of economic security and social stability. Everywhere the demand was for security. Each state tried, as far as possible, to live economically within itself, even the newly-carved post-war states. In an uncontrolled market, nations were planning their own economic systems according to advanced principles of the welfare state and social democracy.

The Weimar Republic was in principle highly democratic, but very remote from anything socialistic. No industries were nationalized, no agrarian reforms were undertaken (as in the new states of eastern Europe), no property changed hands. There was almost no confiscation; even the property of the Kaiser was not confiscated. Moreover, in the republic of which the Social Democrats were the main supporters, officials of imperial

Germany – civil servants, police agents, educators and countless others – remained at their respective posts side-by-side with the implementation of devices then favored by the most advanced democracies. Even the old army, though vastly reduced, remained essentially intact, with officers from predominantly aristocratic families. Changes *were* introduced, but without terror and fanaticism, creating the illusion, inside and outside of Germany, that the Germans had accepted the rule of democracy.

Yet the Weimar Republic, no less than the Treaty of Versailles, was a product of the defeat of Germany in the war. While there were many in the republic who genuinely favored democracy, very few, even among the Social Democrats, accepted the treaty and the new German frontiers as either just or final. Economic distress or any other hardship, which could be ascribed to the treaty, could easily threaten the newly-established regime and the appeal of democracy. In fact, if the American Dawes Plan had not been issued (a plan which made it possible for the republic to borrow money abroad to assure the flow of reparations from Germany to the Allies and from the Allies to the United States), the inflation of the early twenties (caused by the French insistence on German reparation payments) might have destroyed the republic as early as 1923. By wiping out all outstanding indebtedness within the country, however, the inflation made it possible to start afresh. American investments in German government bonds and industrial enterprises helped, in no small measure, to put Germany on its feet again, resulting in several years of prosperity. But the glorious days of the republic (so experienced by many after the turbulence of the war, the impact of the October Revolution, and recent memories of the inflation) were accompanied by a seething undercurrent that would soon surface again with the depression of 1929, paving the road for the National Socialist Worker's Party to seize power in 1933.

Though World War I dealt a mortal blow to the ancient institutions of monarchy and aristocratic feudalism, marking a victory for democracy and the right of national self-determination, it gave no answers to the basic problems of modern civilization – industrialism, nationalism, insecurity and competitive struggle. Even while democracy was advancing, business and propertied interests that lived in terror of communism favored Mussolini and endowed him with dictatorial powers. Although Italy had enjoyed parliamentary liberalism since 1861, he denounced democracy as historically outmoded, claiming that it accentuated class struggle and selfishness, that it split nations into countless parties engaged in empty talk. The evils of society, according to Mussolini, are offsprings of liberalism which, in the final analysis, undermines national solidarity. National solidarity and state-management of economic affairs, he preached, call for vigorous action under a strong and efficient leader.

Fascism thus came to be regarded as a possible alternative to parliamentary government, as a corrective to problems whose reality no one could deny. Unlike Mussolini, Hitler was never a socialist, nor did he suffer from intellectual pretensions, but like a good pupil he absorbed the lesson taught by Mussolini, adding a few observations of his own to the list of evils his teacher set out to cure. He neither liked the trappings of nobility nor the mixed nationalities of the former empire. He despised international Marxism and above all the Jews who had become assimilated into German culture and, thanks to a century of liberal influences, had attained many distinguished positions in business as well as the free professions. Without the Depression Hitler might have faded from history; the circumstances attending the Depression, however, gave him unlimited power. Beclouding all issues, he favored the "right kind of socialism" for the little man, members of the *volk* – "pure Germans." The Jews, who were found in all political camps, became anathema because of Jewish capitalists, and a horror because of Jewish revolutionaries, not to mention the fact that none of them could be considered "pure Germans." In anti-Semitism, Hitler found the lowest common denominator with which to appeal to all parties and classes. Anti-Semitism, however, no matter how prevalent, neither explains the rise of the Nazis to power, nor their success in retaining it as long as they did. The yearning of most Germans for some kind of national rehabilitation, which Hitler seemed to embody, is what blinded the masses, and converted even those who did not like his methods. Anti-Semitism, at this stage, did not constitute *the cause*; it served as an effective instrument. But even as instrument, the Nazis only gradually increased the severity of its application, not knowing themselves how far it would lead.

How a common denominator so low could succeed not only to rally the masses but even to silence the custodians of justice and enlightened thought in the country of Goethe and Schiller – illustrious citizens of the city of Weimar – remains debatable to this day; it certainly worked "wonders" in World War II, for which the thirties were but a prelude. One thing cannot be denied, however: Culture (with a capital C) is evidently no guarantor of either individual or social sanity. But who knew in those trying days what is common knowledge nowadays? It must be remembered that the facts of the pre-war crises were then largely unknown, nor could the sickest mind conjure up what was yet to come. When World War I came to an end, people were trapped in a nightmare whose causes they could not comprehend; they reveled in slanted portrayals of the enemy, indulging themselves in unwarranted self-righteousness for comfort.

Much has been written on those bewildering days which enabled Hitler to ride the wave of mass discontent in Germany, and much will still be written. However, at the close of the century, there was no doubt in the minds of historians that the aftermath of World War I goes a long way towards explaining the crucial factors that precipitated World War II. With the Russian Revolution in their midst, the two World Wars led, as we all know, to the subsequent Cold War and to the eventual collapse of the USSR. The list of major events that mark the century would be incomplete, however, without mention of the *Jewish* state. More than the fulfillment of an age-old dream, the establishment of the State of Israel in 1948 represents a brief moment of soul-searching and penitence. The horrendous atrocities committed on the Jews in World War II made people cognizant, more than ever before, of the enormity of evil of which man is capable.

Robert Lachmann: Representative of a Deceptive Ideal

Of Jewish descent, Robert Lachmann, born in Berlin, lived his early childhood in an enlightened bourgeois world – comfortable, hospitable and friendly. His father Dr. Georg Lachmann, teacher at a humanistic gymnasium, gave his three children the education expected of *gebildete Menschen* (well-bred people). Perhaps because his mother had been born in England, Robert pursued his linguistic studies not only in German universities but in England as well. Thus, within the confines of his family, he breathed the air of cosmopolitanism and discovered the world of *Bildung* with its ideals of humanism, reason, self-discipline, liberalism, pluralism and aesthetic sensibility. *Bildung*, so cherished by the greater part of German Jews after the emancipation, went beyond the separate histories of Germans and Jews, emphasizing the unifying factors that transcend nationality and religion.[5] This kind of universalism was logically coupled with achievement, with implications for individualism (rather than collectivism), relationships that are role-specific (rather than diffuse), and affective neutrality (rather than affectivity). All these describe the liberal ideals which, to begin with, enabled Jews to become part of German culture and which ultimately gave them (at least the well-educated) the feeling that they had actually succeeded.

If there were any areas of special Jewish concentration in Germany these were in liberal causes, both national and universal, and in areas of newness created by industrial society where rationality was the rule and achievement could be measured. This became even more pronounced in the second generation after emancipation, with the movement away from business, banking and the like to the professions, the liberal arts and academic pursuits. Whether the Jewish heritage gives advantage in these areas is a separate question. Centuries of mandatory literacy, Talmudic mind grinding, and perpetual struggle to survive in alien and mostly hostile environments, are often brought forth, by enemies and friends alike, to explain the acumen attributed to Jews, whether in finance and commerce, politics and reform, or endeavors of an academic nature. Moreover, much insight has been attributed to the Jews *because* of their marginality, which supposedly enabled them to gain the kind of overview, difficult to achieve otherwise.

---

5 See George L. Mosse, *German Jews beyond Judaism* (Bloomington, 1985); David Sorkin, "Wilhelm von Humboldt: The Theory and Practice of Self-Formation (*Bildung*), 1791–1810," *Journal of the History of Ideas* 44 (January 1983): 55–73; Uriel Tal, *Christians and Jews in Germany: Religion, Politics and Ideology in the Second Reich, 1870–1914* (Ithaca and London, 1974). Also see Abraham J. Peck (ed.), *The German-Jewish Legacy in America, 1938–1988: From Bildung to the Bill of Rights* (Detroit, 1989).

Whatever the case, the Jewish attraction to intellectual and artistic worlds, for which Germans were widely thought to be peculiarly fit, is better explained by the fact that they conceived these as transcending particularistic traditions. Paradoxically, however, as we now know, rather than becoming ethnically invisible by entering those fields, Jewish concentration made their presence all the more noticeable and vulnerable. It is no coincidence, therefore, that the cultural domain was the first from which Jews were massively expelled after the elections of March 1933.[6] Debasing the Jewish spirit seems, in retrospect, to have prepared the ground for their subsequent corporeal extermination.

Many responded to these first hints; the list of Jewish artists and intellectuals who left Germany early in 1933 comprises some of the most impressive figures of the very culture they decided to flee. The list, however, included non-Jews as well, not only left-wingers, but all sorts of people who disapproved and feared what was taking place in their country. Many Eastern European Jews were also prone to disregard comforting remarks uttered, among others, by their German Jewish compatriots, and managed to get out of Germany in time to save their bodies and souls. But the majority of German Jews wanted desperately to believe that the terrors they encountered represented the actions of a fringe group that had gone mad, so trusting had they become of the culture they had adopted.

It is important to remember that, between the two World Wars, the Jews constituted only one percent of the German population. Few though they were, they did not perceive the rise of Nazism in a unified way, nor react in a unified manner, but none had the knowledge that hindsight and hard study have given us today. Jews, as a whole, continued to live in hope and confidence long beyond understandable limits. If an ethic of universalism and achievement had actually been established – that is, if

---

6 Saul Friedländer, *Nazi Germany and the Jews.* See "Into the Third Reich," in *The Years of Persecution* (New York, 1997), 1, chap. 1. Also see Peter Gay, *Freud, Jews and Other Germans: Masters and Victims in Modernist Culture* (New York, 1978); Jacob Katz, *The Darker Side of Genius: Richard Wagner's Anti-Semitism* (New England, 1986); Frederic V. Grunfeld, *Prophets Without Honor* (New York, 1979).

the ideal had become real, as most German Jews, including the Lachmann family, wanted to believe – things would have gone better. But as it turned out, German society deviated, to say the least, from the liberal model, reaching perverted dimensions in the thirties and forties.

Of the major organizations of Jews in Germany, the various *jüdische Gemeinden* (Jewish communities, that were publicly recognized as "corporations under public law"), seemed least capable of fighting against the rising menace. The *Central-Verein Deutscher Staatsbürger Jüdischen Glauben* (the Central Organization of German Citizens of Jewish Belief – the C.V.), *the* representative organization of German Jews, was also ineffective in its reaction to the changing tide, probably because it had accepted, as a liberal and liberating idea, the reduction of Jewish historic consciousness to that of a mere religious identity. Led, since its inception in the 1890s, by prosperous middle class intellectuals with a liberal orientation, the C.V. opted for German liberal national lines far too long, unaware that they had turned sour. In rejecting the Eastern Jews, whose number had increased considerably following World War I, the C.V. distanced itself primarily from their "folkish ways," endorsing, instead, trends prevalent in the society at large. By the end of the 1920s, the C.V. had fully accepted the Weimar Republic, and had also come to consider it the culmination of Jewish civic emancipation. Its perception of anti-Semitism, therefore, remained primarily rationalistic and intellectual.[7] The Zionists, on the other hand, viewed the Jews as a *national* group (with group values, cohesion and consciousness), placing the "Jewish problem" in a worldwide context; the return of Jews to their own homeland in Palestine seemed an optimal solution to their abnormal condition. In fact, the liberalism professed by the majority of German Jews was their major opponent. While liberalism owed much to the higher German cultural tradition that was rooted in the enlightenment, Zionism shared roots with other forms of 19th century European nationalism, inspired by

---

7   See Herbert A. Strauss, "Essays on the History, Persecution, and Emigration of German Jews," 6 in *Jewish Immigrants of the Nazi Period in the USA* (New York, 1987), pp. 79–94.

romanticism. It was liberalism, however, which enabled the Jews to get out from their ghettos, not the two millennia of longing for Zion.

In 1911, Lachmann enlisted for a year to serve his country; he did so of his own free will.[8] He had good reason to feel patriotic. He had just passed his *Abitur* (qualifying exams for higher education) with flying colors, causing great satisfaction, not only to his parents, but to himself as well. The achievement could not be overestimated, since the requirements of the humanistic gymnasium were, to begin with, very high, making those who were accepted feel they belonged to a select group. But now...; yes, there was no question in his mind that he had made it. This feeling was enhanced, paradoxically, by the fact that, unlike vocational and trade schools, the humanistic gymnasium only gave a *perpaedeutic* education. It was an education, however, for which one had good reason to be grateful.

At the outbreak of World War I, Lachmann, naturally, enlisted in the army. By then he had not only studied English and French on a university level, but Arabic as well. He was greatly disappointed when in 1916 he was sent back from the front, due to illness, to serve as an interpreter in a prisoner-of-war camp at Wünsdorf (Brandenburg). Little did he know how vast an influence this new experience would have on his professional life. The camp contained North African and Indian soldiers from the French and British armies, who, off duty, resorted to their own milieu including their traditional musical repertoires. Having been exposed to music from early childhood (he was a fine musician and violinist), Lachmann became fascinated by the unfamiliar sounds he heard. This was his first encounter with non-European music. So interested and involved did he become that he not only listened to the prisoners' songs, but transcribed them as well. The Arab music of North Africa, as we now know, eventually became the central field of his research endeavors. While Lachmann was still at camp, these transcriptions drew the attention of scholars like Johanness Wolf, Curt Sachs, Erich M. von Hornbostel and Georg Schünemann – pioneers of the Berlin School of ethnomusicology – who, unlike Lachmann at the

---

8   Document 5, appendix I.

time, were aware of Robert Lach's work, a Viennese musicologist who was collecting the songs sung by Russian war prisoners in Austria.[9]

Lachmann: A Member of the Berlin School of Comparative Musicology

The so-called Berlin School was essentially interested in the *comparative* aspects of the study of music. Like all comparisons, the music of different cultures was expected to reveal commonalties, while highlighting differences, or the other way round. Comparative musicology, in fact, sought after the uniqueness of music as a universal human expression, no less than its different manifestations. The comparative aspects go a long way to explain both the scholarly network which it succeeded to create, spreading far beyond Berlin, as well as the attentiveness of its members to methodological questions. The network consisted primarily of a subgroup of musicologists – with the addition of some psychologists, anthropologists, and others – who took an interest in non-European music, attempting to apply scientific rigor to the study of the *unfamiliar*. It is so easy to fall into the trap of understanding other people by one's own criteria, but what passes unnoticed within one's own culture becomes extremely prominent across cultures, requiring special attention and care.

The interest in remote cultures, including their music, has, of course, a long history. Missionaries, explorers, colonialists, and numerous others contributed greatly to making Europeans aware of ways of life other than their own. The prominence gained by the *Vergleichende Musikwissenschaft* around World War I and through the Weimar Republic, however, may be attributed to the specific social-political conditions that affected the various

---

[9] See Edith Gerson-Kiwi, "Robert Lachman: His Achievement and His Legacy," *Yuval*, III (Jerusalem, 1974), pp. 100–103. Also see Dieter Christensen, "Erich M. von Hornbostel, Carl Stumpf, and the Institutionalization of Comparative Musicology," Bruno Nettl and Philip V. Bohlman (eds.), *Comparative Musicology and Anthropology of Music* (Chicago, 1991), pp. 201–209, and Robert Lach, *Gesänge russischer Kriegsgefangener* (Vienna, 1926). Preliminary reports appeared in 1917 and 1918.

empires, as well as the changed status of the colonies under their rule, calling greater attention to their existence. While remote worlds had before been ignored or taken for granted, they were now brought home and widely discussed, gaining the kind of saliency which they had never enjoyed. To this one must add the developments that had taken place in the field of musicology around the turn of the century, making the field, more and more, into an academic discipline. Nor should technological developments be ignored.

We neither wish to trace the historical development of musicology nor that of ethnomusicology; it has been done by others and more is yet to be done.[10] As in the study of history at large, specific developments are traced and retraced, yielding continuously new information. Histories of all kinds are made by historians, no less than the other way round. The study of historians, moreover, adds to the history of what is being studied. It is a continuous process which shapes and reshapes our understanding of the past. Since vision *and* revision are an integral part of history, the understanding of any given moment on this continuum requires the unveiling of its own contiguity and contingencies. Logical as this may sound, it is often disregarded by those who want to take an active part in changing the course of events; in their attempts to affect the future, they tend, wittingly or unwittingly, to distort the past. The attempt here, at any rate, is to position Robert Lachmann at the unique junction, the crossroads, as it were, that affected his life, activities and untimely death in Palestine.

After what has been said so far, it should not come as a surprise that Lachmann in 1929, at the height of the Depression, saw fit to address two

---

10 For comparative musicology see, for example, Erich M. von Hornbostel, "The Problems of Comparative Musicology," eds. and transl. Klaus Wachsmann, et al., *Hornbostel Opera Omnia* (The Hague, 1975), pp. 249–270, "Carl Stumpf und die vergleichende Musikwissenschaft," *Zeitschrift für Vergleichende Musikwissenschaft* 1 (1933): 22–28, "Das Berliner Phonogrammarchiv," *Zeitschrift für Vergleichende Musikwissenschaft* 1 (1933): 40–45; Curt Sachs, *Vergleichende Musikwissenschaft, 2. neu bearbeitete Auflage* (Heidelberg, 1959); Walter Wiora, *Ergebnisse und Aufgaben vergleichender Musikforschung* (Darmstadt, 1975); Alan P. Merriam, "Definitions of Comparative Musicology and Ethnomusicology: An Historical-Theoretical Perspective," *Ethnomusicology* 21 (1977): 189–204.

seemingly unrelated issues. The first pertained to a nuisance he had to get rid of, while the second concerned his identity, now that he was professionally committed to the study of music. Encouraged by Stumpf and Hornbostel (following his prisoners-of-war experience), he had studied musicology under Johannes Wolf and Stumpf and obtained a doctorate (1922), with a dissertation on urban Tunisian music.[11] Since then, he had undertaken several extended recording expeditions to North Africa, visiting Tripoli (1925), Tunisia (1926/1927), Kabylia (1927), Tunisia again (1929), the Isle of Djerba and Morocco (1929). All of these expeditions resulted not only in valuable recordings, which he deposited in the *Berlin Phonogrammarchiv*, headed by Hornbostel at that time, but in numerous publications as well.[12] The year 1929 was an especially fruitful year, for he had managed to publish that year not only his *Musik des Orients,* but also to contribute a major piece to the Bücken Handbook on the music of "non-European civilizations."[13] With all of these behind him, now was the time to take care of two small matters he had somehow neglected, but should have attended to earlier: 1) to step out, in a certified manner, from the *jüdische Gemeinde* (October 31, 1929),[14] doing finally away with a troublesome nuisance, and 2) to engage in an autobiographical sketch which would include a vivid description of the life at the prisoners' camp, where he performed his duty to the *Vaterland*![15]

However tricky and convoluted the paths of history, and regardless of the degree of human folly, could anybody as much as suspect the enormity of the deception that fate had in store? In Greek tragedy, Man always pays beyond his guilt, blinded by circumstances that are not within his

---

11 See Robert Lachmann, "Die Musik in den tunesischen Städten," *Archiv für Musikwissenschaft* 5 (1923): 136–171.
12 See Edith Gerson-Kiwi, "Robert Lachmann: His Achievement and His Legacy," op. cit.
13 Robert Lachmann, *Musik des Orients* (Breslau, 1929); idem, "Die Musik der aussereuropäischen Natur und Kulturvölker," *Handbuch der Musikwissenschaft* (Potsdam, 1929).
14 Document 6, appendix I.
15 Robert Lachmann, *Autobiography* in "Briefe unserer Autoren über ihre Werke," *Hirts literaturbericht* 66–67 (Breslau and Leipzig, 1929), pp. 941–942.

control. Astute as the great tragedians were, even those familiar with their works cannot draw instructive lessons from them, dealing, as the tragedians essentially did, with the condition of man *as* Man. Can one blame more mundane role players for failing to perceive *their* parts in a tragedy that will yet outdo all tragedies? However bizarre in retrospect, yes, Lachmann continued with business as usual, pleased to have been employed as a librarian at the music department of the Berlin State Library (1927–1933) and overjoyed by the attention he received from his colleagues.

In 1930 the *Gesellschaft zur Erforschung der Musik des Orients* (The Society for the Study of Oriental Music) was formed under the guidance of Johannes Wolf, Curt Sachs, Georg Schünemann, Erich M. Hornbostel and Lachmann himself. He had, by then, not only become a full fledged colleague of his former teachers, but the first editor of the *Zeitschrift für Vergleichende Musikwissenschaft* (Journal of Comparative Musicology), an international annual, which they had founded at the same time. The initial list of subscribers included ethnographic museums, institutes of various kinds, university libraries, and practically all of the, already then, renowned musicologists, and some who would become famous later on.[16] It is amazing how extensive a network these diligent scholars were able to create. It spread beyond Germany, or, for that matter, beyond Europe, to encompass musicologists as well as other interested parties – anthropologists, psychologists, folklorists, and natural scientists of sorts, who approached the subject from different perspectives, and who contributed their share to the consolidation and definition of the discipline.

Given his expertise, Lachmann was also asked to head the *Phonogramme Kommission* at the first International Congress of Arabic Music, held in Cairo in 1932. The congress was attended by artists representing many Arabic countries and music centers. Under Lachmann's supervision, their performances were expertly recorded. It should be borne in mind that recording was not a simple matter those days; it required, in addition to familiarity with the musical materials, some technical sophistication as well. Lachmann was highly qualified for both. The recordings of the

---

16 See document 7, "Initial List of Subscribers to the *Zeitschrift für Vergleichende Musikwissenschaft*," appendix I.

congress, as it turned out, have served many a scholar concerned with the *maqamat* tradition in later years.[17] Though rich in theoretical treatises (largely medieval), Arabic music, in practice, seemed to defy theoretical generalizations. Given its different and varied manifestations, the aim of the congress was to discover the common traits of Arabic music as practiced by different groups in different musical centers at the time. More than it solved critical problems, the congress drew attention to important issues – substantive and methodological – that were never before raised, and were dealt with only subsequently.[18]

While Lachmann's contribution to the Cairo Congress of 1932 is well known among scholars of Arabic music, there is much to be learned from the (obviously) little-known letters he wrote home about this, his last extended expedition. The world those days seemed much larger; to get from one place to another often involved roundabout connections, making stops to visit friends and colleagues. Letter writing, however, was the foremost way to keep in touch with those with whom one wished to share information, as well as personal experiences. Thus Lachmann's letters to his *"Liebe Eltern"*[19] contain not only a record of the people he met on his way to Egypt – scholars with whom he had been in touch, including some who had already left Germany – but also impressions he wished to share with his parents. The letters vividly detail the difficulties he encountered on his way, the colleagues he met at the congress, his view of the congress's scientific value, the new contacts he made, the social and physical milieu of the communities he visited, etc., all written in a lucid and amiable style. While of special interest to musicologists, the letters are a gold mine for whoever might be interested in a genre that has all but disappeared from our world. They also reveal how essential a part was played by the cultivated middle class Jewish family in the lives of its members who

---

17 See Ali Jihad Racy, "Historical World Views of Early Ethnomusicologists: An East West Encounter in Cairo, 1932," S. Blum, P. V. Bohlman, and D. M. Neuman (eds.), *Ethnomusicology and Modern Music History* (Champaign, Ill., 1991), pp. 68–91.
18 For a comprehensive study that deals with Arabic music in practice and addresses the problems it raises, see Dalia Cohen and Ruth Katz, *A Maqam Tradition in Theory and Practice* (Chicago, 2003).
19 See Lachmann's letters to his parents, appendix II.

sought entrée into cultured German society. As such, they are a multi-layered historical document, not only echoing the times, but revealing the human relationships that were taken for granted by enlightened Jewish families, whose members understood each other and lent each other support. And support they needed.

Back home, as editor of the *Zeitschrift*, Lachmann attended almost single-handedly to all of the needs of this young new series; he kept in touch with its subscribers, kept meticulous financial records, and, above all, engaged in extensive correspondence with contributors and potential contributors.[20] The first volume appeared in 1933, and under mounting difficulties (he had already been dismissed from his post at the library), Lachmann managed to produce two more issues for the years 1934 and 1935. By then, some of his German colleagues and subscribers to these volumes – a repository of ways of thought and research during the formative years of comparative musicology – had already left Germany, on account of their Jewish origin or political persuasion. The émigrés, however, kept in touch with each other and with their colleagues who stayed behind. While professional matters still constituted the major subject of their correspondence, aspects of a more personal nature, like housing arrangements, financial problems, potential university posts, etc., were increasingly discussed by the "uprooted," as the situation in Europe worsened.[21]

The Uprooted

In his classic essay on Weimar culture,[22] Peter Gay vividly describes the Weimar spirit and effectively claims that those who shaped it were not at

---

20 For his notebooks and accounts of the journal, and a collection of letters from his professional correspondence during that period, see B: "Personal Documents," in *The Lachmann Archive,* housed in the National Sound Archives of the music department of the Jewish National and University Library, Jerusalem, Israel.
21 See ibid., *The Lachmann Archive.*
22 Peter Gay, "Weimar Culture: The Outsider as Insider," Donald Fleming and Bernard Bailyn (eds.), *The Intellectual Migration: Europe and America, 1930–1960,* (Cambridge, Mass., 1969), pp. 11–93.

the heart of public affairs. They met, interacted with, and influenced "insiders" without really becoming insiders themselves. Post-war Germany, argues Gay, was in search of roots *and* novelty; those he calls "outsiders at home" primarily sought the latter. Revolution and democracy became the living realities of the new Weimar after the war. While the longing for human and cultural renewal had already ripened prior to the formation of the republic, it now found unprecedented opportunity for success. Painters, musicians, poets, playwrights, philosophers, architects, psychologists and many others, who had already been engaged in an international commerce of ideas and were part of a Western community on which "they drew and which they fed," felt liberated to pursue ideas towards which imperial Germany was hostile, giving them real content. However, in the quest for national renewal, the hostility of the old regime, which reflected a basic resistance to anything "modern" (the new in art and the social sciences) managed to marginalize the modern trend and its representatives – socialists, democrats and, above all, Jews – more than ever before.[23] The "audacity" of the latter was especially irksome. The Jews, after all, were never central to the larger society: how dare *they*, who belong at any rate in the periphery, challenge the national agenda!

The republic, nonetheless, had its moments of greatness, and though "its end was implied in its beginning," says Gay, "it was not inevitable, because there were republicans who took the symbol of Weimar seriously."[24] As it turned out, however, the quest for reform – political, social and economic – that would lead to harmony and unity, and the belief in the superiority of German culture, did not fare well together. The combination was differently understood by different segments of society, representing not only different social classes, but different fields of intellectual endeavor. Unlike artists and psychologists, the political scientists were more involved in the life of the republic and sought to influence its course. However, while the *Deutsche Hochschule für Politik*, for example, which stood on the ground of bourgeois liberalism, was too radical for most Germans, it was not radical enough for the *Institut für*

---

23 See ibid., pp. 14–19.
24 Ibid., p. 13.

Sozialforschung in Frankfurt (the famous Frankfurt School of Social Research), whose members were mostly neo-Marxists. The mission to extol and preserve German culture also created differences in outlook among historians, emphasizing different aspects of German history. The quest for unity and harmony led a *literat* like Hofmannsthal to advocate a "cultural organism" in which the German *spirit* and the imperatives of life might join. Gay claims that "the hunger for wholeness" was born from fear of modernity – incomprehensible artistic styles, dehumanizing machines, capitalist materialism, godless rationalism, rootless society, and cosmopolitan Jews – revealing a desperate need for roots, community and guidance. The political world of its chief spokesmen, concludes Gay (wearing his psychoanalytic hat), was a "paranoid" world filled with enemies.[25]

Indeed, the frightened are often more frightening than those they are threatened by, forcing the latter to flee. Among the musicologists who left Germany before it was too late, there was a disproportionate number of Jews. Of those who stayed behind, there were but a few, still wavering between what they wanted to believe and the reality they were forced to confront. While those who left, Jews and non-Jews, kept in contact with each other on a personal basis, their growing contacts with American musicologists rested primarily on professional grounds. They hoped to secure academic positions in what was perceived, compared to the European turmoil, as paradise on earth. While America became for many of the uprooted a land of hope and expectation, the uprooted, in turn, were regarded with new promise by those American intellectuals who looked to Europe for guidance in molding their own culture. The development of musicology in America, like that of some other intellectual domains, benefited greatly from those who actually moved to the United States, whose ideas and attitudes were communicated through direct

---

25 Ibid., for the discussion of the political scientists see pp. 42–47; for the discussion of the historians see pp. 59–66; for the discussion of Hofmannsthal's "cultural organism," see pp. 57–58. For the anti-modernity of the German movement, its philosophical and psychological vagaries, also see Fritz Stern, *The Politics of Cultural Despair: A Study in the Rise of the Germanic Ideology* (Berkeley, 1961).

personal contact. But unlike scholars in physics, psychology, history and architecture, who encountered a high degree of readiness among their American counterparts,[26] musicology, compared to its European counterpart, was still in its infancy. While symphony conductors and other virtuosi would have been in and out of the United States even if Hitler had never existed, it is hard to imagine the long list of European musicologists who settled in America without the turbulence he caused.

Members of the *Bildungsbuergertum,* who saw their rabbis in Goethe and Humboldt, were forced to probe their Jewish existence anew by those who banned Lessing's *Nathan the Wise* from the German stage. The Nazis taught marginal Jews that there is no escape from one's *inherited* identity; surely, it could not be what the Nazis thought it was. Deprived of their secular identity, with its high priority for individuation, they were treated by the Nazis as a subhuman flock. Some, as a result, did become more Jewish, but all experienced the oppression of a Grand Betrayal. Ultimately, but too late, the fact that the German Jews were a relatively educated and assimilated group helped call attention to their plight as innocent victims; it certainly prompted the recognition of the State of Israel. An anecdote told by a reporter of *Stars and Stripes,* who visited the concentration camps in 1945, relates that the Jewish survivors expressed a preference for the United States when asked in private where they wished to go, but when questioned by post-war officials they answered "Palestine." Asked to explain the contradiction, one of them volunteered the following: "What I do is my own business, a Jew should go to Palestine."

Palestine was even less attractive in the thirties; it was hardly perceived as a land of opportunities by non-Zionists. Impressive as the achievement of the early pioneers might have been, the budding of a Jewish homeland was not on the minds of cosmopolitan Jews, who in many respects saw themselves as citizens of an enlightened world. Robert Lachmann was one of them. If he entertained the thought of going to Palestine in 1935, it was not as a believer but as an observer; it was because of the ethnic mix of the place. Though small and underdeveloped, the population of this ancient/new country consisted of Palestinian Arabs (Muslims and

---

26 See op. cit., *The Intellectual Migration: Europe and America, 1930–1966.*

Christians), old Christian sects (Eastern and Western), and a variety of Eastern Jewish groups, in addition to European Jews. Given his professional interests, Palestine seemed like an ideal laboratory, offering unique research opportunities. Luckily, the newly-established University in Jerusalem extended invitations, upon serious professional recommendations, to some of the needy who seemed to fit its own, still groping, plans. Lachmann was not in want of recommendations.

Lachmann naturally expected to ally his scholarly activities with the University. He may have heard of other Jewish scholars who migrated to Palestine in the hope of securing an academic position for themselves. What he, in all likelihood, did not know is that this young and forward-looking institution was still in the throes of old debates over the nature, and indeed the very establishment, of a "University of the Jewish People." A brief prehistory of the institution in which Lachmann placed his future is thus necessary in order to comprehend the fateful interaction which ensued between a determined but insecure immigrant scholar and a University, equally determined, but as yet unsure of its direction.

PART TWO

"THE UNIVERSITY OF THE JEWISH PEOPLE"

The idea of a homeland was not a novel one among the Jews, who for centuries had longed for Zion, recalling the days prior to their dispersion. The tie to the Land of Israel was not based solely on the Bible; it was enshrined in daily and holiday prayer, and in post-biblical literature. This focus on place of origin made for a bond among Jews, everywhere. Notwithstanding their diverse lives, their spiritual being depended on a common "virtual reality," which used to be real in ancient times. Indeed, today's "Jewish bookshelf" (as it is sometimes referred to by secular Jews in Israel) continues to foster the idea of a "center" in both time and space, the one which gave rise to their spiritual being as a people.

The Jews and Higher Education

The secularization of this text-based dream of Return underlies the European Zionist movement. It should come as no surprise, therefore, to find that the establishment of institutions of higher learning in Palestine was given such high priority in the Zionist program. Indeed, the idea of a University of the Jewish People at (or as) the restored "center" of the Jewish people intertwines both traditional and secular strands of the Jewish national movement.

One strand, alluded to already, is at the very core of traditional Judaism, whose sacred texts derive from the major study centers of Palestine, both before and after the exiles. The continuous tradition of studying these texts, and the cumulative process of commenting on them orally and in writing, accompanied the Jews throughout their dispersion. They supplied the language, the myths, the heroes, the rituals, the legal structures which unified Jewish communities and connected them to each other.

In Europe, the crowning institutions of Jewish learning – up to and beyond the Enlightenment – were the Talmudic academies, the yeshivot, which flourished both in East and West. These were training grounds not only for rabbis, but also for the lay elite. The ancient sages and their academies in Palestine and in Babylon figured prominently, as an everyday presence, in the European yeshivot. There was also continual longing for the reestablishment of a supreme rabbinical authority – possible only in the homeland of a reunited people – whenever an unsolvable problem of legal or ritual principle arose. It is no wonder, then, that the thought of the renewal of higher Jewish learning in Eretz Israel should be prominent in the traditional imagery of redemption. It is also no wonder that this heritage of literacy and learning should have been translated into the passion for secular learning with the coming of the Enlightenment, or the so-called Jewish emancipation.

Overall, Jewish emancipation in modern times refers to the granting of rights and duties of citizenship to Jews, equal to those of other citizens. Its origin is in the enlightened political and social thought that affected the governance of most European countries since the 18th century. It is easy to see how this movement channeled the Jewish motivation for learning into secular and professional pursuits, as opportunities to participate in the larger society presented themselves. Ostensibly, the process should have led to the intellectual and social assimilation of European Jewry, but in true dialectic fashion, it led also to its opposite, that is, to a renewed (albeit scientific) interest in the social and religious history of Judaism and Jewry, and, eventually, to the idea that a University of the Jewish People in Palestine should be the flagbearer of the Zionist movement. This is the secular strand that converged with the traditional one.

Liberalism, Civic Rights and Higher Education

Jewish emancipation, thus, became a measure of social openness in European culture. Throughout its complex history, it was primarily supported by liberals, who cherished liberalism in actual life, and opposed by reactionary groups, on ideological grounds. The fight for emancipation resulted, at first, in a readiness on the part of many Jews to assimilate, but later on, in the 19th century, it became associated with a renewed Jewish loyalty and, eventually, with the fight for autonomy, which was considerably precipitated by 20th century events. Naturally, the different political and social conditions encountered by the Jews in their host countries affected the manifestations and the pace of this three-fold development. Regardless of the differences among the countries where Jews resided, however, civic equality and participation in civic life became focal issues in the lives of Jews in their various places of residence.[27]

Worthy and attractive as enlightened political and social thought might have been, its a-historical attitude harbored new opportunities for individual Jews, while challenging their shared historical existence. Throughout the ages, Jewish identity has been determined by the interplay between internal and external forces, by feelings and thoughts that grew from within and those that developed outside. Jewish identity was never solely a matter of self definition, nor was it controlled by individual self consciousness. In enlightened thought, Jewish society confronted an attitude that was favorably inclined toward the individual Jew while inimical toward his traditions and social cohesion. The growth of centralist states demanded, on rational grounds, a disavowal of diverse national and ethnic identities within the state in favor of a unifying overall national culture. Between extreme individualism in theory and collective assimilation in practice, Jewish existence in modern times witnessed the greatest individual successes and the most distressing tragedies.

The hope and opportunity for civic rights and civic participation stimulated new tendencies in the world of learning and education among Jews. A secular general education became necessary in order to promote, as well as benefit from the imagined or actual new openness of the host societies. A better grounding in the national language and culture became credentials for further pursuits. While general knowledge weakened the

---

27 For a summary of the three periods in the history of Jewish emancipation and a brief description of its different manifestations in various countries, see *Encyclopaedia Judaica*, VI (Jerusalem, 1971), Cols. 698–718.

case for Jewish separateness, it created a new self awareness as well. More and more, Judaism was viewed, by enlightened Jews, from a broader perspective, as part of the unfolding of history. As such, it gave rise to the comprehensive and scientific study of Judaism itself, based on literary and historical documentation pertaining to its cultural heritage and the totality of conditions under which it existed and faced its destiny.

Subjecting Judaism to criticism and modern methods of research, however, was not solely academic. It gave support to some Jewish intellectuals who wished to dispel the image held by gentiles of the Jew as a deficient human figure, and to others who wished to counteract the indifference and estrangement of modern educated Jews, whose contempt for Judaism endangered their own existence. Thus, while revealing an intricate and fascinating narrative about the predicaments and achievements of Jews through the ages, the Science of Judaism (*Wissenschaft des Judentums*) is, in and of itself, a product of their predicaments and achievements. For that matter, so is the increased participation of Jews in the world of secular knowledge, and their excellence within it, in disproportion to their overall number.

The entrance of Jews into universities to obtain higher education depended on the political and social outlook of their host countries and on the condition of the Jews within them. It should be remembered, however, that the universities, themselves, developed at a different pace and performed different roles, depending on their social-political environments. All of these factors differed not only from place to place, but were subject to additional temporary whims, introducing sudden and unanticipated changes. On the whole, the situation in Western Europe was more favorable to Jewish participation in higher education than was Eastern Europe.[28] However, even in Western countries such opportunities were not evenly distributed. Jewish students, consequently, traveled long distances to escape biases in admission to higher learning, inadvertently creating a sophisticated and cosmopolitan student body. Not all of them returned

---

28 For the situation of Eastern Jews consult Israel Bartal, "Eastern European Jews and Higher Education," Shaul Katz and Michael Heyd (eds.), *The History of The Hebrew University: Roots and Beginnings* (Jerusalem, 1997), pp. 75–89 (Heb.).

home to apply their newly-acquired knowledge and skills; in fact, many established new lives for themselves where greater opportunities presented themselves, mostly in the places which had offered them higher education.

Though they were few in number, the conditions of Jews have always been a kind of barometer reflecting changes in the atmosphere of Europe as a whole. The conflict between Empires and states, between group assimilation and universal emancipation, between religion and secular science, and more, weakened the grounds on which liberalism stood, affecting not only the Jews. The theoretical belief in the liberty of the individual person capable of the free use of reason, regardless of class, race, church and nation, was proven unreasonable in practice. While rational men were deemed capable of reaching agreements by rational and peaceful means, reality continued to foster differences of interests rather than solutions based on compromise. It was because liberalism thought all men potentially reasonable that liberals favored education. Education was necessary to insure religious tolerance, constitutional government, and *laissez-faire* free trade. Nobody was more ready to adopt this agenda than were the Jews.

The "Land of Israel": Place of Refuge, Cultural Center, or Both?

While the spread of liberalism was slow and uneven, its waning, from the end of the 19th century and onward, was rapid. The prevalence of liberalism, as postulated, allowed the Jews not only to free themselves from old legal discriminations that had been imposed on them from outside, but also from the bonds of their own Jewish community, raising the fear that assimilation would lead to a loss of Jewish identity and perhaps even the disappearance of Judaism itself. Like other peoples with similar fears, the Jews launched, toward the end of the century, a national movement of their own. Jewish nationalism expressed itself in the hope of establishing a Jewish state in Palestine, in which Jews from all over the world might find refuge. Given the resurgence of anti-Semitism toward the end of the century, it seemed only natural to look for a place of refuge.

The idea of a homeland was, of course, not a novel idea among the Jews, who for centuries had longed for Zion, recalling the days prior to their dispersion. Over the centuries, some Jews turned the hopes expressed in their prayers into reality; on purely spiritual and religious grounds, they returned to the cradle of the Jewish people to live and practice their Judaism in the Holy Land. It should be remembered that the tie to *the land*, i.e., the land of Israel, was not solely based on the Bible, but on post-biblical literature, created mostly in exile, that referred to the *geographic* area where the group was first molded, giving it substance and expression. This focus on place of origin made for a bond among the Jews, despite their dispersion. Notwithstanding their diverse lives, their spiritual being depended on a common "virtual reality" which used to be real in ancient times. Indeed, the "Jewish bookshelf" continued to foster the idea of a core – a "center" – which gave rise to their spiritual being as a people.

The gains and losses that followed the Jewish Emancipation, however, called for some kind of *tangible action* that would serve as a new integrative force. There were those who favored the cultivation of a tangible "cultural center" in the legendary homeland that would radiate out to the Diaspora. The idea of a cultural center in Palestine seemed like a natural outgrowth of traditional thought, which under the new circumstances gained in impetus and momentum. By comparison, political Zionism – the aspiration to re-establish the homeland *itself* – was a daring idea; it was seriously entertained only toward the end of the 19th century. But even then, it did not kindle the imagination of most religious Jews, nor of those who had gone astray, leaving Judaism far behind.

After all, for the future Jewish state to function as a viable enterprise, it had to take into account the world of nations, to which the designers hoped the new state would belong, albeit with a uniqueness of its own. Moreover, in order to normalize the lives of Jews, who far too long had labored under anomalous conditions, required the renunciation of separation between daily affairs and ethnic-religious existence. By eliminating the predicaments which Jews had to overcome in exile, the rebirth of the Jewish people in their ancient homeland was expected to free the individual to integrate his Jewishness naturally, so that his potential as a *human being* could be realized to the fullest. No longer need the Sabbath preserve the lives of Jews, but Jews would be free to keep their Sabbath.[29] Given the great heritage of the Prophets, not only will Torah come forth from Zion but, hopefully, also light for the nations.

The realization of the quest for a homeland in Palestine had to meet not only with the approval of the powers that could deliver the goods, but required fervent belief in its feasibility by those in need of deliverance. Paradoxically, the broader perspective of political Zionism required some distancing from the familiar in order to overcome what might be labeled a "trained acquiescence," so well exemplified in the phrase "it is difficult to be a Jew." It is worth remembering, however, that the *a priori* acceptance of the difficulty of being Jewish worked wonders for Jewish survival through centuries fraught with hardships and threats. Indeed, it is often easier to continue with the familiar, however difficult, than to entertain an unknown, however promising. To be sure, the renewed homeland was expected to safeguard not only the physical existence of Jews, but their spiritual survival as well. It was expected, moreover, to create a new environment, conducive to unhampered Jewish creativity and development. A tall order.

"The University of the Jewish People"

The idea of establishing a Jewish university in Palestine predates the first Zionist Congress, which convened in 1897.[30] The congress, however, was the first representative Jewish forum committed to the formulation and undertaking of *actual* steps that would gradually lead to the full realization of the Zionist dream. It presented a platform for all who wished to voice

---

29 The sentence is based on a well-known saying by Ahad Ha-am: "More than the Jews kept the Sabbath, the Sabbath kept the Jews." Ahad Ha-am, an important Jewish essayist, is primarily identified with the "cultural center" idea.
30 See the illuminating article by Israel Kolat, "The Idea of a Hebrew University in the Jewish National Movement," Katz and Heyd (eds.), *The History of The Hebrew University*, pp. 3–74.

an opinion about the actions deemed necessary for its implementation. United around overall aims, the delegates to the congress did not necessarily agree about priorities and procedures. Though the question of establishing a Hebrew university was not overlooked at the first congress, it did not command the attention that some delegates thought it deserved, because political/diplomatic issues occupied the greater part of the delegates' attention. Subsequent congresses, however, showed an ever-growing concern for the institutions of those who had already settled in the homeland, and with the measures needed to pave the way for others.

Education, of all sorts, loomed large in this respect. To begin with, striking roots in the *Altneuland* created a demand for more applied knowledge, i.e., agriculture, engineering, and the like, which had to be deployed if the experiment was to succeed. In addition, new opportunities loomed for bridging between Jewish and secular education, between the particular and the general, between the parochial and the universal. A genuine chance presented itself to capitalize on the changes that had taken place in the intellectual lives of Jews in modern times, giving vent to its repressed potential.[31]

Four main concerns affected the shaping of the idea of the University. It had to reckon with the ways in which the institution would represent the Jewish heritage; it had to relate, in one form or another, to the world of knowledge at large; it had to consider local needs and conditions; and last, but not least, it had to offer a solution to the problems faced by Jewish students everywhere in their attempts to obtain higher education. Even these agreed-upon objectives raised questions with regard to their relative priority and the balance to be struck among them. On the whole, those who placed greater weight, or exclusive emphasis, on Jewish studies were more representative of the school of thought that saw in Palestine a cultural

---

31 Major trends in the history of the Zionist movement have been amply documented by qualified historians, whose writings are widely available. Mindful of their work, the attempt here is to raise only those issues which had a bearing on the subsequent struggles that accompanied the establishment of The Hebrew University, leaving lasting marks on its development. They certainly go a long way to explain the infighting, in its formative years, which directly affected the "Lachmann Case."

center in the making that was destined to be meaningful for Jews in the dispersion. Others favored a this-worldly attitude; they wished for an institution that would materialize the Zionist dream as quickly as possible.

Debate over the nature of an institution of higher learning reflected in miniature the desires and conflicts of a collectivity which saw in "the university of the Jewish people" its actual or desired image. The university, thus, became one of the major institutions which embodied the process of the "homeland on its way." As such, it commanded a great deal of attention, engaging the full spectrum of Jewish leaders who wished to influence the course of events.[32]

Assorting Commitments

Almost fifty years elapsed since the idea of a University was first raised and its official inauguration on Mount Scopus in 1925.[33] Overlooking the Judean desert and the Dead Sea, the inauguration ceremony took place in the presence of the High Commissioner for Palestine, Sir Herbert Samuel, and Lord Arthur James Balfour (former British foreign secretary), whose name became associated with the famous declaration of 1917 that viewed "with favor the establishment in Palestine of a national home for the Jewish people."[34] The Chief Rabbi, Abraham I. Kook, was there to bestow God's blessing, and, of course, some of the leading Zionists of the world were

---

32 In addition to Kolat's article, ibid., see for example the following articles: Zev Rosenkranz, "A 'High-Level' Cultural Center or a House Wasted by Cockroach? Albert Einstein's Involvement in Matters Concerning the Hebrew University," Hagit Lavsky, "Between the Cornerstone and the Opening: The Establishment of the Hebrew University, 1918–1925," and Aryeh Goren, "A View From Mount Scopus: Y. L. Magnes and the First Years of the Hebrew University," Katz and Heyd (eds.), *The History of The Hebrew University,* pp. 386–394; 120–159; 363–385, respectively.
33 For the early unfolding of the idea, and the transformations it underwent, consult Kolat, ibid. For the crystallizing stages that led to provisional openings of the University and the final inauguration ceremony, consult Lavsky, ibid.
34 Exact citation from the declaration communicated (in a letter dated November 2, 1917, and made public a week later) to Lord Rothschild by Balfour in his capacity as foreign secretary.

also present, headed by Dr. Chaim Weizmann, whose indefatigable efforts on behalf of the University deserve special mention.[35] The guests included local men of letters, headed by the poet laureate of the Hebrew language, Chaim Nachman Bialik, and the newly-assembled academic staff.[36]

By this time, however, the institute for chemistry and microbiology and the institute for Jewish studies had already been established, after considerable debates over their priority and their nature as institutes – research, teaching or both. Teaching had commenced early at the Institute for Jewish Studies, since the necessary infrastructure was there from the start, i.e., scholars in the various areas of Jewish studies and related fields. A number of first-rate Jewish Orientalists, who took an interest in the "University project," had already expressed their willingness to join.[37] Oriental studies, which had attracted a goodly number of Jews in their pursuits of higher education, were the locus of Jewish studies in European universities and, thus, the relationship between Jewish and Oriental studies had already been established. The University library, one of the major projects undertaken by American Jews, was also already functioning, and a new institute for physics and mathematics – The Albert Einstein Institute – was well on its way, as was the transfer to the University of the Agricultural Experimentation Center.

The University – an idea that was born in the Zionist movement and reflected its national and cultural aspirations – was preoccupied with

---

35 Weizmann, as is well known, was president of the World Zionist Organization for many years (1920–1930 and 1935–1946) and eventually became the first president of the State of Israel. It is less known, however, that in the very year in which he took the initiative of Zionist advocacy in British governmental circles (1916), a year when the prospect of Allied victory was dim, he was successful, as a biochemist, in establishing a process that would yield acetone, a solvent needed for the production of munitions. Weizmann's scientific success, which brought him into contact with influential people in the British government, might have aided the Zionist cause.

36 For the inauguration ceremony and the telling speeches that were held on the occasion, see *The Hebrew University Jerusalem: Inauguration April 1, 1925* (Jerusalem, 1925). For an analysis of some of the speeches, see *The History of The Hebrew University*, op. cit., pp. 311–362.

37 See Menachem Milson, "The Beginning of Arabic and Islamic Studies at The Hebrew University," *The History of The Hebrew University*, pp. 575–588.

questions pertaining to academic standards, not least because of the way it came into being. The idea of commencing with research institutes reflected a basic commitment to open inquiry and a desire to participate in the advancement of knowledge on a universal basis. It also reflected a great deal of caution; after all, there was no point in establishing a University that, to begin with, is anything but first rate by world standards. Only as such, it was believed, could the University hope to attract Jewish scholars who had already made names for themselves in distinguished universities elsewhere. Moreover, given the Zionist aspiration, the University could contribute to the solution of problems and issues raised by its geographic location and its immediate social environment. With research secured, the proper grounds will have been provided for the initiation of others, i.e., for the teaching of students to follow suit.

An orientation of this kind could not, however, provide an immediate solution to one of the major problems which prompted the establishment of the University of the Jewish People, i.e., the predicament of students, whose attempts to acquire a higher education were barred because of their Jewish affiliation. High standards and urgency of needs do not always fare well together, they are usually related inversely. Immediate solutions tend to impose compromise, while high standards tend to delay solutions. Paradoxically, the more committed one was to the idea of establishing a Jewish state in the near future, the more support one lent to long range plans that would justify the efforts invested in them.

Assorting commitments is never an easy task, the more so when it involves the lives of others. With a turbulent *familiar* history weighing on one's shoulders, the undertaking of responsibility for corrective measures, guided by an *envisaged* future, is certainly not easy. All those who stuck out their necks to influence the policy making of the University knew that, in the final analysis, they would be held accountable by the Jewish people at large. Conflicting desiderata are often affected by a time element which circumscribes relevance. Acuteness of immediate needs often overshadows general needs. Indeed, the early history of the University reveals that universal concerns had to yield, more often than not, and understandably so, to particular concerns. Humanity at large seemed less relevant, for the time being, than the people whose condition one set out to ameliorate. There were also some particular dictates of the place itself – of its physical location, of the special mix of its population, etc. – that required precedence. As is often the case, the immediate does not always suit the long run, but neither is foresight a commonplace.

Between an Envisaged Future and an Ambiguous Past

It is not surprising that those determined to mold their future should also be preoccupied with their past, especially if they have chosen to return to their place of origin in order to constitute their new life. From philosophy through archeology, histories of all kinds mushroomed early in the curriculum of the new University. The unearthing of the past, whether distant or recent, implied recourse to disciplines that could yield significant information about Judaism and the Jewish people. In step with the enlightened thought that led to the critical study of Judaism, these disciplines placed the Jewish people in a wider historical context from which the particular circumstances that affected its destiny could be extrapolated. Questions of historical methodology were continually at play, for if the history of the Jews was affected by the various histories in which it unfolded, the Jews, in turn, left their own marks on those who affected them. Given this entanglement, what was the best way to study history? The broader context clearly required an understanding of its own, if scientific justice was to be done with all parties concerned. Jewish history, too, called for its own perspective, if internal developments, not only external influences, were to be seriously considered. Of course, neither need exclude the other: it is only a matter of emphasis. Interestingly, the dilemma between the general versus the particular had its own way of reappearing through the back door, albeit inadvertently.

The immediate social environment could not be overlooked either, if the Jews were to re-integrate into the region. Nor could one ignore the differences among the Jewish groups themselves, those already present and those who were yet to come. Though united by fate and tradition, they had absorbed much of the cultural characteristics and norms of their places of origin. While guided by ideology towards the creation of a melting pot, the ingathering of the exiles presented unique opportunities for the social-scientific study of cultural *differences*. A better understanding of ethnic differences was necessary, at any rate, in order to subsume the various groups in the vigorous, forward-looking image inspired by the Zionist movement.

Once Hebrew was desacralized and secured as a vernacular language suited to instruction and Jewish studies taken for granted, the University could afford to look beyond old debates. The more established the University became and the more it could count on basic (assured) resources – financial and otherwise – the more ready it was to deal with both horns of the dilemma which shaped the inner structure of the University – the one which favored a limited number of research institutes and the other which favored instruction in a large number of subjects. Research and instruction soon came to be stressed equally at the University. The founders, after all, had never made the establishment of research institutes their ultimate object, they only wished to safeguard the academic standing of the University and its ability to contribute toward the solution of problems involved in the material development of the country. While admitting that research and instruction are mutually stimulating activities, the training of a staff of younger people, to assist in research work, became indispensable. Moreover, Jewish students all over the world were demanding ever more insistently that the doors of the University be opened to them, and public opinion supported their demands.

In addition to the activities of the Zionist movement on behalf of the University, the appreciation of the University's work by the Diaspora took on other tangible forms. In many countries Friends of the Hebrew University were organized to raise funds by appealing to their members and the public in general.[38] Pressing needs commanded greater attention among these societies than did the academic debates over the relative merit of different objectives. Some societies undertook special projects, like, for example, the National and University Library, the medical school,

---

38 For the relationship of the University and the Diaspora in the early years, see *The Hebrew University Jerusalem: Its History and Development* (Palestine, 1939), pp. 18–22.

specific research laboratories, equipment and aid for students who wished to study at the university, etc. Though societies of friends were organized in many countries, the earliest measure of assistance came from the American Friends.

By comparison with other Jewish communities, the American Jewish community was both prosperous and unabashed about its Jewishness. "*A goldene medina*" ("golden land") summarized the Jewish view of both the unique democratic nature of America, as well as its social and economic opportunities. Nonetheless, American Jews had to work hard in order to capitalize on these opportunities; and diligent they were. Interestingly, it is precisely the country of unlimited opportunities which created an unprecedented *respect* for money, even among those who made it in a big way. Accordingly, a new kind of philanthropy was introduced in America, a business-like philanthropy, whereby all parties involved stood to gain, including the donor. It is not the tax reduction, however, which is intimated here, though that is significant. Rather, it is the impact of designating money to worthwhile causes and the degree to which it involves its donors that we wish to emphasize. Explaining the worthiness of causes is always easier when addressed to the already convinced. More often than not, however, the already convinced have opinions about how best to spend their money, especially if they worked hard to earn it and amassed a good deal of experience in doing so. The more dedicated donors feel more strongly about voicing opinions, all the more so when it concerns large sums. Looked at from the receiving end, the more dependent an institution on the goodwill of donors, the more marked becomes their influence.

Indeed, the more dependent the University became on American resources, the more pronounced became the tendency of the American Friends to voice opinions, expecting them to be heard. While the administration of the University gave much thought to the development of the Societies of Friends of the Hebrew University, especially the American society, the administrative development itself was influenced by the University's "big" friends. While the apportionment of power between the academic staff and the administration of a university is invariably complicated, public authorities as a rule exercise considerable influence on the autonomy of the academic staff.

Since The Hebrew University regarded itself as the University of the Jewish people, its Board of Governors became the trustee for the Jewish People, exercising supreme authority in the University's affairs. The board was composed of members representing the various societies of friends (including that of the Jewish community of Palestine), the Zionist Organization, learned circles of eminent Jewish scholars, and, last but not least, individual philanthropists prominent in the economic field.[39] Despite the equality among its members, all tried to sway the opinions of those who, in the final analysis, could deliver the goods. The latter, whether members of the board or not, were often approached directly in order to influence the decisions of the board. However, since the board met only at long intervals, it delegated the administration of the University in Palestine to an Executive Committee composed of the chancellor and his deputy. It was left to the chancellor to appoint the advisory members to the Executive Committee. Thus much power was vested in the hands of the chancellor. As long as the leading role in the development of the University was still in the hands of the responsible authorities, rather than in the hands of an academic staff, the chancellor had a great deal of influence on the shaping of academic matters as well.

J. L. Magnes: First Chancellor of The Hebrew University

J. L. Magnes must have been well connected to have been chosen the first Chancellor of The Hebrew University. Given the initiative and extreme involvement of eminent European and Eastern European Zionists with the University project, the selection of a U.S. reform rabbi to run the institution seems somewhat odd at first glance. Born in San Francisco in 1877, Magnes attended the Hebrew Union College, where he was ordained as a rabbi in 1900. Subsequently he spent a number of years (1900–1903) studying in Berlin and Heidelberg, where he met some of the outstanding Jewish scholars engaged in Jewish studies and related fields. While in

---

[39] For the organization and administration of the University from its beginnings see ibid., pp. 23–29.

Germany, he visited several Eastern European countries and was profoundly moved by the Jewish life he encountered. Though already sympathetic toward Zionism prior to his European sojourn, the German and Eastern European experience transformed his sympathy into active commitment. Along with several distinguished rabbinical posts, he served as the secretary of the American Zionist Federation (1905–1908) and as president of the *Kehillah* – the New York Jewish Community (1908–1922). In each of these capacities his hope was to intensify and modernize Jewish religious life and Jewish education. As a communal leader, he emerged not only as a competent guide and spokesman, but as a superb fund raiser, persuasive and effective.

As a member of the American delegation to the Zionist Congress in 1905, Magnes encountered, for the first time, almost all of the then prominent leaders of the Zionist movement and the camps and factions which they represented. United and committed as they were to the general cause, they differed amongst themselves with regard to priorities and the appropriate paths to their attainment. Magnes had moved toward religious traditionalism by then, and as a Zionist he had become a disciple of Ahad Ha-Am and his teaching, i.e., more devoted to the establishment of a cultural center in Palestine than to the establishment of a Jewish political entity, though he did not rule it out. He took great interest in the discussions concerning education in general and those pertaining to the establishment of a University for and of the Jewish people, in particular.

Magnes's commitment to broader issues that concerned the Jewish people induced him eventually to leave his congregational work altogether and to devote himself solely to Jewish public service. In 1908 he helped establish the American Jewish Committee while strengthening, at the same time, his ties with the East European Jews. Well versed in American politics and Jewish affairs, familiar with secular and religious life, knowledgeable about the world at large and the place of the Jews within it, made Magnes an exceptional leader *because* he was an American. Dualities of this sort may have characterized some European leaders as well, but only in the New World was the commitment to the general and the parochial fostered as a natural combination, without spelling conflict. Nonetheless, upon the U.S. entry into the war in 1917, the Jewish community, concerned over possible imputations of disloyalty, felt it had to support the move as a *monolithic* group. Magnes, however, opposed the move out of pacifist convictions and undermined his leadership thereby. His communal career in America came to an end because of his personal convictions during World War I.

In 1922 Magnes emigrated to Palestine, determined to devote all of his efforts to the establishment of the University. He had already taken an active part in the debates that accompanied the process of its actualization, but now, given his former connections, he became actively involved in raising funds for the University and for its special projects. He also tried to secure personal donations that would facilitate some of the University's immediate needs, and successful he was. Thus, despite the fact that he was more inclined toward Jewish studies than were other active members, and more desperate to solve the predicament of Jewish students by focusing on teaching rather than research from the start, he was, nevertheless, an apt candidate to head the University as it approached its official opening. For ten whole years (1925–1935) Magnes served as all-powerful chancellor. His "promotion" to the role of president in 1935 marks the decline of his power and the rising power of the academic staff.[40]

Robert Lachmann spent four of the most precious and fateful years of his life (1935–1939) in Palestine, connected in one form or another with the University and in the shadow of Magnes's power, both in ascendance and decline. Magnes, after all, was the man to whom the letters recommending Lachmann were sent, and Magnes was the man responsible for having brought Lachmann – "the qualified scholar, deserving of note" – to the University. Magnes was the chancellor whom Lachmann addressed in the hope of securing a University position in Palestine. Magnes remained Lachmann's chancellor until the latter's untimely death in 1939, though it was Magnes, the president, who put up the fight on his behalf, shortly after Lachmann's arrival in Palestine.

---

40 For a biography of Magnes see N. Bentwich, *For Zion's Sake* (1954). Also see Aryeh Goren, op. cit., and his "The View from Scopus: Judah L. Magnes and the Early Years," *Judaism* 95 (1996): 203–224. For a broader picture that concerns Jewish studies see David N. Myers, "History of Jewish Studies," ibid., pp. 142–159.

The Docudrama

ACT I
EXPLORING NEW HOPES

While the biographies (in various reference books) uniformly mention that Robert Lachmann died in Palestine, none seems to have an inkling of the special import of his last years. It is, of course, these least known years (1935–39) that are the subject of this study. Had he lived longer, these are the years that would have marked a major turning point in his spiritual being, and, in all likelihood, in his scholarly work as well – a kind of new beginning rather than an unfortunate end. As it turned out, however, these unfortunate years tell a story which goes far beyond Lachmann's individual case.

Since history circumscribes choices, knowledge of the array of choices – those encompassed by history at a *given* moment and those actually opted for – enhances our understanding of what might be denominated "a man-made world." Having situated both Lachmann and The Hebrew University in their respective social and cultural settings, we may now consider their interaction.

Lachmann Makes Contact with The Hebrew University

The letters recommending Lachmann to the University authorities were most impressive; so were those who wrote them. Their contents could make even a conceited candidate blush, so profuse were they in praise of Lachmann and his scholarly achievements. Yet, given the University's financial difficulties and still indecisive policy with respect to its academic expansion, making commitments to new staff members, however qualified, was not a simple matter. The exigency which beset German Jewish scholars in the thirties confounded the situation even further, since more than a few of them looked to "The University of the Jewish People" in the (reasonable) hope that their unanticipated problems might be solved. Expectations of this sort added a major new concern to the long list of dilemmas that characterized the University.

The letters which follow Lachmann's initial contact with the University tell a story to which no summary or analysis, however insightful, can do justice. Verbatim, they produce an emotional impact of which their writers could hardly have been aware, lacking, as they naturally did, the historical perspective of the present-day reader. Betrayed by the country he loved and the life of reason in which he believed, Lachmann appealed to a University which was fostered by people who had themselves long since despaired of the naive promise of Enlightenment. That this visionary University should have been compelled, because of its own uncertain circumstances, to address the Lachmann case as *pragmatically* as it did creates a further irony.

No less compelling than the irony is the circular chain of dependencies which these letters reveal. While Lachmann was awaiting the University's verdict, the University's final decision hinged, in turn, on the financial support of its American friends, whose resolve, however, was conditioned by the University's overall needs, as officially defined. The absorption of a new staff member, accordingly, depended on how well he fit into a development scheme. Aspects of a humanitarian nature *were* taken into account, once the basic needs of the institution were properly resolved. It is not surprising, therefore, to encounter a pleasing tone in the letters which Magnes dispatched to some of the American Friends on behalf of Lachmann; the "music" is that of a good salesman advertising his product, aiming to satisfy the expectations of the "buyer." By comparison, the letters which Magnes addressed to Lachmann, especially the realistic demands which they contain, sound somewhat harsh. Lachmann, for example, was increasingly challenged to take into account the University's condition and was asked to contribute his share to the solution of his problem, i.e., to secure, by himself, some of the resources that would enable the clinching of the transaction between him and the University. Good salesman though he was, Magnes was also forced, as chancellor of the University, to play the part of middle man. Sensitive to the plight of German Jewish scholars, and all too familiar with the immediate problems of the institution which he headed, how conflicted he must have felt with regard to Lachmann – a most qualified scholar who needed the University more than the University, at the time, thought it needed him!

Trained to be reasonable, Lachmann tried to accommodate. The more the burden of securing funds for his position at the University shifted back to him, the more creative his suggestions became with regard to possible solutions. Taking account of his German pension, so as to reduce the salary the University would have to be responsible for, is an idea that came up quite early in the negotiation. The problem of equipment for the research institute which he was supposed to initiate (especially recording and editing equipment which was still very costly at the time) could be solved, he suggested, by donating his personal equipment, though the operating expenditure was to be covered by the University. In the absence of funds for a rudimentary reference library, Lachmann volunteered his personal library until "rosier times." When even this much goodwill and understanding did not suffice, Lachmann set out to solicit support from personal friends – a loan to the University that might ease the financial burden on his behalf. The loan, however, the University insisted, should be made into a gift "for a worthy cause"!

It must be stated in fairness that Magnes was eager to interest some of his American friends in the "Lachmann project." The more effort he exerted on Lachmann's behalf, the more he, himself, became persuaded of its desirability. The documentation of the musical heritage of the Jews seemed especially attractive to him; he was well aware that the ingathering of the exiles presented unique opportunities for comparative studies. Latent features that characterize *Jewish music* might yet be "scientifically" revealed despite manifest differences; he speculated that residues of a bygone past may have lingered on in the very variances that attest to the dispersion of the Jewish people.[41] Moreover, mindful of the local

---

41 Magnes was aware of the pioneering work of A. Z. Idelsohn (the son of a Lithuanian cantor who received his musical education in Germany), who collected the various traditions of Jewish music, East and West, during his stay in Palestine (1906–1921). More than he sought to spell out the differences among these traditions, Idelsohn was after the discovery of what might be legitimately termed "Jewish Music." Magnes was also aware of Rosowsky's work (see footnote 53), who like Idelsohn believed

non-Jewish population, especially the Arab population, he saw in Lachmann an ideal musicologist – a scholar amply qualified to bridge between East and West, present and past. Naive though he sounds with regard to *Musikwissenschaft*, Magnes seems, nonetheless, to have adapted his rhetoric to suit the particular candidate he was promoting. This also goes a long way to explain why Lachmann was preferred over Curt Sachs (whose name also came up in the correspondence with the American Friends), though the latter was, already by then, a more widely known musicologist.

It is hard to tell whether Curt Sachs – a fellow Berliner, eleven years Lachmann's senior, likewise deprived of all his academic positions in 1933 because of his Jewish origin – would have agreed to migrate to Palestine had the University offered him a position. At any rate, Curt Sachs looms like a giant among musicologists in retrospect, not least because of his phenomenal ability to synthesize countless facts into comprehensible wholes. Lachmann, by comparison, appears like a promise not fully realized, not only because of his untimely death, but also because of his finicky, at times excessive, concern for detail, though both ventured courageously into unexplored territory. Since there is no telling what might have happened to Sachs had he landed in Palestine, it is futile to speculate on the University's loss, since the University hardly came through with regard to what it did bargain for. Lachmann, like Sachs, might have soared even beyond the praise that was justly heaped upon him in the letters which introduced him to the University had he been given a fair chance. It is hard to abstain from "what if" speculations, but history does not take kindly to such inferences.

A Revealing Correspondence

The following letters appear in chronological order so as to convey the *dynamics* (in the multiple sense of the word) of their unfolding. The letters,

---

that the ingathering of the exiles presented unique opportunities to discover a common ancient heritage.

as a whole, are also intended to display the interactive process whereby makeshift solutions are fit to urgent problems, though the issues they address may call for fine tuning. Nonetheless, the correspondence displays genuine goodwill and a great deal of trust in the human networks which it involved.

Most of the following letters were written in English (Lachmann, as already mentioned, was well-versed in the language). Others were originally written in German, and some – those internal to the University – in Hebrew. Where necessary an English translation is provided. Occasional remarks will be added either to bridge between issues or to clarify matters that need elucidation.

We begin with a letter of introduction from Johannes Wolf, praising Lachmann as linguist, musicologist, orientalist and outstanding library official. Lest the reader misunderstand Lachmann's role of librarian in the Prussian State Library and the role of Wolf as director of a department, it is important to stress that such positions required scholarly standing in the fields under their jurisdiction. Wolf therefore equates "outstanding library official" with his description of Lachmann as linguist, musicologist and orientalist. Wolf himself became the director of the all-important Department of Music in the Prussian State Library because his scholarly record seemed to befit the rich and significant collection of manuscripts and incunabula which the department housed. In addition to his post as head of the music division of the *Staatsbibliothek*, Wolf was also professor of music at the Berlin University and chairman of the *Gesellschaft zur Erforschung der Musik des Orients*.

PRUSSIAN STATE LIBRARY
MUSIC DEPARTMENT

Berlin NW7, August 29, 1933
Unter der Linden 29

<u>To Whom It May Concern</u>[42]

Dr. Robert Lachmann, linguist (German, English, French), musicologist, orientalist and outstanding library official, has had an extraordinary record as a musicologist. He is rightly regarded as one of the foremost experts in the music of the Orient, which he became familiar with through his own experience in the course of several research travels, and which he has made accessible by lecturing and writing. His command of the Arabic language facilitated an unhampered contact with the common man, thereby ensuring unadulterated results. The success of the Congress in Cairo in 1932 dealing with the reform of Arabic music was largely due to his skill in the treatment of the Oriental musicians. But even beyond this particular field, he is acknowledged as one of the outstanding representatives of comparative music research and definitely deserves recognition also as an expert on the musical situation in the Occident. He is a resourceful and conscientious worker who is capable of meeting any task in his field.

(signed)
Prof. Dr. JOHANNES WOLF
Director of the Department of Music

Please note the date of the document. It obviously predates the letter informing Lachmann about his "retirement" (September 19th). The director of the music section of the library must have supplied Lachmann with the above document at Lachmann's request. Did Lachmann fear what was coming despite wanting to believe otherwise?

Much can be learned from the curriculum vitae prepared by Lachmann himself. His short biographical notes call attention to the importance attached to field work and the areas of responsibility entrusted to him. In

---

42 Translated from the German.

both cases it is assumed that the reader is privy to the scholarly qualifications that these activities require. While his publications in the capacity of librarian display his competence and expertise in Western music, his other publications – which he calls "private studies" – all deal with non-Western music. The list, however, reveals that Lachmann was not only interested in Arabic music, but also intrigued by other non-European musical systems, including that of *"Natur voelker"* (primitive peoples), which he wished to understand and compare in terms of familiar musical dimensions. Whether in search of principles, origins, uniqueness or commonalities, he always knew in advance what he was after.

Dr. Robert LACHMANN[43]

Biographical Notes

Born: November 28, 1892, at Berlin.

University Studies: University College, London; University, Berlin.

Degrees and Diplomas: Staatsexamen in German, English and French, 1920. Dr. phil. in Musicology and Arabic, Berlin, 1922.

Positions held: During the war: interpreter in a Muhammedan prisoners' camp.
1923: library service; since 1927 at the Staatsbibliothek, Berlin, Department of Music; collection of MSS and old prints.
1925, 1927, 1929: Musical Studies in Tripoli, Tunisia, Algeria.
1932: Chairman of the recording committee at the Congress for Arabian Music at Cairo; subsequently musical studies in Egypt and Sinai.

---

43 Lachmann's curriculum vitae as prepared by Lachmann himself.

Publications

A. As a librarian:

1. Die Schubert-Autographen der Staatsbibliothek zu Berlin (Zeitschrift fuer Musikwissenschaft. 11. 1928)

2. Die Haydn-Autographen der Staatsbibliothek zu Berlin (Zeitschrift f. Musikwissenschaft. 14. 1932)

B. Private Studies:

1. Die Musik in den tunisischen Staedten. Thesis (Archiv fuer Musik-wissenschaft. 5. 1923)

2. Musik und Tonschrift des No (Bericht ueber den 1. Kongress der Deutschen Musikgesellschaft in Leipzig, 1923). On the music of the ancient lyrical drama of Japan.

3. Muhammedan music (Grove's Dictionary of Music, 3. Ed. Vol. 3. 1927).

4. Zur aussereuropaeischen Mehrstimmigkeit (Beethoven-Zentenarfeier Wien 1927).

5. Musik des Orients Breslau 1929. Spanish translation: Barcelona 1931. English translation to be published.

6. Die Musik der aussereuropaeischen Kulture- und Natur voelker, Wil-Park-Potsdam 1929 (Handbuch der Musikwissenschaft, ed. E. Buecken).

7. Die Weise vom Loewen und der pythische Nomos (Festschrift fuer Johannes Wolf. Berlin 1929). Comparative study of Bedouin and ancient Greek instrumental music.

8. Musikalische Forschungsaufgaben in vorderen Orient. Berlin 1930. Paper read at the first meeting of the "Society for research in Eastern music" and repeated, in French, at the 8th Congress of the Institut des Hautes Etudes Marocaines at Rabat in April 1933.

9. Al-Kindi: Ueber die Komposition der Melodien, edited and translated with

a commentary. Leipzig 1931. The most ancient treatise on music in Arabic.

10. Asiatische Parallelen zur Berbermusik (Zeitschrift fuer vergleichende Musikwissenschaft. 1. 1933).

11. Das indische Tonsystem bei Bharata und sein ursprung (Zeitschrift f. vergleichende Musikwissenschaft. 1. 1933).

12. Editor of the "Zeitschrift fuer vergleichende Musikwissenschaft," an international review in German, English, and French, and the first one to deal exclusively with Eastern and primitive music.

(signed)
ROBERT LACHMANN

The biographical notes, together with the previous document by Wolf, were attached to a letter which was apparently not filed. It is clear, however, that it was written on February 7th, 1934 (see Magnes's letter to Lachmann from the 21st).

Here is another letter from Johannes Wolf. The letter is clearly addressed to Magnes. Note that Wolf had apparently visited Jerusalem and had been in touch with Magnes, who saw fit to extend his hospitality to Wolf. What brought Wolf, in those days, to Palestine? It would be nice to know more about that visit. Also note that Wolf claims to have heard that the University was looking for a "comparative musicologist." Was Wolf in touch with the American group (see Magnes's reply of February 15th)?

Berlin-Charlottenburg　　　　　　　　　　　　　February 4, 1934
Bismarckstr. 12

My dear Colleague,[44]

As I have heard, you are looking for a comparative musicologist for the University under your administration. As it happens, the Law for the Reconstitution of the Civil Service has affected one of my most competent collaborators in the State Library, one of our most outstanding comparative musicologists, <u>Dr. Robert Lachmann</u>, the publisher of our Journal of Comparative Musicology. Although Jewish, he is not familiar with colloquial Hebrew, but does have command of English, which, as a matter of fact, is his mother tongue (his mother being English).

You will find in him a brilliant collaborator who will surely contribute to the reputation of your University. In fact you have had the opportunity of communicating with him in writing when we tried to interest you in the planned Society for Research of the Music of the Orient. Under separate cover we are sending you our completed first annual volume, further numbers will be dispatched as soon as they appear.

I would like to know how you are doing, and what became of the plans of your son who intended to devote himself to music. I fondly remember your hospitality in Jerusalem and hope to meet you again in person.

Dr. Lachmann will write to you himself within the next few days.

With sincere greetings and best regards to your wife,

Yours,
Prof. Dr. Johannes Wolf

Though Wolf clearly knew the reason for Lachmann's dismissal, he describes the matter in prosaic terms – referring to the "Law for the Reconstitution of the Civil Service" in the second line of the above letter – confident that Magnes, too, knew perfectly well why Lachmann

---

44　Translated from the German.

was discharged. The letter, however, reveals that while taking part in the establishment of the Society for Research of Music of the Orient, Lachmann apparently tried to interest Magnes in the project. Since the population of Palestine was largely oriental, the new University, he thought, might take interest in the study of their music. Lachmann clearly gave some thought, even before having been "retired," to the research challenges which Palestine seemed to offer.

Professor Dr. Johannes Wolf,   February 15th, 1934
BERLIN-CHARLOTTENBURG.
Bismarckstrasse 12.

Dear Professor Wolf,

It was very pleasant to have your letter of February 4th. And I thank you for your interest.

    Thus far we have not heard from Dr. Lachmann himself. If he has not already done so, it would be advisable for him, in connection with his letter, to send us a curriculum vitae and a list of his publications, as well as a plan as to how he conceives his subject at the Hebrew University.

    Every scientific worker at the University is required to learn Hebrew in the course of time.

    There is in America a committee of well-known musicians, including Lazare Saminsky, Ernest Bloch, Ossip Gabrilowitsch, Arnold Schoenberg, Joseph Achron, and Joseph Yasser,[45] who are interesting themselves in the development of music at the Hebrew University. It may be that we could persuade them to supply funds for Dr. Lachmann, but that is not certain as yet. Unless extra funds of the sort were furnished, we could not unfortunately be in a position to pay for Dr. Lachmann's services.

    You are very kind to ask about my son. He is continuing his study of the violin with Mr. Emil Hauser, who is now the director of the Jerusalem Conservatory of Music, and he is studying theory and voice with Mr. Karl Salomon, who is also a

---

45 Note the list of musicians included in the American committee.

teacher at this Conservatory. The musical life of Palestine is developing in a most satisfactory way.

My wife wishes to be remembered to you, and with kind regards,

I am,
Yours sincerely,
J. L. Magnes

JLM/m

Some days later, Magnes received a second recommendation from Professor Eugen Mittwoch. Mittwoch was a distinguished German linguist and Lachmann's revered teacher who ushered him into the Arabic language. Note that Mittwoch's letter was sent from Paris. On account of his Jewish origin, he, too, was compelled to seek his fortune elsewhere. This letter, like Wolf's, reflects Magnes's skill in establishing good human relations with his academic correspondents and his presumed familiarity with Jewish and academic networks.

AMERICAN JOINT DISTRIBUTION COMMITTEE
European Executive Offices

Presently, Paris, February 19, 1934

My dear Dr. Magnes,[46]

Two days after I wrote to you last time, I received your kind letter concerning Mr. Polotsky, for which I thank you very much. I hope that the matter will be settled satisfactorily. In this outstandingly gifted young man, the University will not only gain a very competent Egyptologist, but also an Iranist and semitist of great quality.[47]

---

46 Translated from the German.
47 Polotsky, the "outstandingly gifted young man" recommended to The Hebrew University by Mittwoch, eventually became a world figure in his field.

If today I am again recommending somebody, it is because I personally know him and value him highly. The person in question is the musicologist Dr. Lachmann who, as he told me, wrote to you eight days ago, applying for a position. Dr. Lachmann is not only a general musicologist and historian of music but, in particular, also one of the foremost experts in Arabic music. For this purpose, he has thoroughly studied the Arabic language with me some years ago. He also has in an exemplary fashion edited and prepared an Arabic manuscript on music by Avicenna. He was repeatedly in the Orient where he carried out phonograph recordings of Arabic music. I know that Prof. Wolf and Prof. von Hornbostel (a cousin of Mrs. Max Warburg) hold him in high esteem. Up to now, Dr. Lachmann was employed in the Music Department of the State Library in Berlin, but has lost this position. With him, the University in Jerusalem would gain a most competent and qualified lecturer.

Today I return to Berlin and would be glad to have news from you concerning your plans.

In the meantime I remain,

with cordial greetings to you all,
Your,
Eugen Mittwoch

The following letters contain the initiating stage of an enduring correspondence between Lachmann and Magnes, which was to last until Lachmann's untimely death. While Lachmann's letters (below) are addressed to Magnes as the sole representative of the University, Magnes addresses his letters to all of those, including Lachmann himself, who might enable the University to commit itself to Lachmann. The reader will notice that Magnes often writes several letters on the same day, whenever the "Lachmann case" emerges on his agenda, not forgetting, of course, that the goodwill of some of the people he is addressing has to be maintained, beyond the particular issue discussed.

Dr. Robert Lachmann, February 21st, 1934
Klopstockstrasse 20,
Berlin. NW.87. Germany.

Dear Dr. Lachmann,

Permit me to acknowledge your letter of February 7th, together with its interesting enclosures.[48]

Professor Johannes Wolf had already written to us about your intention to seek a position at the Hebrew University.

There are no funds available for this post at the present time. There is, however, a Committee in America interested in the development of music at the University, and I am taking the liberty of forwarding to them the material which you were good enough to send me. It may be that this will make its appeal to them, as I sincerely hope it may.

Meanwhile, I shall be interested in securing from you a tentative working budget. It would be advisable to make out two budgets – one for an absolute minimum and the other a budget that would be by no means a maximum but that would give this Section the opportunity of steady even though slow development.

Could you send me, as far as you possess them, copies of the material which I have received from you? Also an additional set of the Zeitschrift which Professor Wolf was so kind as to let us have, not forgetting also another copy of your "Ja'qub Ibn Ishaq al-Kindi" publication.

I am,
Yours sincerely,
J. L. Magnes.

JLM/m

Given the way Magnes operated, he was interested, no doubt, in two versions of a tentative working budget – the "absolute minimum" one for

---

48 Lachmann, obviously, sent a letter to Magnes following Wolf's introduction on February 4.

internal use, and the short of "maximum" one for money-raising purposes. The following letter beautifully exemplifies the way in which Magnes set things rolling.

Herbert Askwith, Esq.,   February 21st, 1934
American Friends of the Hebrew University,
New York City. U.S.A.

Dear Mr. Askwith:[49]

I am sending you herewith material received from Dr. Robert Lachmann, of Berlin, and Prof. Wolf, a List of Material sent to the New York office in connection with Dr. R. Lachmann, which is of the utmost importance in connection with the development of music at the University.

    As you will observe, Dr. Lachmann is anxious to come here and if we are to have a Section of Music dealing particularly with Oriental music, Dr. Lachmann is recognised by many music students and researchers as the eminent man in this field. I recall that at the Congress for Oriental Music at Cairo in 1932, Dr. Lachmann played a central part. His knowledge both of Arabic and of music in all of its aspects made him a central figure.

    Prof. Johannes Wolf, a copy of whose letter I am also enclosing, is Professor of Music at the Berlin University and head of the Music Division of the Staatsbibliothek, and he is also Chairman of the Gesellschaft zur Erforschung der Musik des Orients. He is not a Jew, and is one of Dr. Lachmann's most fervent admirers.

    Mr. Kurt Schindler, who is, I believe, now at the College at Bennington, Vermont, also attended the Congress at Cairo and spoke a great deal about Dr. Lachmann.

    I would suggest that this material be laid before Mr. Saminsky and his Committee. If they could raise the funds, it would be a great thing for musical investigation here. Naturally Jewish music has its background in the "Oriental"

---

49 Herbert Askwith was the Director of the American Friends of the Hebrew University at the time.

music that is Dr. Lachmann's field of research. The Committee would thus be establishing here a fundamental division in the hands of a good man, and it would also be helping a German Jewish scholar to come to Jerusalem.

I am sending a copy of this letter to Mr. Saminsky.

I am,
Yours sincerely,
J. L. Magnes

JLM/m
Enc.

List of Material sent to the New York office in connection with Dr. R. Lachmann:
1. Letter from Dr. R. Lachmann dated February 7th.
2. Copies of Testimonials by Dr. Kruss and original by Dr. Johannes Wolf.
3. Copies of Testimonials to Dr. Lachmann's Work.
   "Journal of the Royal Asiatic Society."
   "L'independence."
4. Bericht über die 1. Sitzung der Gesellschaft zur Erforschung der Musik des Orients.
5. Publication on "Ja'qub Ibn Ishaq al-Kindi," by Dr. Lachmann and Mahmud el-Hefni.
   Four other pamphlets are enclosed.

Magnes was highly diplomatic in his letter to Askwith. Note that before presenting Lachmann as an eminent scholar, he implies that there is interest in the development of music at the University. Knowing the sentiments of his addressee, he highlights, in the concluding paragraph, Lachmann's possible contribution to the study of Jewish music.

Mr. Lazare Saminsky, February 21st, 1934
1, East 65th Street,
New York City. N.Y.

Dear Mr. Saminsky,

I am enclosing herewith copy of a letter which I have just written to Mr. Herbert Askwith, Director of the American Friends of the Hebrew University.

As you will see from the list of the material we are sending Mr. Askwith, Dr. Lachmann's work is really of the highest calibre and of the first importance as far as the music of the Orient is concerned.

In connection with the plan for the development of a Department of Music which I sent to you upon the receipt of your recent letter, he takes precedence over Professor Curt Sachs, of Berlin.[50]

I am,
Yours sincerely,
Encs. J. L. Magnes

If Lachmann's name may elude some musicologists today, this can hardly be the case for Curt Sachs, who was already by then the more established scholar. As is well known, Sachs had a serious stake in the study of non-European music, in addition to his manifold interests in Western music. The fact that Lachmann took precedence over Sachs in the plans for the possible, but still remote, development of a music department at the University reveals how eager the University was to adapt itself first to its locale, to the needs and challenges it presented. Lachmann's special interest in the Orient and, in particular, his command of Arabic must have played a major role in preferring him over Sachs.

In the meantime – but very quickly – Lachmann prepared a meticulous reply to Magnes's request for a budget (really, two budgets) to outline a

---

50 Curt Sachs was obviously suggested in an earlier letter.

proposed program of work. The document may be read as a kind of "manifesto," revealing Lachmann's overall conception of musicology, comparative musicology, and their interrelationship. It is fair to assume that it reflects the contemporary understanding of the entire field, not Lachmann's alone, despite the tailor-made issues which it addresses.

March 6th

Dear Dr. Magnes,

Accept my best thanks for your letter of February 21st in which you ask me to send you a tentative working budget for a musical section at the Hebrew University. Professor Wolf tells me that you have written to him as well and that you have suggested, with regard to my request, that I should draw up a plan as to how I conceive my subject there.

I think that a musical section at the Hebrew University should serve several purposes. One of them would be to acquaint students with the problems and methods of <u>general musicology</u>. This subject should not be missing among the disciplines taught at the Hebrew University, not only for its own sake, but also with regard to its relations to other subjects, among which I may mention arts and languages (phonetics) on one hand and ethnology and the history of civilisation on the other. For this part of the programme the usual training as provided at Western universities may safely be taken as a model. Students would have to be taught the elements of musical acoustics, psychology, and aesthetics as well as the outlines of musical history in Europe from antiquity down to the present day. As to the past, it would be desirable that they should gain a good general knowledge not only of the music itself, but also of musical theory in its different stages and of the various ways of musical notation, the latter being essential for an independent study of musical documents in the Middle Ages and later (instrumental tablatures). As to modern music from the 18th century onward, the university training should be in close touch with a training in musical practice as provided by conservatories like the one existing already at Jerusalem.

The chief object of all these courses would be to make students familiar with the main lines of musicology and to prepare them for doing research work.

Another part of the programme would include <u>non-European, and especially Jewish music</u>. In fact, this part may be expected to find special attention and care at a musical section of the Hebrew University which, owing to the history and geographical situation of Jerusalem, might well develop into a centre of research in Eastern music. For this purpose, however, an institute of a purely educational character would not do; besides teaching students the results arrived at up to now, it would be indispensable to undertake new and original investigations.

These investigations, again, have to be divided into the <u>study of literary sources</u> and of musical practice. The literary sources pertaining to Eastern music would have to be studied in the same philological way as those pertaining to European music, with the difference that they require a knowledge of Eastern languages. I am particularly thinking of medieval Hebrew and Arabic treatises some of which are mines of information and far from having yielded all their secrets.

But in spite of the interest afforded by these studies I would consider them to be of minor importance as compared to the <u>study of musical practice</u>. While books and manuscripts can be read, in reproductions, throughout the world Eastern musical practice has to be studied in its natural surroundings and as forming part of the life of the respective people. And while books and manuscripts can be preserved in libraries for an indefinite time, the unwritten music of the East, being the most volatile of utterances, is endangered by the rapid spread of Western civilisation.

It would, therefore, be the chief care of an institute for Eastern music to study the music still extant, and to collect as many specimens as possible of every class of it, both vocal and instrumental. The most reliable method is that of recording them by means of the phonograph (and, if possible, the sound picture). At the same time, special attention has to be paid to the shape, tuning, and handling of the instruments in use.

The advantages of the phonographic method over the old-fashioned one of taking down melodies in staff notation from direct hearing are self-evident. Records render the music such as it really is whereas notation from direct hearing can, at its best, give us an approximate idea of melody and rhythm, and none at all of delivery and timbre.

The records thus taken after a careful study of the music which they are destined to represent can be useful in several ways. But as the original wax records are easily injured they must not be used themselves except for obtaining matrices by an electrotype process; from these matrices any number of copies can be made.

A <u>collection of records</u> has a documentary value increasing in proportion as the music itself from which it has been taken dies out. At the same time the records offer the only reliable material for analyses of Eastern music: for rendering the tunes in staff notation (which can be revised over and over again) and for an exact measurement of pitches and time. These analyses should be undertaken soon after the music has been recorded; it often happens that the analysis draws our attention to points which had not been noticed before and which oblige us to revise our former observations or to make additional records.

A collection of records established at Jerusalem should not, of course, aim at universality. It would be preferable to start with the music within easy reach, that is, Jewish sacred and popular song and the music of the Arabs of Palestine and to proceed from these to kindred music as that of the Jewish communities of North Africa, Syria etc. and of the different branches of Islamic civilization.

In connection with an institute of research in Eastern music it would be desirable to arrange <u>lectures and training courses</u>. Music must not be collected haphazardly, nor can it be transcribed from records without practice; in both cases students have to work under tuition for a considerable time until they can do independent research work. In the same way they have to be instructed in the analysis, and in the study of the theory and history, of Eastern music. It is to be wished that a fair number of students will attend these courses; the subject is vast and requires as many trained specialists as can be had.

Besides, the collection and the studies based on it should attract several other groups of persons. The professional singer of sacred Jewish music may find models here as well as curious variants of the tradition and students of neighbouring disciplines such as Oriental languages or ethnology can amplify their knowledge and ideas. Permit me to quote, as examples, the relations existing between the musical form and the prosody or between the musical practice and the manners and customs (marriage ceremonies, funeral rites, etc.) of Oriental people.

As to my personal qualification for carrying out the above programme permit me to refer you to my former letter and its enclosures of which I am sending you copies as you have asked me to do. The tentative working budget which you have advised me to draw up is appended to this letter; its items are arranged in correspondence with the items of my programme of studies.

I am
Yours sincerely
Robert Lachmann

Enclosures:

1. Tentative working budget
2. Curriculum vitae (Education)
3. List of publications
4. Certificate by Professor Wolf
5. Three reviews of my publications
6. A copy of my edition of a treatise of Al-Kindi
7. A copy of the Zeitschr. F. vergleichende Musikwiss., Vol. 1
8. A copy of the report on the first meeting of the "Gesellsch. Zur Erforschung der Musik d. Orients"

P.S. Items 6-8 are dispatched under separate cover.

Appendix

Tentative working budget						Minimum Average
								In Reichsmark

A. for courses in <u>general musicology</u>

1. a room for lectures containing a piano and a gramophone.

2. books of references including dictionaries, manuals of the different subjects to be treated, a selection of standard editions of European music and musical theory, especially of the past.
I venture to hope that part of the library and, perhaps, the piano may be obtained as gifts from friends of the institute. Besides, it would be possible, in the present circumstances, to purchase books and collections of books at an exceptionally cheap rate owing to the fact that many collectors have been, or will be, forced to sell their libraries. It is, therefore, extremely difficult to figure out the cost of the objects enumerated under 1 and 2, even approxi-mately. Perhaps a sum of RM 2000.- would be sufficient as a beginning.	2000.-	8000.-

3. Periodical expenses						<u>per annum:</u>
   a) the principal reviews and journals on musicology	200.-	300.-
   b) the principal series of publications of music and musical literature	200.-	500.-
   c) gramophone records of standard recitals of classical and modern music, especially orchestral, an excellent help for the study of partitions and their authentic interpretation.	200.-	500.-

B. for <u>research in Eastern music</u>

1. A special <u>library</u> including dictionaries; printed editions and manuscripts (in photographic reproduction) of original works on Eastern musical theory; important modern publications;

at the beginning	200.-	500.-
per annum	150.-	300.-

2. A <u>laboratory</u>
   a) fittings and tools for making matrices and copies of records by an electrotype process — 600.- / 600.-
   b) phonograph (Excelsior) a piece: — 85.- / according to demand
   c) tonometer, metronome, electric pick up — 300.- / 300.-
   d) wax cylinders for recording music (RM 1.05 a piece), 240-400 pieces: — 252.- / 420.- <u>per annum</u>
   e) matrices (RM 3.- a piece) — 720.- / 1200.-
   f) copies (RM.-40 a piece) — 96.- / 160.-
   g) gramophone records of Oriental music — 150.- / 300.-
   h) fees for musicians singing and playing for the collection — 500.- / 1000.-
   i) international correspondence with scholars and institutes — 100.- / 100.-
   j) cost of shipment (wax cylinders) — 40.- / 40.-

The expenses under B might, like those under A, be diminished by occasional or permanent donations. As to No. 2, g, for instance, Jewish gramophone firms might offer specimens of their production gratuitously.

As to No. 1 and No. 2, b, c, I should be willing to place part of my own books as well as my phonograph and other instruments at the disposal of the institute until its finances are firmly established.

C. Personal budget

This would include my own payment as well as that of an assistant who would have to do all the technical laboratory work, and be of help, generally. As I am ignorant of the conditions in Palestine I must leave it to you to make a proposal in this respect. I would, however, point out two things. On one hand, after having lost my position at the Staatsbibliothek I receive a pension of RM 189.- a month. On the other hand, if I obtain a post at the Hebrew University, I shall have to return to Germany every year, which involves the cost of coming and going. Apart from personal reasons – my mother is a widow and in bad health – I suppose that at least a regular temporary residence in Germany is necessary for me if I am to keep my pension which, as you will understand, I do not wish to lose. You would greatly oblige me if you would kindly consider these points.

Robert Lachmann

This important document, together with its tentative working budget, serves as a much-needed reminder that serious scholarly research rests on a well-grounded education that supplies both proper tools and perspectives. Musicology, therefore, is broadly defined: it does not apply only to the study of Western art music, as opposed to other music, but constitutes the umbrella for all musical problems, providing method and guidelines adaptable to the study of musical traditions of whatever kind. A brief glance at the list of subjects which Lachmann included under the heading of general musicology well explains why he and his colleagues felt well prepared to undertake the study of non-European music.

As for the study of non-European music, it must be based primarily on musical practice in its natural surroundings, hence the importance of field expeditions and the perspectives they supply. Music must not be collected haphazardly, for the recordings of these materials carry paramount significance not only for research, but for the preservation of the musical traditions themselves. Familiarity with the literary sources pertaining to the specific musical traditions – where such exist – and careful study of the cultures that choose their own idiosyncratic expressions, is essential to the understanding of music. These precautions are perhaps more relevant nowadays, when musical influence seems to be flowing in all directions, and when the long-standing threat of Westernization – however ubiquitous in the field of technology – no longer applies in a simplistic way to contemporary cultures and identities. In short, the ways in which the bearers of a musical tradition understand their own music should guide the understanding of those who study it, rather than the other way round.

The analysis of the recorded music, Lachmann insists, depends on adequate transcriptions that enable systematic observations and comparisons. Such transcriptions, however, like the recordings themselves, should not be done hastily; they require practice and a prior acquaintance with the materials one wishes to transcribe. While the records offer reliable material for exact measurement of pitches and time, they do not tell us which aspects are significant in the music and in what ways they ought to be notated.

Lachmann, naturally, incorporated in his prospective budget a list of essential publications and laboratory equipment, estimating their costs. These lists may, no doubt, come as a surprise to young musicologists who have learned to take not only the phonograph for granted, but the computer as well.

Don't overlook Lachmann's casual mention of the possibility of purchasing books and collections of books at an exceptionally cheap rate "owing to the fact that many collectors have been, or will be, forced to sell their libraries." There was apparently no need to explain why.

How unprepared the University was to receive Lachmann, despite the rhetoric that was dispatched abroad, may be surmised from the following document.

21/3/34

To: The Committee dealing with the matter of Dr. Robert Lachmann
   Here

<u>re: Dr. Robert Lachmann[51]</u>

Dr. Lachmann is well known as one of the higher quality musicologists, especially in the realm of non-European music. For this reason I am requesting that Prof. Meir and Prof. Fodor consider his coming here. Dr. Lachmann also serves as assistant to Prof. Wolf, head of the Department of Music at the Berlin Staatsbibliothek, and I am therefore asking Dr. Bergman to be appointed a member of the Committee.[52]

The University does not possess the funds to bring Dr. Lachmann here, but there is a special committee in America which is interested in the development of music at the Hebrew University. If we can procure the means from them, I would like to receive answers to the following questions:

1. What is Prof. Meir's opinion concerning Dr. Lachmann as an Orientalist, and what position can an expert like Lachmann occupy at the Institute for Oriental Studies?

2. Does Dr. Bergman think that he will have a position for him in the Library?

3. What attitude should there be towards an external Music department, in Dr. Fodor's opinion?

Regarding music in general, there is great and growing enthusiasm here in this country especially regarding "Jewish music." It seems to me that if the University can acquire someone of Dr. Lachmann's stature, then the possibility exists that in the near future some basis can be worked out for teaching, researching, and expressing "Jewish music."

Yours sincerely,
Y. L. Magnes

YLM/ra

---

51 Translated from the Hebrew.
52 Prof. Meir was a member of the School of Oriental Studies; Prof. Fodor was head of the University's planning committee; and Dr. Bergman was in charge of the National and University Library.

Recall that in his letter to Askwith, Magnes implied that the University was interested in the development of a music section. Addressing University members, however, he saw fit to mention "a special committee in America" interested in the development of music at the University. Neither does he forget to harp on the Jewish angle, claiming that there is "great and growing enthusiasm" in the country regarding Jewish music, which Lachmann, as it so happens, is best qualified to teach and research. The following letters clearly show that the "special committee" still needed persuading.

Mr. Lazare Saminsky,   March 21st, 1934
1 East 65th Street,
NEW YORK CITY. N.Y.

Dear Mr. Saminsky,

Further to my letter to you of February 21st. concerning Dr. Robert Lachmann, I am enclosing you herewith a copy of his letter to me of March 6th, as also copies of letters from Professor Johannes Wolf, of Berlin.

Dr. Lachmann is undoubtedly a genuine authority in his subject, and, in the opinion of some, he is the very best man to be secured for the scientific and practical treatment of the music of the Near and Middle East. If we could have a man like him giving us the general scientific and practical background, the work of a man like Rosowsky[53] could be made infinitely more valuable than it otherwise might be.

It seems to me that this is a real opportunity for laying the foundations for a

---

53 Solomon Rosowsky, the son of a noted Russian cantor, was a student of Rimsky-Korsakov, Glazunov and Liadov. He was the co-founder of the Society for Jewish Folk Music in St. Petersburg (1908) and the founder of the first Jewish Conservatory of Music (1920) at Riga. He immigrated to Palestine in 1925 where he started his systematic research on biblical cantillation. His *The Cantillation of the Bible* was published in New York in 1957. He was a pioneer in his quest for a modern Hebrew style based on traditional and oriental elements.

genuine and sincere centre of musical research. This can have great influence not only upon Palestine and the music here, but upon musical development in this whole part of the world and also among the Jews of the world. With a man like Dr. Lachmann here, we would be treading on sure ground.

With kind regards,

I am,
Yours sincerely,
J. L. Magnes

JLM/m
Enc.

Mr. Herbert Askwith, DirectorMarch 21st., 1934
American Friends of the Hebrew University
New York City.

Dear Mr. Askwith,

I am sending you herewith further material relating to Dr. Robert Lachmann of Berlin, whom we would like to have here in connection with Oriental (including Jewish) Music. It will not be possible to invite him, as I think I have already written you, out of German funds. Perhaps, however, the Committee of which Mr. Saminsky is Chairman could provide for bringing Dr. Lachmann here and for setting up what is required in order to have a real laboratory for research in Eastern Music.

I am,
Yours sincerely,
J. L. Magnes

JLM/m
Encls.

Still other letters are addressed to prospective donors. Please pay close attention to Magnes the fund-raiser. His smooth language and clever rhetoric engage the interest of a potential donor. Note that each letter is tailor made, so as to meet the assumed expectations of the addressee. Also note the "personal touch," that invariably intimates that the group with which the addressees identify is already interested. Magnes is obviously not only a shrewd fund-raiser, but equally astute with regard to the organizational nets needed in order to promote specific projects. He often creates these nets himself, by selling the supposed interest of its members to each other.

Mr. Ossip Gabrilowitsch,   March 21st., 1934
Detroit Symphony Orchestra,
Orchestra Hall,
DETROIT. Mich. U.S.A.

Dear Mr. Gabrilowitsch,

I am sure you will be interested in a copy of a letter to me from Dr. Robert Lachmann, of Berlin, dated March 6th.

He is a man whom we ought really to try to get here. There is a great deal of loose talk as to the nature of Jewish music. Certainly if there is to be any scientific basis to Jewish music, Dr. Lachmann is the very best man to secure. With him here, the more specialized work that Rosowsky is doing would find its natural background.

There is a great deal of musical feeling in Palestine, as you know. The presence here of a scientist of music could do much to deepen and purify musical feeling.

Unfortunately we have not the funds to invite Dr. Lachmann here. There is, as you know, a committee of which Mr. Lazare Saminsky is Chairman. They have prepared a rather elaborate plan for music at the University. I do not know if you are in touch with them, but I hope that you are. If you are not, Mr. Askwith, at the office of the American Friends of the University, in New York, will be glad to put you into touch with them.

We have had press reports here of the very great success of the concert which you and others were good enough to give on behalf of the funds of the American Jewish Physicians' Committee. It is encouraging to all of us to see how you are continuing your interest and your efforts on our behalf.

When will you come here again?

With kind regards to you and Mrs. Gabrilowitsch,

I am,
Yours sincerely,
J. L. Magnes

JLM/m
Enc.

Here is a similar approach to Leonie Ginzburg who was involved with the activities of the University from the start. She had a particular interest in music, as will become evident later on.

Mrs. Leonie Ginzburg,   March 21st, 1934
c/o Mr. Harold U. Ginzburg,
18 East 42nd Street,
NEW YORK CITY. N.Y.

Dear Mrs. Ginzburg,

I am enclosing herewith a copy of a very interesting letter from Dr. Robert Lachmann, of Berlin. He is one of the great authorities, some say the greatest authority, in the field of Oriental Music. From his list of publications you will see that he is at the same time a scholar in the field of music as also a man of great practical experience.

When the Congress for Oriental Music was held in Cairo under the auspices of the King of Egypt three years ago, Dr. Lachmann was one of the most important participants. The "Zeitschrift fuer vergleichende Musikwissenschaft," of which he is editor, is a most important publication.

He is among those who have lost their positions in Germany because they are Jews and he is exceedingly anxious to come here and we are exceedingly anxious to have him.

Are you interested and able to help us get him here?

It is possible that I shall be coming to America in connection with a proposed meeting of the Board of Governors of the University. Beatrice will not come. I hope that you are in good health and that I shall have the opportunity of seeing you if I come.

We are all well, and with kind regards from Beatrice and myself,

I am,
Yours sincerely,
J. L. Magnes

JLM/m

In the midst of this juggling, Magnes does not conceal from Lachmann that he is unable, under the prevailing circumstances, to bring him to Jerusalem. In the following exchange, Magnes reiterates his interest and presses again for Lachmann's "cooperation." And, once again, Lachmann readily acquiesces.

Dr. Robert Lachmann, March 27th, 1934
Klopstockstrasse 20,
BERLIN. N.W.87.

Dear Dr. Lachmann,

I beg to acknowledge the receipt of your very interesting letter of March 6th and the accompanying material. You have given us just what we need.

Let me repeat that we should be glad to have you here in view of the very great interest we have in your subject. On the other hand, as I informed you, the University has at the present time no funds that it could use in order to bring and maintain you here. We have, however, sent copies of your material to America, to the Committee on Music there, and we have asked them if they could secure the necessary funds.

In case part of the necessary funds could be secured but not all of them, which items on pages 5-6 of your appendix[54] could you, in case of urgency,

---

54 Pages 5–6, mentioned in paragraph three of this letter, refer to the original document

strike out? Moreover, would an assistant be an absolute necessity at the present time?

I realise that this is asking a rather difficult question, but you will gather from this merely a repetition of what I have said to you above, namely, that we would like to have you here and that we have not any guarantee of securing funds at the present time.

I am,
Yours sincerely,
J. L. Magnes

JLM/m

Dr. Robert Lachmann
Berlin NW87
Klopstockstrasse 20

April 7th, 1934

Dear Dr. Magnes,[55]

In answer to the questions in your kind letter of March 27th regarding reductions from my working budget, I would, first of all, point out that the sums figuring in my former letter represent a minimum for the programme of studies I have outlined there. Reductions from there sums, therefore, carry along with reductions from the programme itself.

If this is inevitable I should suggest cutting down all the sums serving for the purchase of books and periodicals. This would mean that the educational part of the institute would have to manage with a very modest library at the beginning. I may repeat that I am willing to place part of my own books at the disposal of the institute.

On this basis, the sums under A, 1–3 and B, 1 might be diminished considerably.

(see Lachmann's proposal of March 6th) which conveyed Lachmann's tentative estimate of a working budget for a music section at the university.

55 Compare the present letter to the initial proposal from March 6th. Notice the emphasis on field and laboratory work.

A, 2–3, for instance, might be halved; as to B,1, only the annual sum of RM 150.- might be retained.

Once the institute is established, even on a small scale, it may be easier to obtain donations of any kind than before it has been started. The all-important point, in my opinion, is to prove, as quickly and as clearly as possible, that the institute is doing serious and important work. It will probably take years to train students for it; but it would be possible to record music and publish it without much delay. It would, therefore, be advisable to direct the first effort to field and laboratory work (B, 2 of the budget).

Here, too, expenses may be reduced temporarily. I can start the work with my own instrument; in this case, items B,2,b,c (with the exception of the electric pick up) would drop out. Further, B,2,g, as serving educational purposes, may be struck out.

Lastly, the assistant. I quite see that a second person may at first seem to bring about an additional and, perhaps, unnecessary expense. But according to my experience both the field and the laboratory work will profit immensely by the help of a capable man as the one I am thinking of. Collaboration with an all-round technician would ultimately save expenses instead of increasing them. The person I have in view would enable me to concentrate upon my study undisturbed by technicalities. He would not only carry out the different technical processes connected with the records (which, otherwise, would have to be done in Berlin), but also all the manipulations and frequent repairs occurring in the field and the laboratory; in fact, there would be no need to employ another workman in cases of emergency. Besides, he is trained to do photographic work, which, I think, might be a successful and appreciable side-issue and, perhaps, become a source of income for the institute, pictures of musical practice being extremely rare. Permit me to add a personal remark. While a difficulty might be seen in the fact that the person referred to is not a Jew, I can warrant his perfect loyalty which, as you can easily imagine, has been tried on more than one occasion in the recent past.

I am, dear Dr. Magnes,

Yours sincerely,
ROBERT LACHMANN

The idea of bringing along an assistant, while the funds for Lachmann, himself, were hardly in sight, must have, indeed, appeared as an unnecessary expense, especially to those who were unfamiliar with the kind of work that Lachmann was engaged in. Even today it strikes us as a luxury under the circumstances which Lachmann was forced to face. It strikes us thus, however, because we can no longer even imagine the technical complications and difficulties which recording involved.

At any rate, while the correspondence between Magnes and Lachmann concerns the establishment of a music section at the University, the letter that follows reveals how ill prepared the University was to absorb Lachmann, even in the library.

Dr. J. L. Magnes,   April 10th, 1934
C/o American Friends of the University,
New York City.

Dear Dr. Magnes,

1. Dr. Bergmann writes you as follows on the subject of Dr. Lachmann: (His note is dated April 5th, reaching us today.)

"In reply to Dr. Magnes's query of March 26th, whether Dr. Lachmann could find a place at the Library, I would say that after examining the material, I find that Dr. Lachmann was employed in Berlin in the Musical Department in the <u>collection of ancient musical manuscripts and prints</u>. Such work is not available with us. It might be possible to employ him if we could for instance get a large budget to extend the Music Section."

2. I am sending herewith Dr. Eig's budget, as worked out with Professor Warburg, for the Botanical Garden. Mrs. Horowitz, S.C. Lamport's sister, is leaving for America, and was insistent that you should get this revised budget. Dr. Eig explains why the sum he now gives is larger than that originally quoted to Mr. Lamport. You may care to take it up while in New York, if you have the time.

Yours sincerely,
J. L. Meltzer,
For the Registrar.

Enc.
M

Undeterred, Magnes offers another glimmer of hope.

Dr. Robert Lachmann,　　　　　　　　　　　　　New York, May 17, 1934
Klopstockstrasse 20,
Berlin. NW.87.

Dear Dr. Lachmann:

I am glad to say that I have found someone who is ready to contribute a very minimum amount, in accordance with your letter of April 7th, to the working budget of a section in non-European Musicology.

This leaves the question of your salary and that of your assistant.

In view of the fact that you have a pension, I would like you please to let me know what is the very minimum for which you and your assistant could come.

I should like to say that we have some splendid young scholars here who have been willing to come from Germany for £200 annually, and we have assistants who are coming for from £100 to £150 a year. These scholars and assistants have no pensions.

The highest amount that we are paying to German refugees is £400 to a professor. The section in Musicology, as I have written you, is not as yet to be included in our regular courses, and we have no provision for a professorship or even a regular lectureship. I am, personally, very anxious, together with some others, to make a beginning on this work, and with you I believe that if a beginning be made, it will be possible to develop this work in the way we should all like.

Will you be good enough to write me frankly about the situation as you see it?

A group of musicians here who have formed a society for the support of music at the Hebrew University, have pledged themselves for the coming year for a limited sum to support the work of Mr. S. Rosowsky on Biblical Cantillation. The next point in their program for next year will be in addition, helping the musical library. There are other groups here also who are interested in helping the library.

In the third instance, the society I mentioned is greatly interested in your work and will endeavour to contribute towards it in the future, but they cannot pledge themselves for the present.

I do hope we may come to some satisfactory conclusion.

Sincerely yours,
J. L. MAGNES

In the attempt to reach some "satisfactory conclusion," a number of letters were exchanged between May 17th and October 23rd. Though progress was made during these months it was not enough to enable Lachmann to make the final move. It was Lachmann, however, who was asked to make adjustments, including the expectation that he would raise funds by himself.

Dr. Robert Lachmann   October 23, 1934
Klopstockstr. 20
Berlin N.W. 87
Germany

Dear Dr. Lachmann,

Since your letter to me of September 25th, you must have received Mr. Ginzberg's letter of September 17th in which he replied to some of your questions.

It is not likely that we shall be able to find the rooms required by you in the University. It will probably be necessary to arrange for a couple of rooms in town. This will necessitate an increase of your budget by some fifty pounds.

Glad as I would be to see you working here as soon as possible, I consider it much more advisable not to hurry your departure from Europe, but to wait until you feel that you have done all you could, over there, to secure the additional funds required to cover your budget for three years. Work in Music cannot, of course, be included in the ordinary budget of the University, and it would be a great pity if your activities here had to be discontinued prematurely because our music funds had run out. We both agreed on that point during our talk at Zurich. I can well understand your natural wish to start at once. Nevertheless, under the circumstances, I would urge you to go on with your fund-raising efforts. I hope you will be successful and that the delay involved will not prove too long.

It is not advisable to apply to the authorities for visas for you and your assistant until the time of your coming draws nearer. The University's applications for visas are generally dealt with quickly, and we do not anticipate delays on that account.

I am
Yours sincerely,
J. L. Magnes

Klopstockstr. 20   November 15th, 1934

Dear Dr. Magnes,

Some friends of mine have made a proposition which, as it seems to me, overcomes the financial difficulties existing with regard to my work. They have offered to lend me an amount equal to £500 so as to complete the sum provided in my three years' budget. Of this sum, about £150 will be used in Germany for preparatory expenses as stated in my budget (under A, a–c). The remainder of £350 will be transferred to Palestine in small rates within three years.

My friends are ready to annul the debt if, in spite of further efforts we are expected to make in the meantime, we should not succeed in finding donations from other sources. If, on the other hand, additional funds can be raised, the debt is to be repaid in so far as the repayments do not interfere with the development of the section.

I hope that this proposition will appeal to you as much as it does to me and that, once the section has been started on this basis, it will be far easier to obtain additional sums than before.

Looking forward to your decision,

> I am, dear Dr. Magnes
> Yours sincerely,
> Robert Lachmann

On November 22nd, Magnes added to the above document a comment addressed to the treasurer of the University saying that "the condition is now ripe to invite Lachmann."

From the minutes of The Society for the Support of Music:[56]

RESEARCH IN ORIENTAL MUSIC.

There appears to be a possibility of Dr. Robert Lachmann, expert in non-European music (especially Oriental Music), establishing a research institute for Oriental Music in Palestine. The question of affiliating this undertaking with the Hebrew University was considered by the University Council on June 13, 1934, and it was agreed, after obtaining opinions from Prof. Johannes Wolf, Prof. Mittwoch, Prof. Mayer and Prof. Weil, that Dr. R. Lachmann possesses the necessary qualification for an academic appointment (perhaps in the rank of Lecturer). The funds for his work would not come from the regular budget, but, for the present, a temporary association with Dr. Lachmann was contemplated on the basis of earmarked funds promised for this work for a period of three years, if these funds are found sufficient.

---

56 See Magnes's letter to Lachmann from May 17th in which he mentions the society. The society was established by refugee musicians who sought to further the study of music in Palestine, as well as to solve their own problems of livelihood.

The following document clearly reveals that the money needed to enable Lachmann to continue his work in Palestine was not to come from the University's regular budget. His association with the University, moreover, was conceived in temporary terms. Ironically, Lachmann himself was one of the sources of the earmarked funds that would gain him the desperately needed University blessing.

December 27, 1934

Estimate of the Income and Expenditure
Dr. Lachmann – for three years.

I. Expenditure:
1. Non-recurring
   a) Laboratory Equipment (Apparatus for the electrotype process, pick up, tools for manufacturing wax cylinders) £ 100
   b) Transport 20
   c) Journey to Palestine and Return 50
   d) Unforeseen Expenses (not included in Dr. Lachmann's estimate) 30
   £ 200
2. Annual Expenses
   a) Material for preparation of records £ 50
   b) Excursions in Palestine for the purpose of Collecting Music 10
   c) Fees for Musicians 10
   d) Rent (not included in Dr. Lachmann's estimate) 50
   e) Light, Heat, Service (not included in Dr. Lachmann's estimate) 30
   f) Salary of Technical Assistant 200
   g) Salary of Dr. Lachmann 220
   £ 570
   For Three Years 1,710
   TOTAL £ 1,910

II. Income:
From Mrs. Ginsburg of New York $ 4,000   £   800
From Friends of Dr. Lachmann   500   1,300

Estimated Deficit for three years   £   610

Dr. Robert Lachmann   January 1st, 1935
Klopstockstr 20
Berlin N.W. 87.

Dear Dr. Lachmann,

I beg to acknowledge your letter of November 15th, 1934.
 Will you be good enough to thank your friends for their kind offer to loan you a sum equal to £500 so as to supplement your three years' budget.
 You and your friends will not, I am sure, regard it as in any way showing lack of appreciation if we say that we are not greatly enamoured of accepting loans which have to be repaid.
 We are not, unfortunately, in a position to make extra efforts on behalf of music out of our regular budget. The situation may some day change but we cannot build upon that hope in view of the large number of lacunae in our regular University structure for which funds will have to be secured. All that we can hope for is that friends interested in music may from time to time place sums for this purpose at our disposal.
 If such sums are placed at our disposal, it is not encouraging to have to say that the money is to be used in repaying loans.
 For this reason, I would suggest that you try to persuade your friends that they place this sum at your disposal without any conditions whatever.
 From the revised budget enclosed herewith, you will find that there is a difference of £600 in the total amount. The items in which this difference occurs are checked. Perhaps you can go over the budget to the end that there be no deficit.
 The budget should, it seems to me, be reduced on the point of traveling expenses. Inasmuch as you are receiving a pension, this seems to me to be a

not unreasonable suggestion. Moreover, I would point out to you that a number of our staff coming here from Germany do not have their travelling expenses refunded to them.

£80 of the additional expenditure in our revised budget is due to the fact that, unfortunately, we have no space at the University for your section. As it is, we are having constant struggles between departments as to the use of rooms already occupied. We are hoping that this situation will be remedied in the course of the next two years through the addition of some buildings. It may therefore be possible to remove £80 from the budget for the third year although this should not be definitely counted upon.

The salary of your assistant has been raised from £110 as proposed by you to £200 because we have here a collective agreement with the workers' union in accordance with which a fully skilled technical worker, such as your assistant seems to be, will have to be paid something like that amount.

I am
Yours sincerely,
JLM/ieb
J. L. Magnes.

Once more we note that music was not part of the "regular University structure," nor was its prospect very bright. Only an ad hoc appointment resulted from the negotiations in which Lachmann's salary remained negotiable. Paradoxically, only the salary of his assistant was assured; it was even raised due to the strength of the workers' union.

All of the contradictions and ambivalences – ranging from talk of a "new department" to a hesitant "appointment for the moment for one year" – are incorporated in the following official document.

The budget for Lachmann's appointment
(Oriental Music)

---

a. According to the budget submitted by Dr. Lachmann and amended by the University administration, expenses for the new department (Research of Oriental Music) will amount to £1910 for three years.
b. The above budget was sent by Dr. Lachmann on January 1st of this year and received by us. His suggestion to organize the required funding is as follows: In addition to the £800 ($4000 placed at the University's disposal for this purpose by Mrs. Ginzburg of New York), Dr. Lachmann places his <u>pension</u> at the University's disposal, which amounts to £650 for the three-year period. He hopes to raise the remainder – £550 – from a number of people to whom he has applied; however, if that sum is not raised, he is ready to cover the difference from his private pocket. Professor Wolf of Berlin, Dr. Lachmann's teacher and friend, has confirmed the above in a conversation with H. Ginzburg on 3 March 1935.
c. The administration must now decide whether the above financial situation is sufficient as a financial basis for deciding to establish the department. The first step will be requesting visas for Dr. Lachmann and his assistant, which will require an undertaking by us to the Government to employ them on a long-term basis.

<u>Note</u>: Regarding the above question:
1. Dr. Lachmann's salary has been estimated in the budget as the small amount of £220 per year, since we took into account the pension he is due to receive; however, if this sum will be spent on department expenses, Dr. Lachmann will then receive a very low salary when compared to his responsibilities.
2. It is not clear whether Dr. Lachmann's salary will definitely be received for three years, if he receives the appointment in Jerusalem.

A possible solution may be that he should be appointment for the moment <u>for one year</u> (the money from America should cover this).[57]

6.3.35

Upon which, the University turns to Lachmann as follows:

Dr. Robert Lachmann March 28, 1935
Klopstockstr. 20
Berlin-Germany

Dear Dr. Lachmann,

With reference to your letter and enclosures of February 14th, I beg to inform you that the University authorities are prepared to accept the budget as submitted by you, for three years including as part of the income your pension for three years (about £560) and the special income of £550 which you undertook to collect from a small number of interested friends, or failing that, to guarantee it from your private means.

In view, however, of the uncertainty attached to these two sources of income, your appointment at the University will, at first, be for one year. When you come here, we shall discuss with you the arrangements necessary for the prolongation of that appointment.

We have applied to the Jewish Agency for a visa for yourself and to the Government Department of Immigration for your technician (the law does not permit a non-Jew to enter on the Agency's certificate). We are making every effort to secure these visas as soon as possible and shall forward them to you upon receipt.

In order to import the machinery required for your department duty-free, it will be necessary for you to send us the bill of lading, or dispatch notice, with a

---

57 Note what little risk the University was willing to undertake (see item C, paragraph 2).

covering letter informing us of the shipment. Please take care, however, to address the machines directly to the Hebrew University and not to any intermediary agent, since otherwise the exemption from customs cannot be granted. We assume that the machines are required for your scientific work only, and not for any commercial purposes as the exemption is granted only on that condition.

I am,
Sincerely yours,
Max Schloessinger
Deputy Chancellor

Lachmann must have been pleased to read Schloessinger's letter informing him that the University authorities had accepted the budget he submitted that would enable the University to receive him. The letter made sure to remind him that the proposed budget included his pension fund and the money he undertook to collect from "interested friends" or otherwise to guarantee from his own "private means." However, given the uncertainty attached to these two sources of income, he was informed that the University would be willing to give him an appointment, at first, for one year only!

Despite these irksome, painful reminders and the University's embarrassingly cautious decision, Lachmann was bound to feel relieved. Impressed with Magnes's effort on his behalf and genuine interest in his work, Lachmann had learned, in the tedious process of negotiation, to empathize with the plight of the institution which Magnes headed. Determined to realize his dream, he, too, spared no effort, eager to display as much goodwill as he could possibly mobilize. Of course what might have struck the negotiators as symmetrical hardly strikes us the same way in retrospect.

Fourteen months elapsed from the initial contact with the University until Lachmann, accompanied by Walter Schur (his German technician), debarked in Haifa. The date was April 1935.

Walter Schur (Lachmann's technician)

ACT II
DREAMS CONFRONTED BY REALITY

Early Impressions

With problems seemingly solved, at least momentarily, it must have been exhilarating to arrive at a haven which also harbored so many exciting professional promises. Jerusalem, in particular, must have seemed like no other place Lachmann had ever visited. The barren hills, gradually rolling into the Judean desert, set a primordial frame to the city on high. But Jerusalem was not just another ancient city surrounded by mountains. As the meeting place of the three great monotheistic religions, it abounded in relics, monuments, edifices and sites attesting to its well-known history, which had turned familiar, as the terrestrial became spiritually endowed. The Jerusalem which Lachmann encountered defied the imagination of artists, who for centuries had depicted The Heavenly City as an elevated medieval town hugged by a city wall. Yet reality surpassed all that an informed mind could conjure up with regard to a place which had witnessed glorious, and not so glorious, chapters in the history of mankind. Within the confines of the Ottoman wall, built on earlier layers, there were countless monasteries, covering the long history of the monastic movement, from individual cells to community organizations. Amidst the many places of worship stood the famous Church of the Holy Sepulchre, entrusted to the various denominations still fighting for custody of Jesus' burial place. The Temple Mount, not far away, proudly supported the magnificent Mosque of Omar with its glistening dome, and the all important Mosque of El-Aqsa, hiding the ancient western part of the Wailing Wall, which came into sight only after meandering through narrow cobble-stoned streets. The mini pilgrimage one had to undergo in order to reach the Wall, and the inability to grasp it in one gaze added a spiritual dimension to its significance. For those addressing their prayers to heaven while scrutinizing the remnant of a Golden Age, longing and hope merged into a unique spiritual experience.

However possessed the historic sites had become, their significance was maintained by religious practice, which had evolved into crystallized forms – outward manifestations, as it were, of well-seated beliefs. These forms served as sources of reference for legacies that inevitably underwent change in the course of time. Christians, Moslems and Jews expressed their heritage in unique rituals and customs, relying, in no small measure, on canonical texts and sanctioned musical utterances. What a feast it must have been for someone interested in the comparative study of music to encounter in so small an area so great a variety of musical traditions. The fact that these traditions hark back to critical moments in the history of both Eastern and Western civilization, affecting their subsequent developments, was surely an added attraction. The sheer ubiquity of different musical traditions could be addressed with the hope of gaining new insight into important musical developments. Naturally, the ability to put the right questions depends on a broader frame of prior knowledge. Lachmann was well equipped.

Given his special interest in Arabic music, Lachmann could now forgo the extended expeditions that characterized his previous field studies. The country to which he migrated was very small, despite its large historic claim. There were countless Arab villages, scattered all over the country, some within the immediate vicinity. The Arab municipal centers, outside of Jerusalem, could also be reached quite easily. Given his sensitivity as a photographer,[58] Lachmann could not fail to be impressed by the picturesque hamlets with their protruding minarets, hugging the terrain in a way that made them appear like an integral part of the topography. In the quiet of the night he could even hear the powerful voice of some muezzin intoning the *adhan* – the Muslim call to prayer.[59] All considered, he could hardly have landed at a place with more inviting vistas. He was ready to go to work!

---

58 Lachmann was an expert photographer; he often supplemented his field trips with exceptional pictorial documentation.

59 The structure of the call for prayer – the *adhan* – is determined by the phrasing of the text which does not vary from region to region. Musically, it is composed of twelve phrases setting a seven-line text, with repetitions. Unlike the text, the melodies, with their relatively free rhythm, vary from region to region, though all are related to Arabic folk music.

The making of music in its "natural" environment

Lachmann's photographic depiction of a rural market in Tunisia

Getting Established

Magnes was most willing to help Lachmann get started. He wrote letters to whomever might assist Lachmann and his research activities. These letters reveal that Lachmann set out, at first, to collect everything that seemed of interest and worth recording. On May 27th, 1935, accordingly, Magnes asked Mr. Maliah, at the National Committee, to assist "our expert on non-European music" in contacting the cantors of Sephardic synagogues and other Oriental groups, while four days later he asked Mr. Foots, District Officer of Nablus, to facilitate the recording of the music of the Samaritans by "the University's great expert on chants and dialects of various peoples and sects of this part of the world." Lachmann writes Magnes to thank him for these letters which further his plan to establish a significant sound archive. At the same time, surrounded by so great a number of research opportunities, Lachmann can hardly curb his appetite. Though he knew well that limited budgets do not fit grandiose plans, his mind was constantly roaming, busy discerning what could be done if only…

House Himelfarb   June 1st 1935
Bezalel Str.

Dear Dr. Magnes,

Accept my very best thanks for the letters serving to prepare my stay at Nablus. I am very much looking forward to the recording of this and other music during the next weeks, especially since a considerable improvement has been made in the machine after you have heard it.

    As to the various points you raised the other day, I would –

    1. remind you of the permission I shall need, on my second arrival, to introduce discs and cylinders from my Berlin collection and additional tools, bulbs etc., for the laboratory.

    2. The Institut français d'archéologie et d'Arts musulmans of Damascus publishes two series of a philological and archeological nature. But one of the publications is also concerned with an ethnological subject. I think that a

connection with the Institute might become useful for musical studies in the Hauran or in Syria, generally.

I enclose a few remarks on the broadcasting programme hoping that this is about what you wanted.

I am,
Yours very sincerely,
Robert Lachmann

While paving the way for Lachmann, Magnes made sure to present the University to Mr. Nurock – a British government official – as an enlightened academic institution, appreciative of its staff members and their scholarly excellence. Though Lachmann, no doubt, deserves the praise Magnes heaped upon him, Magnes clearly misrepresented Lachmann's position within the University, having unfortunately *not* been made a member of the staff of the School of Oriental Studies (see Schloessinger's letter of July 16, 1935).

It should be noticed that while emphasizing (in paragraph five of the letter) the importance of a record-archive in order to secure an "exact knowledge" of the music of the region, Magnes sees fit to claim that what makes Lachmann's presence in the country "doubly valuable" is the fact that he brought from Berlin his own recording machine together with his mechanic. Recording, evidently, was not only novel and rare, but an intricate matter that required considerable knowledge of those in charge. The subsequent letter, written by Lachmann, makes this point abundantly clear.

Max Nurock, Esquire   June 5, 1935
Government Offices
Jerusalem

Dear Mr. Nurock,

I have pleasure in enclosing a most interesting statement from Dr. Lachmann on the broadcasting of music from the Jerusalem station.

You may be aware that Dr. Lachmann is regarded as one of the world's foremost experts in what is technically called non-European Musicology. He is still the editor of the foremost periodical on this subject "Die Zeitschrift fuer vergleichende Musikwissenschaft," which appears in Berlin under the auspices of the Society for Oriental Music. He was the Librarian for Old Musical Prints and Manuscripts in the State Library at Berlin. Owing, however, to the new regime in Germany, he was compelled to give up this post.

Dr. Lachmann was one of the prime figures in the Congress of Oriental Music convened by King Fuad of Egypt at Cairo in 1932.

In addition to having written a great deal on this subject, he is the editor of the first Arabic treatise on music (Al-Kindi: On the Composition of Melodies, 9th Century).

What makes Dr. Lachmann's presence in this country doubly valuable is the fact that he has brought from Berlin his own recording machine together with his mechanic. This will make it possible for him, in the course of the years, to record everything that is worth recording for the purpose of securing an exact knowledge of the music of this region and for the purpose of establishing an archive of such records. This is the indispensable basis for any natural development of Arabic, Jewish or any other kind of non-European music. The Hebrew University regards it as its good fortune to have been able to bring Dr. Lachmann here and to have made him a member of the staff of the School of Oriental Studies at the University.

I am sure that it will be most helpful in arriving at clarity in this complicated subject of so-called oriental music and of establishing high standards in this music if Dr. Lachmann were brought into consultation with those responsible for the programs of the Broadcasting station.

Sincerely yours,
J. L. Magnes

House Himelfarb   8.6.1935
Bezalel Str.

Dear Dr. Magnes,

This is the list of the objects which are needed for the section of non-European music and which I intend bringing from Germany in autumn:[60]
1. for the laboratory
    a) an amplifier for alternating current;
    b) a recording machine for alternating current;
    c) a contrivance for loading accumulators;
    d) ten valves as reserve;
    e) 100 gelatine blank discs for recordings;
    f) some minor reserve parts.

These objects cannot be had here. Nor can they be ordered by letter from England or elsewhere; they must be bought personally in order to make sure that they exactly fit the purpose for which they are intended. (The items under a) and b) will enable us to record music in the laboratory by means of the ordinary street current, and reserve the expensive batteries for recording in the field.)
2. for the archive:
    a) 60-100 gramophone discs from my personal collection, all of them used. These discs were recorded by different firms 15–25 years ago. They are no more on sale, but of great value for demonstration and studies.
    b) My collection of Oriental music recorded on about 100–200 phonograph cylinders on my various travels in North Africa. Same purpose as Nr. 2a.

The budget of the section is altogether too small for paying duty on these objects. On the other hand they are partly indispensable, partly most desirable for my work here. It would, therefore, be of great importance for the section

---

60 Since it was still possible to go to Germany in the mid-thirties, Lachmann went back several times to visit his family.

if you could obtain permission to have them imported free of duty. In case this is granted I should be grateful for precise directions how to handle the matter.

Yours sincerely,
Robert Lachmann

Though naive about his surroundings, Lachmann was anything but a naive collector. He knew his métier well and managed, under the new circumstances, to keep abreast with relevant developments elsewhere. He was pleased to have been able to display his recording machine to Magnes, who was duly impressed with the new "wonder machine." If Magnes was also willing to lend his ears to Lachmann's detailed requirements, in spite of everything else he had on his mind, it was because the idea of securing an "exact knowledge" of the music of the *region* appealed to Magnes, who never lost sight of the fact that the country was not only inhabited by Jews. Moreover, he saw in Lachmann's envisioned archive a sound base for the future development of an indigenous musical culture. Echoing Lachmann, he agreed that the radio station could benefit from Lachmann's unchallenged expertise in order to assure high standards with regard to the broadcasting of Oriental music.

The conflict between cultural experts and officials who wish to accommodate the groups' own interest in their traditions is often symptomatic of situations characterized by continuities in the face of change. While most experts have a vested interest, as it were, in cultural purity – in unadulterated versions of well entrenched practices, the bearers of a given culture may, wittingly or unwittingly, enhance their own tradition by what they have come to appreciate in cultures other than their own, or through concessions to subtle processes of acculturation. Indeed, the scientific attitude is often regarded as antiquarian by bearers of a *living* tradition. Lachmann was bound to work hard, trying to create a new self awareness in the eyes of those whose music he wished to preserve. In the meantime, it was advisable to record as much as possible, to be on the safe side. The archive was, thus, destined to serve a double function: as custodian of a treasury of musical traditions (living and extinct) and as a database for research.

Although not easily accessible to other people, Magnes seems to have befriended Lachmann, who needed his advice and protection. Lachmann, apparently, felt free to share his thoughts with Magnes, involving him, as well, in minor practical details. Magnes, though unsure that his new academic acquisition knew how to manage his own affairs, completely trusted Lachmann's judgement insofar as music was concerned.[61] The following letter, which was attached to Lachmann's first official report about the Section for the Study of Non-European Music, clearly reveals that Lachmann, in gratitude to Magnes, was eager to present a united front vis-à-vis other University officials.

14.6.1935

House Himelfarb
Bezalel St.

Dear Dr. Magnes,

Please find enclosed the first report of my section. I may add that I am deeply indebted to you for your kind help and suggestions and for bringing me into contact with people who can advise me and advance my work. I did not mention this in my report because I thought that you might not like it.

I saw Mr. Epstein, of the Jewish Agency, a few days ago and I am particularly grateful to you for this interesting and pleasant acquaintance. Following my invitation he attended the recording last Thursday.

Following your hint I visited the gramophone shop at Mea Shearim. But I have not yet heard enough records to come to a conclusion.

We go to Nablus on Sunday.

---

61 He also seems to have consulted Lachmann about the future education of his son, who was interested in contemporary composition and preparing to go to the States to further his musical studies. The mention of Henry Cowell (in the letter attached to Lachmann's First Report; see below) apparently came as an answer to a query.

Would you please give the enclosed card to your son. Mr. Cowell is a composer of disputed talents and undisputed oddity. Above all, he is a most kind and pleasant person, and knows a great many musicians. He usually spends his holiday at Menlo Park, Calif., but is sure to be in New York for his courses at the New School for Social Research (66 West 12th Street) in Autumn.[62]

In case you should have my report type-written I should be obliged for a copy.

Yours sincerely,
Robert Lachman

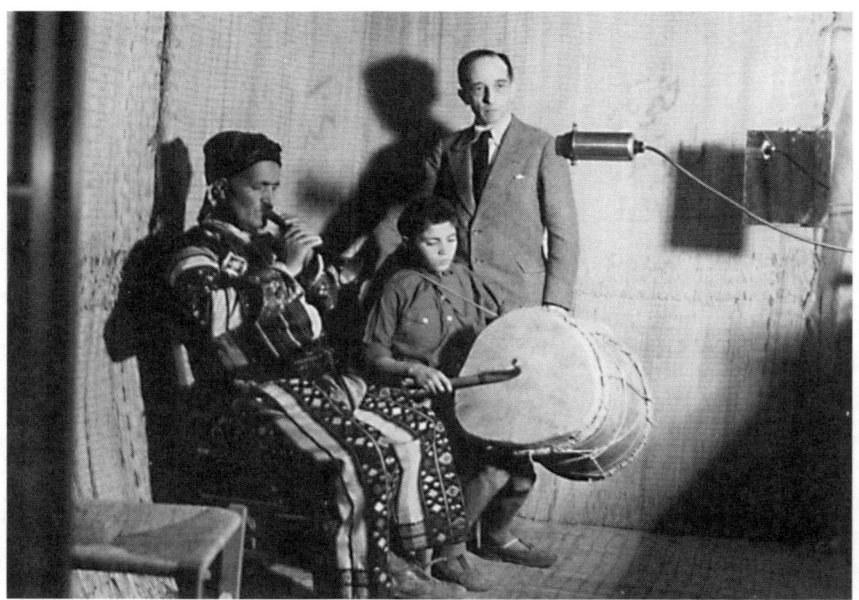

Lachmann in his recording studio with a Kurdish Zurna player
and a Dolla (drum) player

---

62 Lachmann apparently knew something of Cowell's experiments with new musical sounds and his persistent advocacy of the avant garde. He also must have met him in 1931–1932 in Berlin, since Cowell, who became interested in non-European music, worked closely with some of the better known comparative musicologists that year, including von Hornbostel.

14.6.35

SECTION FOR THE STUDY OF NON-EUROPEAN MUSIC

First Report

The first few weeks after our arrival in Jerusalem, on Monday, April 29, were spent in trying to find suitable rooms for the archive and laboratory and in gathering some rudimentary information as to opportunities of obtaining Jewish and Arab traditional music both in town and elsewhere.

The question of the rooms could not be settled definitely, owing to financial considerations. Until further arrangements, a wing at Himelfarb House, Bezalel Street, was hired as provisional work-rooms.

As regards the work itself, expectations as to a vast field of research offering itself in Jerusalem and in the country at large were not deceived. It may be hoped that in the course of time it will be possible to study the ritual song not only of the different Jewish traditions, but also of the Christian Oriental communities of Palestine and, perhaps, recitations of the Koran, all of them in reliable renderings. Moreover, there still exists a wealth of secular song and instrumental music especially on the part of Arab peasants and Bedouins.

While it had been proposed to spend the first months on sketching a comprehensive programme for the next few years it now appears that it will be wiser not to proceed on fixed lines, but to seize opportunities as they present themselves (sometimes suddenly and unexpectedly) of studying the repertoire of a particular singer or musician or the musical aspect of a ceremony, sacred or secular. Opportunities of this kind have turned up already, owing in the first place to the constant and ready help and advice of the University, but also to the keen interest that the Education Department as well as a number of private persons are taking in the work.

Owing to delay at the customs, it was not until the end of May that the recording machines and the other objects imported for the laboratory work could be mounted. Sittings for recording Oriental music were started on Tuesday, June 4th. Up to now, specimens were obtained of

1. Singing to the accompaniment of the Rabab al-sha'ir
2. Popular Arab song in Jerusalem
3. Psalm-singing by a Roumanian Jew

4. Singing to the accompaniment of the 'ud.

The last item is of special interest. At my request, the singer and player, a well-known amateur of Jerusalem, Wasif Gauharija, started a series of instrumental preludes and vocal introductions representing the different melody-types (maqamat) of Arab classical music, and promised to complete it on the next occasion. These records will be particularly useful for anybody who wishes to obtain a precise idea of the traditional Arab system of melodies and scales. Of course, no summary of this kind can be found on records of industrial firms.

The records taken so far amount to a total of 12 double-faced discs.

Jerusalem, June 14, 1935   Dr. ROBERT LACHMANN

As mentioned, Lachmann could not help but be impressed with the vast research opportunities which the country offered. It offered no less than the opportunity to study the musical traditions of *all* three monotheistic religions – Jewish, Christian and Arab – and the possible relationships among them. What a feast! From a sheer professional point of view, it was, indeed, more advisable not to sketch in advance a comprehensive program of studies, but to collect first as many representative specimens that could be obtained so as to enable the charting of such a program. However, while collecting these specimens, Lachmann, as expected, did not overlook opportunities, when they presented themselves, to secure musical renditions which, in and of themselves, could provide answers to important scholarly queries, like, for example, Mr. Gauharija's renditions of the different melody-types, concerning the workings of the *maqāmāt*.

Having become increasingly involved with Lachmann and his scholarly activities, Magnes needed some reassurance, since his enthusiasm was not shared by other staff members of the University, as will be shown below. In this connection it is of interest to note that Magnes saw fit to report to Wolf about Lachmann's progress, echoing, as it were, Wolf's recommendation in the first place. This can be surmised from the following reply from Wolf to Magnes:

Berlin, June 20, 1935

My dear Colleague,[63]

I most cordially thank you for the letters concerning the University which I have read with the greatest sympathy. You know that I wish your Institute only the best and that I am glad to have rendered you a service, however modest. You may already have realized that Robert Lachmann constitutes an intellectual potential which must be utilized for the University, and that musicology is not just an also-ran discipline, but one that must be fully incorporated into the corpus of University disciplines.

I wish you a restful vacation and with the best regards to your wife and your son.

I remain
truly yours,
Johannes Wolf

Wolf knew well what he was talking about. Musicology had not yet been incorporated even in the curricula of the majority of German universities, though they certainly did not consider the field as "just an also-ran discipline." While musicology, on the whole, was still an unfamiliar field at the Hebrew University, this was not the only reason why it failed to rally support.

Even while Wolf's letter was being written, Lachmann was delivering his Second Report to Magnes. This impressive document is a portrait of Lachmann the careful and disciplined ethnographer; he always made sure he knew why and what he was recording. However, it should be mentioned that discs were still relatively expensive in those days, and most informants had to be paid for their services. Constrained by a limited budget, Lachmann was compelled, at any rate, to discriminate between the "what"

---

63 Translated from the German.

and the "whom" to record. Luckily, he was equipped to make educated choices. While the Second Report vividly portrays what has been said, it also suggests that Magnes may have been the sole reader of these reports, filed under "Lachmann." The reports, justifiably, emphasize accomplishments under difficult constraints, re-enforcing Magnes's trust in Lachmann, and his efforts on Lachmann's behalf.

SECTION FOR THE STUDY OF NON-EUROPEAN MUSIC

Second Report

Immediately after the first report had been written several opportunities were offered of hearing and recording songs outside Jerusalem.

A. Mr. D.N. Barbour had the kindness of conveying ourselves and the recording machine to Artas, a village near the ponds of Solomon, in his motor-car. He introduced us to Madam Louise Baldensperger who occupies a singular position in the village, having spent a life-time among the natives, and enjoying their full confidence. Being herself a Student of Arab manners and customs she readily used her influence to make people play and sing for us at her house. We recorded:
    1. a romance (qusida) about the invasion of Tunisia by the Beni Hilal, sung by a young villager to the accompaniment of the Rabab al-shair;
    2. women's songs, partly ritual, partly profane, sung by a blind elderly woman.

B. On the following day (Sunday, June 16th), on our way to Nablus, we stopped at Bira, the Arab village close to Ramallah, where, by recommendation of Omar Effendi Salah Berguthy and in his presence, we were invited to hear two men, one singing and playing on the Rabab al-shair, the other playing on the shibbaba (a flute).

C. At Nablus, the main object was to record specimens of the liturgical song of the Samaritans. On the first day (Monday, June 17th) while negotiations as to the payment of the Samaritan singers were conducted, there was time to record:
    I   a number of women's songs (with devotional texts), from two . . .

II a number of Arab songs of Bedouin character, sung by a group of men from Nablus.

In the meantime it had been agreed that the High Priest of the Samaritans should assemble six of his priests, and recite a number of songs and cantillations with them. I had, before starting from Jerusalem, made a list of passages from the Tora and of other chants which it was desirable to obtain in the Samaritan version, and had also received some additional hints from Professor Pick. The chants recorded at the house of the High Priest and partly executed by himself were:

III 1. Recitations peculiar to the five high feasts;
2. the "Song of the Sea" from Exodus;
3. specimens from the ten commandments (with special regard to the Samaritan 10th commandment), both chanted and read.
4. Chants on special occasions (wedding, circumcision, and burial), and a song for general festivities.

The Samaritan cantillations show signs of high antiquity, a fact which I hope to be able to prove by an analysis of the records and a comparison with the cantillation of other liturgies. It would certainly be premature, after this first hearing, to attempt a guess as to the exact, or even to the approximate, time to which the present state of the tradition may be dated back. But I think that it will be possible to show that the Samaritan style of liturgical recitation belongs to a layer prior to that of most other Oriental cantillations, and intermediate, perhaps, between it and the magical recitations typical of shamanism. But this cannot be said definitely until after a close study of the specimens obtained. At any rate, the Samaritan claim as to the faithfulness of their tradition is fully justified.

The fragmentary character of the records, or of most of the records is explained by the enormous length to which every sentence of the texts is stretched in the solemn delivery of them in the service. Owing to this and to the responsorial rendering of many of the prayers, it would have been impossible to record any of them at full length. The "Song of the Sea", e.g. covers two double-faced discs although only the beginning, the middle, and the end were recorded. This must chiefly be regretted from a philological point of view whereas it is hoped that the specimens will permit to form a fair idea of the chant which, of course, abounds in repetitions. But even if, from the point of view of research, it should appear to be desirable to obtain more specimens the money question would be a serious impediment; an immoderate price was demanded and paid for the three sittings during which the records were made.

We returned to Jerusalem on Tuesday night.

The number of records taken on the various occasions is:

A (Artas): 3 double-faced discs
B (Bira): $4\frac{1}{2}$
C (Nablus):
   I: $1\frac{1}{2}$ "   "   "
   II: 3   "   "   "
   III: 17 "   "   "

    29 "   "   "

The archive now consists of 41 discs numbering from 1a, b to 40a, b, 41, 42.

Jerusalem, June 21st, 1935

An Arab playing the Rabāb

In addition to his interesting and vivid ethnographic descriptions, Lachmann's spontaneous reaction to the Samaritan style of liturgical recitation is quite remarkable. Considering the fact that he had never before heard Samaritan cantillation, his impression of the antiquity of the music can be attributed only to his thorough acquaintance with other ancient styles of recitation. It beautifully exemplifies, albeit in minuscule, the comparative nature of the field which Lachmann helped to promote.

Lachmann's utter seriousness and scholarly rigor is interestingly reflected in his account of the recording of the "Song of the Sea." He bemoans, for example, the fact that he was unable to record the entire song, though it abounds in repetitions, due to the "money impediment." It is particularly regrettable, Lachmann tells us, from the philological point of view of which he always took account.

Even while occupied with his own problems, professional and personal, Lachmann became an address for other uprooted individuals who hoped to find refuge in Palestine. Lachmann was hardly in a position to take care of his own affairs, as will become increasingly apparent, let alone other people's problems. Still, he lent an attentive ear to the needy. For example, the following letter shows Lachmann trying to help Mr. Benno Balan, a Jewish publisher who had music written and photocopied for Lachmann in Berlin. As usual, he turned to Magnes (see the last part of the letter).

The suggestions he makes concerning additional activities for his project are especially interesting, for they raise issues and offer solutions to problems which are of pertinence to this very day. Committed to traditional music, as he was, he sought to address the needs of those whose attention he wished to engage, offering his services as an adviser and an expert. Lachmann proposed that activities of this kind might help stir developments in directions that could prove useful to larger publics, and to national institutions such as education and broadcasting.

7.7.1935

Dear Dr. Magnes,

With reference to our conversation on last Wednesday permit me to draw your attention to the following points:

1. The question of my rooms has found, or will shortly find, its solution. I have seen a most suitable flat, the ground-floor of Beth Rav mi-Gur, at the back of Himelfarb House, with a large garden (which is important for persuading country-folk to sing and play), at the price of £P32

2. With regard to the budget, and especially to the sums of £P10.- each provided for musicians' fees and travelling expenses, two months; experience has shown that no considerable results can be arrived at in the future unless it becomes possible to open up new sources of income. Permit me to remind you of the sums spent on Samaritan sacred song which amounted to about £P10.- (including the trip) and which would have been even more disproportionate if it had not been possible to take other interesting records on the way and at Nablus during free hours. On the other hand, the Samaritan records are an outstanding feature of the collection. I grant that, in the course of time, I may learn to get musicians at lower prices, but any such diminution will certainly not be sufficient to balance the budget and to secure a satisfactory range of activity for the section. Apart from the exaggerated demands of some musicians, there are cases where singing and playing is offered without any fee, but where it seems impossible to take up the singer's time without any remuneration. The Jewish lute-player of Baghdad, e.g. who is mentioned in the enclosed report, and who offered to play gratuitously owing to our friendship formed at the Egyptian Congress, has to struggle for his and his family's existence and I felt I could not accept his service without paying for it.

I would suggest to try and find additional funds by interesting a larger public in the work of the section without for a moment straying from the lines as proposed in the original programme. This might perhaps be done by throwing stress on these points connected with the work which, as I had numerous occasions to observe, are most discussed and felt to be important by the general public.

The general public seems to be less interested in the work as far as it aims at a careful and fairly complete preservation of traditional music from a point of view of history than in the question as to what part of traditional music may be, or may become, important for future developments. Strange as it seems to me, it is a fact that both among Jewish and Arab musicians there is a strong tendency towards asking expert opinion and advice. Even today I was asked by an Arab musician what I could do to bring about a reform of their music. I think that this confidence in scholarly judgment, of which the above question is only one instance, should not be left hanging in the air. It might encourage

a) to lecture every now and then, perhaps three times a year, before a general audience on observations made in the course of the work (with musical illustrations), and especially on observations which may be fruitful for present day music. More generally, it might be useful to impress upon these audiences the value of historical research as showing on what lines music has proceeded and, therefore, indicating on what lines it may possible proceed in the future.

b) to apply the experience gathered by the study of traditional music to teaching. The problem of school-music has been attacked successfully in Egypt and there is no reason why it should not be done here. In Egypt the expert opinions laid down by musicologists at the Congress in 1932 have become the foundation for musical training in boys' and girls' schools. Owing to these opinions, a number of traditional musical instruments, e.g., have been revived and are now in the hands of the young generation. It would be advisable to communicate with the educational authorities and they would, I think, accept advice as to how a programme of school music could be built up and be a firm hold for musical instructors at schools instead of allowing them to follow their own and, maybe, wrong ways or instead of neglecting school music altogether.

c) to take an active influence on the programme of the future broadcasting station as far as it is concerned with non-European music. I have stated some points with regard to this programme on a former occasion. In the meantime I have noticed that, in this respect as well, the general hearer in this country is much more interested in questions connected with the work of the section as I had foreseen, and here again, hints as to a sound evolution of traditional music will not be wasted. Formerly, e.g., I was hesitating about the utility of making the music and songs of the more primitive parts of the population a feature of the programme. But since it has become known that the rural population will be led to take an interest in the broadcasting programme I am positive that it is not only desirable but necessary to include their music and, moreover, that it will be essential to be as careful in the selection of it as in that of any other kind of music.

With regard to Jewish music it will be most useful to perform typical folk songs from every one of the diverse Jewish communities and to recall to the minds of the Jewish listeners how rich and varied their music can be. They will then be more able than at present to choose from this inventory and to arrive at a clear idea of a Jewish style in music.

Perhaps, if these suggestions could be put into practice, some financial aid for the section might result from them. As to point (a), the entrance fees for the lectures might yield a small sum. As to points (b) and (c), the respective organisations, schools and the broadcasting station, if they can be convinced that expert advice and help, given temporarily or continually, is really essential for their work, may be expected to pay for it and thus to strengthen a source from which they benefit themselves.

3. I enclose a letter addressed to me by Mr. Benno Balan whom I mentioned the other day. He now tells me that the appreciable work he had done by having music written and phototyped for me and others at a very reasonable price in Berlin can be continued here, and that he has learnt to do it himself. I think that his proposal can be very useful indeed and that there is no objection to recommend him for immigration if his statement as to his being able to write the music himself is correct. He has published numerous compositions, chiefly by Jewish authors.

I remain, dear Dr. Magnes,
Yours sincerely,
Robert Lachmann

P.S.1 I should be grateful for obtaining a type-written copy of the 2nd and 3rd reports of the section.

2 enclosures

P.S.2 I received an invitation from the High Commissioner for dinner on Saturday night. He appeared to be vividly interested in the work of the section and I had to answer numerous questions as to the music of this country, Jewish and Arab, and its history.

Sociologically astute, Lachmann discerned that the general public, both Jews and Arabs, were far more interested in what their musical heritage was likely to become than what it actually was in the past. The question of identity, or concern over identity-loss, must have preoccupied some segments of the population already then. The idea of turning to experts for advice, not shunning the possibility of introducing deliberate changes into musical traditions, so that they might continue to serve as viable hallmarks, clearly points in this direction. If Lachmann considered the possibility of giving an occasional lecture to a general public, it was certainly not only for the purpose of raising additional funds for his work, or in order to make his work more widely known. Rather, his scholarly commitment impelled him to persuade the bearers of the different musical traditions to take pride in their musical heritage and carry it forward. His plan to introduce traditional music into boys' and girls' schools (as, we learn, was done in Egypt after the congress of 1932), as well as his intent to exert influence on the musical programs of the broadcasting station, were equally motivated by his commitment to understand and to value authentic cultural expression for the bearers themselves and for others. This proposal implies an intuitive awareness of the importance of representation in a multi-cultural society.

Lachmann's progress report accompanied the letter of July 7th:

SECTION FOR THE STUDY OF NON-EUROPEAN MUSIC

Third Report

After the excursion to Nablus no further recording took place outside Jerusalem. Still, the collection could be increased by two series of records.

Mrs. Gerbell informed me of the presence in Jerusalem of a Jewish lute-player from Baghdad, Azuri Harun, who has settled down here some time ago. As a matter of fact, this player can be considered to be one of the foremost Oriental musicians of the present day. He is remarkable both for his technical skill and his wide knowledge of the repertoire. I made his acquaintance at the Congress for Arabian music at Cairo in 1932, where he was a member of the

Iraqian group of musicians. When I asked him to play for my collection he at once agreed, being one of the few musicians here who fully understand the scope of the work. We started a series of records similar to that one executed by Wasif Gauhariya (cf. First Report) and demonstrating the different melody-types prevalent in Iraq.

A second series was recorded from a Bedouin singer who accompanied himself on the Rabab al-shair. His readiness to sing and play for me was due to the influence of Omar Effendi Salah El-Berguthy whose interest in the work of the section was duly recognised in the second report. He deservedly has the reputation of being one of the best musicians in his genre. Besides a number of characteristic songs I obtained some valuable information as to the system underlying the playing on this kind of Rabab, a system which is a more rudimentary form of that existing in the time of Al-Isbahani's Kitab al-Aghani and, therefore, throws some light on medieval practice.

The collection now contains 51 doublefaced records.

A second set of records was started by playing over records from cylinders to discs by means of an electric pick up constructed by Mr. Schur. The result was most satisfactory, the records being rendered on the discs more loudly and without any additional noises. This is important for the archive of the section as it secures making copies on discs of all the records I have taken systematically in Egypt, Tripoli, and the Maghreb in former years.

Jerusalem, July 7th, 1935   Dr. Robert Lachmann

Even though Lachmann considered the sketching in advance of a comprehensive program of studies inadvisable, he never overlooked an opportunity to introduce some kind of theoretical order in the musical materials he collected. Thus the Iraqi Jewish lute-player – Mr. Azuri Harun [Ezra Aharon], whom he first met at the Cairo Congress – was expected to supply musical renditions of the different melody-types prevalent in Iraq, that would enable a comparison between his and Mr. Wasif Gauhariya's renditions of the *maqāmāt*. A comparison of this kind was bound to yield further insight into the workings of the *maqāmāt*, which shares a common theoretical base with other music in the region. Also notice the way Lachmann's mind works: While recording some characteristic songs rendered by a Bedouin singer, Lachmann shifts his interest from the songs to the rudimentary system that underlies the playing of the *Rabab*, the accompanying instrument. The erudite scholar is able to recall Al-Isbahani's *Kitab al-aghani*, at this point, which suggests to him that what he is hearing is a more rudimentary form of accompaniment than the one described in the aforementioned treatise; it may, hence, "throw some light on medieval practice"!

The elimination of "additional noises," which Lachmann mentions in connection with the copying of recorded materials, is particularly relevant, nowadays, with regard to initial recordings, which may be subjected to electronic analyses of sorts, such as melographic analysis, for example.

Lachmann made sure that the people he recorded were the kind who knew their business – competent musicians who faithfully represented the traditions they voiced. Determined to enlarge the collection as much as possible, Lachmann was nonetheless guided by musicological queries such as melody-types, instrumental techniques, performance practices, etc. Nor did he overlook queries of an anthropological nature. The archive, after all, was expected to provide a reliable data base for future musical research. Lachmann, too, knew his business. Indeed, the cautious recordings were matched by meticulous records concerning each item that joined the collection.

Limited though the project's budget was, it was hard to resist temptations; the accessibility of so much music of great interest inspired new ideas. It was possible, for example, to enlarge the collection by way of exchange with other institutions in the region that were establishing their own archives. Having been involved with the Congress of Arabic Music in Cairo, 1932, it was only natural that Lachmann wished, in the first place, to obtain those recordings which he, himself, had supervised.

The following letter was sent from Berlin. Lachmann, most likely, visited the Berlin Sound Archive while visiting his family, for he had hoped to obtain copies of their collections, at least of those to which he himself had contributed. It was still possible, incidentally, to go in and out of Germany without trouble.

Act II

14.7.1935

Dear Dr. Magnes,

My trip to Cairo will, I think, have the desired result. Dr. El-Hefny, the Inspector of Music at the Ministry of Education, told me that their Music Department would be glad to get into connection with the Section for non-European Music at the Hebrew University. He said that they would certainly send us their series of about 160 double-faced discs recorded by His Master's Voice in 1932, in exchange with our records, of which I had taken two samples to Cairo which highly satisfied them. The series, he said, would be sent to Jerusalem if the University officially applied for it to the Minister of Education. He suggested a text set out as follows:

> To H.E., the Minister of Education, Cairo
>
> Your Excellency,
>
> We beg to inform you that the Section for Research in non-European Music at the Hebrew University, Jerusalem, would be very much obliged to obtain copies of the complete series of gramophone records registered especially for the Congress of Arabian Music held at Cairo in 1932. We declare our readiness to exchange them for an equal number of records from our Phono-Archive.
>
> Moreover, we should be most grateful for sending us the "Report on the Work of the Congress" both in Arabic and French.
>
> We hope, for the sake of scientific research and mutual benefit, that our request will meet Your Excellency's kind attention.

. . . .

This, of course, is merely a draft. Permit me to ask you to send the request to Cairo as soon as possible, firstly, because it is now fresh in their memory, and secondly, because, if it were delayed until October, we could scarcely hope to obtain the discs this year. Since the records were made at Cairo under my direction it might be worth while mentioning in the letter that the Section for which the copies are requested is under my direction too.

There is only one set of copies left. I fear they might send it to some other institute if we hesitate. There is every reason to be keen about it. It represents the only full collection of classical Arab music that has ever been recorded.

I am, dear Dr. Magnes,
Yours sincerely,
Robert Lachmann
Klopstockstr. 20
Berlin NW 87

Lachmann went to Egypt to make sure that the Inspector of Music in the Ministry of Education in Cairo knew about the proposed transaction and granted his approval. Given the Egyptian willingness to accommodate, nothing seemed more simple to Lachmann than the immediate transfer of the desired collection to Palestine. But it was not as simple as he thought, for it involved the cumbersome Custom Authority.

Dealing with bureaucracies was not exactly his forte. His affiliation within the University was far from settled, nor had a location been found for his recording studio. His budget turned out to be more limited than he had thought, and now he was confronted by yet another problem. If he wished to proceed with his plans, including the importing of record collections and other technical items necessary for his work, he was forced to deal with mundane matters, however ill equipped he was to handle them. Indeed, one wonders whether he was aware of how much trouble he was giving to the academic bureaucracy. Consider Schloessinger's letter to Magnes, for example:

July 16, 1935

Dr. Magnes
From Dr. Schloessinger

DOCTOR LACHMANN

It was a technical question – not a personal one – amongst the members of the School of Oriental Studies, whether Dr. Lachmann's subject belongs in the School of Oriental Studies or in the present or a future Musical Department of the University. There was a majority view in favor of the latter.

But there is no objection in principle to Dr. Lachmann's being attached to the Department of Oriental Studies giving him the right to work in that department in connection with his subject. It is understood that he has the status of a Research Fellow (Chaver Mechkar) and that he will not lecture in the School of Oriental Studies <u>nor be a member of the teaching staff of the Department.</u>

I hope that this will settle the matter.

Handwriting: Might I know what the underlined words mean? 16.VII

Dr. Schloessinger was a member of the Executive Council of the University, which apparently also dealt with particular problematic cases. Since the closing words of the second paragraph of Schloessinger's letter were underlined, Magnes asked for clarification of the statement "nor be a member of the Department," upon which the statement was corrected, by hand, to read: "nor be a member of the teaching staff of the Department."

Or, consider the following letter addressed to Magnes and written, in all likelihood, by Mr. Ben-David who was Assistant Registrar at the University. While in Germany, Lachmann had written Ben-David to inquire about working space.

<u>Dr. Magnes</u>,[64]

Concerning Lachmann, my advice is <u>not</u> to promise him rooms on Mount Scopus; he needs rather large rooms, and this will cause us great difficulty. It would be more reasonable if he were to take a flat in town (has this been approved?). But then we must consider the cost concerning his budget.

A pressing question, he asks about the quality of the electricity flow in order

---

64 Translated from the Hebrew.

to adjust his machines. The flow is different here and in town (one is Gleichstrom and the other is Wechselstrom).

17.X   (illegible signature)

Lachmann's name, apparently, came up in many administrative conversations as a "problem." In due time, the internal correspondence will, in fact, refer to all that pertains to Lachmann as "The Lachmann Problem." In light of the University's Grand Vision, each member, whether faculty or administration, considered himself, in those pioneering days, a trustee of the Jewish people! Such diffusion of authority, needless to say, undermined realization of the very goals to which, paradoxically, all adhered. At any rate, unable to affect primary decisions, members of the University, regardless of position, seem to have exercised the utmost power within *their* jurisdictions, often turning trivial issues into major obstacles. It is their unsympathetic leanings that gave "The Lachmann Problem" the salience which it eventually acquired. In University circles the man began to be characterized as a "nudnik," thus redefining Lachmann's professional persistence via caricature. Magnes was awake to the injustice being done to Lachmann and tried, whenever possible, to intervene. No wonder, therefore, that Lachmann addressed almost all of his queries, small and large, to Magnes – his sole protector – to whom he attributed powers far beyond those he actually possessed.

Shifting Concerns

It is hard to establish whether Lachmann was privy, as was Magnes, to the lack of goodwill which accompanied the handling of his affairs at the University. The difficulties spelled out by all kinds of University officials sounded quite reasonable as a rule. Nobody could deny the fact that the University was short of money, space, equipment, and a host of other things, not least of which was the in-fighting over academic priorities. Under such tight and competitive conditions, it is those who are defined marginal who are more likely to provoke formalistic replies to their "unreasonable" requests. Whatever the official policies, Magnes knew that these could be circumvented whenever it could be agreed that an issue or case called for special attention and care. Magnes, evidently, did not succeed in persuading administrative officials, or members of the staff, to join him in understanding and solving "The Lachmann Problem." Bearing this in mind, one cannot help but be struck by Lachmann's utter naiveté as one reads the following letter:

November 13th, 1935

Dear Dr. Magnes,

In today's Palestine Post I find a notice about "no less than 500 records of Arabic songs having been acquired for the Wireless Programme of local music". Being, of course, greatly interested in all questions concerning records of Arab music, I should very much like to know whether the statement is correct and, if it is, to what kind of records it alludes. The Palestine Post goes on to speak, in this connection of "the monotony of the desert having given rise to some plaintive airs"; this might imply that the discs in question contain Beduin or villagers' songs. During my long experience, I have hardly ever come across industrial records of rural music, and certainly not of rural music of this country; the firms do not make them because there is no market for them. So I am led to think that the discs, most probably, are records of Egyptian urban music or records coming from another urban centre. Of these records, indeed, any amount can be had as long as the quality is disregarded. The only selection of Arab urban music which has been made so far purely from a point of view of musical value, is the one recorded by His Master's Voice for the Congress of Arabian Music, Cairo 1932. The series is in possession of the Egyptian Department of Education, and is not, as far as I know, available generally. But this collection, a complete set of which has been promised as a gift to our Archive of Oriental Music, amounts to less than 200 discs.

Permit me to mention some additional considerations regarding the plan, if it exists, of introducing industrial records into the Wireless Programme.

(1) Supposing the records are reproductions of Egyptian urban music, I do

not think that their inclusion in the Programme would be attractive to any part of the population of Palestine. Not only are records of this kind heard in Cafes, shops, and private houses throughout this country; the original musicians themselves who supply these records, are easily accessible by listening to the broadcasting stations of Cairo and of Istanbul, and are heard, as a matter of fact, by large masses of the population. I have witnessed concerts of this kind at Nablus, at Haifa, and at the Damascus Gate, Jerusalem, where they are transmitted in Arab Cafes by means of loudspeakers. In broadcasting records of these or other musicians, the Jerusalem station, therefore, would at most supply reproductions of music accessible through neighbouring stations in the original. Besides, as far as the simpler groups of the population, villagers and Beduins, are concerned, they would, again, be made to hear urban music instead of their own songs, which vastly differ from it, and thereby be influenced in a direction greatly detrimental to the conservation of their own traditions.

(2) Those members of the Arab population, with whom I am in touch, are looking forward to the musical programme of the Palestine Wireless Station as a means of intensifying the general love of music and of encouraging its practice. These expectations are, I think easy enough to fulfil, if the wireless program is prepared to take them into account. But there is little hope for any enthusiasm to be raised by reproducing discs instead of giving the different parts of the population opportunities of taking an active share in the programme. The audience would, of course, much rather hear local music from their favourites, who are known to them personally, than the urban music of Egypt etc. on which they are being fed to weariness. As to the singers and players, urban, rural and Beduin, of this country, among whom there are excellent and inspired performers, they would, I am sure, be deeply disappointed at being invited to hear records from other countries instead of being given a chance of displaying their own abilities. The hope of intensifying musical life in this country by encouraging local singers, and by holding out, to unknown singers, the possibility of being discovered by and for the wireless, would be extinguished. As a matter of fact, would it not be a more gratifying task for the Jerusalem Station to support the original music existing in this country, and thereby to promote its development instead of offering their audience records, bought from elsewhere, of music being available through foreign

stations in the original?

Yours sincerely,
R. Lachmann

What exactly did he expect of Magnes? Why couldn't he find out by himself whether the notice which appeared in the Palestine Post was correct and, if so, to what kind of records it alluded? As for the rest of the letter, he must have known that he was preaching to the converted. Magnes, we know, was keenly aware of the local Arab population and not at all oblivious to their needs and aspirations. Supportive of Lachmann and his project, the alleged broadcasting policy concerning Arabic music might have suggested a convenient battlefield. Did Lachmann expect Magnes to put up a fight on this issue to which he was professionally committed? While it is hard to attribute such cunning to Lachmann, it is fair, nonetheless, to assume that having failed to draw attention to his subject within the University, he became increasingly involved with the cultural life of the country using his professional vantage point, and encouraged by the approval of his patron. Moreover, since there was little hope for a teaching program in the near future, the archive commanded the greater part of his time. The more he invested in its creation the larger became its scope, guided by an ever growing ambition to establish, in this forsaken part of the world, the most encompassing Archive of Oriental Music. Lachmann may never have heard of Ahad Ha-am, but the idea of creating a spiritual center of sorts was a contagious one. Lachmann could hardly have avoided being affected by it, for it permeated the atmosphere. Alongside political Zionism, cultural Zionism was gaining in strength and undergoing a process of secularization. Rather than disappearing, it was incorporated into the political agenda, constituting a major driving force. Although not made explicit, this theme is consonant with Lachmann's Fourth Report, which also assumes a new, more realistic, name for the unit.

17.11.35

ARCHIVE OF ORIENTAL MUSIC

Fourth Report

We left Jerusalem on July 10th. On our way to Germany we stopped in Egypt for three days to discuss possibilities of collaboration between our archive and the Royal Institute for Arabian Music at Cairo. I met the director of the Institute, the Vice-Minister of the Ministry of Education, and the Inspector of Music at the Ministry of Education who is at the same time Secretary of the Institute. At this Institute, the first congress of Arabian music had been held in 1932; on this occasion, a selection of typical recitals of urban music from most Arab countries had been recorded on discs under my direction. The Ministry of Education promised to send this collection (which, to this day, has remained the only one satisfactory both as to technical finish – it was recorded by "His Master's Voice" – and from the point of view of musical research) to our archive as a present as soon as a complete set of it would be available. The Report on the Proceedings of the Congress, a bulky publication containing a great number of important papers on various aspects of Arab music, has been received, both in Arabic and French, in the meantime. In return, our archive will have to send a number of specimens of its records to the Institute for Arabian music at Cairo. Further ways of collaboration were taken into regard. Possibly, the archive may hope to be granted facilities or occasional support in its activities by the Egyptian government. A notable increase of our collection, beyond the above-mentioned series of discs, can hardly be expected from them although they are planning to establish a phonogram archive.

In Berlin our work was in two parts:

(1) As a result of the experience gathered in Palestine in spring, a number of machines and tools had to be acquired in addition to those which already belong to the laboratory of the archive. They were partly bought, partly constructed by Mr. Schur. The most important item was a recording machine only to be used in houses provided with electric current and a wall-jack. This machine serves:

a) to make discs at the archive and, occasionally, in other Jerusalem houses. Hence, our first recording machine (which is independent of public electricity) can be reserved for use on expeditions, and its spring be saved from being speedily worn;

b) to make copies of the original discs, for which purpose both the old and the new machine are required.

(2) The Berlin phonogram archive is in possession of all the records of Oriental music that I have made on former occasions, partly in Berlin, but for the greatest part in North Africa. These records include a full collection of Bedouin music, vocal and instrumental, in Tunizia, songs and instrumental pieces from Morocco, Algeria, Tripoli, Egypt, Turkey, and Persia, and a series of songs from Japanese No-plays. Part of these phonograms (which were all recorded with an Edison machine) only existed on the original wax cylinders; the rest were already copied by means of an electrotype process. By kind permission of the present director of the Berlin archive we could make copies of the originals by means of a pick up specially constructed by Mr. Schur for the purpose of transferring sound recorded on cylinders to discs. In the same way we were allowed to "pick up" a collection of cylinders containing records of Jewish Oriental songs, and of Jewish and some Samaritan cantillations made by A. Z. Idelsohn in Palestine in 1913 and presented by him to the Berlin archive. In addition to these discs I brought copies, in cylinder form, of all those of my records which had been electrotyped already; these will be transferred to discs here. Owing to the imperfection of the recording process on an Edison phonograph and of the material used for it, a great number of all these records are not satisfactory technically. But still, transferred to discs, it will be possible to use part of them even for public demonstration while most of them will, at least, be sufficiently audible for research and analysis. These records, therefore, are a valuable addition to the collection of the archive considering that it can hardly be hoped to obtain records from the Maghreb again before long.

The collection of the archive has been increased, further, by about 180 double-faced discs containing music from various parts of the East (Japan, China, Siam, Java, India, and the Near East). These discs were made by different industrial firms. I bought them, as representative of their respective kinds, for my private use in the course of many years; they are now at the disposal of the archive.

Jerusalem, November 17, 1935   Dr. Robert Lachmann

The University's budget for the archive, as we have seen, hardly covered the limited plan; it certainly held no promise for the more extended vision. However, since Lachmann's extended vision no longer took into account the University as its sole reference, other parties, who might view with favor the establishment of a unique and significant *Phonogramarchive* in Palestine, could now be approached. Unlike Magnes, Lachmann was unaware of the fact that the University might not take kindly to such private actions. After all, the idea of interesting the High Commissioner, for example, came from Mr. Rendall, one of Magnes's friends (see the following letter). Impatient with the bureaucracy he headed, Magnes, himself, tried to engage the interest of some of his wealthy friends, overlooking the halfhearted attention the Archive received within the University. As president of the University, he must have known that he was free to use his position to raise as much money as he possibly could, but that his power to affect its allocation was limited, curbed by decision making bodies other than that of the president. His influence and attention inspired Lachmann, no doubt, to be alert to other potential donors, leaving all else to Magnes to sort out.

Beth Ha-Rav mi-Gur   25.12.35
oppo. Ettinger House
Ben Yehuda St.

Dear Dr. Magnes,

Permit me to add a few remarks to the two points raised the other day at the concert:
   (1) I just received the following lines from Mr. Rendall:
      "I am just off for 4 days to Haifa.
      "This note is to let you know that I have been thinking over our very interesting discussion, but I shall not be making any further suggestions to you until the beginning of January, when I hope to have the opportunity of discussing the matter with His Excellency, the High Commissioner, who will be away until the end of the year."

(2) In connection with the impending visit of Mr. Blumenfeld I forgot to mention another chance of obtaining money for the Archives apart from Frau Maschke's action. Since about a month I have given private courses in the history and theory of Oriental music to a student of musicology, a young lady from Leipzig, who has come to stay in Palestine for good. Her father is a merchant of considerable wealth, formerly at Leipzig (where a synagogue and a hospital were built at his expense), now, I believe, in Brussels. She had the idea of taking her degree in musicology here, but heard from Dr. Bergmann that, in his opinion, this would not be possible during the next 5 years, if then. This lady is quite ready, and thinks that it would be possible, to obtain funds for the Archive from U.S.A., through her father's connections with rich friends of his, there.

This opportunity, too, would be destroyed if the University insisted on applying the principle of "not admitting individual actions" to the Archives. On the other hand, as long as no hope is held out to include the Archives into the ordinary budget of the University, individual action is the only resource, otherwise the Archives will be left without any means at the end of two years. It does not seem to be premature to think of this now because opportunities like those which are being offered now may not be available then.

Hoping that these two points will find your kind consideration I am

Yours sincerely,
Robert Lachmann

It cannot be said that Lachmann sat by idly awaiting solutions to his problems. He invited Mr. Blumenfeld, and a host of other potential donors, to visit the Archive. All were duly impressed and expressed willingness to help. As he reported to Magnes, he was careful not to mention the question of "private actions." He also had met with the High Commissioner, who subsequently invited him to tea, so impressed was he with this unfortunate educated German Jew. Nothing, however, materialized from all of these efforts. The University archive contains a vast number of letters that Magnes dispatched to friends and acquaintances on behalf of Lachmann. In addition to his genuine goodwill, they also reveal his increased frustration over not being able to assist in the way he thought Lachmann deserved. In due time, "The Lachmann Problem" became an obsession with Magnes, a test case, as it were, for his own standing in the University.

Lachmann and his associates engrossed in a problem

Lachmann and Sofia Lentschnez transcribing recorded music

ACT III

LACHMANN AND MAGNES: THE MERGING OF TWO BATTLES

Towards the end of that year Lachmann produced two telling documents, one in German, the other in English. Both documents summarize his activities since he migrated to Palestine. But whereas the one in German emphasizes the *raison-d'être* of his work, the one in English emphasizes accomplishments and needs. The latter was written at Magnes's request. It describes the present state of the Recording Laboratory and the Music Library in objective terms, as it were, spelling out the financial needs for their future developments. Magnes, evidently, requested an official document of sorts, which he expected to use in order to raise money. It is not altogether clear for whom the one in German was intended. It is a very personal account which weaves together past achievements, present accomplishments, and future objectives, all subjected to an *exposé* about comparative musicology. Whatever their intent, both documents reveal Lachmann's own understanding of his endeavor – its objectives, its methodology, and the technical equipment it implies. These documents reflect the thoughts and conceptions that guided the founding fathers of comparative musicology. Having absorbed their legacy, much of it no longer sounds new. Yet, much can still be gained by attempting to emulate the broad vision, the conscientious attitude, the discipline, and the sense of mission which accompanied their work.

Lachmann Summarizes his Enterprise

Annual Report 1935-1936 [65]

Archive for Oriental Music

53 – 2[66]   Personnel
Director: Dr. Robert Lachmann, born Berlin, November 28, 1892. Studied English, German, French (State Examination for Work in Higher Schools, Berlin 1920) as well as Musicology and Arabic (Examination for Doctoral Degree, Berlin 1922). 1923–1933 scientific functionary in the Prussian Library service, since 1927 at the Music Department of the Prussian State Library in Berlin, since 1931 Library Councillor, since 1934 retired. Research on oriental music, see 55 – 1.
   Technician: W. Schur.

53 – 3 Field of Activity
Of the Director: Study of the genres of instrumental and vocal music extant in Palestine and the neighboring regions, also with regard to their social environment and ethnological significance. Selection of samples of these genres for sound recording purposes. Recording of the texts of vocal music. Work on the logbook and the card index of the recordings. Scientific processing of the recordings. Writing down the recorded music in musical notation. Analyzing the pieces. A special activity consists in the recording of speech samples from personages of importance for the history and the cultural life of the country.
   Of the Technician: Preparation of phonograph discs, recording on such discs, preparation of copies of these discs as well as of other recordings (not originating in the collection being created here). Maintenance of the recording equipment and of the workshop. Improvement of the equipment as based on the technical literature and on his own experiments.

---

65 Translated from the German.
66 The meaning of the numbers that precede several of the paragraphs is not clear. However, since they must have designated something for Lachmann, they are included here.

55 – 1 The program of the Archive consists mainly in the collection and the scientific processing of traditional vocal and instrumental music in Palestine and the neighboring countries, preferably of such music as has come down by ear only. This program aims at fulfilling a task to be set not only from the point of view of musicology, but also of the history of civilization, of folklore and of ethnology. Given the growing influence of Europe and the increasing traffic between peoples and population groups of the Near East which formerly, separated from one another, had cultivated their own lives, their vocal music is in danger of losing its own characteristic features, or even of altogether disappearing. Science has thus a compelling interest in ensuring the survival of whatever traditional music is still extant. To this end it is not sufficient to note down melodies by ear. A reliable basis for future research is ensured not only by preserving the subjective jotting down of the music, but by recording the music itself in as many samples as possible. In other words, a collection of traditional music is of scientific value only if supported by sound recordings. Only with the aid of such recordings is it possible to objectively measure pitch and tempi, and only with their aid can the reliability of notation by ear be checked.

This is not to say that recordings are the only basis in this field of research. Sound recordings serve to demonstrate the manner in which a certain piece of music was once actually performed. (Given the peculiarities of handing down such music by ear, such performances will each be different. In important cases it is therefore useful to record several performances of the same piece.)

The aim of research, however, is not the preservation of single pieces, but the grasping of their essential qualities. The collection of melodies must therefore be preceded by the study of the musical genres cultivated by the population group concerned. Examples of each genre must be collected; from these, a comprehensive picture emerges.

Understanding musical practice presupposes its integration into a certain sphere of life and realm of ideas. This part of the research already borders on the above-mentioned allied disciplines.

Finally, the relations must be investigated between present practice and the past. This necessitates going into details of the history of oriental music with the aid of ancient and medieval sources. It has been frequently shown that the aural tradition has to this very day preserved features of ancient practice as known from literary sources.

<u>55</u> – 1 These aspects determine the work of the Archive which began on May 1, 1933. From them emerges as the most urgent task the collecting of the corpus of melodies threatened in their existence, and to ready them for scientific processing.

Due to my earlier activity in this field I was able, already upon its establishment by myself, to put at the disposal of the Archive a collection of a considerable extent.

My activity began in the war years with prisoners-of-war colonial troops from North Africa, from whom I was able to write down about 300 pieces, including their texts. A number of these are phonographically supported.

After the war, collections of Moroccan, Persian, Turkish and Japanese vocal and instrumental pieces were established with the help of reliable informants who were temporarily staying in Berlin. All of these collections consist of these phonographic recordings with the addition of material written down by ear and are accompanied by remarks concerning the system and practice of the respective music, as well as by collected texts. Further material I have picked out and acquired from the Berlin store rooms of phonograph firms. Its particular value resides in the fact that it consists largely of recordings from the prewar period, and represents a musical situation already in the past. The copper matrices of these recordings no longer exist, and thus no further copies can reach the market, so that the discs acquired by me are of unique value.

Starting from 1925, I have undertaken further studies on occasion of various travels to North Africa: in 1925, in Tripoli; in 1927, in Tunisia and Algeria, and in 1932 in different parts of Egypt, including Sinai. On all of these travels numerous recordings were made, altogether over 400 examples of Jewish and Arabic music.

The Egyptian journey took place upon the conclusion of the Congress for Oriental Music in Cairo, in which I participated upon the invitation of the Egyptian Government. As I was elected Chairman of the Department for Music Recording, it was my duty to select the music pieces to be recorded and to oversee the recording sessions. This activity produced the record collection of the Congress, which comprises about 400 music recordings from almost all parts of the Near East.

In 1932 the Society for Comparative Musicology entrusted me with the founding and publishing of the sole scientific organ in the field of non-European music. This organ, the Journal of Comparative Musicology, has so far attained three yearly volumes (1933-1935). While at the end of last year I resigned from the management, I hope to return soon to this or a similar journal. In that case, the Archive will have at its disposal an organ for the results of its research work.

55 – 1 The entire body of sound recordings which were produced or acquired by me in the course of the above-described activities are now accessible for research in the Archive. The originals of the recordings made by me during my travels consist of wax cylinders which are the property of the State Phonogram Archive in Berlin. Mr. Schur, the technician of the Archive, has invented a device facilitating the transfer of these originals onto discs. This made it possible to obtain copies from them for local use.

The vocal recordings made in Jerusalem in the years 1912-1913 by A. Z. Idelsohn, which are the property of the Berlin Archive, were also copied by the same method, the copies having been transferred here.

Finally, by transferring my private library, I have made accessible to the Archive a collection of the special literature on non-European music, comprising the largest part of the important publications in this field. It consists of source material from antiquity and the Middle Ages, of monographs, numerous off-prints and complete series of periodicals.

55 – 2-3 Since the establishment of the Archive in the past year, and to the present day, 420 discs have been recorded. They contain various groups of Jewish music: performances of liturgical texts in different oriental communities, *Piyutim* and music for modern Hebrew poetry. Further represented are examples of Samaritan liturgical and secular songs, and many more. Texts have been noted down for all vocal recordings. For each recording there are provided the data essential for scientific processing: category of scale and rhythm of the piece of music as given by the informant; extraction of vocalists and instrumentalists, and function of the piece in liturgy and social life. The recordings were first of all consecutively listed in a logbook which also contains additional

observations concerning practice and systematics. Furthermore, a card index has been set up and partly finished, which cross-indexes the recordings according to all relevant criteria.

Recording was carried out partly in the recording room of the Archive, but partly also outside of the Archive and of Jerusalem. The latter was made possible by the mobile equipment designed by Mr. Schur and not dependent on the main current.

Recordings were always preceded by determination of the available genre, thereby avoiding indiscriminate recording of pieces of the same kind. For this type of work it was necessary to continuously search for suitable informants. For mediating personal contacts I owe thanks to various gentlemen within and without the University. It would singularly advance the work of the Archive if also in the future, and to an increasing degree, the help of representatives of neighboring countries was put at the disposal of the Archive.

For future collection activities, Jerusalem still offers an inexhaustible source of traditional vocal material. But it is increasingly necessary to include in the work also other parts of Palestine and the neighboring regions.

After recording, each disk is at once played back, which is impossible with the recording methods of the phonograph factories. In this manner it can be verified if, technically, the recording was successful. At the same time, the musicians are offered the opportunity to hear the reproduction of their voices or their playing. Experience has shown that this encourages even the least cooperative to improve their efforts.

Having been replayed, the originals are then only used to prepare copies. It is these copies that serve for demonstration and, primarily, for the scientific work.

This work includes first of all listening and putting down the music in proper notation. Tempi are determined with the aid of a metronome, pitch is measured using a tonometer. In its present state, the collection already affords the possibility of representing various self-contained types of music. It should, however, be borne in mind that, given the rapidly progressing decay of local music, collecting activities proper must have precedence over the literary evaluation of the collected items.

55 – 22 Although the Archive is not associated with any public teaching activity,

two persons have been found that are ready to participate in the scientific processing of the already available and the still to be collected material. Both are now in the initial stage of their training. The Archive offers opportunities for work to a far greater number of persons. According to their qualifications, some of them could be given practical tasks (writing down of melodies, observation of musical practice), others, theoretical ones (study of sources).

In my opinion, the Archive can also serve pedagogical purposes. The level of music instruction in schools can be considerably raised, if teachers are afforded an insight into the history of oriental music with the aid of the tenacious oriental tradition going back for many centuries, rather than via one-sided European attitudes or their personal tastes. Which musical style will be adopted by future generations cannot be foreseen. There is, however, no reason to withhold from them the native style, which for part of the Jewish population is also the customary one. The Archive offers the opportunity to get acquainted with the traditional music, perhaps only as a historical document, but perhaps also as an art capable of new developments.

55 – 367 For May this year I am invited by the University of Basle and the Geographical-Ethnological Society in Basle to give guest lectures on my field of research.

55 – 379 Following a request by the Palestine Broadcasting Service, I have declared my readiness to advise them on oriental music on a voluntary basis.

52 – 2 Publications Dealing with non-European Music

    A. General Summaries
1. Mohammedan Music (Grove's Dictionary of Music).
2. Music of the Orient, Breslau 1929. Translated into Spanish: Musica de Oriente, Barcelona 1931.
3. Music of the non-European Civilized and Primitive People. Potsdam 1930. In: Handbuch der Wissenschaft, published by E. Bücken.
4. Musical Research Tasks in the Near East. (In: Bericht über die 1. Sitzung der Gesellschaft zur Erforschung der Musik des Orients, Berlin, 27.4.1930.)

Summary in: Actes du 8ᵉ Congrès de l'Institut des Hautes-Etudes marocaines, Rabat-Fèz, 1933.
5. Publications of the Zeitschrift für vergleichende Musikwissenschaft.

B. About Theory and Systematics

6. On non-European Polyphony. (Kongressbericht der Beethoven-Zentenarfeier, Wien 1927.)
7. Al-Kindi: Risala fi hubr ta'lif al-alhan. Translation, introduction, commentary, facsimile and emended text. (With Mahmud El-Hefnï.) Leipzig 1931. (The oldest Arabic music treatise.)
8. Review of A. Z. Idelsohn: Jewish Music. (Zeitschrift für Musikwissenschaft. 15. 1923–33.) Comprises fundamental discussions concerning the system of synagogal music.
9. The Indian Tonal System with Bharata and its Origin. (With E. M. von Hornbostel.) (Zeitschrift f. vergleichende Musikwissenschaft. 1. 1933.)
10. Rapport de la Commission de l'enregistrement. (In: Recueil des trafaux du Congrès de musique arab au Caire en 1932. Le Caire 1934.) Comprises a comprehensive proposal for the setting up and the operation of a record archive.
11. Music systems and Music Conception (I.) (Zeitschrift für vergleichende Musikwissenschaft. 3. 1935.) Historical position of Jewish and other religious music.

C. Specific Descriptions of Musical Practice

12. Music in Tunisian Towns. Ph.D. thesis. (Archiv für vergleichende Musikwissenschaft. 5. 1923.)
13. Music and Music Notation of the No. (Bericht über den 1. Kongress der Deutschen Musikgesellschaft. Leipzig 1925.)
14. Songs from East Turkistan. In: A. v. Le Coq: Von Land und Leuten in Ostturkestan. Leipzig 1928.
15. (59 – 2) The Song of the Lion and the Pythian Nomos. (In: Festschrift für Johannes Wolf. Berlin 1929.) On the relationship between the respective musical practices of today's Orient and ancient Greece.
16. Asiatic Parallels to the Music of the Berbers. (With E. M. v. Hornbostel.) (Zeitschrift für vergleichende Musikwissenschaft. 1. 1933.)

17. Review of: M. Rida and M. El-Hefny: Dirasat al-qanun. (Zeitschrift für vergleichende Musikwissenschaft. 3. 1935.) Discusses present problems of the music of the Near East.

59 – 2 This year I have finished a series of publications which all relate to the field of research of the Archive. The recordings that were used in Nos. 2 and 3 are part of the collection of the Archive.
1. Al-Kindi: Risila fi igza habariya al-musiqi. Translation, emended text.
2. Songs of the Jews on the island of Djerba.
3. Music of the Algerian Kabyles.

56 – 1 For the time being, the Archive is privately accommodated, that is, until the Muharrem 1937, in the lower floor of the Beth harav mi-Gur, in the vicinity of Ben-Yehuda Str.

56 – 2 Apart from my study, the Archive comprises two working rooms: a workshop and a recording studio. The latter consists of a partitioned section of a hall which is used for performances. The workshop has a floor area of 20 m^2, the hall, including the studio, a floor area of 44 m^2.

56 – 31 Furniture

Workshop: 2 shelves for records
1 working bench
1 table for mounting of the equipment.
Hall: 3 benches
The studio consists of a wooden trestle lined with straw mats.

56 – 32 Equipment
1. Electrical equipment for inside recording of discs
2. Portable electrical equipment for sound recording without need for mains connection
3. Microphones: a) 1 electrostatic m.
b) 1 ribbon m.
c) 1 carbon m.

4. Guiding device for acoustic recording of discs
5. Edison phonograph for cylinders
6. Excelsior phonograph for cylinders
7. Sound box for sound transfer from cylinders to discs
8. Pick-up with motor and speaker for electrical reproduction of sound
9. Portable phonograph
10. Stationary phonograph
11. Two battery preamplifiers
12. Galvanic equipment for producing copper masters from a wax master
13. Rectifier
14. Tonometer
15. Metronome
16. Device for repeating disc sections

<u>56</u> – 32   Hand tools, e.g., for preparing wax cylinders

<u>56</u> – 5   Sound recordings (see also <u>55</u> – 1, 2)
1. Original discs of the Archive: 420
2. Copies of earlier recordings: 600
3. Factory-made discs: 180

<u>56</u> – 6 The Archive has no library of its own, but shares the room of my private professional library.

Budget
So far, the Archive has no part in the University's budget. It is maintained by the following means:
1) Donation of £P 800 from the USA
2) £P 158.780 from a collection in Prague
3) £P 410 – my private property, transferred to Palestine

The sum under 1) was given under the condition that the Archive's work was to be ensured for at least 3 years. Under this assumption, the sums under 2) and 3) were made available, which complement the sum under 1) to produce a minimum budget.

From this budget are defrayed the salaries for myself and the technician, as well as the current expenses for the work (replenishment of tools and equipment, rent for the premises, travel allowances for studies outside of Jerusalem, and fees for musicians). However, the budget is not sufficient for a full year's work, so that I can stay here only part of the year, being compelled to spend the rest of the year in Germany.

Costs of the equipment etc. used for the work of the Archive were not defrayed from the budget, but by myself. The same is the case with the costs of copying the recordings made prior to 1935.

What a document! For those interested in the confines in which he conducted his work, Lachmann supplies a vivid description. For those seeking information about his working-budget, Lachmann spells out its sources and sums. For those interested in the equipment used at the time, Lachmann provides an exact list. For those interested in the musical materials he collected in Palestine, Lachmann furnishes information. For those interested in his publications concerning non-European music, Lachmann supplies the references. The division of his publications into categories – General Summaries, Theory and Systematics, and Descriptions of Musical Practice – does not simply reflect his own systematic thinking, but the methodical approach that guided the founding fathers of the field. By these rules, careful study of musical practice and all that it entails must precede the theoretical extrapolations that enable comparisons among musical cultures, while "general summaries" are expected to contain syntheses that rest on the specifics studied.

It is his discussion of working procedures, however, which is most illuminating. Thus we learn from Lachmann that collecting activities must have precedence over the literary evaluation of the collected items and that a collection of traditional music is of scientific value only if supported by "sound" (noun and adjective) recordings, i.e., those that (1) make possible the objective measurement of pitch and tempi, and (2) are preceded by the study of the indigenous musical genres. The texts of vocal recordings must, of course, be noted down as well. However, since most of the collected music is of the kind that is handed down by ear, and the recordings only serve to demonstrate the manner in which a certain piece of music "was once actually performed," it is important to obtain several performances of the same piece. For scientific purposes, we are told, it is essential that the data referring to the piece include the following information: category of scale and rhythm "as given by the informant"; social extraction of vocalists and instrumentalists; and function of the piece in liturgy and social life. The understanding of musical practice, Lachmann insists, depends on its integration into a specific sphere of life and ideas. As such, it may also offer an opportunity to investigate its relationship to the past.

Though much of the above no longer sounds new, the conscientiousness and broad vision that accompanied comparative musicology from its inception may serve, nonetheless, as a powerful reminder for those to whom the field was bequeathed.

The following document, written in English, then goes on to summarize Lachmann's activities since he migrated to Palestine. Though he himself wrote the document, it is written in an objective manner, describing the Archive of Oriental Music that was started at the University under the direction of Dr. Robert Lachmann. It must certainly have been written at Magnes's request.

January 8, 1936

I. RECORDING LABORATORY

An Archive of Oriental Music was started by the University in April 1935, under the direction of Dr. Robert Lachmann. Its stock, at the beginning, was a collection of records taken viz. acquired in former years, and a laboratory on very modest lines. The laboratory contains two machines for recording on discs, one of them to be used in the studio, and the other, which is independent of public electricity, for recording at any place, even in the desert. The second machine was specially constructed by Mr. Walter Schur, who is in charge of the laboratory, and who has also constructed a highly sensitive microphone, and pick up for playing over records in cylinder form (Edison type) to discs (which made it possible for the Archive to get copies of valuable old records, as, for instance, the collection of Jewish songs made by A. Z. Idelsohn in Jerusalem in 1913 for the Berlin Archive).

Hitherto, about a hundred records have been made in Palestine including, among other things, a series of Samaritan Liturgical cantillations (the Ten Commandments deserves special mention). A publication based on records from Jews of the isle of Djerba (Tunisia) who, according to tradition, settled there immediately after the destruction of the Second Temple, is being prepared by Dr. Lachmann.

But although the costs of recording have been kept down to a minimum, the progress of the work suffers from financial difficulties. The scanty means of the Archive – which do not consist of an annual income, but only of a fixed one-time sum secured from private sources – do not allow the research work to be carried on as quickly and as thoroughly as would seem necessary considering the imminent decay, owing to European influence, of Oriental musical tradition.

At present, the most urgent requirements for developing the Archives are:

1. an increase of the funds and, possibly, a regular periodical.
   Income to be used:
   a) for paying fees to musicians, the experience having been that hardly any of them will sing or play without remuneration; about £P 100
   b) for financing occasional tours in order to widen the range of the work and to find music and song at remote places where they are better preserved than in large centres; about £P 150

The regions to be visited are in the first place, the various parts of Palestine; thus a kind of "musical topography" will be established. Further, the work is to extend to Syria, where there are several important Jewish communities, and to Transjordan. At a later stage, tours to Iraq (Mandeans!) and Nejd may be considered; in this case, the annual budget would have to be increased.

2. An increase of the laboratory outfit:
   a) a machine with two turntables serving to record music and songs which extend over more than

> one disc (e.g., music from broadcasting stations);   about £P 70
> b) an instrument for measuring the electric current used at the various stages of the recording process;   about £P 18
> c) recurrent expenses: batteries used for recording music in the field, etc.   about £P 20
> d) means available for testing the most important of the many innovations which are constantly made in the technique of recording;   about £P 20

II. MUSIC LIBRARY

Up to the present, the University Library has not collected music and books on music systematically. Apart from some valuable publications, which have been received incidentally, nearly all the standard works, or, at least, the latest editions of them are missing. A serious study of any branch of musicology (acoustics, psychology, aesthetics, history, theory, form) cannot be undertaken on this basis. But the establishment of a library fulfilling this purpose would require a vast sum of money to start on and a considerable annual budget. It would be necessary, e.g., to acquire the authoritative editions of the complete works of the great composers (J.S. Bach: 100 vols; Mendelssohn, about 30 vols; etc., etc.), and to subscribe to the equally expensive series of national monuments of music.

As long as no chair in general musicology is provided for by the University it hardly seems justifiable to enter upon this vast field. It would be sufficient for the present to acquire the principal works of reference, handbooks, and bibliographical works, in short, the literature supplying a general knowledge of the subject and its progress.

On the other hand, every possible effort should be made towards collecting books on Jewish music and on Oriental music, generally. Considering that Jerusalem is an ideal centre of Oriental music, both sacred and secular, all facilities should be provided for research in this field. In just recognition of this, the University has taken a first step by establishing an Archive of Oriental Music under Dr. Lachman's direction; a library of important special works on the subject should be collected as a necessary complement of the Archive. In this way the Hebrew University, by concentrating its efforts on the particular branch of musicology for which it is specially suited, can attain unique results.

It is therefore suggested that about two-thirds of any funds obtained for a musical library should be spent on Oriental books, and the rest on general musicology. A small list of books, recommended by Dr. Lachmann, is enclosed. (See Appendix).

For the future development of research in Oriental music it would be most desirable to obtain photostats of all, or, at least, the most important unpublished manuscript treatises on Jewish, Judeo-Arabic, and other Oriental music, chiefly mediaeval. Thus, a large amount of material from the great manuscript collections of European libraries would be at hand. It has been proved on many occasions that the study of musical theory of the past is indispensable for a real understanding of present day practice. Besides, these documents present an important aspect of the learning of the Middle Ages when music, along with astronomy, arithmetics, and geometry, was considered to be an essential part of scholarly and philosophical knowledge.

APPENDIX

Books (ca 20 £)

(1) Beiträge für Akustik u. Musikwissenschaft, Ursg. V. Carl Stumpf. 9 Hefte. 1898-1924.

(2) Seewald, Otto: Beiträge sur Kenntnis der Steinzeitlichen Musik instrumente Europas. Wien: A Schroll 1934. (Bücher für Ur und Frühgeschichte, Urag. V. Oswald Menghin. Vol. 2).

(3) Kirby, Percival R.: The Musical Instruments of the Native Races of South Africa. London: Humphrey Milford (Oxford University Press) 1934. (Ca. 36 sh.).

(4) Monumenta Musicae Byzantinae. Copenhague 1935 (?) Vol. 1: Complete facsimile of a Sticherarion from a ms. At Vienna.

  Subsidia: I,1: H.J.W. Tillyard: Handbook of Middle Byzantine Musical Notation.

       I,2: Carsten Ho g: La Notation ecphonétique. (To be acquired by subscription)

Photostats: (ca 40 £)

(1) London. Ms. British Museum Or. 2361, fols. 236v.–238v.

(2) London. Ms. Royal Asiatic Soc. Ms. 58 (K. Al-shifa', Chapt. 12).
(3) London, Ms. India Office. Ms. 1811, fols. 152v–174v.
(4) Oxford. Bodleian Library. Ms. Pocock 109, fols. 74v.–308v.
(5) Oxford. Bodleian Library. Ms. Pocock 250, fols. 74–93v.
(6) Berlin. Staatsbibliothek. Ms. Wetzstein 1240, fols. 22–31.
(7) Leyden. University Library. Ms. 1427. 123 leaves.
(8) Milan. Biblioteca Ambrosiana. Ms. 289. 195 leaves.
(9) Escorial. Ms. 96. 182 leaves.

If the acquisition of photostats is approved it is recommended that Dr. Lachmann should be charged with ordering them at the respective institutions so as to give them full details (size of reproduction, etc.).

As expected of a document that was meant to solicit financial support, it contained information about the Archive, its aims and needs. As far as Magnes was concerned, the document was to serve a double function – to appeal to potential donors and to persuade the University's staff that the Archive justified his efforts on Lachmann's behalf. Since its potential readers were primarily Jews, the document naturally emphasized the importance of retrieving *their* heritage before it was too late. But it also left no doubt that the vision of the Archive of Oriental Music was wider than that. As a repository of Oriental music – secular and sacred – it was to enable the Archive to turn into an important research center for the study of Oriental music in the broadest possible sense. Section II that discusses the Music Library, and the Appendix that specifies its immediate needs, make this abundantly clear.

Lachmann believed sincerely that Jerusalem was an ideal center for the study of Oriental music; he certainly acted as though it already was. Close attention to the list of books and photostats he requested as carrying first priority makes evident what was uppermost on his mind, namely, the material he needed in order to proceed with his own research work. Research on Oriental music, after all, was his mission; he was not collecting for its own sake.

The *Zeitschrift* as "Catch 22"

Given Lachmann's commitment to the field, it is not at all surprising that he should have wanted to see the *Zeitschrift für Vergleichende Musikwissenschaft* – the pioneering journal to which he had contributed so much as editor – continue in Palestine, undisturbed by current political events. Furthermore, it might be a good idea to transfer, as well, the Berlin *Phonogram Archive,* at least to make sure to have copies of its important holdings. Intimately involved with the early stages of the Berlin School of Comparative Musicology, it was hard for Lachmann to sever the concerns for himself from those pertaining to the field he helped initiate. Yet, he was right in assuming that redeeming the journal, or safeguarding the Berlin Archive, could enlist more support than "saving Lachmann." Having sold the idea to Magnes, Magnes handled the *Zeitschrift* like one of those designated, but indisputable, items for which he was, apparently, able to raise money.

WERTHEIM & CO.
Members New York Stock Exchange
120 Broadway, New York

January 7, 1936.

Dear Judah,

Replying to your recent letter regarding your desire to continue the Zeitschrift für Vergleichende Musikwissenschaft, with Dr. Lachmann as editor, I am pleased to enclose you herewith £50 for this purpose.
    To this fund the following gentlemen contributed: E. M. M. Warburg, Walter E. Meyer, Eugene Untermyer, Dr. A. S. W. Rosenbach and Maurice Wertheim.
    I hope all is going well with you and yours and that the University is marching along under your leadership to further achievements. I imagine you must be very busy in the present chaotic state of the German situation and receiving more and more German refugees.
    Can one expect to see you here this winter?

With best regards to you and Beatrice, believe me,

Sincerely,
Maurice

Dr. J. L. Magnes,
The Hebrew University,
Jerusalem, Palestine.

It is worth noting that Mr. Wertheim treated the continuation of the *Zeitschrift* as an idea that originated with Magnes. The money was, consequently, sent to Magnes. Rather than adding the money to the funds which stood at Magnes's disposal (funds he was free to assign at his discretion), somebody in the administration took the liberty to hand over the money directly to Lachmann. This seeming innocent act infuriated Magnes; how dare *they*, who were so reluctant to help Lachmann, allow themselves to pass him by? While the act of handing over the money to Lachmann may have resulted from a misunderstanding (see the letters below), the fact remains that it undermined Magnes's sole control of the situation – a situation which evolved against his better judgement, but which had come to affect him personally, albeit in a roundabout way. Psychological subtlety may help explain his anger, yet, given the ambiguity of the issue involved (not to speak of the modest sum), his protestation sounds somewhat pathetic. Indeed, it is doubly sad to see those who have been wronged make fools of themselves by choosing, in their overall desperation, the inappropriate issue or moment for protestation.

31/1/36

To the Administrator.⁶⁷

Re: the letter from Dr. Lachmann of 30/1.

I am amazed that the £50 that were received were handed over to Dr. Lachmann. I had intended that Dr. Lachmann be asked to prepare for me a plan how this money was to be used.

If I remember correctly, I had not given any instructions that the money should be passed on to Dr. Lachmann.

Please supply me with the appropriate documents.

Signed: J. L. Magnes.

(In handwriting, from Ben-David):
This is the documentation.
After receiving the letter to Dr. Lachmann, he came to me and asked what will happen to the money. Since this money was not part of the budget for his work at the University, I told him that in my opinion the University should not keep the sum, and he received it in order to keep it in a special account, separate from his private account, in the bank. If I did not understand your intention, I apologise for that.

4.2.36

To: Dr. Ben-David

I have asked Dr. Lachmann to prepare me a plan for using the sum of £50 received. Please approach him again on this subject, so that there should be no misunderstanding.

---

67 Translated from the Hebrew. Though Magnes knew that Dr. Ben-David, the secretary of the Standing Committee, gave the order to transfer the money to Lachmann, he addressed the letter facetiously "to the Administrator." In the letter from the 31ˢᵗ Lachmann informed Magnes of the money he had received. The answer, added by hand to Magnes's letter, was written by Ben-David.

I think he should return the money to the Music Fund at my disposal. The money was sent to me, and is my responsibility.

The University has several sums of non-budget funds, and I have not heard of any sum being given to interested recipients without special instructions. I would like the money to be registered as money belonging to the University, which is at my disposal. In future, I shall give more detailed instructions.

Signed: J. L. Magnes.

Dutifully, Lachmann informs Ben-David that he is returning the money:

February 10, 1936

Dear Mr. Ben-David

Mr. Schur is bringing you the £P50 for transfer to the University Fund at the disposal of Dr. Magnes.

Last Friday I had the opportunity of talking to Dr. Magnes about the disposition of the sum. We agreed to wait for a report on the position of the Society for Comparative Musicology, which I hope to receive within the next days. If nevertheless a new plan is to be drawn up, I am clearly ready to do so, and am awaiting your reply.

Please forgive me for not having shown up to personally talk things over with you. But I am busy with work that cannot be put off.

Sincerely yours,
R. Lachmann

Naïve though he was, Lachmann was aware of the sentiments that drove Magnes to act the way he did. With considerable self-effacement, Lachmann tried to gloss over what was defined as "an unfortunate incident." He trusted Magnes's judgement more than he trusted his own, and had no reason to doubt his commitment. Obedient yet sensitive, Lachmann became increasingly aware of the fact that his Arch Protector was in no position to have things his way. He witnessed too often the fights Magnes had to put up in order to assert himself. Moreover, it had become increasingly clear that their fights to survive, each in the domain he carved out for himself, got inextricably intertwined. This goes a long way to explain why Magnes acted the way he did when the question of Lachmann's employment was reopened towards the end of his first year at the University. The requisite conditions for continuation were apparently not fulfilled to the satisfaction of the Financial Secretariat. The *Zeitschrift*, it goes without saying, had to wait until the more pertinent problem, concerning its would-be editor, was solved. This time, hopefully, in unequivocal terms.

The Reopening of the Lachmann Appointment

The new year began the same process over again. Time was up for the one-year arrangement, and now what?

THE HEBREW UNIVERSITY

Financial Secretary's Office
Jerusalem

28.2.1936

To:
Dr. J. L. Magnes,
Here.

Dear Dr. Magnes,[68]

In the days preceding Mr. Schocken's departure, a meeting was held with Mr.

---

68 Translated from the Hebrew. Mr. Schocken was Chairman and Honorary Treasurer of the Executive Council. Mr. Ginsberg was the Administrator.

Ginsberg, during which continuation of Dr. Lachmann's employment was discussed.

Mr. Schocken agreed with you that if Dr. Lachmann's contract was officially approved by the Board of Governors for just one year, his employment should be continued according to the conditions of the earlier negotiations which you held with him – that is, for another two years, but under the same conditions on which Dr. Lachmann's budget was based, and which were laid down in your letter to Mr. Ginsberg of 4.12.1934, and in the budget proposal of 27.12.1934.

According to the above conditions, the University's obligation to Dr. Lachmann is limited to the sum of £P 800, promised to you, as you wrote to Mr. Ginsberg on 4.12.1934, by Mrs. Ginsberg in New York.

Therefore, the University can only undertake Dr. Lachmann insofar as Mrs. Ginsberg keeps her promise, given to yourself, and we can arrange payments to Dr. Lachmann only when we receive the contribution from Mrs. Ginsberg, as is our custom with all similar instances which are external to the budget.

However, if you think that it would be fitting to sign a contract with Dr. Lachmann with the Board of Governors for two years without the particular above-mentioned condition – that is, without limiting our obligation to Dr. Lachmann of the above-mentioned sum – Mr. Schocken is ready to agree to that if he receives a promise from you that if for any reason we do not receive Mrs. Ginsburg's contribution, you will provide the treasurer of the University with those sums needed for this purpose from other sources which are held by the treasurer to be used at your disposal.

Yours sincerely,
M. Schneersohn

To the above letter Magnes added (by hand) "Please address Mrs. Ginsburg. She will send all that she has promised." To which Schneersohn replied "have already written." Mr. Schneersohn, however, wrote his letter to Mrs. Ginsburg almost a month after this little exchange between him and Magnes took place.

The Hebrew University, Jerusalem

23/3/1936

Mrs. Leonie Ginsburg,
Mamaroneck, New York

Dear Mrs. Ginsburg,

About a year and a half to two years ago you were good enough to undertake to provide the sum of $4,000 over a period of three years for the maintainance of the researches of Dr. Lachmann, the authority on Oriental Music; this sum, you will remember, you promised to pay as follows: $2,000 during the 1934/35 Session and two separate payments of $1,000 during each of the two following years. We are well aware, from your previous efforts on our behalf, that you are both punctual and punctilious in carrying out your obligations toward the University; but at the same time the Regulations of the University do not permit expenditure on account of expected income which is not within the scope of the Regular Budget; such expenditure is made only as and when the specially contributed and allocated sums are received.

You are doubtless aware that, despite the scientific importance of Dr. Lachmann's work his Department is not yet included in the Regular Budget of the University and is therefore entirely dependent upon the regular receipt of the sums specially allocated from the contributors. We would therefore esteem it a favour to learn from you roughly about when you can forward your Annual Contribution in accordance with your undertaking for this and next year, in order that Dr. Lachmann may continue to work undisturbed and so that we may pay his expenses in due season.

We take this opportunity of reminding you that during the past year, as you wrote to Dr. Magnes on October 17th, 1934, you intended to forward the University $2,000, of which we only received $1,000. As a result we were $1,000 short last year, and had to advance this amount from General Funds as a loan on account of your contribution. We shall be very grateful if you settle this particular matter at the same time as the other.

Thanking you in advance for the information and settlement requested, as well as for your long-standing interest in the University.

Yours faithfully,
M. Schneersohn
Financial Secretary

9.4.1936

To: Mr. S. Z. Schocken
From: Mr. M. Schneersohn

Clarifying details of the Contract with Dr. Lachmann[69]

Dr. Magnes conducted negotiations with Dr. Lachmann concerning his employment at the Hebrew University already in 1933, on the basis of an agreed sum of University participation in his employment budget; this sum was finally fixed at a limit of £P 800.- for three years.

Dr. Magnes received a promise from Mrs. Ginsburg of New York to provide this amount, which she would pay over a period of three years: the first year – $2,000; the second year – $1,000; the third year – $1,000.

The budget settled in December 1934 for a period of three years was a sum of £P1910.- per year, of which £P 1,110.- would be solicited by Dr. Lachmann and £P 800.- would be the University's participation.

Mr. Schocken, honorary treasurer of the University, did not want to sign on a three-year contract for the following reasons:

1. Since all the money promised by Mrs. Ginsburg was not yet in our coffers, and if anything happened, all financial responsibility would fall on the University;

2. Due to caution, since it could happen that after the three years are over, responsibility for the continuation of Dr. Lachmann's employment would have to be paid out of the University's budget.

It was therefore decided to invite him for only one year, from 1.4.1935 until 1.4.1936, and that Dr. Magnes would inform Dr. Lachmann about this decision.

---

69 Translated from the Hebrew.

Since Dr. Lachmann was not here at the time, Dr. Schlesinger wrote to Dr. Lachmann on 28.3. a copy of which I attach.

Two months before the end of the year, the question of continuation of Dr. Lachmann's future employment was discussed with Mr. Schocken. Mr. Schocken made two suggestions:

1. To behave concerning Dr. Lachmann as is done concerning other employees – i.e. Rosowsky, Stecklis, and others – and to inform Dr. Lachmann that our obligation to him is only insofar as we receive the promised money from the donor in America; we will pay his salary when the above-mentioned money is received;

2. If Dr. Magnes is willing to accept responsibility for the money to be received from Mrs. Ginsburg so that if for any reason the money from Mrs. Ginsburg is not received, Dr. Magnes will provide the Treasury with money that is held at his disposal. In that case Mr. Schocken is willing to sign a contract with Dr. Lachmann for the coming two years.

These two suggestions were passed on by Dr. Magnes both in writing and verbally. Dr. Magnes contends that the new administration must honour his obligations given as Chancellor of the University, even if it is possible to cancel them through legal means.

We do not find it possible to give any obligations. In his opinion, Mrs. Ginsburg's promise which is in his possession guarantees Mrs. Ginsburg's donation.

I have written a letter to Mrs. Ginsburg, a copy of which I herewith attach, and a copy of which has been sent by me to Dr. Magnes.

I feel it necessary to add that Mrs. Ginsburg is particularly interested in musical matters and has occasionally in the past sent special sums to be used for the History of Music, which we used mainly to purchase books on Musical Science. The sum of £P 307 – which we have kept to be used as reserve – was transferred to the Chancellor about two years ago.

I have suggested that this sum should be set aside by Dr. Magnes as a reserve for Dr. Lachmann's budget, if we do not receive the promised sum from Mrs. Ginsburg.

Dr. Magnes most emphatically rejected this suggestion.

After the letter he had sent to Magnes involving Mr. Schocken,

Schneersohn made sure to equip Mr. Schocken with the details he either never knew or had long forgotten. From the order of events, it is clear that Mr. Schneersohn took upon himself the initiative to reopen the Lachmann case. In all fairness, given his position at the University, he could hardly ignore financial matters. Still, his overeagerness in this case, and the cunning way in which he handled it, suggests that he, too, knew in which direction the wind was blowing. More than compromise Lachmann, he managed to put Magnes in an awkward position.

Here is what Lachmann was told. It offered little hope for the long run. Rather, it extended the existing arrangement for two additional years – without betraying the extent to which Magnes, personally, bore the brunt of it.

23.4.1936

Dr. R. Lachmann,[70]
Here

Dear Sir,

It is my honour to inform you that the University administration has agreed to extend your employment by the University until 1.4.1938.

In so doing, the University does not accept any additional responsibility regarding the budget agreed between us when arranging the initial agreement – that is, the whole budget for three years – from 1.4.1935 until 1.4.1938 – will be in the amount of £P1,910, of which £P1,110 will be raised by yourself, and the sum of £P800 for the three years will be the responsibility of the University.

We feel that it should be emphasized that when the above-mentioned period ends – i.e. 1.4.1938 – the University will have no financial or institutional responsibility for the continuation of your employment at the University.

Yours sincerely,
M. Schneersohn
Financial secretary

---

70 Translated from the Hebrew.

It is difficult to interpret Lachmann's reply, since it neither acknowledges nor questions Schneerson's letter. It simply changes the subject to issues of housekeeping.

April 27, 1936

Dear Mr. Schneerson,

I am forwarding to you the agreement arrived at with the representatives of the Rabbi of Gur, which is signed by both of them (Eisner and Weinberg). I should like you to keep this document with the rest of my papers and to make use of it, should the occasion arise.[71]

Concerning the arrangement with Mr. Schur, I assume that, following our conversation of yesterday, his salary for the month of May will be disbursed without problems in a month's time. With regard to further months, I should like to ask you to honor the lists, countersigned by me, of work performed.

I would further ask you to honor invoices, to be signed by Mr. Schur, for purposes of Archive work, current invoices for electricity and water consumption, as well as the pay for a charlady.

Many thanks for your efforts and cordial greetings,

Your
Robert Lachmann

Notwithstanding Lachmann's tendency to deal with detail in a meticulous fashion, the kind of bureaucratic minutiae that were imposed on him, which he was forced to address despite himself, must have taken its toll. Yet, outwardly, he kept his calm, always maintaining a civilized posture. Nothing, it seems, could shake his confidence in the course he was pursuing. However much he wished to be better integrated in the University, his real group of reference was composed of professional colleagues, not in Jerusalem, but the world over. Abreast of developments

---

71 Lachmann had to arrive at an agreement with the Rabbi to ensure that religious practice would not be violated and that proper payment would be guaranteed.

in his field, he kept in touch (as we shall again see) with many who knew his whereabouts, understood what he was trying to achieve, and lent support to his efforts. At the same time, due to his relentless effort to record and document vanishing musical traditions, he had become more familiar and involved with the population of the country, sensitive to its plight and aspirations. Having created for himself a bubble, as it were, within which to survive, the decisions and conduct of members at the University struck him as lacking foresight, more than acts of intentional malice. The truth, of course, resided somewhere in between. Nonetheless, as a foreigner in a new land, Lachmann relished the kind words that Magnes – a member of the establishment – was willing to spare on his behalf, whether in letters addressed to friends or to himself.

Extract – Dr. Magnes's letter to Mrs. H.A. Ginzburg, 941 Park Ave., New York

3.V.36

Dear Leonie,

Thank you ever so much for sending your $500 to the University. I shall ask the Treasurer's office here either to get into direct touch with you as to the further payments or to have the American office do this.

Dr. Lachmann, whom you are helping to maintain here, is doing exceptional work. With his home-made recording machine, he and his assistant have now almost 500 new recordings to add to the Archive of Oriental Music which is now a valuable part of the University's collections. Dr. Lachmann is also the trusted adviser of the new radio on non-European music.[72] He has just gone to Germany on leave where his mother and brother still live. There is an idea of transferring to Jerusalem the publication of the Quarterly "Zeitschrift für Vergleichende Musikwissenschaft," of which he has been editor since its beginning.

There is being sent to you a typed copy of four lectures of his on Eastern Music. Please return when you have finished.[73]

---

72 See appendix III: Twelve Radio Talks.
73 See appendix IV: Four Lectures on Eastern Music.

<u>The Hebrew University</u>

Jerusalem, 27.7.36

Dr. R. Lachmann,
Klopstockstr. 20
Berlin NW. 87

Dear Dr. Lachmann,

The Hebrew University is greatly interested in the furtherance of your work and would welcome additional support for it.

The Archives you have been able to establish during the past winter are of the utmost value for the scientific elucidation of non-European music, and there is no doubt that with the development of your important and fascinating work its practical application and use will become clear.

Sincerely yours,
Dr. J. L. Magnes

Several additional months elapsed since Mr. Schneersohn reopened the case until Lachmann, at Magnes's request, produced an account of his recent activities. This time, however, the report was supposed to be in Hebrew and circulated among members of the faculty of the University. Magnes had hoped to rally their support, especially the support of those who were in the position to appreciate what Lachmann was trying to accomplish. Also, the document was to reveal that he had an international standing and was sought after by institutions abroad.

The short document which Lachmann produced was in perfect Hebrew, Lachmann had by then mastered the language. He began taking Hebrew lessons from the day of his arrival in Palestine, trying, as well, to perfect his Arabic. Though extremely gifted linguistically, it took some effort to master these languages in the way he did.

REPORT OF ACTIVITIES OF THE ARCHIVE OF ORIENTAL MUSIC [74]

From May 1936 to January 1937

A. My activities last summer

The bad financial situation of the Archive forced me, as in 1935, to spend the summer months in Germany. I left the country at the beginning of May. On my way to Germany I spent 3 weeks in Switzerland to lecture at the University and before the Geographic-Ethnological Society in Basel. My lecture before this organization took place on 8.5.36, on the subject: Oriental Music and Antiquity. At the University I gave a series of six lectures from 11.5-16.5, on the subject: Musical Cultures of the Near East. The musical examples used in order to explain the subjects on these two occasions were taken, amongst others, from the discs of the Archive.

During my stay in Germany I dealt with Archive matters in two directions:

1) Purchasing specific machines and instruments for the Archive laboratory (see part D)

2) Analyzing discs from the Archive material, whose results I shall shortly publish.

B. My Activities in Winter 1936/37

I arrived back in Israel on 23 October, and continued my work at the Archive. Discs recorded from the beginning of November can be categorized as follows:

1. Discs of Music of Oriental Jews
    a) Yemenites: readings from the Bible, and songs
    b) Kurdish songs
    c) Maaravi'im (Western): Liturgical songs
    d) "Bene Yisrael" (Indian Jews): Songs I acquired through Dr. Olschwanger
    e) Spanish songs
    f) Various Oriental songs
2. Discs of Christian Music
    a) Copts: Hymns

---

74 Translated from the Hebrew.

b) Armenians: Readings and Songs, including the Christmas ceremony and songs in Bethlehem
   c) Greek Church: Christmas ceremony and songs in Bethlehem
3. Discs of Arab Music
   a) Readings from the Koran
   b) Urban songs, instrumental music
   c) Songs accompanied by the Rababa
4. Discs of Scottish bagpipes

No. of discs added from 3.2.36 until 23.1.37	178
Previous number	<u>437</u>
Total	615

In addition to the above-mentioned discs, copies were made from commercial discs which can be divided into two categories:
a) Indian urban music
b) Southern Spanish (flamenco) songs

C. The Activities of the Participants in the Scientific Work of the Archive

In the past year, three female students began to participate in the work of the Archive:
a) Dr. Edith Gerson-Kivi. Her subject: Western liturgical songs and instrumental music.
b) Kitt Flaxman, M.A.: The Yemenite Bible Reading
c) Sofia Lentschner: Oriental Urban Instrumental Music

D. The Laboratory

Last summer I bought several machines and instruments for the Archive Laboratory: Gramophone lamps, spare lamps, cutters, Potentiometer.

During the winter, the following jobs were done besides recording:
a) A new room was furbished for voice recording.
b) Important improvements were made in the recording machines.
c) The instruments were arranged on special shelves built for them.

For the sake of progress, it was necessary to acquire another recording machine.

This concise, well-written report conveys the spirit of action, of activities in progress, not only of work already accomplished. It certainly conveys the message that Lachmann, though hardly known "at home," is professionally well-known abroad. Unfortunately, the six lectures he delivered could not be found either in his personal files or in the University's archive. It would have been nice to read what he saw fit to emphasize, under the heading of Musical Cultures of the Near East. The report, at any rate, emphasizes the mix of the local population – its musical heritage, largely in connection with entrenched religious practice, raising the possibility of a historical relationship among the musical traditions of the religious groups involved.

Following this account, Magnes asked Lachmann to submit a new budget – an estimate of his needs, based on his experience in the country. Magnes was determined to settle the issue once and for all. He made his position known to whomever he was in contact with, primarily, but not only, to those who had a say over financial matters. According to Magnes, Lachmann apparently was not the only one who was mistreated. Having lost much power since his "promotion" from Chancellor to President, Magnes was still the University's best bet as a fundraiser. He knew he was, and began using it as a threat.

<u>The Hebrew University</u>
<u>Office of the President</u>

Jerusalem, 11th February, 1937

<u>No. XII</u>

To the Administrator

<u>Subject</u>: Budget of Department of Non-European Music

Upon the basis of the attached budget submitted to me today by Dr.

Lachmann, it appears that for his work from now until April 1938 there is available only the sum of £P 307.649.

His department should have a budget of about £P 680 per annum.

I should like to know what the attitude of the university's administration is towards the continuation of Dr. Lachmann's work in general and towards supplying him with an adequate budget up to April 1, 1938.

I should like to know as much as possible about this before the visit here of Mr. and Mrs. Roger Straus. This is an instance of what I mean when I say that it may be necessary to persuade them, or others, to contribute funds for some of the stepchildren of the University.

J. L. Magnes
President

An Arab playing the Nāy

Act III

12th February, 1937

To the President

Subject: Department of Non-European Music

Note No. XII from the President, together with the budget for this department, has been transmitted to Mr. Schneersohn for Mr. Schocken for his views as to supplementing the budget of this department up to April 1, 1938.

At the same time I would suggest that either Dr. Lachmann or yourself – if you wish to initiate such a proposal – ask the Rector in his capacity of Chairman of the Senate and of the Standing Committee of the Senate, to bring before those bodies for consideration the question of whether Lachmann's department should be included in the problem of the development of the University, i.e., to be included among the chairs and departments that the Senate recommends to establish or to start as part of the regular University structure.

In the absence of Professor Bergmann,[75] such a note should be addressed to Dr. Ben-David, as secretary of the Standing Committee, who would see to it that this comes on the Agenda.

S. Ginzberg
Administrator

P.S. Personal comment:- I would suggest an amendment in terminology. You refer to Lachmann and others as stepchildren of the University. I would suggest that they are in the nature of distant relations offered temporary hospitality?

Mr. Ginzberg may have intended his amendment to Magnes's terminology as an improvement. In retrospect, it reveals that the Jewish population in Palestine was so self-absorbed that the difficulties which their "distant

---

75 Professor S.H. Bergmann was the Rector of the University.

relations" were forced to face did not completely strike home. As a matter of fact, the extent of the sensitivity of the Jewish population in Palestine to the calamity that was in the offing has been called into question in recent years, provoking serious debate.

Whatever the intent of Ginzberg's reply, Magnes seems to despair of the *ad hoc* arrangement and the exclusivity of his personal patronage:

12th February, 1937

Dear Dr. Lachmann,

In relation to the future of your work, I would suggest that you consult with Professor Mayer, head of the School of Oriental Studies.

Professor Mayer and his colleagues will have to consider whether or not they wish to bring the continuance of your work before the University authorities. The programme of the University's development is, as you know, receiving constant consideration.

I am hoping that Professor Mayer and his associates and the University authorities will realize the great value of your work for the country and for the University.

Yours sincerely,
J. L. Magnes
President

cc. to Prof. Mayer
the Administrator

Indeed, the program for the University's development was constantly reviewed. All of those involved were familiar with the commitments and agreed priorities that guided this development, watchful not to stray from its course. Thus Magnes's threat, that he might persuade Mr. and Mrs. Straus to contribute funds, elicited the following letter which put both Magnes and Lachmann in their place. Mr. Schocken reminded Magnes that he was by no means free to divert donations to the University as he saw fit, and that Lachmann had not fulfilled his obligation as promised.

15/2/37

Dr. J. L. Magnes,
President of the Hebrew University,
Here

Dear Dr. Magnes,[76]

Re your question as to the position of the University administration concerning Mr. D. Straus's contribution and also concerning Dr. Lachmann's budget, I would like to reply that:

a) It is my clear opinion, with which you agreed in one of our recent conversations, that the financial situation of the University demands that all efforts should be made to use donations in order to take the load off the University treasury – that is, in order to fulfill its financial obligations both in the regular budget and in additional budgets.

I would therefore suggest that Mr. Straus's donation be set aside to cover the "Moadon" building. As you know, the deficit on this building is already more than £P 1,600. Mr. Straus's donation in the sum of £P 1,200 could cover most of this deficit, which would release our treasury from the great burden, and Mr. Straus would also get satisfaction from this, as his donation would not be swallowed up into the regular annual budget, but be remembered for a specific purpose (by placing a plaque in the building).

It would also be possible – if the donor would prefer it – to set aside £P 1,000 for the above-mentioned purpose and use the rest of the money for publishing Prof. Klausner's book which we already approved over and above the regular budget without ensuring that we could cover it.

b). Re continuation of Dr. Lachmann's employment at the University until the end of the three-year period, my opinion is that this question should first be

---

76 Translated from the Hebrew.

brought before the Senate – so that they can state their opinion concerning the fitting place for this effort in the framework of the development plan of the University.

c) Re the deficit in Dr. Lachmann's budget until 1 April 1938 which reaches the sum of £P 365 according to our latest accounting with Dr. Lachmann, I am sorry that with the present financial situation of the University I cannot see any possibility of finding a source to cover the deficit from University funds. I must point out that if such a deficit has occurred, it is only through Dr. Lachmann's not fulfilling the financial obligation he gave when originally employed. The obligation the University undertook to cover part of the budget up to £P 800 will be fulfilled by us.

According to the budget approved by you on 2 December 1934 and approved by Dr. Schlesinger in his letter to the Chancellor of 28 March 1935 (copy attached), Dr. Lachmann undertook to raise the sum of £P 1,110, of which £P 560 was to come from 3 years of his pension, and the remaining £560 from donations which he undertook to solicit from a small number of his friends interested in him or – if that did not succeed – from his private means.

Our condition was, therefore, that Dr. Lachmann receive donations from sources interested especially in his subject, and not directly in the University – that is, his efforts should not jeopardise donations that the University could raise in any case.

I therefore suggest that Dr. Lachmann continue in his efforts among his friends. We will of course be happy if you find it possible to assist these subjects. On the other hand, if funds which the donors were willing to donate to the University are set aside for Dr. Lachmann's project, the University thus is losing funds and is *de facto* participating in funding Dr. Lachmann from its own pocket, and this contradicts the spirit of the agreement of his appointment for the above-mentioned three years and also contradicts the possibility of realizing it at this moment.

Hoping that you agree to the administration's position,

Yours very sincerely,
S. Z. Schocken

Mr. Schocken's adamant letter was accurate in describing the situation in factual terms. Reading the letter, Magnes must have felt challenged enough to address a semi-confessional letter to Mrs. Ginzburg – the major source of Lachmann's budget.

22.2.37

Mrs. H. A. Ginzburg
941 Park Avenue
New York, N.Y.

Dear Leonie,

Your letter of February 2nd, with its check for $500, has just arrived. Let me thank you for your great kindness. I am informing the University that you will try to send $250 a month until you pay up the promised amount.

Professor Bergmann, Rector of the University, left on Friday morning for a trip to Europe and then to the United States in April on behalf of the University. I gave him a letter to you at his request.

The work that Dr. Lachmann has been doing in Oriental and Non-European Music generally has now received great recognition, and we must all of us thank you for giving him and us this great opportunity. Oriental Music, as you may know, is not a usual subject in a university curriculum, and there are so many gaps in our regular university structure that many have said – and with a great deal of reason – that we must endeavor to fill in some of those fundamental gaps before we undertake work like that of Oriental Music, interesting and important as this may be. Nevertheless, life does not always work out in regular, logical sequence, and I am personally very glad that through your understanding we have been able to establish this subject in such a way as now to have won the support of a number, if not all, of the members of our Senate.

Dr. Lachmann's budget up to April 1, 1938 shows a deficit of some £P 300, or about $500, and I am anxious to be able to raise this sum. If it is raised from special funds such as yours, I would accept these additional funds only on condition that Dr. Lachmann and his subject be made an integral part of the

University structure. Under such conditions, do you think that you would be able to contribute all or any part of this $1500?

What you say about this awful world and about the happy people who are nevertheless to be found in it is something that I constantly think about. I happen also to be one of those happy people, and I am sure that that is due to good health as much as perhaps to any other thing. When I see someone with good health, I can hardly sympathize with any of his material or spiritual problems; and yet I know that these problems are the most important thing for him and for everyone else. If I were running the world and were asked to grant one fundamental for men's happiness, it would be to give them good health. If they then could not be happy, it would certainly be their own fault – as it is indeed largely now, even though there are a lot of people sick and diseased physically, mentally and spiritually.

Roger and Gladys Straus and Arthur and Iphigene Sulzberger are here and are being rushed to death. They are greatly impressed by much of what they have seen, and deeply worried about what may take place here because of the tense relations between Jews and Arabs. I am worried about that too, and sometimes I think, now that I am almost sixty, that I ought to give up everything else and spend all the years that may be left to me carrying on the good old political fight, as years ago I used to. It is not a pleasant prospect, but they do say of old war-horses that they stamp and rear when the trumpet sounds and think themselves young again.

We have pleasant letters from Benedict and Jonathan. I wonder when you saw that very healthy and happy Benedict last. Why do you not persuade Jimmy and Lenore to come this way with you?

We are both well.

Judah

The last two letters speak for themselves, for they dramatically juxtapose Magnes's *formal* difficulties with staff and faculty of the University and his *amicable* relations with those who supported it financially. Though possibly able to raise the money for Lachmann, Magnes was cornered into a position which challenged his loyalty to the institution he headed. His confessional letter to Mrs. Ginzburg reveals the pressure he was under, and how very tired he had become trying to sort out his conflicting commitments.

Lachmann, by contrast, continued to spin dreams, independent of his personal predicament. In fact, while Magnes's doubts – concerning the way he had chosen to express his own commitment to the Zionist enterprise – kept mounting, Lachmann came to accept the local struggles, more and more, as inevitable. While Magnes was juggling his competing commitments, Lachmann came to appreciate the enormity of the tasks which all involved had taken upon themselves. It was legitimate, he found, to continue to fight for causes which could be justified as contributing to the future of the country and its place in the world. Thus, despite the difficulties of which he was aware, Lachmann resubmitted his plan for the journal. This time, however, he approached the issue with greater confidence, attesting to the matter in concrete terms. He had even thought of a new, more appropriate, name for the Journal, so sure was he that it would, somehow, resume.

March 10th, 1937

Dear Dr. Magnes,

The enclosures refer to the journal to be established. I think it will be practical to start the journal <u>at the beginning of 1938</u>.

Enclosure (1) contains a preliminary budget worked out by Mr. Ibn-Sahav. The figures are based on information obtained from <u>the Azriel Press</u> who would print the text and from Mr. B. Balan who would supply the musical appendices. The question of who is to sign as publishers has not yet been decided.

Enclosure (2) contains the prospectus to be sent to possible subscribers. The costs of printing 1000 copies of it are estimated by Mr. Ibn-Sahav at £P 1,500. Nor would the costs of distributing the Journal four times per annum be considerable. Still, it may be wise to add another £P 6 to the costs as calculated before arriving, thus, at a total of £P 125 (cf. Enclosure 1). Correspondingly I should have to count on 8 more subscribers.

Enclosure (3) enumerates articles to be published in the first few issues of the Journal. Nos. 3, 7, and 8 are being done by my pupils.

Yours sincerely,
R. Lachmann

The other reports for which you asked me today will follow as soon as possible.

(2) Prospectus
Journal of Eastern and Primitive Music

This new publication addresses itself to all those who take an interest in the study and preservation of music and song outside the sphere of modern European civilization, to the general music lover as well as to the musical historian, the student of folklore, the Orientalist, the ethnologist, and others. It will be conducted on much the same lines as the Zeitschrift für vergleichende Musikwissenschaft, the editorship of which I resigned in October 1935 and which has ceased to exist after the completion of its third volume.

The Journal will include essays, notes and discussions, reviews of books, a bibliography, and copious musical illustrations. Through the collaboration of specialists it is hoped to cover the whole field of Eastern and primitive music. In particular, it will be possible to draw on the material of the Archives of Oriental Music established, under my direction, in 1935, as a department of the Hebrew University in Jerusalem, and serving to preserve the traditional music in the Near East.

The prevailing language will be English, but contributions in French, German, and Italian will also be accepted.

There will be four issues a year amounting to a total of 132 pages apart from musical and other appendices.

The annual subscription is 15 sh. payable by money order or cheque to

Dr. Robert Lachmann
University, Jerusalem

(3) Articles To Be Published
in the first few issues
of the Journal of Eastern and Primitive Music

(1) Cantillation and songs of the Jews on the isle of Djerba
(2) A treatise on musical rhythm and cosmology by Al-Kindi (died about 874); facsimile, emendated text, commentary, English translation
(3) The modes of the Yemenite Jewish Bible and prayer cantillation
(4) The modes of Samaritan Bible cantillation
(5) Musical systems among Arab Bedouins and peasants and their history
(6) The musical system and practice on the Turkish tanbur
(7) The modal preludes of Oriental urban music
(8) The music of Moroccan Jewish piyyutim
(9) An appreciation of the work of E. M. v. Hornbostel (died 1935), the foremost scholar in primitive music in his time, with a complete bibliography of his writings
(10) The Archives of Oriental Music at the Hebrew University, Jerusalem, its collection and activities[77]

The change of name of the proposed journal is noteworthy, for it reveals that Lachmann really intended to turn Jerusalem into a place befitting the study of non-European music. Nonetheless, examining the list of subjects that the early issues of the journal were expected to address, it must be remembered that no other journal existed at the time for the publication of articles on these subjects, certainly not lengthy ones. It is worth noting that most of the promised articles were of a theoretical nature, enabling comparisons among different musical traditions, like the modal systems, for example.

---

77 Enclosure (1) – the preliminary budget worked out by Mr. Ibn-Sahav – is omitted from the document presented above.

The Highlights of the Struggle

From the following letters it is evident that Magnes was more interested in Lachmann's budget becoming a part of the University's budget, and in Lachmann becoming a regular member of the staff, than he was in the journal. The fight, at any rate, which *he* was engaged in, centered around Lachmann, since the case had become symptomatic of his own crumbling authority.

18.3.37

Dear Dr. Wertheimer,

In connection with our conversation concerning the work of Dr. Lachmann, I understand you to be ready to guarantee a minimum sum of £P250 a year for three years.

I have discussed this matter with some of my associates at the University.

I am personally greatly interested in having Dr. Lachmann's budget become a part of the regular budget of the University and having him become a regular member of the University staff. He is, as you are aware, a distinguished man in his field, and I regard his being here as adding to the prestige and scholarly capacities of the Hebrew University.

It is not possible for the authorities of the University here to determine how far such a collection on your part would be approved by the Society of Friends of the Hebrew University in Prague. If, for whatever reasons, they object to your making a public and formal collection, I would suggest that you collect this money privately and only from such persons as would be willing to give an additional sum to the Society of Friends.

It was very pleasant meeting you.

With good wishes for a safe journey back to your home, I am

Sincerely yours,
J. L. Magnes
President

Act III

Dr. P. Wertheimer
S.S. Galilea
Port of Haifa

24th March, 1937

Dr. R. Lachmann
Beth Ha-rav Migur
Opp. Pension Ettinger
Rehov Ben-Jehudah
Jerusalem

Dear Dr. Lachmann,

This is to inform you that I have proposed to the University that you be made a regular member of its staff.

The budget which you have submitted is large. It should, I think, be reduced considerably in connection with payments to persons who are to record for you. The item for rental, etc. is also very large.

I am proposing to the University that at least the latter item be taken over by the regular budget of the University. The other items – although to be included in the regular budget, if my proposal is carried – must nevertheless be made up, for the time being, from special funds.

In any event, whether you are made a member of the regular staff or not, I think you should prepare to go to America. That will help your work in every way. If you are made a member of the regular staff, any money that would be collected would have to be turned over by you towards the regular budget, which would thus be enabled to cover the expenses of your laboratory. Should you collect more than the amount necessary to cover your budget, you would then get into touch with the American office of the University and the University here to consider in how far that surplus should be used for the extension of your work or should go for general expenses in the regular budget.

In connection with the whole question, I should like to inform you that there are special funds which, together with Dr. Wertheimer's pledge, should be sufficient to provide for your reduced budget for a year and a half or two years, as also your deficit for this year.

Until a definite decision is reached, I do not think that you should proceed with the preparations for a periodical, particularly in view of the fact that there would be a deficit also on this score.

I would urge you, together with Professor Mayer[78] and Professor Bergmann when he returns, to take the matter up vigorously and press for a decision one way or another.

You need not be assured further of my own regard for you and for your work.

Sincerely yours,
J. L. Magnes
President

Magnes did not just threaten, he meant every word he wrote. He insisted that the case be brought before the Senate (composed of all professors and other elected representatives of the staff[79]) and that a decision be reached, "one way or the other," concerning the prospect of including Lachmann and the Archive in the development plans of the University. Fearing the outcome, Magnes supplied himself with a document that left no doubt in the eyes of its beholders that he, at any rate, was determined not to let Lachmann down.

Magnes, clearly, now takes a strong academic stance – vis-à-vis the faculty, not his administrative staff. Having been favorably disposed from the start, he learned a great deal from Lachmann in the interim. The document, in fact, summarizes most of what he learned, and a good student he was. While the three-fold division of Lachmann's publications (see Lachmann's extensive German report) suggests that Lachmann might have helped, this document, unlike the others, must have surely been supervised by Magnes himself. The substantive information which it contains naturally

---

78 Professor Mayer was a renowned Islamicist in the School of Oriental Studies, to whom Magnes directed Lachmann in his letter of February 18.
79 At the beginning of the academic year of 1937-38 the Senate had 31 members (17 professors, 9 professors *ad personam*, 4 lecturers, and 1 senior assistant).

rests on Lachmann's progress reports, which had been languishing, anyway, in his own drawers.

April 1937

<u>The document</u>

The Archives of Oriental Music were established in Jerusalem on the 1st of May, 1935, as a section of the School of Oriental Studies of the Hebrew University, under the direction of Dr. Robert Lachmann.

Dr. Lachmann was born in Berlin in 1892, where he studied English, German, French, Arabic and Music, receiving the degree of Doctor of Philosophy in 1922. From 1923 to 1933, he was Librarian of the Musical Section of the State Library in Berlin. Under the new political regime, he went into forced retirement in 1934. An account of Dr. Lachmann's work and publications in the field of Oriental Music is given at a later point.

The purpose of the Archives is to promote the study of the music and song of the Near East, particularly that which is preserved through oral tradition, before such song is lost to us through the gradual seeping in of Western influences which are growing more and more evident. This involves:

a) the acquisition and recording of material from native performers, for which purpose Jerusalem is the most ideal situation for Archives of such a nature,

b) writing down this traditional music in musical notation,

c) a scientific analysis of such music, based on these recordings and transcriptions,

d) the publication of the results of work done through the Archives,

e) and the bringing-out of hitherto unpublished theoretical works on the subject of Oriental Music.

It is evident that a work of this nature is of foremost importance not only from the point of view of Musical History, but also from the sociological, ethnological and philological standpoint, and will throw considerable light on the historical and cultural life of the peoples in question. Furthermore, this institute – because of its ideal situation and the infinite scope of its work – could become the unique centre for the study of the music of the Near East. It has at present three students, each occupied with one particular aspect of this music, namely:

the Cantillation of the Yemenite Jews, the Modes of Urban Arab Music, and the Music of the Moroccan Piyyutim (Poems).

Dr. Lachmann's activities in the field of Oriental Music began about 1915, when he wrote down a large collection of music and songs performed by prisoners of war from North Africa. After the War he undertook a number of travels in Tripoli, Tunis, Algeria, Egypt (including Sinai), in order to collect further material. Copies of this material – about 600 discs – which was collected for the Berlin Phonogram Archives, are now included in the Archives. The Archives also possess copies of the material collected by Idelsohn before the War, as well as about 200 commercial discs which are no longer available as the matrices were destroyed.

Since the establishment of the Archives in 1935, about 800 discs have been made. These records cover various fields of music and song to be found in Palestine and the neighbouring countries:

1) Jewish Music and Song
   a) Yemenite cantillation of the Bible, and songs male and female.
   b) Kurdish cantillation.
   c) North African Sephardic songs and cantillation.
   d) Babylonian cantillation.
   e) B'nei Yisrael from India.
2) Christian Oriental
   a) Coptic hymns.
   b) Armenian cantillation and secular songs.
   c) Greek Orthodox Christmas ceremony.
3) Arab
   a) Koran reading.
   b) Peasant and Beduin songs, male and female.
   c) Flute and viol music.
   d) Urban music and song.
4) Samaritan cantillation, hymns and secular songs.

The records are made after preliminary information relating to the kinds of music and song existing in the respective group or community has been obtained. Through this preparation, it is assured that the records are not taken in a haphazard way, but represent typical specimens of the various kinds.

The original records are copied at once by means of a Pick-up. (For details of the technical apparatus, see further.) These copies, and not the originals, are used for research and analysis. The contents of the records are transcribed in staff-notation with all possible exactness, and with the help of a Metronome and a Tonometer for measuring the pitch. In the case of vocal music the texts are also noted.

The material thus obtained is worked out as a basis for publications, and even at this stage it is possible to work out a number of subjects, each independent and complete in itself, as for instance: Samaritan Cantillation, North African Jewish Lyrical Songs, Forms of Beduin and Peasant Songs, etc.

The Archives can also serve pedagogical purposes. The standard of music-teaching in schools can be raised considerably, if teachers – instead of keeping to their one-sided European point of view – use the Archives and thus obtain an insight into Oriental musical traditions.

The study of present-day oriental music – as made possible by the collection of the Archives – throws light on the earlier stages of this music, because of the conservatism of the orientals who have handed down their music orally with very few changes from the Middle Ages, and in some cases even from antiquity. The study of historical musical documents is thus enlivened by bringing it into connection with present-day practice.

Another important aspect of the collection is the connection of Eastern music with the principal features of the peoples' social life. Descriptions of their manners and customs would remain greatly deficient if the part played by music in their social life were not given its full estimate.

So far, only a beginning has been made. The material to be collected in Palestine itself is far from having been exhausted, in view of the great diversity of ethnical groups assembled here. Besides, the study of music in the neighbouring countries opens up a vast additional field of research. All this material should be collected as quickly as possible, so as to secure the invaluable musical tradition before it comes to be transformed or altogether destroyed by the growing European influence. Some of the subjects to be tackled in the near future are:

1) Kurdish Jewish Cantillation and Songs – hitherto quite unknown.

2) Mandean Religious Songs (Mesopotamia).

3) Beduin forms of song in the Syrian Hauran and in Nejd.

4) Ethiopian and Maronite Church Music.

For recording purposes a Laboratory has been installed and is being constantly improved upon, according to modern technical principles. There are mainly two apparatus, one for recording at the Archives, while the other is portable and can be used even in the desert. Dr. Lachmann states that, to his knowledge, this is the only, and at any rate the first, Institute to use electric recording of discs in the field. The Laboratory also has a specially-constructed pick-up for transferring on to discs – and improving upon – records originally made on cylinders of the Edison type. Thus it has been, and will further be, possible to preserve collections which are unsatisfactory technically, but are invaluable as containing music which has, in the meantime, disappeared from living practice.

The following is a list of Dr. Lachmann's publications on Oriental Music:

A: Comprehensive Works

1. Muhammedan Music (Grove's Dictionary of Music)
2. Musik des Orients, Breslau 1929. In Spanish translation: Musica de Oriente. Barceloni 1931.
3. Musik der aussereuropäischen Kulture- und Naturvölker. Potsdam 1930. In: Handbuch der Musikwissenschaft, edited by E. Bucken.
4. Musikalische Forschungsaufgaben im vorderen Orient. (In: Bericht über die 1. Sitzung der Gesellschaft zur Erforschung der Musik des Orients. Berlin, 27.4.1930.) – Zusammenfassung in: Actes du 8me. Congrès de l'Institut des Hautes-Etudes marocaines, Rabat-Fès, 1933.
5. Editor of the "Zeitschrift für vergleichende Musikwissenschaft," until 1935. A new Journal of Eastern and Primitive Music is now in the course of preparation and will be started, in English, at the beginning of 1938.

B: On Theory and Systems.

6. Zur aussereuropäischen Mehrstimmigkeit. (Kongressbericht der Beethoven-Zenterarfeier. Wien 1927.)
7. Al-Kindi: Risala fi hubr ta'lif al-alhan. Translation, Introduction, Commentary, Facsimile, and corrected Text. (With Mahmud el-Hefni) Leipzig 1931. (The oldest Arabic treatise on Music.)
8. Review of A. Z. Idelsohn: Jewish Music. (Zeitschrift für Musikwissenschaft. 15. 1923-33.) Contents, fundamental discussions on the system of Synagogal Music.

9. Das indische Tonsystem bie Bharata und sein Ursprung. (With E.M.v. Hornbostel.) (Zeitschrift für Vergleichende Musikwissenschaft. 1. 1933.)
10. Rapport de la Commission de l'enregistrement. (In: Recueil des travaux du Congrès de Musique arabe au Caire en 1932.) Le Caire 1934.
11. Musiksysteme und Musikauffassung (I) (Zeitschrift für Vergl. Musikwis. 3. 1933)

    C: Monographs on Musical Practice.

12. Die Musik in den tunisichen Städten. Phil. Dissertation. (Archiv für Musikwissenschaft, 5. 1923.)
13. Musik und Tonschrift des No. (Bericht über den 1. Kongress der Deutschen Musikgesellschaft, Leipzig 1925.)
14. Gesänge aus Ostturkistan. In: A.v. Lecoq: Von Land und Leuten in Ostturkistan. Leipzig, 1928.
15. Die Weise vom Löwen und der pythische Nomos. (In: Festschrift für Johannes Wolf. Berlin 1929. On the connection between present-day oriental and ancient Greek musical practice.
16. Asiatische Parallelen zur Berbermusik. (With E.M. v. Hornbostel.) (Zeitschrift für Vergl. Musikwiss. 1. 1933)
17. Review of M. Rida and M. El-Hefny: Diresat al-qanun. (Zeitschr. für Vergl. Musikwiss. 3. 1935.)

The document has a neutral air – it states facts, emphasizes the importance of the Archive, and describes the qualifications of the man in charge. It stresses the historical and theoretical significance of Lachmann's undertaking, making salient the scholarly responsibility involved. No mention whatsoever is made of the difficulties, save for the urgency to collect "the invaluable musical traditions" before they "transform." Such a document clearly can be used in different ways and for different purposes. Before using it in any way at all, however, it made sense to await the Senate's verdict. Paragraph 13, of the agenda submitted to the Senate for its meeting on the 28th of May, reads as follows:

Paragraph 13, Senate Meeting of 28.4.37

Archive of Oriental Music[80]

In 1935 Dr. R. Lachmann was appointed as a research fellow for Oriental Music for three years. The question arose concerning the continuation of his activity in connection with the Archive of Oriental Music which he created, as one of the fixed departments of the University. The administration requests that the Senate give its opinion regarding the situation of this Archive in the University building, and also regarding its development programme.

We are attaching a list of the developments of the Archive since its establishment.

25.4.37

Discs of the Archive for Oriental Music in Jerusalem
(as of 10 April 1937)

I. Discs prepared by the Archive (from 1 May 1935 until 10 April 1937). Gramophone plates only.

1. Jewish music
   a) Kurdish   12
   b) Yemenite   75
   c) Western   51
   d) Other communities   25
   e) Contemporary   <u>34</u>   197

2. Samaritan   233

---

80 Translated from the Hebrew.

3. Arabic
   - a) Beduin — 23
   - b) Peasant — 119
   - c) Religious — 39
   - d) Women and children — 9 — 190

4. Oriental urban music — 92

5. Christian — 42

6. Gypsy — 6

7. Miscellaneous — 9

Total — 769

II. My private collection, prepared or purchased by me abroad, which also includes the instruments necessary for recording and copying.

a) Edison rolls
   1) Jewish — 28
   2) Tunis (rural) — 113
   3) Berbers — 53
   4) Tripoli (rural) — 15
   5) Egypt (rural) — 60
   6) China — 12
   7) Persia — 12
   8) Japan — 37

   Total — 330

b) Edison rolls copied onto plates (discs)
   1) Jewish — 76
   2) Samaritan — 15
   3) Western — 6
   4) Tunis and Algeria (rural) — 93

5)	Tripoli (rural)	6
6)	Egypt (rural)	64
7)	Japan	8
	Total	268

c) Commercially produced discs (most of them unavailable today)

1)	Morocco	14
2)	Algeria	44
3)	Tunis	30
4)	Andalusia	6
5)	Egypt	107
6)	Syria	20
7)	Turkey	25
8)	Bulgaria	5
9)	India	16
10)	Siam	9
11)	Java and Bali	20
12)	Tibet	2
13)	China	7
14)	Japan	29
	Total	334

```
769:  I
330:  II   a) ) brought by
263:  II   b) ) me from
334:  II   c) ) Germany
1701*
```

* The texts of the songs in I, IIa, IIb, and some of IIc can also be found in the Archive.

prepared by R. Lachmann
25.4.37

Professor Mayer, evidently, presented the case at the meeting, and against his better judgement and recommendation, the Senate reached the following decision:

From the Protocol of the Senate[81]

2.6.37

The Archive of Oriental Music

Professor Mayer gives details about the Archive, stressing its important work in the field of Jewish and Samaritan music, and the fact that students come from abroad to study at the Archive. He suggests incorporating the Archive as one of the fixed regular departments of the University.

Decisions:

a) The suggestion is rejected.

b) The Senate, while expressing its complete admiration for the work of the Institute and its director, delegates to the Steering Committee responsibility for finding ways of strengthening ties with the Institute without at present affirming it a permanent place in the University.

It cannot be said that Lachmann did not try to publicize his work among faculty members; in fact, by June 1936 he had already published a lengthy report on the Archive in *The Information Bulletin of the Hebrew University*, hoping to familiarize the academic staff with its activities. Trusting that the Senate would vote in his favor, he composed (after he had completed the brief résumé which was used at the Senate meeting) a supplement to his 1936 report, also to be published in the *Bulletin*. What makes this supplement especially engaging is the way in which it caters to the imagined interests of its potential readers. Without distorting fundamental facts, the information it conveys, and the manner in which some of its

---

81 Translated from the Hebrew.

particulars are discussed, reflect Lachmann's profound respect for, and perception of, the scholars whose attention he tried to attract. Though they knew little about the field he represented, they were not addressed as "newcomers" to its research objectives. By emphasizing those aspects to which they could easily relate, Lachmann harbored the hope of dispelling the conception that musical studies were marginal to their own interests, or, for that matter, to the interests of the University of the Jewish People.

Playing and listening to music

Act III

Supplement to the Report on the
Archives of Oriental Music of the Hebrew University
Jerusalem

May 4th, 1937

Since the publication of the report in the INFORMATION BULLETIN of the Hebrew University in June 1936, the work of the Archives of Oriental Music has made considerable progress.

Several branches of oriental music have been studied closely with the object of publishing collections of tunes fully representative of each particular branch.

I. Above all, a very full collection of <u>Yemenite Jewish</u> records has been made. Fortunately, it has been possible to find among the Yemenites residing in Jerusalem, individuals born and bred in Yemen, who are in full possession of their musical tradition which, since their immigration into Palestine, tends to dissolve under the influence of their new surroundings. This Yemenite collection falls into three groups:

1. <u>Liturgical Cantillation</u>.

A thorough investigation is being made into the different kinds of biblical modes or "neginoth" on the basis of records, each mode being represented by a number of records.

2. <u>Hymns and Songs</u>.

This group covers the whole repertoire of songs as used for sacred and secular purposes. They are interesting not only from a musical but also from a literary point of view, most of the tunes being sung to poems of famous medieval poets, such as Shlomo Ibn Gabirol and Yehudah Halevy. It is planned to devote a special study to the relation existing between musical and poetical metre, in connection with these records.

3. A full collection has been made of <u>women's songs</u>. These very simple types of song represent an early stratum in oriental musical development and have been recorded for the first time.

The songs and recitations collected make it possible to furnish a complete musical supplement to the study of the manners and customs of the Yemenite Jews. The Archives possess examples of every kind of song involved in the different events and ceremonies of their social life – a fact which should be greatly appreciated by students of ethnology who, in most cases, have to content themselves, with regard to oriental nations, with the knowledge that their social life is constantly accompanied by music and song, without being able to state the nature of these songs.

It is proposed to make a similarly complete collection of <u>Kurdish Jewish</u> cantillation and song next winter. Up to now, only a number of specimens have been recorded.

II. The Archives are making a complete study of the musical modes or melody types of <u>Oriental Urban Music</u>. This is being done by recording, analysing, and transcribing into staff-notation the preludes in "free rhythm" of all the musical modes now in practice, and the modulations which occur between any of these modes. This collection, which is being recorded from musicians belonging to the different schools of tradition, will be completed towards the end of this year.

The <u>Samaritan</u> collection which at the time of the publication of the BULLETIN numbered 60 records, has been greatly enlarged as a preparation for a study of this music, and now numbers 250 records. This will be a sufficient basis for a monograph on a similar plan to that of Yemenite music, including liturgical cantillation as well as secular songs.

The unique importance of collecting and studying Samaritan musical tradition lies in the fact that the Samaritan community has dwindled down to less than 200 members, including women and children, and that only a handful of people – all of them old men – are keeping up this tradition.

III. All other kinds of music and song mentioned in the BULLETIN report have been given further attention since then.

The Arab section has been enriched by a series of recitations from the Koran, and by a complete program of peasant wedding songs.

Records have been taken of the Christmas service of the Greek Orthodox and Armenian churches, and specimens from the liturgy of other Christian oriental communities – Coptic, Abyssinian, and Syrian.

The total number of records, which at the time of the report was about 250, has now risen to 800. This would have no special significance had the records not been made with special regard to their being as fully representative as possible.

The Archives have already begun to attract the attention of students. At present, three collaborators are using the material for independent research.

Of these, one is preparing a monograph on Yemenite Jewish Cantillation; the second, on Musical Modes of Urban Music; and the third, on Moroccan Jewish Songs.

Apart from these research studies, the Archives are beginning to exercise an influence on the musical education in the schools. The Director of the Model School at Beth Hakerem (Jerusalem) has communicated with the Archives, and several demonstrations of the recorded material have been given, with explanations, and have found such ready response that it has been planned to continue this on a larger scale next winter.

A similar connection has been established with the Arab Model School in Jerusalem, and the Director of this school asked for and printed in the School Journal two articles on musical education to be established in Arab schools.

Dr. Lachmann's private collection of oriental musical instruments, which he has now incorporated in the Archives, is also constantly being increased.

The publication of the supplement did not alter Lachmann's position. Naturally, following the Senate meeting, an active exchange of letters took place in the attempt to accommodate the spirit of its decision. No solution, however, could be found that would secure Lachmann's position, and that of his Archive, to the satisfaction of the negotiating parties. The more impatient Magnes became, the more adamant became those who protected the budget, i.e., the agreed-upon development plans of the University which had no room for Lachmann. Magnes knew he was fighting a lost battle, for his former colleagues turned their backs not only on Lachmann but on him, casting doubts on his commitments as president. What had begun in Magnes's mind as a contribution to the development of the University was being construed as a selfish concern for an individual at the expense of the University. Uneasy with the deterioration of the situation, Magnes felt the time had come to reconsider the whole Lachmann issue and, possibly, his own position as well. After having exerted enormous efforts on the realization of a Vision, i.e., the establishment of a *Hebrew* University in Palestine, the resultant reality seemed beyond his powers. Angry and upset, he contemplated Lachmann's utter dissociation from the University, convinced he could do more for him outside the institution. Lachmann, too, entertained the possibility of dissociating himself from the University; outside its confines, he felt, he might be able to do more for the country with which he had become involved. Ironically, the two men responded in opposite ways to the shrinking of *Lebensraum* at the University. Magnes felt weakened, while Lachmann seemed to derive more and more strength from an emotional space which kept growing inside of him!

November 14th, 1937.

Dear Dr. Magnes,

Dr. Senator,[82] on Wednesday, gave me to understand that, with regard to my position towards the University, three possibilities suggested by you had been discussed by the Senate and the Administration:

(1) that the Archives should be definitely taken over into the regular budget at once;

(2) that the Archives should figure, as before, among the temporary institutions, and should be kept going for another three years, and then be taken over into the regular budget;

(3) that the Archives should be dissociated from the University and that you would endeavour to establish it as a permanent and independent institution.

Since your suggestion under 1 has been rejected both by the Senate and the Administration it seems useless for me to comment on it any further. Professor Mayer pointed out to me that the Senate's decision was not due to a lack of appreciation of my work. It must be due, therefore, to a conception of what is the essential and immutable programme of the University which I cannot but regret. I should, perhaps, leave things at that, but you will permit me repeating my own point of view on this occasion. From the beginning, my hope for the Archives to be definitely incorporated in the regular programme of the University was founded on two points:

(a) I held the idea which, as I know, is shared by many scholars abroad, that the University was laying particular stress on subjects out of the reach of

---

82 Dr. Senator was a member of the Executive Council in the capacity of administrator.

universities abroad and through the investigation of which the Hebrew University might gain a unique and central position in the Near East; namely, subjects pertaining to Jewry, to the population of the Near East in general, and to natural conditions in this part of the world.

(b) I further thought that among these subjects preference was due to those the investigation of which cannot be postponed indefinitely. This, obviously, applies to traditional music and song which, like a number of other manifestations of the Eastern spirit, is being swept away by the recent changes in Eastern social life. We have examples of such music having been neglected until it was too late to collect it. Future generations of scholars will not understand why, in spite of warnings, repeated over and again, a similar omission should have been made here by a body like the Hebrew University who ought to know better, and priceless material have been left to perish while an institute stands ready for its preservation.

The institute, in the course of my two and a half years' work, has attracted four students three of whom intend using the material of the Archives for their theses here or, if this should be impossible, at foreign universities (Basel, Johannesburg). This, in view of the fact that the University has done nothing to encourage students to work on this line, and has actually tried to discourage one of them, tends to prove that the Archives, once its work were recognized as an official subject of teaching, might very probably become a feature also as regards academic education.

Against these remarks, the objection may perhaps be raised that in order to enable the Archives to go on collecting musical material and their incorporation in the regular budget of the University was not indispensable, and that a less permanent arrangement would be sufficient for the purpose. To this, I would reply in the first place that the work of the Archives, if it is to be done thoroughly, cannot be completed within the next three years and that it is, of course, preferable to secure its steady progress at once instead of making it depend on a new decision which may cause it to be broken off suddenly; and secondly that the incorporation would suit the educational aims of the Archives as mentioned above infinitely better than any other arrangement.

As to your suggestion under 2, I was told that the Senate and Administration objected to it on two points; firstly that they were unwilling to commit themselves as to the continuation of my work after the new three years' term; and secondly that they considered their financial share under this proposal as too big. On the other hand, they were ready to accept this solution provided that they were not to contribute more than, I believe, £500 to the budget, and were not legally or morally bound to keep the Archives beyond three years.

The value of arrangement 2 depends, of course, on the decision to be taken after three years. I cannot undertake to predict whether or not it will be favourable. If the present ideas on the part of the Senate as regards the programme of the University remain unchanged, the Senate, at that time, will again refuse to take the Archives over into the regular budget and no additional success obtained by the Archives in the meantime will alter their view since, according to Professor Mayer, they even now take my merit as a scholar for granted. Nor is the Administration likely to change their attitude. There is, however, a point in favour of the arrangement. It regards the educational activities of the Archives. As long as the Archives belong to the University, students may hope, as some of them do now, to attain their academic degrees through work performed at the Archives, whereas, otherwise, only persons independent financially would be able to devote their time to studies which offer no practical advantage.

In all other respects, arrangement 3, as aiming at a definite instead of a temporary solution, is obviously preferable to No. 2; it would be the more so if, as you said, arrangements could be made to keep up some kind of connection with the University enabling students to continue their work with me.

Permit me to say a few more words on the possibilities which this arrangement – i.e., No. 3 – may provide. When, more than three years ago, we first discussed the plan of establishing the Archives, I was thinking of their incorporation in, or, at any rate, their close connection with, the University as a matter of course. I now have to consider what a dissociation from the University would mean for the future work of the Archives.

From the experience made during my work in the past I am inclined to think that the separation would enable me to pursue my work with more freedom. I have been at pains, on many occasions, to explain that the investigation of traditional Jewish music cannot be carried out satisfactorily unless neighbouring subjects, the music of the Oriental Christian Churches as well as Arab music, are studied along with it. I cannot help feeling that, outside, of course, the School of Oriental Studies at the University, this point is not generally accepted and that the reasons why it is not accepted are irreconcilable with a disinterested attitude towards research work like my own or, as a matter of fact, research of any kind.

My work necessitates free intercourse with all the different ethnical groups in this country and the Near East generally. It may therefore be made to contribute, however modestly, towards aims beyond its immediate scope, towards a better understanding between Jews and Arabs. This contribution, I think, could be made or, at least, tried to be made with some hope of success in a neutral atmosphere rather than in my present surroundings. When I consider a change in my relations to the University this point rather than my personal interest would carry most weight in favour of a dissociation.

I am not familiar enough with local conditions to be able to judge in what way this change can be effected; but I should like to venture a few suggestions. To secure Arab cooperation I should be willing to share the direction of the Archives with an Arab provided that we can be sure of his fully understanding our intentions as regards both research work and cultural contacts. Further, it might be advisable to try and find a neutral background which would enable both parties to collaborate with each other without being accused of illoyalty by their own people. I do not know whether the British government could or would furnish a label for this undertaking. One might, perhaps, think of the American School, or of the Carnegie Foundation, but this is mere guesswork.

I wish, however, to express very clearly that these suggestions are not meant as an indispensable part of your arrangement No. 3. I am submitting them to your kind consideration because I think they might facilitate my task; but I shall be quite satisfied if you decide on other methods of attaining our ends.

I fear that by your suggestion to dissociate my work from the University you are loading a new financial burden on your shoulders for many years to come and I should feel very uncomfortable about this if I were not convinced that we agree on all the main issues of this work and that the broader outlook which my work is to have in future, will justify new efforts.

I may add that I have not mentioned my new plan – if it is to be called a plan – to anybody except Professor Mayer.

Sincerely yours,
R. Lachmann

This letter clarifies the options which Lachmann now confronted, having failed to obtain a permanent place in the University for himself or his Archive. In this letter, however, Lachmann also allows himself for the first time to criticize the University's policy, albeit in a subtle manner. His hopes for the Archive, he reminds Magnes, were founded on the assumptions, shared at least by many scholars abroad, that the University might gain a unique and central position by (1) laying particular stress on subjects out of reach elsewhere, and (2) by giving preference to subjects which cannot be indefinitely postponed. He stressed the Archives accomplishments despite the obstacles that were put in its way. He points out the narrow-mindedness of those faculty members who did not understand why Arab and Jewish music needed to be studied side by side, and the possible contribution of such interaction to reducing the potential conflict between Arabs and Jews, knowing full-well that the future of this relationship occupied the thoughts of many a Zionist leader. It was certainly uppermost on Magnes's mind. Trusting the man, and grateful for the efforts he exerted on his behalf, Lachmann expressed readiness to accept whatever decision Magnes might deem appropriate for the furthering of their "common" cause – "our ends," to use Lachmann's words. Having said all that, the letter displays, above all, Lachmann's methodical thinking and unwavering commitment.

Gasping for Life Against the Current

However petty and shortsighted it all may seem in retrospect, nobody experienced the situation this way at the time. The Hebrew University, after all, was conceived as more than another institution of higher learning, striving towards academic excellence. It was considered, no less, as an important step towards the establishment of a national home in Palestine. Indeed, the division between basic needs and those considered luxuries largely rests on the definition of the roles they are meant to fulfill. In light of the multiple roles the University was expected to perform at one and the same time, and given its perennial shortage of money, it is surprising that issues facing the University did not get more confounded than they actually did. In this sense, music could hardly compete with the needs of the young medical school and the industrious agricultural center. Nor could music compete with the basic sciences and the canonic Jewish studies. Though recognized as a legitimate area of study, the investigation of music seemed like a luxury one could ill afford. Even the sciences, those days, were more occupied with issues relevant to the development of the country than to the development of scientific thought in general.

Given this frame of mind, the University authorities and most of its staff had little reason to feel guilty about acting towards Lachmann the way they did. As far as they were concerned, Lachmann's insistence only highlighted the degree to which he had remained an outsider, despite his efforts to understand, be understood and become integrated. Empathy aside, there were many other newcomers in the country, including professionals of all sorts, who adjusted to the conditions which they encountered. In fact, within the norms prevailing at the time, adjusting to the trying conditions of the country symbolized one's commitment to a cause transcending oneself. Having genuinely internalized the aspirations of the new society, Lachmann could not help but feel rejected by those he wanted to join. Nobody treated Magnes as an outsider, of course; his opinions were simply overruled. For reasons implied throughout, and still others unknown, Magnes saw Lachmann as an unusual find, both for academia, community relations and the cultural Zionist project; but he failed to convince the faculty to depart from its priorities. For one whose opinions had carried enormous weight not so long ago, it was hard to take. Disappointed and upset, he deplored the shortsightedness of his colleagues, adding to it other grievances which had accumulated over the years, but which he had been too busy to attend to.

With all the talk about Lachmann's severance from the University, Magnes was in no hurry to encourage the move when it finally seemed imminent. Despite threats and promises, he could not see clearly how to assist Lachmann, once divorced from the University. Inevitably, he would have had to appeal to those who already had the welfare of the University at heart, or to those whose support for the institution he could enlist. As president of the University, however, he could ill afford to disapprove of the institution publicly, or to be viewed as a traitor by his immediate associates. What a trap to be caught in!

After further exasperating negotiations which echoed the earlier ones, a settlement was finally reached, in the spirit of "better a bird in hand than two in the bush." Magnes, if not Lachmann, was aware that the settlement only permitted a fallen bird still to flutter, allowing it to believe that it could soar once again with the changing current of the wind.

The decision of the Executive Committee[83]

Paragraph 3, Meeting of the Executive Committee, 12.5.38

The Archive for Oriental Music

After lengthy negotiations the following agreement was reached concerning the employment of Dr. Lachmann (Archive of Oriental Music):
1. The arrangement is for three years.
2. This budget will be covered from three sources:
    a) A special fund (Roger Straus), to be distributed at the discretion of the President of the University £P 200 p.a.
    b) Money from Mrs. L. Ginsburg, for the President of the University to dispense for Dr. Lachmann's work £P 100 p.a.
    c) From the Hebrew University £P 200 p.a.

The Administration of the University is considering approaching Mrs. Ginsburg with the request to increase her donation for the 3 years 1938-1939-1940. This increase would be used to officially enlarge the Archive's budget to the sum of £P 600, and the balance, if there is any, will be reckoned against the University's participation.

The University accepts no financial responsibility over and above the aforementioned £P 200 for three years.

---

83 Translated from the Hebrew.

Act III

3.5.38

Archive of Oriental Music

Decisions:
The Executive Committee approved the suggestion that the University participate from its own budget to the amount of £P 200 per year for a period of three years in the budget of the Archive of Oriental Music, under the following conditions:
    a) The University will have no obligations at the end of those three years;
    b) Appropriate steps should be taken to ensure that the University has rights of possession over those discs of the Archive in which the University is interested.
    (Executive Committee Meeting, 12.5.38)

Disappointed and dejected, Magnes helped Lachmann spin his last dream – the resurrection of the *Zeitschrift für vergleichende Musikwissenschaft* under the title *Journal of Comparative Musicology*.

May 14th, 1938

Dr. R. Lachmann
House Turgeman
Saad & Said
Jerusalem

Dear Dr. Magnes,

I enclose a copy of the prospectus of the journal. The indication at the end of the last sentence as to where subscribers should send their annual fee has been left open and I would ask you kindly to consider this point.
    According to my former experience, payment through a bank is the simplest way for me to be constantly and quickly posted as to the total sum at the journal's disposal at any given time. To have the money sent to the University would mean a loss of time for the secretariat as well as for myself.
    I should be very glad if you would agree with me in thinking that the most

practical method is to establish an account with Barclay's. In this case, the sum hitherto collected will have to be paid over to the bank. The account would have to be in my name since the chief accountant informed me that they do not, as I suggested to him, open accounts in the name of an anonymous institution such as "Journal of . . ."

As soon as I have your answer I shall send the prospectus to the printing press.

With kindest regards,

Yours sincerely,
R. Lachmann

PROSPECTUS

Since, in 1935, the "Zeitschrift für vergleichende Musikwissenschaft" ceased to exist, research in non-European music has been left without a periodical publication of its own. This gap is now to be filled by a journal which will be conducted on much the same lines as the former one.

The title of the periodical will be

JOURNAL OF COMPARATIVE MUSICOLOGY

Its major preoccupation will be with research into oriental and primitive music; yet, its contents are intended also to include other provinces of the subject and thus to demonstrate its variety and the progress being made in its study.

This task cannot be carried out except by a system of collaboration and with this aim in view the following have agreed to act as members of a committee in assistance of the editor:

J.S. BRANDTS BUYS, Wiragoenan wétan, Jogjakarta, Java

A. CHOTTIN, 32 Avenue de Metz, Rabat, Maroco

Dr. H.G. FARMER, Stirling Drive, Bearsden, Scotland

Professor P.R. KIRBY, University of the Witwatersrand, Johannesburg, South Africa

Dr. M. KOLINSKI, Hradesinska, 64, Praha XII, Czechoslovakia

Dr. J. KUNST, 53 Hobbemalaan, Bilthoven, Holland

MESUD CEMIL, P.T.T. Istanbul radyosu, Türkiye

Miss H. H. ROBERTS, High Watch, Tryon, N.C., U.S.A.

Professor C. SACHS, New York University, New York City, U.S.A.

A. SCHAEFFNER, Musée de l'Homme, Palais du Trocadère, Paris 16e, France

An enlargement of the committee is under consideration.

The journal will include original articles, reviews of books, and comprehensive bibliography. Among the articles to be published in the first few issues are these:

Les notions de qualité et de consonance dans la psychologie musicale, par JACQUES HANDSCHIN.

Jewish cantillation and song in the isle of Djerba, by R. LACHMANN.

An unpublished treatise by the Arab philosopher Al-Kindi (9th century), critically edited by R. LACHMANN and M. EL'-HEFNY.

Articles on the music of Arab peasants, of the Algerian Berbers, and of the Samaritans.

The annual volume will include about 128 pages of text, 32 pages of music, occasional pictures, and reproductions of manuscripts. The volume will be published in instalments, preferably quarterly. The proposed form of publication will be seen on the reverse page of this prospectus.

Articles and notes intended for publication and copies of books and articles for review should be addressed to any of the members of the committee or to the editor.

The annual subscription will be sh. 12 ($3), to be sent to

Dr. Robert Lachmann
Editor
c/o Hebrew University, Jerusalem, Palestine

Jerusalem, May 1938

The reader may recall that Lachmann acted once before in a manner of "business as usual," refusing to comprehend the signs, though obvious they were. Now again, *mutatis mutandis,* he acted in the same way. While the first time called for, no less than, a total denial of all he was taught and learned to trust as a human being, this second time called for a temperance of his professional identity. Lachmann was in no position to accommodate.

Cultured through and through, he was ill prepared to digest cultural deformities of whatever nature, even, possibly, justifiable ones. His well integrated personality caused Lachmann, paradoxically, to shield himself against anomalies by turning cognitive dissonance, as it were, into illusory harmony.

A brief glance at his Prospectus reveals how wisely Lachmann made sure that the journal would reflect the comparative nature of the field. Among the people he managed to enlist for the editorial committee and as contributors were some of the best known scholars in the area. That he was able to interest them attests to his own standing in the field. From the list of articles that the first issues were expected to include, it is evident that the renewed journal aimed to maintain the high standards established by the original *Zeitschrift*. By including some of his own studies, Lachmann wished to indicate the seriousness of the enterprise, for he had no difficulty publishing his work – in book-form – elsewhere. Strange as it might sound, he honestly hoped to transfer, not only the journal, but most of the Berlin School's activities to Jerusalem. Given the multicultural nature of the country, Jerusalem, he honestly believed, was a more suitable place for it. Had the University been less preoccupied with solving its immediate problems, and more ready to look further ahead, Jerusalem might have indeed become the leading center of comparative musicology. Though nobody knows whether it would have actually succeeded, it is nonetheless fair to think of it as an opportunity missed. Lachmann is not the only one whose dream was overlooked in this way.[84]

Totally absorbed in his plans for the journal, Lachmann also tried to solve, as quickly as possible, the problem he raised in his letter to Magnes (May 14th) concerning the administration of the journal's future accounts. From a subsequent letter he sent to Magnes (May 18th) we learn that the secretariat of the University refused to attend to the financial administration of the journal. Less sanguine than Lachmann, Magnes was still preoccupied

---

84 See, for example, David Bar-Gill, "The Social-Psychology that Might Have Been: Kurt Lewin and The Hebrew University," in *The History of The Hebrew University*, op. cit., pp. 627–645. Also see Avner Horowitz, "Zigfried Landhaus and the Absence of Canonical Social Sciences in the Yishuv," ibid., pp. 661–671.

with attempts to improve Lachmann's own financial arrangements. To an inquiry concerning the eventuality of a surplus in the Ginzburg grant, he received the following answer:

The Hebrew University, Jerusalem

15.V.38

Dear Dr. Magnes,

Your inquiry with regard to a possible surplus in the Leonie Ginsburg grant over and above the £P 500 budget of Dr. Lachman:

The intention is merely that Dr. Lachmann's budget should not be increased by any such surplus.

The question as to who would benefit from such a surplus is being left open.

When the matter was dealt with at the Executive Council, I made a statement explaining the situation.

David Werner Senator
Administrator

(Handwriting added at bottom of letter): My attitude is that Dr. Lachmann's work should be helped. 17.4.38

Lachmann's inquiry concerning the accounts of the journal resulted in the following rebuke:

22.V.38.

Dear Dr. Lachmann,

Dr. Magnes has sent me your letter of May 18th, from which I learned that the vague plans for the appearance of a journal – of which you once spoke to me – have begun to materialize.

Permit me to call your attention to the rule that copies of correspondence of members of the staff with University authorities – aside from private matters

– are to be sent to the Administration for its information and action, if required.

This procedure has been adopted in order to integrate University handling of its business.

I enclose copy of the form letter sent to all heads of departments in this connection.

Yours sincerely,
David Werner Senator
Administrator

In light of Lachmann's "misbehavior" and Magnes's "audacity," Dr. Senator saw fit, in order to avoid future misunderstandings, to repeat the decision reached by the Executive Committee clearly and succinctly, and to ask Lachmann to commit his acceptance of its conditions in writing. How humiliating!

27.5.38

Dr. R. Lachmann,[85]
Here

Dear Sir,

I must inform you of the decision of the Executive Committee of the University of May 12th, concerning continuation of your employment as a Research Fellow in Oriental Music.

The Executive Committee decided to allot from the University's regular budget the sum of £P200 per year for three years (1938, 1939, 1940) for the above-mentioned purposes, and another £P300 per year from special sources for the duration of three years. In addition, the Executive Committee noted that if funds from "special sources" exceed expectations, they can be added to your budget up to the sum of £P600 per year. On the other hand, the University

---

85 Translated from the Hebrew.

accepts no responsibility for any funds exceeding £P200 approved from the general budget. At the end of the above-mentioned three-year period the University will have no obligations to your work.

The Executive Committee fixed that as a condition to its decision, the University should be assured of acquisition of the Archive's discs which were recorded during the Archive's existence in Jerusalem, and also of the machines and instruments acquired for the Archive during that period. Please contact the Administration on this matter.

Yours sincerely,
Dr. D. W. Senator
Administrator

copy to Treasury

29/5/38

The Financial Secretariat[86]
Here

Dear Sir,

1) I herewith confirm to you that the financial secretary, Mr. M. Schneersohn, informed me that the Administration of the Hebrew University has agreed – as per the special agreement arrived at between it and Dr. J. L. Magnes, President of the Hebrew University – to allot to the Archive of Oriental Music the sum of £P 500 (five hundred Palestine pounds) per year for a period of three years, beginning in October 1937 and ending in September 1940.

2) I hereby declare that, at the end of those three years – if the University has not in the meantime voluntarily renewed its agreement with me according to these conditions or any others – that I will have no complaints or claims against the University concerning my past or future employment; furthermore, I relinquish any claim for compensation either for myself or any of the employees whom I will employ during my work.

86 Translated from the Hebrew.

3) Arrangements for payments and expenses for the Archive of Oriental Music within the range of the above-mentioned budget will be according to the fixed procedures which apply to all other departments of the Hebrew University.

4) Regarding handing-over of property and scientific material of the Archive to the Hebrew University, an agreement will be drawn up between myself and the University's administration. But I hereby obligate myself to hand over to the University a list of property so that it can be recorded in the files of the "Inventar" of the Hebrew University. In any case I undertake to prepare double recordings of all material gathered by me, to be kept in my Archive, and they will be the property of the University.

Yours sincerely,
Dr. Robert Lachmann

While "The Lachmann Problem" was far from solved, the idea of the journal was, evidently, less far fetched. Without divulging Lachmann's *real* difficulties at the University, Magnes was able to arouse interest in the journal among potential supporters. Interesting, though not surprising, as long as the journal was considered a University contribution to music, there were many who were ready to lend a hand.

The Musicians' Committee of Mailamm
The American-Palestine Music Association
Affiliated with the Hebrew University in Jerusalem
Steinway Hall, One Hundred and Thirteen West Fifty-Seventh Street, New York, N.Y.

Leopold Godowsky, *Honorary President*

Mischa Elman, Bronislaw Huberman, *Honorary Vice-Presidents*

Honorary Associates: Ernest Bloch, Samuel Chotzinoff, Aaron Copland, Mrs. Clara Gabrilowitsch, Dorothy Lawton, Joseph Levine
Boris Morros, Arnold Schoenberg, Ernest Toch, Arnold Volpe

Central Music Committee: Isidor Achron, Joseph Achron, A.W. Binder
Erick Jacobi, Salomo Rosowsky, Joseph Yasser

October 7th, 1938

Dr. Judah Magnes
Hebrew University
Jerusalem, Palestine

Dear Dr. Magnes,

The prospectus of a Journal of Comparative Musicology edited by Dr. Robert Lachmann, of the Hebrew University, was shown to me the other day.

I am very curious to know whether the Journal is to be considered a University contribution to Music or what its status is in connection with the University. Will it in any way be subsidized with University Funds?

It would indeed be gratifying to know that the Journal of a Comparative Musicology was to be a University project. It would add prestige to the University in the field of Music which is at present one of the weak branches of your institution.

With holiday greetings, I am very truly yours,

Mrs. Frank Cohen (Ethel Cohen)[87]

4.XII.38.

Mrs. Frank Cohen
113 West 57th Street
New York, N.Y.

Dear Mrs. Cohen,

Dr. Lachmann's Journal of Comparative Musicology is to be regarded as a

---

[87] Mrs. Cohen was a well-off woman, interested in music, and an active member of the Mailamm Committee.

University project. It is being financed out of special funds collected from a number of sources.

I am glad to know that you are interested in this publication, and when it appears you will see, as you perhaps already know, that Dr. Lachmann is a first-class authority in his important field, and that other authorities throughout the world so regard him.

I hope that it may be possible for you to aid this Journal in every possible way.

With best regards, I am,

Sincerely yours,
J. L. Magnes, President

Notwithstanding its stationery heading, the Mailamm Musicians' Committee did not organize, originally, as an association affiliated with the Hebrew University. It was organized from the start to assist Jewish musicians who were driven by circumstances to find refuge in America. Note the list of musicians that decorated the stationery of the association. Since a good number of musicians also found refuge in Palestine, the association enlarged its scope of activities to include them as well. Huberman,[88] the Honorary Vice President of the association, made several appearances in Palestine to raise money for refugee musicians. In 1936, as is well known, he assembled in Tel Aviv a number of experienced refugee musicians, raised the financial backing, and founded the Palestine Orchestra (later the Israel Philharmonic Orchestra), thus creating a full-fledged concert life in Palestine. At Huberman's request, Toscanini agreed to conduct the orchestra's opening concerts. The orchestra thereby acquired an immediate international standing.

The American Society for Comparative Musicology, naturally, took an active interest in the resurrection of the much appreciated *Zeitschrift*, the more

---

88 Huberman, who as a child prodigy played the Brahms violin concerto in 1896 in the presence of the composer, refused to play it in 1933 at Furtwaengler's invitation because of the measures introduced by the Nazis against Jews.

so since the new journal was to adopt English as its official language. Needless to reiterate that its most famous members were German speaking Jews.

28.X.38

Mr. Wallace D. Brock
Bursar
American Council of Learned Societies
907 Fifteenth Street
Washington, D.C.

Dear Mr. Brock,

Permit me to thank you for the check of $175 forwarded in your letter of October 7th, at the request of Dr. Herzog,[89] Treasurer of the American Society for Comparative Musicology. Receipt of the Hebrew University is enclosed herewith.

This money will be used towards the publication of Dr. Lachmann's "Journal of Comparative Musicology."

I am sure that Dr. Lachmann will be happy to hear of this remittance. He has been seriously ill but we are glad to report he is making a good recovery.

Sincerely yours,
J. L. Magnes
President

Last Blows and their Aftermath

While support for the Journal was increasing, Lachmann, unfortunately, lost his own private income. It will be recalled that his original arrangement

---

[89] Born in Hungary, George Herzog pursued his higher education in Berlin. Between 1922–1924 he was an assistant to Hornbostel at the *Phonogramm-Archiv*. Herzog was one of the most important founders of ethnomusicological studies at American academic institutions.

with the University took into account his "steady income" – his German pension. With the mounting atrocities against the Jews, the Germans cut off these sources of income, including their pension funds. By then, needless to say, nobody believed that it was just a passing nightmare. Still residing in Germany, Lachmann's family, nonetheless, tried to intervene on Robert's behalf, but to no avail. Luckily, they managed to get out of Germany, in the nick of time, and migrated to England.

Lachmann's problem, clearly, no longer centered around his position at the University, but on much more. This last blow seems to have curtailed his individual freedom to the point of overshadowing all else, the more so, since his health began to betray him. Listen carefully to the subdued tone of his last report. His total surrender and profound acquiescence take the form of a few sentences relating, as it were, simple facts.

REPORT[90]

on my activity as Research Fellow

The Institute of Oriental Music

during the six-month period from 1 June until 31 October 1938

During the above-mentioned period a basic change took place in the Archive. Due to the changes in the financial relations in Germany, my private income has been taken away from me. I now have no means of buying or ordering instruments and discs and any other technical merchandise from Germany. I therefore was constrained to find alternative sources outside Germany; for this reason I used part of the summer to travel to England. I visited factories, especially those that manufacture microphones and discs. The discs are obviously so expensive that the recording work in the Archive will be greatly limited. However, the American products are far superior to their German counterparts, a fact which will be manifested in our winter recordings.

Apart from the technical work, I have prepared the literary side of the recordings of Djerba's Jews. The work is ready to be published in a journal, the

---

90 Translated from the Hebrew.

staff-notes have been arranged. I expect the Hebrew translation to be published before the English translation. This work is being done by Dr. Braun, who will also deal with the musical-lexicographical questions arising out of this work.

R. Lachmann.
8.1.39

After this short report, Lachmann was in no position to continue with his work. Despite temporary brief recoveries, his health was getting worse. Magnes, of course, was most concerned, but so were many others when "The Lachmann Problem" took this unforeseeable turn. They felt the need, however, to let Magnes know how deeply concerned they actually were.

15. III.39

Dr. Magnes,

Dr. Senator has asked me to give you particulars connected with Dr. Lachmann, as follows:

1. Dr. Senator has been intending for some time to visit Dr. Lachmann's laboratory, but this had been put off from week to week. When a time was finally fixed, Dr. Lachmann became ill and the visit was cancelled. After a certain period, during which I heard that Dr. Lachmann was not sufficiently well to receive callers, Dr. Senator asked me to telephone Dr. Spiegel and get particulars concerning Dr. Lachmann's condition.

2. I telephoned Dr. Spiegel, who said that Dr. Lachmann's condition was as satisfactory as could be expected, and that he (Dr. S.) as a physician could not give any details.

3. Dr. Lachmann's condition continued to improve and Dr. Senator and Prof. Mayer were to have visited him – this was only a few weeks ago – when Prof. Mayer informed me again that Dr. Lachmann could not "talk business" although he might receive visitors.

4. About ten days ago, Dr. Lachmann came to this office, dictated to me, made a telephone call, etc. And then left. He seemed well but very weak, as

could be understood.

5. Yesterday I was requested by Dr. Ben-David, in Dr. Senator's name, to make an appointment with Dr. Spiegel concerning Dr. Lachmann. Dr. Senator had heard that "Dr. Lachmann's condition was very serious indeed." I said Dr. Spiegel, months before, had not given any details and was not likely to do so now. Besides I had the impression that Dr. Lachmann was getting better.

6. Later yesterday afternoon, at about 4 p.m. I met Miss Muehlendorf, who confirmed my statement that Dr. Lachmann was quite well and was at that moment with you. I said Dr. Senator seemed anxious about Dr. Lachmann's condition and had wanted to get details from the physician. There was no mention at all of having Dr. Lachmann's work done by someone else or anything in this connection.

My bulletins on Dr. Lachmann I have been receiving through Miss Muehlendorf, whom I have occasionally met, and she had consistently told me he was getting better and had commenced work.

IG[91]

Though it was impossible to ascertain Lachmann's exact ailment, the files make it abundantly clear that he suffered from a life-threatening, terminal disease. Miss Muehlendorf was apparently attending to his needs during this last affliction.

Note the last sentence in the paragraph before last of the above letter; Magnes, obviously, did not trust the sincerity of these belated well-wishers. Also note the last paragraph of the following letter:

---

91 IG are in all likelihood the initials of Mr. Ginsberg from the Administration.

The Hebrew University
Jerusalem, 17.III.39

Dr. Magnes,

In reply to the query indicated by you on my report of the 15th concerning Dr. Lachmann:

Of course each time I have asked about Dr. Lachmann, I have specifically inquired as to whether he had begun work.

On this last occasion, after Dr. Senator had refuted my statement as to Dr. Lachmann's improvement in health, I again asked Miss Muehlendorf "Aber er arbeitet? Kann er arbeiten? Ist etwas seit gestern geschehen?" She replied "Aber nein. Es geht ihm ausgezeichnet. Er arbeitet, macht Plaene, und ist jetzt bei Dr. Magnes." (But he works? Can he work? Did something happen since yesterday?" She replied "But no, he is very well. He works, makes plans, and is presently with Magnes.")

I repeat that there has never been any mention of Dr. Lachmann's place being taken by anyone. Contrary to what you have gathered, this office has done everything it could to reassure concerning Dr. Lachmann's state of health and activity. The other occupants of our room can testify to this. I would personally take it very much to heart if any damage were done to Dr. Lachmann, whom I like and admire. I am unable to ascertain from whom these rumors emanated.

IG

Anticipating the inevitable, there was no shortage of those who wished to cleanse their conscience. With the steady deterioration of Lachmann's health, he turned overnight into an individual one claimed to have liked, appreciated, and even admired. Paradoxically, those who never liked him, and those who failed to appreciate what he was trying to accomplish, could hardly help but admire his perseverance. Indeed, what had been repressed all along burst out in full force, once it could no longer halt Lachmann's tragic departure.

The Hebrew University, Jerusalem

ANNOUNCEMENT[92]

The President of the Hebrew University announces with great sorrow the death of Dr. Robert Lachmann after a prolonged illness.

9.5.39

9.V.39
LACHMANN EDGECO WESDO LONDON

GREATLY	GRIEVED	INFORM	YOU	PASSING
YOUR	DEAR	ONE	LAST	NIGHT
BURIAL	THIS	AFTERNOON	MOUNT	OLIVES
SINCERE	SYMPATHY	OF	ENTIRE	UNIVERSITY
AND	OF	ALL	MEN	OF
GOOD	WILL	EVERYWHERE	WHO	KNEW HIM

The Hebrew University, Jerusalem

To:
Scientific Employees of the University[93]

Yesterday Dr. R. Lachmann, may his memory be blessed, Director of the Archive of Oriental Music of the Hebrew University, was laid to rest in the cemetery of our community on the Mount of Olives.

Dr. Lachmann was one of the refugees from Germany who found here a haven and a home.

He was well known throughout the international scientific community as an expert in his profession, maybe the greatest expert of them all. Besides his

---

92 Translated from the Hebrew.
93 Translated from the Hebrew.

musical knowledge, especially of Oriental Music, he was well versed in the Arabic language and published a text of Al-Kindi; we are shortly hoping to publish the Arabic-Hebrew text of the songs of the Jews on the isle of Djerba to which he devoted a great deal of time and energy.

At the Archive of Oriental Music of the University he managed to collect more than 600 discs, most if not all of which he himself recorded here in Israel and in the area.

His expertise provided him with background and platform for flights of his imagination. He used this expertise not only in the musical and historical sense, but also in the ethnological sense; above all through this expertise he was able to open to us Westerners the souls of those born and educated in the Orient, both Jews and Arabs.

We, his friends at the Hebrew University in the Land of Israel, will keep his memory in our hearts as if we were close family members.

May he rest in peace!

J. L. Magnes (signed)
President

Without doubting Magnes's personal grief, Lachmann – "one of the refugees from Germany" – can hardly be described as one who found "a haven and a home" among his "family members" at the Hebrew University.

Many letters of condolence were received.

17.V.39

Miss Katharine Wambold
American School of Oriental Research
Jerusalem, Palestine

Dear Madam,

I have your letter of the 10th of May and wish to thank you, on behalf of the

University, for your kind words about the late Dr. Lachmann. Science and the Hebrew University have suffered the loss of a unique scholar, the only one in this very important field. We have been privileged to know him and honoured that his work was done here.

Yours faithfully,
A. H. Fraenkel
Rector

What Lachmann was trying to achieve in Palestine, more than it was appreciated locally, was highly regarded by some people abroad.[94] There was nobody in Palestine, at the time, who was fully qualified to assess its value, even among those who took an interest in his work. If the University was unable to place the Archive among its priorities because of the multiple tasks the University was expected to perform, the Archive could, nonetheless, have constituted a major resource for professionals in the field, who recognized its value. Lachmann, as it turned out, succeeded not only in driving home the idea that Palestine was an ideal location for comparative musicological studies, and that some of the musical traditions found in the country harbored answers to questions that transcend these traditions. Given his standing in the field, nobody questioned his judgement, everybody trusted his expertise, i.e., the responsible way in which he collected his data. Though isolated at the University, Lachmann kept in touch with some of his former colleagues and other musicologists, all of whom knew his whereabouts and what he was trying to accomplish in that ancient part of the world.

---

94 The following chapter (Epilogue, Part I) discusses his high standing abroad.

Act III

June 9, 1939

Dr. J. L. Magnes, President
Hebrew University
Jerusalem, Palestine

My dear President Magnes,

I hasten to offer you my condolences for the grave loss the University has suffered through the death of Dr. Robert Lachmann. Every one of Dr. Lachmann's colleagues, scattered all over the globe, will find this loss an irreparable one. I myself had the good fortune to be acquainted with Dr. Lachmann in Berlin, and have followed his work with especial interest since he transferred it to the Hebrew University. I was highly impressed by the possibilities of this work, which he pursued with all the modesty of the true scholar, for the ultimate good and prestige of Science as well as of Jewish Science, and it was a source of great regret to me that his efforts were so slow to receive tangible support in this country. I found it the more impressive that he was able to accumulate in his Archives a rich storehouse of immense historical and musicological value, of recordings of Jewish and other Oriental music, and was looking forward eagerly to the time when his energies could turn from collecting to evaluation and analysis, and when we might share with him the many thrills he must have had.

What distresses me now besides the feeling of personal loss in Dr. Lachmann's death is the knowledge that so few people could at the present time step into his shoes and continue with his work. The number of scholars qualified to deal with the intricate and rich problems vested in Jewish music and the music of the Near East is exceedingly limited. Some time ago we lost Professor A. Z. Idelsohn whom we had come to consider our first authority; and of the small group of German scholars who began to devote themselves to the study of Oriental music early during this century, some are dead, others dispersed. Naturally these considerations make me feel concerned about the future of Dr. Lachmann's Archives. Speaking as I do for a number of colleagues and groups interested, may I ask you what plans you think might be made to insure the continued functioning of these Archives? One matter of especial concern is the position of Jewish music in its setting in Palestine. The invaluable contribution that studies such as Dr. Lachmann's can give us lies in the light they will shed on the history of Jewish music and culture, and the most venerable phases of this history are tied up with the history of the neighboring nationalities of past and present. It is the emphasis of studying the object of prime interest against this background for which the opportunity in Palestine is so unique, and I believe if this broad perspective would be given up for a more narrow interest, there would be also a lessening of the contribution to our knowledge of the history or culture and of music, Jewish or other.

A practical matter of concern is the fear that in Palestine, as elsewhere, there may not be anyone who could be entrusted to carry on Dr. Lachmann's work in full. In case you should find this to be true, may I suggest to you at least a person who was well acquainted with Dr. Lachmann's ideas and aims, as well as with the practical details of administering the collection: Mme Dr. Gerson-Kivi? I do not have the pleasure of knowing Mme Gerson-Kivi and do not know whether or not her qualifications are such that she could be charged with the ultimate leadership of the Archives. I am thinking of her merely as one who through her acquaintance with Dr. Lachmann and the Archives would be eminently suited to safeguard and take care of the collection until further steps may be deemed feasible. I am making my suggestion, at the risk of seeming to meddle, due to the concern to which I must have given sufficient expression in my letter.

May I tell you how much we appreciate the battle you and the University are fighting, in the midst of strains and stresses? I do regret that this expression comes to you at the moment when you as well as we have suffered a loss. I shall appreciate whatever consideration you can give to this matter and of course would be very much interested in whatever plans you think could be made for the safeguarding of the Archives.

I am sending a copy of my letter to the Friends of the Hebrew University.

I wish to apologize to you for placing after my name a number of qualifications; they serve merely to indicate to you the number of groups which are greatly interested in the future of Dr. Lachmann's Archives and for whom I take the liberty of speaking.

With the warmest respect, I am

Yours very sincerely,
George Herzog

Assistant Professor of Anthropology
Vice-President, Ethnological Society of America
Treasurer, American Society for Comparative Musicology
    Assistant Editor and Member of the Council, American Folklore Society
Member of the Council, American Anthropological Association
Member of the Committees in Musicology, on Materials for Research, and on Studies in American Culture, American Council of Learned Societies

Before safeguarding the Archive, the University had to make sure that all of the expenses Lachmann incurred in the last months of his life were properly covered. There were additional expenses which the University, unfortunately, had to cover as well, before addressing, what seemed, like a "less burning" issue.

Expense Account of Dr. Lachmann up to 10 June 1939[95]

Up to March 1939 (our reckoning)	£P	280.523
April		
To Dr. Lachmann by Dr. Magnes, balance of April 39 salary	13.000	
To Mrs. Jeruzalem for visas etc.	0.785	
To First Aid: to Dr. L. for the transfer of his pension	0.300	
To nurse Weissbrod for her work	0.800	
Expenses of transferring the Institute	6.859 £P	21.744
May		
To Pension Zelinger for board	20.180	
To "Kehilat Yerushalayim" – Hevra Kadisha (burial society)	17.000	
To H. Schneersohn, funeral-connected expenses	1.050	

95 Translated from the Hebrew.

Medical:

To "Bikur Holim" (Hospital)	1.500	
To Dr. Brenner	0.450	
To Dr. Klopstock	0.600	
Professor Zondek	3.000	
To Dr. Horn	0.350	
To Dr. Spiegel	<u>14.750</u>	20.650
Expenses of transferring the Institute	1.590	
To "Hadassah" for bacteriological test	1.000	
To "Magen David Adom" for transferring the Deceased to "Bikur Holim"	0.500	
To Lloyds Israel for visas and expenses	2.880	
To Kerubi for paying balance of rent	34.000	
To Mrs. Kaufman (employed)	0.468	
To Pension Zelinger for board	4.085	
Expenses of transferring the Institute	<u>2.250</u> £P 105.653

June

To Mrs. Mollendorf	0.090	
To "Meah Shearim" pharmacy	0.125	
To the Arab for groceries	<u>0.610</u>	<u>0.825</u>
	£P	408.745

Expenses

Balance as of 1/10/1938	51.206	
From the President's Fund for 1938	300.000	
From the University's budget for 1938	<u>200.000</u>	
	551.206	
Expenses up to 10/6/1939	<u>408.745</u>	
Balance of credit up to 10/6/1939	£P	142.461

Examining the balance sheet reveals that there was hardly any money left for the continued activities of the Archive, not to speak of money for a new person to run it, even if a suitable person were available. In any event, there was little likelihood that the University would change its entire attitude to the issue, now that Lachmann was no longer there to press it. Nonetheless, the property of the Archive, including the many recordings it contained, deserved some attention and care, if only to communicate to interested parties that the University was a responsible scholarly institution.

12.6.39

Mr. Schocken,[96]
Here

Dear Sir,

In response to your question no. 41 of 8.6.39, I would like to reply to you that:

All the property of Dr. Lachmann's Archive was brought over to the University building and stored there, according to Dr. Magnes's instructions.

Regarding rights of ownership of the collection: It was agreed with Dr. Lachmann that the University is entitled at any time to receive copies of any recordings it wishes to receive. In addition, the recording instruments produced at the Archive since its establishment belong to the University.

The Executive Committee decided to approach the President and to suggest that he allocate a sum of money from Dr. Lachmann's funds for arranging the remaining property.

Dr. Senator informed the Executive Committee meeting that the Administration will not allocate any more funds for continuing of the Archive's work.

Yours sincerely,
M. Ben-David
General Secretary

---

96 Translated from the Hebrew.

Though the Executive Committee was informed that there would be no more funds for the continued work of the Archive, the remaining property required some "arrangements." The following suggestions were offered by one of the student researchers who worked with Lachmann in Palestine:

July 15, 1939

Memorandum offered to the Hebrew University concerning the
Institute for Oriental Music Research

The Hebrew University has in the Institute for Oriental Music Research an institution of singular cultural value. The following memorandum is offered by its writer, who had the good fortune of being associated with the Institute for three years, at the request of Dr. Werner Senator. The memorandum attempts to give a picture of the role of this institute, and makes some tentative suggestions as to how its continued existence could be safeguarded.

There are in various countries Archives or Institutes devoted to the study and cultivation of national music. Others are concerned with a comparative study of music. The institute in Jerusalem is singular in that it combines both, the national and the comparative, culture-historical interest.

It is hardly necessary to point to the importance of studying Hebrew music. It has often been stated that especially ritualistic Jewish music reaches back into the time of antiquity, that it has intimate connections with the Semitic music of ancient times, and that it has served as a source to the music of the various Christian churches, which in turn have had a profound influence on the development of the cultivated music and folk music of the Western world. It is very fortunate, then, that the Hebrew University realized the great importance of a truly scientific, dispassionate, and sound study of Jewish music and of related sources, and found it possible to house and sponsor the Institute. Its location in Jerusalem lends to the Institute added significance. Comparable scientific institutions must consequently divide their time between their work in the field, and their work in their libraries and laboratories. An institute in Jerusalem can combine both types of facilities, and the scholar can constantly study the cultural and folkloristic background of the music in which he is interested.

When Dr. Robert Lachmann was invited by the Hebrew University to transfer his collections and apparatus to Jerusalem in 1935, he visualized the unusual advantages of an institute of Jewish and Oriental music in Jerusalem, and there gradually developed an institution of international reputation. About 3,000 recordings of Semitic music have been assembled, in the majority Jewish, including vocal and instrumental pieces, ritual and secular music; the largest collection of Oriental music in existence, which in its kind is singular not only in the Orient but in the entire world.

With the much regretted death of Dr. Robert Lachmann, the Institute finds itself bereft of its guiding spirit. In absence of someone qualified to take over the burden of directorship, the Hebrew University may not find it feasible to continue with the operation of the Institute on the same scale as heretofore. However, it would be disastrous if some way could not be found for the Institute to go on with its work, even if on a modest scale, and if its invaluable materials were permitted to deteriorate, without the proper supervision and care.

Due to Dr. Robert Lachmann's prolonged illness and to the transfer of the collection to new quarters at the Hebrew University, a certain amount of work and checking seems necessary, before the material can be utilized for any purpose whatsoever. The needs are as follows:

1. The disks themselves must be kept from damage, from mishandling, playing over, rain, dust, etc. They must be kept in individual paper covers, and in locked cupboards, preferably dustproof. Damage both from rain and playing over are irreparable. The metal of the recordings rusts when exposed to moisture. The recordings are not as durable as commercial recordings and indiscriminate playing over damages them permanently. For that reason no archive copy of a disk should be used for playing or study, only second copies.

2. Since the machinery has been dismantled, it must be mounted again. A radio or sound engineer should be employed for the mounting. If necessary, information could be had from the factories in Germany who manufactured the machinery. However, new connections and improvements have been made on the original machinery, in order to adapt it to local conditions. Once the machinery is set up, its operation does not need expert technical knowledge, but a technician may have to be called from time to time to make repairs and replace parts.

3. All information, catalogues, notes, concerning the recordings must be

assembled and kept safe. Considering the variety, musical, ethnic, etc., represented in the material, without the proper identification the material loses very much of its value, and of its usefulness for anyone interested.

If these safeguards can be exercised, and if the collection and apparatus are housed in an accessible place, the continuity of the work of the Institute may be secure, and it will be able to function, as heretofore, in the following respects:

A. Dispensing of informations. During previous contacts of the Institute with scholars and other institutions, a great many inquiries have been coming in, and will continue to come.
B. Display of the material to visiting scholars.
C. Exchange of copies of recordings with other institutions. This usage is taken for granted between related institutions, and a considerable part of the growth of the Institute was due to the cooperation which existed between it and others. Exchange of this type is, of course, not a commercial transaction, it is on the sole basis of the raw cost of making copies.
D. Cooperation with other specialists at the Hebrew University, and with scientific institutions abroad.
E. New recordings, their extent depending on the budget.

Normally an institution such as the Institute for Oriental Music Research could hardly function without an appropriate budget, but at least equally important is the question of the intellectual guidance. The qualifications that must go into the proper supervision and development of such a research institute are manifold, since the work itself is unusually rich and complex. That rigorous academic training is indispensable may go without saying. Such training ought to contain intimate acquaintance with the problems and methods of musicology, of (semitic) linguistics, and of anthropology, since such are the qualifications of the directors of comparable institutions elsewhere. Collecting of material is not the ultimate end, and the evaluation of the work of an individual or of an institution depends entirely on whether these various disciplines have been sufficiently utilized in gathering information on the background and setting of the music itself.

It is not likely that a person combining these qualifications can be found to take Dr. Robert Lachmann's place. Nevertheless, the Institute could maintain its existence and vitality if someone will be found who is devoted to it, who understands all the practical details connected with its administration, and who can be trusted with the responsibility of safeguarding and keeping intact the valuable collection. Such a curator, even if salaried comparatively modestly, would have to be definitely in charge.

Following the request of Dr. Werner Senator, I am taking the liberty of suggesting Dr. Edith Gerson Kivi as one eminently suited for such a responsibility, and shall describe her qualifications as I see them.

Dr. Edith Gerson Kivi studied in various conservatories and Universities in Germany and acquired a thoroughgoing musical education, both from the practical and scientific angle. The excellence of her scientific work is indicated by the fact that her University financed publication of her studies in 1937. She has the degree of Ph.D. from a German University in musicology. She has also training as a librarian and obtained a degree from the University of Bologna. Since she has been in Palestine, she has had ample opportunity to become acquainted with the land. She speaks Hebrew, German, English, French, and Italian and teaches musicology at the conservatory in Jerusalem where she has proved her ability since years. She has worked with Dr. Robert Lachmann and assisted steadily in the various tasks connected with the Institute. I do not believe there is another person in Jerusalem who has either of her two main qualifications: that of a trained musicologist with a doctor's degree in that field, and of a person who is acquainted with the special requirements of the Institute. I believe that Dr. Edith Gerson Kivi, of whose disinterested devotion I am certain, is the most effective person to whom as curator the Institute could be entrusted. [97]

A budget which calls for a sum comparable to the one, mentioned to me by Dr. Werner Senator, may be set up as follows:

---

[97] Dr. Kivi also migrated to Palestine in 1935. Born in Germany (1908), she was trained as a pianist and harpsichordist at the Berlin Stern Conservatory and the Leipzig *Musikhochschule*. She also studied performance practice and musicology with Gurlit in Freiburg. As an apprentice in the Archive, her encounter with Lachmann effected a change in Kivi's musical interests. Upon Lachmann's death, worried about the future of the Archive and concerned, as well, about her own scholarly activities, Kivi shared her sentiments with those whom she knew to be supporters of Lachmann and his Archive.

I.	Salary of curator of the Institute	$ 600 per year
II.	Rental of room and electricity	$ 240 per year
III.	Materials, postage, expressage, occasional Repairs and replacement of parts, new Recordings	$ <u>360 per year</u>
		$ 1200

I. The salary may be satisfactory for part-time position providing for halfdays work. Dr. Edith Gerson Kivi is active as a pedagogue, both of the conservatory and privately, and it can hardly be expected of her to give up all her other interests unless some more permanent and more lucrative arrangement should be envisaged.

II. Rental of room must be considered since the Institute could not continue to function if located at the University itself. Singers are not as a rule free before six o'clock, and after that time work at the University is not feasible. Consequently, the Institute ought to be located right in the heart of the city. The machinery and the recordings of the Institute would call for an unusually large room or two, and it may be best, also in the interest of saving, to have Dr. Edith Gerson Kivi take a sufficiently large apartment, so as to be able to house the Institute in part of it. This would also provide for greater security and constant supervision for the Institute. The figure of $240 per year may provide for an arrangement of sharing the expenses of rental, heating, cleaning and also for the considerable consumption of electricity the Institute's work entails.

III. This item is somewhat flexible and difficult to calculate exactly.

The suggestions have been made with the assumption that the catalogues of the collection are available and can be located. If not considerable work will have to be done in order to reconstruct them. It is of highest importance to make a search for the catalogues and to check the state of matters in general. For that reason I should suggest that Dr. Edith Gerson Kivi who knows the catalogues and the materials be requested to go through the inventory, Dr. Lachmann's books, possibly belongings, with a representative of the University if necessary, so that planning can be made according to her findings and report. It may be even necessary to communicate for the catalogues with Dr.

Lachmann's family in London, in case his personal effects have been transferred to London already.

Another matter of a practical nature concerns recordings belonging to me which I have deposited in the Institute. My collection of records consists of Arab lute music, played by Esra Aharon, teacher at the Hebrew conservatory, which I referred to in my letter of July 4, 1939, to Dr. Magnes. I would appreciate it if these records could be sent to me as soon as possible, since my present work at Columbia University is greatly hampered by their absence.

In case the family of Dr. Robert Lachmann is willing to make a gift to the University of Dr. Lachmann's private library and scientific correspondence, it would be very fitting if the collection could be kept as a separate unit of the University Library, and housed with the Institute where they would be most needed.

Sofia Lentschner

As Lachmann's student – setting aside the fact that he had no formal students from the University's point of view – Sofia Lentschner clearly imbibed not only his teachings, but his commitment as well. Her letter, written at Dr. Senator's request, made sure to reiterate the importance and uniqueness of the Archive, before offering suggestions as to how to minimize the calamity caused by the premature death of her revered teacher. While in Palestine, she no doubt met the other Lachmann "students," including Edith Gerson Kivi, who actually migrated to Palestine. She must have, likewise, been aware of the difficulties Lachmann was facing at the University. It is fair to assume that, upon Lachmann's departure, Dr. Kivi shared her own worries with her fellow student concerning the future of the Archive.

New York[98]

Dear Dr. Ben-David:

During my stay here I met with Dr. Herzog, Assistant Professor of Anthropology at Columbia University, and Vice-President of the Ethnological Society of America, together with Mrs. Ethel Cohen.

Both are interested in the future of the Institute for Oriental Music.

Dr. Herzog wrote to Dr. Magnes on June 9th. I would ask you to get from Dr. Magnes the letter and have a copy made for our files. Copy of the letter is also here with the American Friends.

Both are interested that Dr. Lachmann's collection be in proper shape and should if possible be continued. I told them that the University would probably not be in a position to continue this grant, but possibly the money would be available and if it would be the question of adding a few pounds, we may consider the proposition. I think it would be wise to get in touch with Mrs. Gerson-Kivi who is mentioned in the letter to Dr. Magnes.

Dr. Herzog and Mrs. Cohen seemed to be genuinely interested in the matter. They told me also the name of a lady who studied at some time at Dr. Lachmann's Institute and who is now in America. This lady will communicate with me and I shall let you know any further developments.

In the meantime you should have the matter in mind.

With kind regards,

Cordially,
David Werner Senator
Administrator

Note to Mr. Finkel   September 19, 1939

Mrs. Frank Cohen of Mailamm called you yesterday. In your absence I spoke to her and the following is her story.

---

[98] The letter is not dated. Based on its content, however, one may surmise that it must have been written sometime between June 12 and July 15.

Dr. Herzog of Columbia University and Sophie Lentschner, a student of the late Dr. Lachmann, communicated with Dr. Magnes during the summer and spoke to Dr. Senator when he was here concerning the Institute of Music at Hebrew University (I believe what Mrs. Cohen meant was that she spoke to Dr. Senator and that the other two wrote Dr. Magnes). Neither of them have had any word from Dr. Magnes.

In the meantime, Miss Lentschner is very eager to know what became of the collection of recordings at Hebrew University. She needs them for her work at Columbia and she insists that nothing is being done about them at Hebrew University – that they are being carelessly housed at Hebrew University – that she wants to know what action is being taken.

Miss Lentschner attended the meeting of the American Musicological Congress last week and was asked about the disposition of the recordings and she had nothing to say and that made a very bad impression concerning Hebrew University.

The crux of the situation is this:

Miss Lentschner is now asking Mrs. Cohen to write a letter to Mrs. Leonie Ginsburg who subsidized Dr. Lachmann at Hebrew University, giving her the facts and asking her to intervene.

The ladies concerned feel that the records are shoved off in a corner in a basement of a cellar at Hebrew University, that they will become corroded, spoiled, etc., and that they must do something about it in a hurry.

Will you please call Mrs. Cohen at Trafalgar 7-0122 before she calls Mrs. Leonie Ginsburg and cooks up a dish.

The note was, apparently, left for Mr. Finkel by some worker in his office. Mr. Finkel was the director of the American Friends of the Hebrew University. Before Mr. Finkel was able to clear the air, he received the following letter from Mrs. Cohen:

THE AMERICAN PALESTINE MUSIC ASSOCIATION
113 West 57th Street, New York, N.Y.
88 Central Park West (home address)

October 1, 1939

Dear Mr. Finkel,

In addition to the request I made, that you communicate with Dr. Magnes, concerning the late Dr. Lachmann's collection at the Institute, I am quoting herewith, from the contents of a letter to me from Dr. Herzog. It seems to me that the matter is so serious that this should be cleared up immediately.

"One thing that is of considerable concern to me is the fact that we have no indication whatsoever that the University of Jerusalem is planning to undertake anything in order to bring out those materials which Dr. Lachmann collated for publication in his planned Journal. We do not know just what happened to the funds that went to Dr. Lachmann, mostly through Dr. Magnes, from various sources in the USA. The amount of money is modest, between $400 and $500 I believe, but I would hate to see any doubts thrown on the integrity of either Dr. Lachmann or the University. A grant of a little over $250 was made by the American Council of Learned Societies in Washington D.C. at Dr. Spivacke's and my request; another grant was made by the American Society of Comparative Musicology, and a third, by the Library Committee, I believe. There is responsibility toward each of these groups. Moreover, the grant by the Society represented membership dues we collected, for which members have not received anything as yet.

At the Congress (the International Musicological) in New York I talked this matter over with Dr. Spivacke, a representative of the American Council of Learned Societies, and a few others interested. Our conference resulted in the decision that we must urge Dr. Magnes to indicate to us just where the matter stands. I was asked whether I would take the responsibility for editing and seeing through the press the material, here, and of course I should only be too glad to do this and clear Dr. Lachmann's name. But I am distressed that the University puts herself as well as many of us in the rather embarrassing situation. I'll have to take the matter up with Dr. Magnes very soon, either on my own or officially, through a joint inquiry by all the groups and donors involved."

May I urge you, Mr. Finkel, to transmit this complaint to Dr. Magnes so that this matter may be immediately cleared up.

Thanking you, I am

Very sincerely,
Ethel S. Cohen

Whereupon, Magnes wrote to Mrs. Leonie Ginzburg but no copy could be found in the University's Archive. Alluding to this letter, Mr. Senator offers comforting reassurances. Few deeds, however, followed to match the words.

3.XI.39
Hon. Samuel B. Finkel
Director, American Friends of the Hebrew University
10 East 30 Street
New York, N.Y.

Dear Mr. Finkel,

In reply to your letters of September 27th and October 2nd with regard to Dr. Lachmann's collection I enclose copy of a letter Dr. Magnes has written to Mrs. Leonie Ginzburg which I think fully explains the situation. I think that this letter of Dr. Magnes can be taken as an authoritative document which should disperse any doubts or fears which may have been entertained by the MAILAMM people or by Dr. Herzog with regard to the state of the material left by Dr. Lachmann.

I am amazed that Mrs. Gerson-Kivi should have made any such allegations and I am taking the matter up with her on the spot.

As you see from Dr. Magnes's letter, nobody is needed at present to take care of the collection.

With kind regards, I am

Yours sincerely,
David Werner Senator
Administrator

"Burial" and "Resurrection"

Inquiries concerning the Lachmann Archive, which poured in heavily upon his death, gradually turned into a drizzle, evaporating completely with the flow of time. The University, at first, pretended to be taking care of matters, but having failed to solve the problem from the start, it was even less inclined to do so once Lachmann was no longer there to shame them into action. His entire project, however, was forsaken in the forties, under the pressure of more urgent issues which engaged not only the University, but the rest of the world.

While neglecting the sound archive, the University was continually devoted to the growth of its library, even during the war. The National and University Library, that was to serve the student body, as well as the country at large, was one of the University's major projects from its inception. It engaged not only the organizations of Friends of the Hebrew University, but influential individuals who roamed around the United States on behalf of the University, as did Albert Einstein somewhat earlier, in search of entire libraries that could either be bought at a reasonable price, or secured for the University through donations. Many of the scholars who transferred their libraries to Palestine saw fit, like Lachmann, to donate books to the library in order to increase and vary its collection. Among the immigrants who still managed to transfer their belongings to Palestine, there were also many who contributed valuable books to the library. Naturally, once a steady budget for the library was secured, the library became more selective in its acquisitions.

Despite the steady growth of a music loving public and despite various collections bequeathed to the University by individuals who had been involved in the music world, the library's music division reflected its sporadic beginnings for a long time. The Jewish National and University Library was primarily shaped by the subjects taught at the University, by the continuous pressure to accommodate academic needs and by the exigency to meet immediate scholarly requirements. Music, unfortunately, vanished from the University's agenda after Lachmann's death, and there was no one in sight, under the prevailing circumstances, to exert the necessary pressure.

The War of Independence, which broke out upon the establishment of the State of Israel in 1948, divided the city of Jerusalem so that the University buildings on Mount Scopus, including the library, remained in Jordanian hands. Consequently, until the construction of the new campus in the western part of the city (1954–1963), all of the teaching and various laboratories were dispersed among several buildings in different parts of the Jewish sector of the city (outside the Old City walls). Needless to say that the absence of the library created more of a problem than did the rest, not that the rest was easy. By special arrangements, and at considerable peril, convoys kept shuttling books from Mount Scopus to their temporary locations according to needs. All of the books, however, eventually found their proper place on the new campus at Givat Ram, primarily in the main library building. The library building, however, was only completed in 1963.

Until the completion of the library building, the music division, including a music reading room, was housed in the Ettinger building, which was centrally located. Under the custody of Edith Gerson-Kivi, Lachmann's equipment and archive were housed in the Terra Sancta building, a former monastery that became one of the major locations at which classes were held. The music books were transferred to the main library upon its completion, together with the rest of the books it was meant to house. The Lachmann Archive, however, found its way to the library only five years after the establishment of the Jewish Music Research Centre (1965) by Israel Adler, located at the Jewish National and University Library.[99] Owing to Adler's initiative, diligence and organizational ability,

---

99 In 1964 Adler returned from his studies in Paris. Given his scholarly interests, and

the center assiduously promoted the development of its sound archive, which was established along with the research center. Lachmann's recordings, naturally, became one of its prize possessions. By then, however, the unattended cylinders required expert treatment. In order to preserve the original recordings intact, it seemed advisable to copy them, hopefully without losing the musical information which they contained. This required, in addition to money, the kind of expertise not available in the country.

After much and prolonged effort, assisted by the Austrian Friends of the H.U., Adler struck a deal with the Austrian *Phonogrammarchiv* whereby in return for its expertise in such matters, and close supervision of the copying procedure, the Austrian *Phonogrammarchiv* was entitled to a copy of its own. This long awaited "resurrection," however, did not take place before the late eighties. By then the department of musicology had already been established and, at Adler's insistence, a complete inventory of Lachmann's files had already been completed by Gerson-Kivi, who also edited Lachmann's *Gesänge der Juden auf der Insel Djerba*, published by the center (1978) as part of its monograph series. Nonetheless, the Lachmann File (bequeathed to the University in its entirety by the Lachmann family) still contains unattended matters. In addition to diaries of recordings, lectures and unfinished works, it contains historical evidence for illuminating chapters waiting to be written.[100]

In his attempts to solicit the support of the American Friends, the reader may recall that Magnes tried to "sell" Lachmann as an able follower of Idelsohn and Rosowsky; the two had already earned reputations as scholars in search of the musical heritage of the Jews. Idelsohn and Rosowsky had succeeded, in all likelihood, because of their familiar backgrounds and single-mindedness. Perceived as an outsider, Lachmann, by contrast, failed

---

under the influence of the International Congress of Jewish Music held in Paris in 1957, he was determined to establish a center for the study of Jewish music in Israel.

100 Appendix III contains his radio talks on "Oriental Music," delivered via the Palestine Broadcasting Station. Appendix IV contains four lectures on "Eastern Music." These lectures may still be viewed as exceptional introductions to their respective subjects. They provide, as well, much insight into Lachmann, the scholar and man.

to convey his message, though he was anchored in a more widely sanctioned scholarly world. In the mid-sixties, however, once the University was ready to endorse musical studies, it was Lachmann, i.e., the kind of scholarship which he represented, that set the desired model.[101] By then, of course, Israel had become an established fact and the University sufficiently developed to allow a shift from local and particularistic concerns to issues and criteria dictated by the international scientific community.

---

101 A year after the establishment of the department of musicology at The Hebrew University, the Tel Aviv, and Bar-Ilan Universities followed suit. Since these universities were established many years after the establishment of "The University of the Jewish People," they did not undergo the trials and tribulations the H.U. was forced to undergo.

Epilogue

PART THREE
PROFESSIONAL SUCCESS AND INSTITUTIONAL FAILURE

Hindsight tends to sort out contradictory messages by re-introducing order and hierarchy into what got divorced, for a while, from the mainstream. In this view, the standing of a scholar, even if temporarily overshadowed by extrinsic factors, depends largely on his contribution, certainly in the long run. This remains true even if we have learned from more recent history, sociology and philosophy of science that such issues are more complicated. We know now that in addition to establishing the agenda of what ought to be investigated, scientists are active in determining the methods they employ and the criteria by which their findings are judged. Scientists also belong to the larger society which may affect their thinking. In short, science is a community-anchored activity, subject to paradigmatic shifts under certain circumstances, affected either from within (due, for example, to anomalies that could not be subsumed by a current paradigm) or impacted from without (due, for example, to social and ideological changes in the society at large). In the final analysis, nevertheless, the validity of one's scholarly work has to be recognized by the scientific community, either contemporaneously or in retrospect. It cannot rise to prominence unless fairly well known, nor can that which failed to be registered in the first place (at least by some) be resurrected, as it were, from oblivion.

This chapter will try to show that Lachmann was not "resurrected from oblivion." He was certainly recognized in his own lifetime by the scientific community to which he belonged, commanding the respect of its members both at home, before he left, and abroad. He surely participated in the establishment of the scientific agenda of the field – i.e., of what ought to be investigated. He clearly partook in designing appropriate methods and, above all, helped forge the criteria by which the findings should be judged.

All of these remained intact – neither affected from within nor impacted from without – despite the turbulence caused by the Nazis and, *mutatis mutandis*, the enormous strides in the realm of technology ever since.

Not that the field stood still. Rather, it gained momentum, in line with the growth of a general interest – anthropological and sociological – in cultural differences. In addition, by making the world look smaller, the mass media, paradoxically, has increased everyone's awareness of its diversity, affecting the self-centered thinking of the West, no less than people's awareness of their own uniqueness. Clearly, the world had undergone significant changes since the days in which Lachmann was occupied with his work and his vision. How is it then that the changes that took place in the world at large – affecting political, economic and social ideas – did not cause a major shift in the field, enough so as to render Lachmann's thinking obsolete? The answer, surprisingly, is quite simple: Lachmann and some of his fellow countrymen were themselves instrumental in fashioning a field that would later gain centrality in the subsequent development of musicology in the New World.

The following pages, accordingly, will first reiterate and expand the evidence that Lachmann was well integrated in the professional network whose contributions to the field at large are still held in great esteem; indeed, many a subsequent study was (and is still being) built on the groundwork laid down by this group. They will drive home, secondly, that the uprooted musicologists – the very same network – who landed in America influenced the development of musicology in their new environment. They will also show that Lachmann, though he went to Palestine, played a significant role in the formulation and definition of the organizational and scholarly activities of the Americans, new and old, who took a particular interest in Comparative Musicology. And last, but not least, they will attempt to do justice to Lachmann's persistent effort to revive the journal which – it will be recalled – was perceived in Palestine as yet another daydream. Put together, these factors – some obviously related, others ostensibly isolated – go a long way toward explaining why Lachmann may be adjudged a professional success, whatever his ostensible failure in Jerusalem.

Lachmann's Unchallenged Scholarly Standing

Lachmann, as we have seen, went through trying times, first in Germany and later in Palestine. In Germany, he was a success both professionally and institutionally, until disqualified altogether, for reasons of race. In Palestine, of course, his being Jewish constituted an incentive to the public recognition of his field of endeavor, as well as his scholarly achievements within it. Nonetheless, since the University's priorities at the time did not make room for the incorporation of his activities, he was, in fact, an *institutional* failure. That Lachmann was never a *professional* failure in the eyes of the relevant scientific community – quite the contrary – highlights his personal tragedy. The injustice done to Lachmann in those pioneering days could be fully comprehended only in retrospect, once the University was less bound by commitments other than purely academic ones. Historic conditions, not of his choosing, closed in on him, making him pay "beyond his guilt," like in classical tragedy.

Luckily, despite insurmountable difficulties, Lachmann had no cause to doubt his scholarly standing. His contribution to the initial phases of comparative musicology was widely known; after all, he played an active part in the molding of methods and criteria of judgement appropriate to the field he helped to promote. Moreover, he was well connected with other leading musicologists, who thought highly of his work and his professional abilities. Naturally, those who followed the German lead, as far as musical scholarship was concerned, were cognizant of Lachmann and appreciative of what he was trying to accomplish in Palestine. Yet it is primarily those who suffered a fate similar to that of Lachmann, and those who empathized with the group on political, not only professional grounds, who kept in touch with him on a regular basis, not least for their own sake. They were all in dire need of mutual support. Indeed, it must have been difficult for these sensible people to concentrate on their narrow professional interests, while witnessing their world crumble into pieces. Even those German musicologists who went along with the policy of their government found it difficult to deny the professional achievements of their former colleagues, because it was tantamount to admitting that they, themselves, had no leg to stand on. Given the times and the specific case in question, the following attestation, written by a well known German musicologist, telegraphically tells both parts of the story.

National Museums

National Museum for Ethnology

Berlin SW II, Stresemannstr.
January 22, 1935

To Whom It May Concern[102]

The Phonogram Archive of the Museum for Ethnology is indebted to Dr. Lachmann for putting at its disposal, in addition to Japanese and Turkish recordings, his largest and best-catalogued collection of North African Music (about 450 recordings). Within the framework of the scientific publications of our Archive, Dr. Lachmann has contributed the following: 1. Music in the Tunisian cities. Arch. F. Musikw. V, 1923. 2. Music and Recordings of the Congress of the German Musical Society, 1925. 3. East Turkistanian Chants in Le Coq, Von Land und Leuten in Ostturkestan, 1928. 4. Music of the Orient, 1929. 5. The Song of the Lion and the Pythian Nomos, 1929. 6. Music of non-European Primitive and Civilized People, 1930. 7. Asiatic Parallels to Berber Music, 1933.

The planned establishment, in Jerusalem, of a Phonogram Archive would also be in our interest, 1. because this would enable us to extend our collection merely by an exchange procedure, without involving foreign currency expenses, 2. because Dr. Lachmann is a well-renowned expert.

Heil Hitler!

Dr. Marius Schneider.
Director of the Phonogram Archive.

---

102 Translated from the German. See a copy of the original letter with its emblem in appendix I, no. 8.

Shared Interests and Mutual Concerns

Among the many letters which Lachmann received, those written by colleagues, with whom he shared both culture and fate, are the most interesting. If we add to shared culture and fate their joint interests and experiences in the shaping of what was still considered a young science, the letters are important at several different levels.

In spite of everything they were occupied, in the first place, with the progress of their chosen profession. Compared to other branches of the humanities, the scientific study of music was still not taken for granted in institutions of higher learning in the thirties, not even in Germany. Most of the *hochschulen,* which specialized in the arts, emphasized the knowledge of the métier, leaving little room for the investigation of their premises. But whereas the plastic arts had already been incorporated into the *Geisteswissenschaften* at universities, musicology was only gradually making inroads (directly or indirectly), especially in Germany.

It is, of course, to the 19th century German model of universities, which promoted the scientific study of the liberal arts, that the above observation applies. While music occupied an honorable position in the *quadrivium,* modern musicology was not seen as a direct descendant of the medieval classification of the seven liberal arts. Nor was it viewed as a direct continuation of the many valuable treatises concerning music, written in the course of several centuries, which later became subjects of modern scientific investigation.

From their correspondence it is evident that these uprooted scholars found it congenial to communicate with each other about such matters. Given their shared background, they could assume familiarity with the issues they were addressing. They could engage in a kind of shorthand, not fearing they might be misunderstood. The letters, accordingly, contain a mix of personal and professional concerns, an *in medias res.* See, for example, the following sample from Curt Sachs's letters to Lachmann:

The New York Public Library

Astor, Lennox and Tilden Foundation

Fifth Avenue & 42 Street
New York

Nov. 29, 1937

My dear Dr. Lachmann,[103]

This is to follow the hon. writer's suggestion and to convey the learned letter of the Benedectine Prior to a more competent authority than myself. I have a sneaking suspicion that you on your part are passing the letter to Mr. Rosowsky via the administrative path – which isn't doing any harm, but I think it would be proper if the relations were to be initiated by the Jerusalem University as such. If – against expectations – financial conditions there should be particularly favorable, I am all for sending the gentleman, together with the letter, a fresh typewriter ribbon.

Mode of address: "Mon père."

I am using the opportunity to tell you about myself, namely that I have had a furuncle in my right ear; that, at an American speed, I have twice proofread, as well as indexed, 448 pages of an English translation of a book on dance, have simultaneously brought the French translation to a happy ending, have read the second galley proofs of my Madagascar book for the Institut d'Ethnologie, and have done several more things.

How are the Bedouin and the lady dyer? Old Galpin[104] has published an extravagantly bad book about the music of the Sumerians, Babylonians and Assyrians. And my wretched self is supposed to review it for a local journal for classical scholars. How does one do that without hurting the dear old gentleman too much?

All the best, in addition to the letter,
from your
Curt Sachs

---

103 Translated from the German. The Benedictine Prior mentioned in his letter must have turned to Sachs with questions concerning biblical cantillation on which Rosowsky was an expert.

104 Rev. Francis William Galpin wrote many articles on old musical instruments in *Music and Letters* and *Monthly Musical Record*.

NEW YORK UNIVERSITY
WASHINGTON SQUARE COLLEGE
Washington Square, New York

Department of Music[105]   June 12, 1938

<u>Anagrammatical</u>. Lieber Lob mach Narren, it took me a night to realize that Robert Lach is not anagrammatizable. Generally speaking, I suffer from sleeplessness.

<u>Veganic</u>. Carlos Vega[106] cannot be acknowledged here, even by Spaniards. But there is no harm in the committee not being complete all at once.

<u>Benedictinian</u>. A letter has arrived here from the slightly unsavory Prior OB, which I am unable to answer and therefore, for reasons of competence, am forwarding to the Alma Mater Hierosolymensis, or whomever seems to you appropriate.

<u>Phonographical</u>. Do you know that a very beautiful set of Kongo records has come out?

<u>Museological</u>. After any number of luncheons, dinners, meetings, reports and letters, I have advanced one step. Or rather two. The first is that the Boards of the Public Library, the Metropolitan Museum and New York University have in principle approved of the plan. What is still missing is only the decision whether a certain substantial legacy can be legally appropriated for our purpose, which point is now being discussed by the lawyers among the Trustees. The second step is that I have been authorized by the Museum to engage two restorators and to begin at once with the setting up of the collection. To be sure, everybody is in the country or just going there and thus nothing much can be expected before the fall. Indeed, the summer is already now rather severe. Imagine that in the warm season one cannot leave a rug, or a painting, or a piece of upholstered furniture without a cover. The air is like in a hothouse, and people are limp.

---

105 Translated from the German.
106 Carlos Vega was an Argentine musicologist who devoted himself mainly to the research of Latinamerican music.

Of Humans. My family is now here in full. That Georg is at Columbia as a hispanist you probably know already; the last arrival, my eldest daughter, has a beginner's job at the Public Library; Gabriele went yesterday for three months to a farm in New England as a kindergartner; the smallest one (but already 18 years old) is going to the Hebrew Technical Institute and is struggling with mathematics.

Professorial. The Professor is not abbreviated, neither Pr nor Pro, nor Prof. The title is only rarely used, especially if one is a Doctor. Relating to me, it should on principle not be used by you.

On Work. When I have time, I am doing a book on . . . Musical Instruments for W. W. Norton, N.Y. There exists nothing comprehensive, neither in English, nor in anything else. For me, the subject is partly very boring, as I happen to know it more or less. It is, however, astonishing how many new problems are created by the new form. I must hurry up, because once I will have to start on the indispensable catalogue of the collection of instruments, I shall no longer find the time for such a book.

Please do write soon about yourself and your work.
Cordially yours,
Curt Sachs.

PS. Mrs. Von Hornbostel is in a very bad state. And I am very angry. In May, it was suddenly reported that, by the first of June, the last money will be gone. This could not have come as a surprise; why, in these $2\frac{1}{2}$ years, did they not start to sell the library? I am trying to acquire at least a part for the Public Library. But so far it was impossible to get hold of even the most tentative list. In the meantime, the Warburg Institute has acquired the Cambridge portion, and here an effort is underway to list whatever is in the basement of Wertheimer's. Mrs. V. H. complains that the preparation of the catalogue produces a commotion in the house. . . . Meanwhile, a collection has been initiated in Holland.

Dr. Robert Lachmann
Institute for Oriental Music
Saad van Said Quarter
Beth Turgeman
Jerusalem Palestine

Dear Dr. Lachmann,[107]

This is to express my joy at the better news from you, brought by Miss Lentschner. It is so often that I think of you – especially on Wednesdays on the subway when, before my oriental lectures, I look up your opinion. In spite of this, I am still not sure of the exact meaning of Pelog. Are you? I am sitting over a six-hundred-page tome on The History of Musical Instruments, which I must deliver by September 1st. Please, please recover soon, for your own sake, and for all the rest of us.

With the most cordial wishes,
Your
Curt Sachs

Much can be learned about Curt Sachs from the letters he wrote to Lachmann. Though totally committed to his field, he maintained a sensible view of life in general and of the activities he was engaged in, never taking himself too seriously. His sense of humor, his ability to adjust to his new environment and to address issues with a degree of detachment, are quite remarkable. The special quality of these letters (not only those written by Sachs), which mix personal and professional concerns, give insight into the personality of their writers, both individually and as a group.

It is the professional tenacity of most of these uprooted musicologists that deserves our utmost attention, for it conveys the spirit of *mission*

---

107 Translated from the German.

which refuses, as it were, to succumb to adverse circumstances. The following letter, by Manfred Bukofzer, was written with the full awareness of the political situation, since he himself was on his way to America around that time, leaving Europe for good.

DR. MANFRED BUKOFZER　　　　　　　　　　　　　　Basle, Rosentalstr. 5
　　　　　　　　　　　　　　　　　　　　　　　　　　　　　7 November 1938

Dear Mr. Lachmann,[108]

Please forgive me for not providing you with an offprint from Anthropos at an earlier date, I simply did not have your address. In the meantime, a remark by Schneider has appeared in the Archiv für Musikforschung, which is not without piquantness, inasmuch as he reproaches Schünemann for having read me all right, but not having credited me (the work in the Z. F. Physik). I have heard this also from another source and am almost sorry for having handled Schünemann as gently as I did.

By the way, the last number of Anthropos contains also a review of Schiffer's dissertation and of the work of Boone on the xylophones of the Kongo. Unfortunately I did not manage to obtain offprints, but the journal is possibly carried by the library.

At the beginning of next semester I am slated to give several guest lectures on the tone system. Much to my pleasure I have succeeded in working out a simpler, and what is more, an empirical theory concerning the origin of the Slendro-scale, which at the same time also satisfactorily explains the mythological tradition on Java. Given more time, I shall explain the matter to you in greater detail. However, still unexplained remains the Pelog-scale, or at least its oldest component: the fourth which, in descent, is divided into a major third and a semitone. I guess there must exist the identical basic situation as with the changing of the asemitonic pentatonic scale into the semitonic one in Japan. If that points to a common primeval race, I don't know. Do you have an explanation for the Japanese transformation? I assume an emergence influenced by vocal music rather than by instrumental music.

108　Translated from the German.

Have the lectures which you gave in Basle ever appeared in print?

Please let us occasionally hear from you and, in case you see her, give my regards to my old fellow student, Miss Kiwi, who is married today and has another name.

Cordial greetings,
Your
M. Bukofzer

P.S.: The offprint leaves under separate cover.

The Lachmann files contain 92 (!) letters from Hornbostel alone. The last of them, those that were sent to Palestine, continue to focus on professional issues as a matter of course. Despite his enormous achievements (which nobody doubted), Hornbostel, too, was dismissed from the university (his mother was Jewish) in 1933. He left for Switzerland that year, spent a short period, subsequently, at the New School for Social Research in New York,[109] and the last month of his life (he died November 1935) in Cambridge, England, working on a collection of recordings at the Psychological Laboratory. In fact, most of his letters to Lachmann deal with methodological questions, problems of measurements, tonal systems, and so forth. Like Lachmann's own unpublished works, they undoubtedly deserve special treatment and publication, because of their historic interest and substantive value.[110] However, it is the admirable commitment displayed by these scholars that is being stressed here. The professional respect they felt for each other enabled them to engage in scientific problems, skipping superfluous introductions. Obviously, they were addressing not only professional issues discernible by the group, but

---

109 The New School for Social Research, as is well known, performed an important role in the absorption of many immigrant scholars. While much is known about its relationship to the Frankfurt School for Social Research, little is known about its contribution to the bridging between German and American musicological research. It seems to deserve a separate study.

110 With the completion of this volume, I hope to address all of these other issues separately.

scientific problems which all were eager to solve, or see solved. Collective problem solving, we are told nowadays, is one of the major earmarks of genuine scientific endeavor.

Given the difficult circumstances which each and every one of these scholars was forced to confront, it is striking how sincerely concerned they were about each other, as if their own survival depended on the functioning and well being of the others. They saw fit, accordingly, to report to each other about their personal situations and whereabouts. See, for example the following letter by Hans David – another well known musicologist, who left Germany for Holland in 1933 and settled in America in 1936[111] – and the letter from the Warburg Institute enlisting Lachmann's help:

THE JEWISH FORUM
305 Broadway, New York

Dear, most esteemed Dr. Lachmann, [112]

I am glad to have the opportunity to write to you – I only hope you will receive the letter. It is two months now that I am here and trying to get a firm footing. My wife and children (since January 1935, there are two of them) are on a visit to Germany and will return to Holland. I hope they will be able to join me here in the fall. I hear that there are some chances for you to receive a call to Cambridge. I hope this is indeed the case and truly wish for you to obtain all the possibilities that you need for extensive work. The other day, I think at Zadora's,[113] the conversation turned to you. The motive for this letter: The Jewish Forum, a monthly with a circulation of about 20,000, is about to be reorganized. Einstein's sons-in-law and Dr. R. Kayser, formerly with S. Fischer (Neue Rundschau), whom you probably know, are the editors. I have taken charge of a music

---

111 David is best known for his Bach studies which he summed up in "Bach: a Portrait in Outline," in *The Bach Reader* (1945), which he wrote with Arthur Mendel.
112 Translated from the German. The letter was undated.
113 Michael von Zadora was a pianist and composer who transcribed for piano several organ and violin works by Buxtehude and Bach.

section, 2–3 pages in each number. I would like to make it as many-sided as possible, historical, comparative, actual (music life here and in Palestine). I consider it as extraordinarily important to ensure your cooperation. Everything somehow connected with Jewish life is welcome. Preferably condensations, if possible in English (of whatever kind). Articles can have 1–3 printed pages, i.e., 3–8 typewritten pages (double-spaced). Payment is $10, unfortunately regardless of extent.

I very much hope to hear from you soon, and to receive a positive answer.

All the very best, most cordial greetings,
Your
Hans David

THE WARBURG INSTITUTE

7 Thames House, Millbank
London, S.W.1 Victoria 8786

Most esteemed Professor,[114]　　　　　　　　　　　　　　　　　March 5, 1937

I am taking the liberty of writing to you following a suggestion by Dr. Klaus Wachsman, who assured me that the matter for which I venture to solicit your help would be of interest for you.

The subject of my endeavor is the widow of Dr. von Hornbostel. As you know, the prolonged illness of Dr. von Hornbostel has eaten up his last reserves. Defrayal of all the expenses incurred by his disease and the necessary move to England was made possible by the generous obligingness of the New School of Social Research in America which for at least one and a half years paid his salary in spite of the fact that he no longer gave any lectures, and by a grant from the Academic Assistance Council, London.

What Mrs. von Hornbostel has been living on so far I do not know, because since Dr. von Hornbostel's death we have had no contact with her. I do, however, hear that she is in need of urgent assistance. Since Dr. von Hornbostel's

---

114　Translated from the German.

death she has been immersing herself with great energy in the work he has left behind and is preparing it for publication. In the course of the last year, since he was no longer able to give lectures, Dr. von Hornbostel has been extensively working for himself, and there must be in existence a number of, most probably, important works. His notes were all written in shorthand, with which Mrs. von Hornbostel is familiar and is already busy with the transcription of these notes.

There exists thus the possibility of saving Dr. von Hornbostel's work of the last years, if Mrs. von Hornbostel is given the wherewithal to complete her work. It goes without saying that the Warburg Institute is ready to provide Mrs. von Hornbostel with all assistance our own Library can offer, and with the procuring of books. There exists also the possibility of publishing some of the articles of Dr. von Hornbostel in the new "Journal of the Warburg Institute," as far as they fit the framework of the journal. Unfortunately, however, we are at the moment quite unable to provide financial means. Our request from you, dear Professor Lachmann, is to advise us as to a possible source of money. I think that a monthly sum of £10 for a year would go far to solve the problem. I would be very grateful if you were to give some consideration to this question.

I hope that for the sake of the memory of this researcher, for whose personality and work we all share the greatest veneration, I have done the right thing.

With the sincerest regards,
your devoted
Dr. Gertrud Bing
Deputy Director

Professor Dr. Robert Lachmann,
Jerusalem University
Institute for Comparative Musicology

These uprooted scholars were in touch with other leading musicologists, as well. Since musicology encompassed only a relatively small number of scholars, largely concentrated in Europe – the birthplace of the discipline – they all knew, or had heard, of each other. A sociometric map would show that most of them were joined in a network whose members were related to each other via a number of mentors, themselves directly or indirectly related to the founding fathers. Our uprooted group constituted a significant part of that network. No wonder, therefore, that musicologists like Jacques Handschin, for example, should be interested in Lachmann and his work. As the unrivalled authority on the schools of St. Martial and Notre Dame, and on English polyphony before the 13th century,[115] Handschin extended his interest in the Middle Ages to Byzantium and Syria, trying to gain insight into non-European music. He depended for sources on the Berlin *Phonogramm Archiv,* and on the experiences of those connected with the *Archiv* and its aims. Jaap Kunst,[116] George Farmer,[117] and many others who had an interest in non-European music likewise continued to be in touch with Lachmann, informing or consulting him. Some even saw fit to invite him to deliver lectures at their respective institutions, knowing only too well that Lachmann was facing difficulties in the Promised Land. All of them supported the idea of resurrecting the *Zeitschrift*, remembering the quality of the first issues which Lachmann had so ably edited.

German Scholarship and the Development of American Musicology

As we have seen, not all of the German universities saw fit to include musicology among the disciplines they offered their students, not even

---

115 Bukofzer wrote his famous doctoral dissertation on the English descant style – a style of improvised singing practiced in England distinct from the continental fauxbourdon practice – under Handschin at Basle University.
116 A Dutch ethnomusicologist whose work centered primarily around Indonesian music. Kunst was, in fact, a founder of modern ethnomusicology, and coined the term "ethnomusicology" as more accurate than "comparative musicology." In his studies he showed the need to comprehend music in the widest possible frame of reference, including social, physical and spiritual.
117 Farmer, a British musicologist, established his reputation with his *History of Arabian Music of the xiiith Century* (1929). He was the only British representative at the Cairo Conference of Arabian Music (1932), where he met Lachmann. Farmer was elected president of the Commission of Manuscripts and History, at that conference. While working on his Al-Kindi project, Lachmann was assisted by Farmer.

by the thirties of the last century. Yet it is the German university system, a system which strongly supported the scientific study of the liberal arts, that created both a framework hospitable to the scientific study of music, as well as an institution of higher learning compatible with musicology as an academic discipline.

Though many countries contributed significantly to the development of the study of music, it was Germany that led the rest of Europe in establishing the academic discipline. The study of music was not regarded as an independent discipline until the second half of the 19th century. Until then, musical questions were handled as part of a general theory of knowledge. True, as a physical phenomenon, music early benefited from the scientific methods developed in the natural sciences. As a cultural phenomenon, however, it had to wait for the development of the cultural sciences and their modes of investigation. Indeed, modern humanistic scholarship only commenced with the Enlightenment, with that current in European intellectual history which was as interested in the worlds created by Man as it was in God's creation.

Most historians of music will agree that the center of gravity of Western music, in the 18th century, moved from the south to the northern countries of Europe. No wonder, therefore, that the contemplative part, which accompanied active music making, should also have enjoyed a growing prominence in these countries. However, serious intellectual deliberations, concerning a field of knowledge, require a proper stage for the exchange of ideas. Beyond societies of sorts, they require newspapers, journals and publications of all kinds. Yet publishing houses, no less than institutions of learning, have to first recognize the value of such deliberations in order to lend them support. While the problem of the chicken or the egg is often difficult to sort out, it seems likely that the principle of supply and demand affected the printing press more readily than the institutions of higher learning. Paradoxically, the more entrenched these institutions were in their respective countries, the less readiness they exhibited to explore new avenues. As is often the case, those who stand to lose more are less willing to dare it; long standing traditions, good or bad, resist changes as long as they possibly can.

Compared to France, England and Italy, the German university system of the 19th century seems to have provided, both directly and indirectly, the institutional framework within which the new field could evolve. German musicology enjoyed not only a record in productivity, but in scientific standards as well, made possible by the ubiquity of other fields of knowledge that had a direct bearing on the study of music. The German printing press, consequently, saw fit to support the publication of critical editions, bibliographies, catalogues, dictionaries, in short all that was deemed necessary for the furtherance of musicological research. All of this, naturally, did not happen overnight.

Given this development, many a student interested in musical research traveled to Germany to acquire an education not obtainable in their countries of origin. Germany, for that matter, was considered a Mecca by scholars seeking scientific rigor in many fields. Yet, what was well recognized in most of the European countries was doubly appreciated in the United States. Thus Oscar Sonneck, the first important American musicologist, chief of the Music Division of the Library of Congress (1902–1917), received his training in Germany. Otto Kinkeldey, another figure associated with the beginnings of musicology in America, was, likewise, trained in Germany; he became the head of the Music Division of the New York Public Library upon his return from Germany in 1914. The first chair of musicology was established, sixteen years later (1930), by Cornell University, and was offered to Kinkeldey. Oliver Strunk, one of the founders of the American Musicological Society (1934), a student of Kinkeldey, spent his early twenties in Germany studying under Wolf, Blume, Sachs and Schering. In fact, the first generation of American musicologists were inspired or came into direct contact with the leading figures of German musicology in those days.

Though musicology was steadily growing in America, it was still in its infancy when so many uprooted musicologists landed on its shores. Only a few universities included musicology in their curricula, and there were but few institutions which could absorb these unfortunate newcomers. However, by giving salience to the field, these newcomers helped create the very jobs which were not available when they arrived. As is well known, it is these struggling scholars who became leading figures in the second generation of American musicology. By transferring their experience with

German musicology to the United States, they contributed immeasurably towards its development.

"Cultural codes" serve well to identify the choices and biases that give cultures their continuity and distinctness.[118] "Crystallization of scientific problems and their solutions" characterize the development of scientific paradigms, as well as the emergence of new scientific disciplines.[119] Such "agreed-on problems and solutions" inhere in "invisible colleges," i.e., in social circles of colleagues whose informal networks of communication nurture the paradigm and fructify it.[120] All of these factors apply to the social network to which our uprooted scholars belonged. The uprooted members of this invisible college admirably exemplified the emergent discipline they helped to make visible.

Lachmann, as we have seen, was an appreciated member of the distinguished circle that left a lasting mark on the development of musicology. Though primarily associated with the Berlin School of *comparative* musicology, he was a well-rounded musicologist, fully entrenched in all of the trends that characterized the study of music at the time. In fact, the distinction between comparative musicology and musicology, those days, was one that designated an area of interest, more than it pointed to two separate branches of musical studies. Indeed, the musicologists who took a special interest in non-European musical expression shared the musicological background of their colleagues. Their interest in non-European musical cultures constituted a kind of theoretical extension, lending the new investigations points of perspective. This, of course, holds equally true for the natural scientists and the anthropologists

---

118 See, for example, Samuel N. Eisenstadt, *Tradition, Change and Modernity* (New York, 1973); Rainer C. Baum, "Authority and Identity: The Case for Evolutionary Invariants," *Sociological Inquiry* (1975); Clifford Geertz, *The Interpretation of Culture* (New York, 1973); and Alfred Kroeber, *Style and Civilization* (California, 1963).

119 See Thomas S. Kuhn, *The Structure of Scientific Revolutions* (Chicago, 1970), and M. K. Mulkay, *The Social Process in Innovation* (London, 1972).

120 See Diana Crane, *Invisible Colleges: Diffusion of Knowledge in Scientific Communities* (Chicago, 1972). Also see E. Katz, M. Levin, and H. Hamilton, "Traditions of Research on the Diffusion of Innovation," *American Sociological Review* 28 (1963).

who were drawn to learn from, or contribute to, the study of non-Western music.

In addition to Lachmann's contact with his former European colleagues, it is important not to overlook his association with the American Society of Ethnomusicology in its formative years. A few of the letters, which span a five-year period starting in 1933, will convey Lachmann's involvement with the American scene. As it turned out, Lachmann was well known in America by those who shared his interests, and was looked up to as an exemplary scholar in the field. In his attempt to revive the *Zeitschrift* and, if possible, the entire *Gesellschaft* as he knew it, he turned to the Americans for help. This helped further their own interests as well, contributing to the cohesion that was lacking on the local scene. Given his overall financial difficulties, Lachmann also hoped to ease his personal lot by an arranged lecture tour in America. The idea to move to the United States altogether hovered as an hypothetical possibility, perhaps even before the move to Palestine, as well as during the period of his failure to become securely established there. But the situation in America was not much more secure, as will become clear from the following letters.

AMERICAN LIBRARY OF MUSICOLOGY

Charles Seeger, *Editor* 1 West 68th Street
Blanche Walton, *Secretary* New York City

66 West 12th Street
New York City

July 26, 1933

Dear Dr. Lachmann,

I think it will be better to keep the subject matter of our letters apart, if only to make filing and record-keeping easier.

I am most interested in your proposed study of Berber music. Actually, it would be more appropriate for inclusion in our series than the more popular

Musik des Orients. But the lack of any general work such as the latter and the abysmal ignorance of the subject among even the best educated of our American musicians leads me to favor it – at least for the present. It would be only in 1935 that we could think of publishing the translation of the Musik des Orients for we are hoping to be able to announce Schillinger's Physico-Mathematical Theory of Musical Composition for 1934. Perhaps, however, funds can be obtained to speed up publication.

We are more and more disturbed by news affecting our musicological interests. I am earnestly hoping that your position in the Staatsbibliothek will not change. If times were not so unsettled in this country we could do a great deal for you but as it is, even we ourselves, who have continually to do even under normal conditions that which you fear for yourself, must do all musicological work as an extra thing – outside of our earning a living by popularising and missionary work. That is why we can point to so little scholarly accomplishment and are generally so far behind the Europeans in our field. The state of affairs is improving rapidly, however. In 1916, in a lecture at Harvard, I prophesied that by 1941 musicology would be accepted as a respectable subject by American Universities. It may be that that guess was a good one.

Miss Roberts is going over the MS of our translation and then I shall send it to you – if it is safe to do so.

Sincerely
Charles Seeger

The idea of including some discs in the book is a very good one, which we have thought of, provided they can be made cheaply and well. How about including discs for the illustration in "Musik des Orients"?[121]

---

121 Lachmann's study of Berber music was never published. It is one of his important studies that still awaits publication. Moreover, a new study of Berber music could make good use of Lachmann's study for comparative purposes of all kinds.

3007 Pershing Drive
Clarendon Virginia
United States of America

Dr. Robert Lachmann January 12 1936
Beth ha-Rav mi-Gur
Opposite Ettinger House
Ben Yehuda Street
Jerusalem, Palestine

Dear Dr. Lachmann,

Owing to my moving to Washington D.C. and undertaking some new work in connection with the government, I have been delayed in sending out the circular letter to the membership of the Gesellschaft für Vergleichende Musikwissenschaft. It has finally gone to Miss Roberts for typing and mailing and you will receive a copy in due time – also a copy of the letter sent to Professor Wolf authorising him to edit the brochure containing number 3 and 4 of the 1935 Zeitschrift, material for which you sent to Miss Roberts. I have begged Professor Wolf to write, or have written, adequate material upon the life, work and death of Erich M. von Hornbostel. I have written to his son for a good picture for reproduction as a frontispiece. He was one of the most lovable men I ever met. His death is a loss to us all.

I am hoping that the last half of Volume 3 will appear before the end of March. But in any event we must begin to get the first number, or numbers 1 and 2 of vol. 4 in one brochure, out before June first. Dues will probably come in very slowly and certainly not in as large an amount as heretofore. But this need not alarm us. The American Library of Musicology, which, as you know, has had to suspend publication (I hope only temporarily) has a small amount of money in the bank, and I think this may be made available to tide the Zeitschrift over at least the first half of 1936.

We think here that it would be unwise, at the present time to publish Volume 4 in Palestine. If you send us the material, we could secure excellent publishers, even sending you the copy for correction, if you so desire. If, however, we put out just two brochures, say, one in May and another in November, there will be time even for this difficult task.

Perhaps you could be relieved of some of the detail of the reviewing and bibliography by entrusting sections of the work to competent workers under your direction. At any rate, please feel that we are anxious to help you in any way we can. We rely upon you, however, to tell us what you want us to do.

We must begin to talk now about the elections in the autumn. When I was notified by Dr. Wolf that the Chairmanship came to me automatically, I understood the situation according to American practice. Here, it is not open to a vice-chairman or vice-president to accept or to decline. He must accept. Hence the absence of any formal acceptance on my part. When, however, I wrote to you that I would not be a candidate for Chairman at the elections next fall, I think I did the right thing. While I would be glad to serve the Society in any way, I do feel that some one who has accomplished more than I have should be elected to the Chairmanship at that time. I should think that Dr. Sachs, Yourself and many others would make better chairmen than I. I am glad to step into the gap made by Dr. Wolf's resignation; and especially glad if I can keep things alive until formal election of new officers takes place. But unless there is absolutely no other person available, I think my original decision should stand.

In concluding, let me say that I am hoping it may be possible for me to go to Europe next fall. If possible, I should like to time my travel so as to be present at the general meeting. I am proposing some questions as to where that meeting might be and shall let you know what comes of them in the near future. It would give me great pleasure to meet you, of whom I have heard so much and whose work I admire.

By the way, the translation of your "Musik des Orients" was so bad that I could not and have not done the second revision. My German is not very good. But Professor Lang of Columbia University has expressed an interest in it, and if he would like to publish it, I would be only too glad to turn it all over to him. I shall have something to say about this, too, in a little time.

With best regards for the New Year
sincerely
Charles Seeger

P.S. Of course, if you decide to publish the Zeitschrift in Palestine, we shall back you to the best of our ability. C.S.[122]

Charles Seeger was no doubt the most prominent American member of the Society for Comparative Musicology. There were of course others, but only a small number of musicologists in America took special interest in this newly-established branch. It must be remembered that musicology in America lagged far behind German musicology altogether. Nonetheless, the United States seemed to harbor possibilities not in sight in Europe at the time, even if the undertaking of serious musical studies still required vigorous persuasion. Looking to European scholarship for guidance, America on the whole was hospitable to European scholars, especially to those who came on lecture tours. Given his financial situation, Lachmann was naturally interested in the arrangement of such a tour for himself.

Division of Music   Library of Congress
                                      Washington

                                                          January 28, 1937

Dr. Walter Grau
c/o Lichstein
Spring Valley Road
Issining, New York

My dear Dr. Grau,

I was very sorry that I was unable to see you again before you left Washington, but my wife's illness turned out to be more serious than I had anticipated. Mr. Strunk reacted very favorably to my suggestion that Dr. Lachmann give a series of lectures at various universities in this country under the auspices of the

---

[122] Lachmann, obviously, was determined to publish the *Zeitschrift* in Palestine for reasons already mentioned. "Correct" decisions are not always realistic!

Elizabeth Sprague Coolidge Foundation. This Foundation is administered in the Music Division of the Library of Congress. The next step is to get Robert Lachmann to apply directly to Mr. Strunk indicating the subjects on which he would like to lecture and the time of year in which he could come to this country.

I have also spoken to Charles Seeger who believes that a short course of lectures might be arranged at the New School for Social Research in New York City. All in all, the outlook for some sort of lecture tour looks very favorably at the moment. Of course, you must understand that nothing is definite as yet.

Please have Dr. Lachmann write both to Mr. Strunk and to Mr. Seeger as soon as possible. Their addresses are given below.

Hoping that your trip to this country proved successful and with best regards from Mrs. Spivacke and myself to the Branaus and the Lachmanns, I remain

Very sincerely yours,
signed: Harold Spivacke

Mr. Oliver Strunk, Chief, Division of Music, Library of Congress, Washington, D.C.

Mr. Charles Seeger, Special Skills Division, Resettlement Administration, Washington, D.C.

Lachmann's lectureship in America never materialized. The following letter written by Helen Roberts goes a long way to explain why Lachmann never made it to America. As a musicologist whose main interest centered on the music of the American Indians, Miss Roberts was an active member of the Society for Comparative Musicology. She was, apparently, well aware of the difficulties and internal intrigues. In addition to the gossip which she shares with Lachmann, she vividly describes the hardships she herself is facing in *her* "land of promise." Altogether, her picture of the state of musicology in America is far from encouraging, particularly her report of the decision at Yale to abandon musicology.

It is interesting to note, however, how central a role their German colleagues played – even those who never set foot in America – in the formulation and definition of the professional and organizational activities in America. Her references to the journal that Lachmann was so eager to re-establish in Palestine make clear how widely it was agreed that

Lachmann deserved to continue its editorship in order to assure its continuity as well as its high standards.

High Watch,
Tryon, N.C.

Feb. 5, 1937

Dear Dr. Lachmann,

I am very sorry not to have been able to answer your letter of Dec. 30th at once. The chances to carry on professional correspondence and work since I moved here have been almost nil. You see, I am all alone in this house, except for occasional guests, and everything that is done at all, must have my personal attention or supervision. After I knew I was not going to be able to remain at Yale, I bought the house a year ago last July – a year before I was to occupy it – for the more conservative business men here feel that we are in for a very strong inflation and no one knows what else, as the result of our present government.

I am so glad you liked my papers. I wrote, and read another at the annual meeting in Chicago, Dec. 29, of the American Musicological Society (which is another than the A.S.C.M.) which was held jointly with that of the Music Teachers' National Association. The A.M.S. had a symposium on Musicology, and asked me to contribute the paper on the "Viewpoint of Comparative Musicology." I will presently send you a reprint. Of course eventually I hope to go on with my research, although probably without a university connection or salary. It was most discouraging to have Yale decide that it could not support musicology any longer. It did not pay, economically, and that is all they judge by, these days. I believe I could have lectured and had students, and I am quite sure I could have made the courses attractive, but I was not allowed to give them, that work being given to Dr. Herzog, and unfortunately he could not hold the interest of his students, or so it has been reported. So it ended the career there of both of us. My archives have gone mostly to the Library of Congress, except the records I hope to continue to work on if I ever get my living conditions in running order, and can acquire the leisure. Possibly I have written you all this but it seems to me that I have not written for a very long time, partly because of the last minute rush or all-year rush at Yale to finish work and pack up all my archives and collections, and partly because I knew you expected to return to Germany and was not sure where you were. I risked the reprints to your Palestine address. And I am very glad to know that you got them safely.

I have copied your letter for Mr. Seeger and Dr. Herzog. Have also written Mr. Seeger. I have not seen him now for more than a year, or Herzog either, and as my funds are limited I shall not be able to get as far as Washington or New York for conference with them. Last fall I got (Dec. 1 or thereabouts) a letter from Mr. Seeger, outlining further plans. Unfortunately he never seems to get much beyond plans. He said:

(1) There seems to be only one thing to do in answer to the pleas of Wolf and Lachmann, and that is to disband, temporarily, at least, the International Society. (I am unaware that such ever existed, if he is referring to the society he proposed to get together with the remnants of the German society, and the American. Perhaps he means the Gesellschaft.) It may be that in a few years it could be resuscitated. I do not know. Herzog thinks it could be. But at least we would be protecting the German position of these two men and we would allow a free development of the Zeitschrift.

(2) I would like him to know from Lachmann how much he would need to have us send him, how soon he could send us copies (I supposed he is referring to the journal continued under your editorship) for our A.S.C.M. members, etc.

(3) In collecting dues for the A.S.C.M. I would propose we make it optional for the members to hold back their 1937 dues until at least Nos. 1 and 2 for 1936 of the new Zeitschrift are in their hands.

(4) In view of the possible need for all our spare cash and to avoid seeming to try to compete with the Zeitschrift, I would suggest we do not announce any yearbook for the present. (The year book was my suggestion for this past year, which would be an American product only, with papers contributed by some of us, which we might send to our members in lieu of the Zeitschrift, since some or most of them expect something of that nature in return for their dues. Few of them are wholly altruistic in their membership. H.H.R.)

(5) (He wanted a meeting some time in Washington, this winter. I cannot go. Apparently we never get anywhere at these meetings except to draw up more plans which are not put into execution.)

He continued that he thinks, by the way, that we should write first to the old international committee (he means the governing board of the Gesellschaft) proposing the disbanding of the society (i.e., the old Gesellschaft). He says they have not paid their dues (that is they did not pay them to Herzog, as was suggested), and he says that in fact the non-payment of dues is alone sufficient reason for abandoning the attempt to keep the thing going, but that as a matter of courtesy to write them would undoubtedly be the thing to do. He was to have sent me a copy of the letter he would draw up for this purpose, but he wrote Nov. 27 and I have heard nothing since. He is very busy, of course, in one of those new Government-sponsored jobs, and has little time, but we wait months on end for action and do not get any. All of this is calculated to cool such interest for our society as we have been able to stir up and keep alive. I wish there were someone not so busy with other things who could assume the presidency and give the problem the attention it deserves. But nobody over here knows the whole international situation as does Seeger, or is as able, in a way, as he is. But societies have to come after the scratch for a living.

Now my comments on his letter are as follows:

I agree with him and Herzog, and yourself, that at present there seems to be no chance of getting together the old society. Perhaps later, if you get a journal started, most of the real scholars, at least outside of Germany, will come in again. I fear many cannot afford to join any group and see their dues bring in nothing but a sense of fellowship. Perhaps many are waiting for order and something definite to come out of chaos and so few realize that journals cannot be published and correspondence continued, without money in hand. I think, however, that it is not up to Seeger to suggest the disbanding of a European group. If they have not responded to his suggestion of a year ago, they should be ignored, as far as we are concerned over here.

Mr. Seeger proposes to help you, at least temporarily, to finance the journal you propose to issue, with our small reserve, which is not over $125.00. I maintain he cannot do this independently of approval of our society, through its council. Not that they are likely to have any objections. But Seeger is very apt to get high handed with money, over which he has not complete control. I have told him this. So discount his suggestions until you have a formal notice of the reaction of the society to this plan. He probably also is wondering how much in dues you would need per year of American members.

Now as to answers to your questions:

I think by all means a journal of some sort should continue, and I have been distressed that we had nothing to offer our members this past year, and at Seeger's procrastinations. Several people have written me asking the fate of our society and the Zeitschrift, and I have not had anything definite to tell them. I can understand your not wishing to continue the Zeitschrift as it is. But I do wish you would consider giving the new journal an English title which would be a virtual translation of the German one, and would take it up where the other left off, that is, with 1936, even if the publications were over a year behind, and some issues had to be combined, as they were before. My reason for this is that it would preserve, practically unbroken, a journal devoted to comparative musicology, which has already had a four years' start. Since you were so prominent in the other one and nobody has attempted to keep it up since the debacle, I think you are fully justified in attempting to keep it continuous. This would please librarians and others, who might still subscribe for back issues. By the way, where are the back issues, and were there any reprints of the 1935 one, or any spare copies? I received no reprints of my paper and would like very much to have some, if not too hopelessly late. I did not know to whom to write, and would very much like more than my single issue for this I subscribed. Hitherto, there have been sent us some extra copies, for filing or distribution, but of this last year we got none. Could you find out from Dr. Wolf if there is still a chance of getting any?

To return to the journal. I do not blame you in the least for feeling that you have waited long enough, and I think there is no reason why you need hesitate to announce that this Journal will continue the work of the previous one. I should place an announcement to this effect on the title page of the first issue of the new journal. You need not state that it is the same thing, but that it takes up where the other left off. With its new title and English setting, the Germans cannot possibly object. They are still at liberty to continue with the other, if they can. As to including the work by your students, that should be all to the good.

As to contributions, I should be happy to make them when I can and have anything to offer. As I said, the time for research seems even less, now that I am free of an institution, than before, but in time I may be able to devote more time to it. I could give you a paper which sums up the work I recently completed on the music of the Nootka Indians for the Canadian government. This would be a summary of a very large monograph which they are to publish with several hundred pages of music, and would only "hit the high spots" to use an American slang expression. Perhaps, after seeing the paper on The Viewpoint of Comparative Musicology, you might like a sort of summarizing of that, or a paper on some areas still little known, which offer attractive research.

As to your English, you express yourself in it remarkably well. I wish I could do half as well with German. But if I can be of assistance in polishing off certain small roughnesses of expression, I would be happy to run over your papers, *sub rosa*, and help you until you feel in better command of it.

As to your question (2), I have already told you that I have made copies of your letter for Mr. Seeger and Herzog, which I will mail to Seeger with another letter to him, all of which will go in today's mail.

As to your question (3) I feel quite sure that a number, if not all, of our American society members would be glad to have the substitution of a journal more in English than in German. That has been a stumbling block to many – the German articles. Provided the cost of the new journal is no higher than of the other, we could handle it as before, through our membership dues. But in view of the relative cheapness of the most elaborately illustrated and beautiful periodicals which we have in such number here, few people would want to pay very much more. A five-dollar journal is considered expensive, whereas a $2.50 one is reasonable. People also look at the size of a journal, not the value of its contents, I am sorry to say. This is apt to be true of libraries. Most American libraries will not subscribe to a journal which has not proven its power to survive at least two years. That is one reason I wish yours could in some way be linked definitely to the Zeitschrift. We could then hope to increase very materially the interest of librarians in it, who otherwise would refuse to subscribe for at least two years more. Also, an All-English journal will stand more chance in schools and libraries than one with articles in several languages. If Seeger does not procrastinate too long, and our members lose all interest and confidence in the society, I think we can save most of our membership, although the organization of the A.M.S. a year or so ago, was a serious blow to us and a comment on some conditions in our society.

It might be a good idea for you to prepare prospectuses for both our societies of musicology. Then send to me those intended for our Comparative Society members, which I could distribute with the announcement that it replaces the

Zeitschrift, and can be had (if you agree) under the same financial considerations as before, to members of the A.S.C.M. The lot intended for the other society you could send out direct, after obtaining a list of the members from the secretary. There is a new one, just elected, unfamiliar to me, but the one just out, Gustave Reese, c/o Musical Quarterly, 3 East 43rd St., New York, would procure the list for you, I am sure, if you would write him why you want it.

Personally, I shall do all I can to help you.
Sincerely,
Helen H. Roberts

P.S. Please do not pass on what I have had to relate regarding delays. It is well known over here. I dislike to say it, but it has come to a place where you need to know, in order to act.

The above testimony clearly dispels the thought that Lachmann was but a dreamer when he envisaged the continuation of the journal as an important step towards the reorganization of an international society of people interested in the study of non-European music, with Palestine as its base. Focusing on future developments more than on past achievements, Lachmann himself, as we have seen, was of the opinion that English would be more appropriate for a journal seeking subscribers and financial support.

Despite Miss Roberts's grim description, one gets a feeling that musicology was making headway in America. Though she deplores the establishment of the American Musicological Society (1936) – considering the new organization as competing with the extant American Society for Comparative Musicology – it testifies to an increased interest in the scientific study of music. The *Musical Quarterly* – which Miss Roberts happens to mention in connection with obtaining the membership list of the A.M.S. – though in existence from 1915, could hardly claim to have imparted a sense of mission comparable to that which characterized the *Zeitschrift*. The establishment of the A.M.S. naturally changed matters, not only for the *MQ*, but for subsequent journals as well.

As we already know, the re-establishment of the *Zeitschrift*, in whatever form, faced all of the difficulties discussed earlier, long enough, at any rate, to have reached a critical point – the illness of its editor.

**COLUMBIA UNIVERSITY
in the City of New York**

Department of Anthropology

November 2, 1938

Miss Sophie Lentschner
International House
500 Riverside Drive
New York City

Dear Miss Lentschner, [123]

Thank you very much for your lines. I am truly sorry about what you told me concerning Dr. Lachmann's state of health and hope that he will soon completely recover. The journal can wait. We all know that Dr. Lachmann must also overcome other difficulties and I on my part admire him for his energy and single-mindedness. I am about to write to him one of these days in any case and will ask him not to worry on account of the journal and the time lost.

With cordial greetings,
Yours
George Herzog

P.S. Many thanks for the . . . ., which probably reached me through your efforts.

---

123 Translated from the German. The letterhead shows that Herzog's post at Columbia was by then secure, although as a member of the department of anthropology. The P.S. is reproduced as it appears in the original letter.

As promised to Miss Lentschner, Herzog dispatched the following letter to Lachmann:

**COLUMBIA UNIVERSITY
in the City of New York**

Department of Anthropology

December 9, 1938

Dr. Robert Lachmann
House Turgemann
Saad van Said
Jerusalem, Palestine

Dear Dr. Lachmann,[124]

Miss Lentschner, with whom I just had a lengthy meeting, showed me your last two letters addressed to her. With Miss Lentschner's help and gentle "reminders" I shall certainly be more effective in extending my help. I am truly glad that you are already so much better.

We talked 1) about the possibility of having you here, at least for a year or so. Miss Lentschner has told me a few things about your plans and the situation in Jerusalem, and I think I am informed. In the meantime I have learned that, while he was here, Bake had a deficit and therefore I can hardly believe that a commercial agency which handles lectures on a business basis will be able to cover as little as possible of your costs. Another possibility is to motivate one of the "Foundations" to contribute to your stay (and travel expenses). I shall now try to inquire how matters are and will be in touch. It would be helpful if you could meanwhile inform me what the costs would be, especially travel costs. Clearly, if anything can be done, people will get in touch with you, all I can do is to prepare the ground. It is hardly necessary for me to tell you how

---

124 Translated from the German.

glad I would be to see you here and, hopefully, in the course of time, also have you in the U.S. for good.

2) About records you will hear from Miss Lentschner. She will hardly be able to send you catalogues, because the records (i.e., home recordings) are mostly made by people who make the recording machines; they then list the prices of the records on their publicity leaflets and sell the records themselves. Miss Lentschner has the addresses from me and will send them to you.

3) Journal. Together with many apologies, I am sending you today the contribution of Kunst, including music examples and photos. For months now, if not years, they were on my desk to be dispatched to you. My contribution concerning xylophone music from Liberia is ready, but requires some last corrections for which I haven't found the time yet. I hope to be able to do so soon, before New Year's Day. Included will be two photos and about 6-7 short music examples. I hope and trust that for the first two numbers or so you have enough material and that the missing xylophone work is not causing you any trouble. I myself would like to complete it very much, since in the recent past I have published very little. A package is under way to you containing various offprints and other matter. No other contributions are ready. To be sure, a huge mass of material has accumulated, not only Indian. One has prepared for us a Toda collection, and we expect also new material from South America and Bali! I hope to be able to provide you from time to time with contributions.

4) Bibliography. I have a card index which is obviously far from complete, but still comprises a lot since 1935. I also have gone over the last years' issues of Afrika, American Anthropologist, Journal of American Folklore, Musical Quarterly, and several more, have entered many items in my catalogue, and have recorded the rest, particularly in the bibliographies. In the goodness of her heart, Miss Lentschner is prepared to compile and type out all this, so that it may be sent off soon. As it is hardly worthwhile to wait for your instructions, I think we shall send you those items that begin from 1934 and were not included in the bibliographies of the Journal, and of course all those that appeared after the discontinuance of the Journal. Many of these items are probably in your possession and, as I said, these things are never complete. I do, however, believe that with the above we have a bibliographical nucleus, all the more so as for the last years I have missed very little of importance. After we shall have your ideas and instructions, it shall possibly be simpler to handle the matter

from here. I receive a great many journals, and naturally even more so our library at Columbia. Due to her lectures with Sachs, Miss Lentschner has a better opportunity to go through the items or journals in the Public Library. Even if you should find it impossible to incorporate the bibliographies of the last years into the journal in toto, you should at least have them. As soon as we have reached 1938 or 1939, it will be easy to continuously compile most of the stuff here, especially with the help of Miss Lentschner, whose helpfulness is a real blessing. In another week, we shall possibly be ready to send off the material to you.

5) What else might we do here or from here to lighten your technical burden?

6) Some years ago you had the idea of now and then publishing reports on commercial records. I have recently gone over the Indian records which are now commercially available, and would easily be able to send you a list and possibly a few remarks.

With the best regards, your
George Herzog

Herzog's letter makes it abundantly clear that Lachmann sought assistance, especially for his dream of the Journal, from colleagues who migrated to America – from those who were both acquainted with his work and able to empathize with him. It is hard to refrain from the thought that Lachmann might have achieved more had he opted for America in the first place. Lachmann, it should be remembered, went to Palestine because of the research opportunities the population of the country seemed to offer. He, of course, made a perfectly rational decision on the basis of what he knew. But, alas, he did not know enough.

Items 3 & 4 in Herzog's letter are of special interest as far as the field is concerned: They reflect (1) the variety of subjects which the field – not only Lachmann's journal – intended to cover; they reveal (2) the importance which the field attached to the collecting of musical materials of as wide a range as possible, and convey (3) the significance which the field attributed to a bibliographic nucleus – necessary for the comparative study of music.

As we already know, Lachmann did not live to see his dreams fulfilled. Nonetheless, he accomplished a great deal in his lifetime, and was never in want of appreciation from colleagues whose judgement he respected. His dreams, to be sure, have long been surpassed in reality. Even if Jerusalem did not become *the* center for the study of non-European music, the study of Oriental music now commands a respectable place – not only at the Hebrew University – owing to the seeds he planted. And comparative study of music has taken great strides, often under the newer (and less telling) title of ethnomusicology.

In retrospect, Robert Lachmann looms even larger than he did in his own lifetime. For it is *because* of him, and his likes – scholars who dared broaden our intellectual horizons as admirably as they did – that we were given a chance to behold new vistas. May his and their memory be blessed!

PART FOUR

FINDING A GENRE THAT FITS

Tragedy, Religious Drama, or History in the Making?

There is something intangibly dramatic about "The Lachmann Case," keenly felt, yet evasive. We know, of course, that the culture which he imbibed double-crossed him. We also know that the other, which he came to appreciate towards the end of his life, failed to absorb him. Betrayed and rejected, he emerges as a heroic anti-hero. Despite the severity of his trials, Lachmann continued to personify the Western ideals of civilized behavior to the very end.

Though outwardly groomed – attentive but reserved, committed yet rational, invariably polite and soft spoken – Lachmann underwent a sensual transmutation. Two opposite forces conspired, simultaneously, to effect this metamorphosis. Ousted by those who deformed the world he loved and respected, he remained inexorably drawn to its cultural attainments as *he* understood them. Betrayed nonetheless, he had to detach himself emotionally from what he believed he knew intimately, but, alas, not as thoroughly as he might have, or should have. On the other hand, though he never concealed his Jewish origin, to the best of his knowledge it had played an insignificant role in his life, until, of course, he was forced to learn otherwise. But what exactly was he supposed to learn? It certainly could not be religious belief, or narrow parochial considerations. It had to tie Jewish identity to universals, in order to minimize, as it were, the "cognitive dissonance" in which he was trapped. Luckily, he could adhere to his professional interests without guilt or remorse. While adverse circumstances hindered his original professional plans, the plans he was compelled to devise under new conditions continued, nonetheless, to be guided by the very same professional precepts. These were never compromised, nor had they become politically tainted in order to ease his load.

Lachmann knew, all too well, that some academicians, even among those who belonged to fields related to his own, went astray under National Socialism, whether inadvertently or intentionally. The German *Volkskunde,* for example, buttressed by Nazi folk ideology and Nazi conceptions of culture, lent itself rather smoothly to a process of Nazification during the Third Reich. Consciously or not, the *Volkskunde* helped provide a "scientific" basis for the mythos of Germanic continuity, a prerequisite to the conception of a *pure* German Folk. The Nazis, as we know, were eager to establish such a conception. In their attempt to create a new overall ideology of rootedness, the Nazis availed themselves of anything that would disguise *real* history and society.[125]

As far as Lachman was concerned, Comparative Musicology could not be so construed, despite its own commitment to "purities" of sorts. Indeed, the Nazi conception of Culture (with a capital C) went against the very presuppositions which guided the field, at least the one *he* helped promote. Of course, the study of musical traditions (including ancient traditions which reveal the origin of subsequent ones) also calls for strenuous efforts to reveal continuity and uniqueness, and to isolate the authentic from the non-authentic. Such studies, however, aim only at the characterization of different musical cultures, based primarily on elements which traditionally inhered in them. The "folk traditions" set out to broaden Man's understanding of the *variety* and *riches* of his musical expression, not to narrow its scope. Comparative Musicology, to the best of Lachmann's knowledge, was committed to unveiling what appears incomprehensible at first, ultimately rendering it more accessible. Rather than mystify the familiar, it aimed to *de*mystify the *un*familiar.

Comparative Musicology was in no position even to entertain the yet unheard-of idea that the past can be invented and that interested parties might actually choose to do so. To be sure, the Nazis were not the first to tailor their past, but the brazen way in which they went about it disclosed

---

[125] See Hannjost Lixfeld, *Folklore & Fascism: The Reich Institute for German Volkskunde,* ed. and trans. James R. Dow (Champaign, 1994). Also see *The Nazification of an Academic Discipline,* ed. and trans. James R. Dow and Hannjost Lixfeld (Champaign, 1994).

what others had tried to conceal, out of shame or guilt. At any rate, ethnomusicologists, like many others, had to deal, subsequently, with "fabricated" traditions. There is no want of groups, nowadays, who choose, for social-political reasons or commercial purposes, to invent their cultural past. This includes proclamations about a musical heritage based on limited vestiges or none at all. Much can be learned from the ways in which people fake their assumed musical heritage, for they disclose a great deal both about the "inventors," as well as about the music with which they choose to identify. Making this latent process manifest has surely contributed to the proliferation of such fabrications and to the ever growing finesse with which such manipulations are accomplished. While this remains a dangerous game, let's hope that we are better equipped to identify its players.

Lachmann was not surprised to find in Palestine a greater attentiveness to the study of Jewish music than to the study of other better known traditions. In fact, nobody knew whether a Jewish music could be said to exist. Indeed, could music, like some of the texts, have survived the dispersion? Could the music of the various Jewish ethnic groups harbor musical relics of a common past? Could current religious practices, based on ancient texts, disclose something about the music of centuries ago? As is well known, Christianity incorporated the psalms into its own religious repertoire; what about the music? Given the uniqueness of the locale, the questions were numerous, and many had already been raised by Jews and non-Jews alike. As we have seen, the need to view Judaism not only from a religious perspective, but as part of the unfolding of history, commenced long before it was endorsed by Zionism. In Palestine, however, it constituted an immediate challenge. Lachmann was in a position to relate to the challenge on purely professional grounds, with or without endorsing Zionist ideology. Whatever the findings of musical studies in the area, they were bound to enrich our knowledge of Music. Lachmann, as we know, spared no effort.

It is often the case that people become attached to their own investments, even when these continue to show signs of diminishing returns. Likewise, the more effort exerted on a task, the less the likelihood of relinquishing it, though it fails to materialize. This irrational behavior may turn, at times, into an obsession which refuses to recognize reality for what it is. Can Lachmann's persistence be viewed in these terms? Can it be called blindness? Not at all, for nobody ever challenged the wisdom of his professional commitment. Quite the contrary, his commitment constituted a response to those who were blatantly evil and cruel, as well as to those who were embarrassingly short sighted. Though each of these sides, each in its way, hoped to remedy the ills of the past, Lachmann was naturally more inclined towards the short sighted. The more he detached himself from the culprits, from those whom he increasingly failed to understand, the more drawn he felt towards their victims, whom he desperately tried to understand, though they were too busy to learn from *him* what he wished to impart to them. Fortified by new insights into the group whose fate he shared, Lachmann hurled himself towards a *"Liebestod"* – towards transmutation into a new spirituality with self-destruction as its highest rapture. The newly "converted," thus, departed from this world in true Germanic fashion. Even Wagner might have been proud of him. Most of us ordinary human beings only sense the aura emanating from Lachmann's departure. The atmosphere surrounding his death has a quasi religious character; it is permeated by Lachmann's devotion to what he firmly believed and unreservedly trusted. It is *we* – who know more about what failed to be apprehended at the time – who experience the aura the way we do. In retrospect, Lachmann's behavior, during the toughest years of his life, reminds us of those who are generally portrayed as impregnated and guided by something greater than themselves, such as religious heroes, saints or true prophets. Like them, he could not help but act the way he did, regardless of cost to himself. In short, "The Lachmann Problem" has all of the makings of religious drama. We feel sorry for its hero, but delight in the triumph of his cause. Since hero and cause are intrinsically related, the genre is able to increase the worthiness of the cause by attenuating the sacrifice of the hero.

To interpret the aesthetic import of "The Lachmann Problem" in terms of religious drama, however, tends to overlook the conflict Lachmann was forced to undergo. Though the conflict was imposed on him from without (it certainly did not emerge from within himself), he was, nonetheless, compelled to deal with it. The condition in which he was caught required, as we know, the unraveling of an intricate and baffling web, which involved each and every part of his entire being. Inflicted from without, with no room for choice, he was confronted by a situation that called for a new integration of self. Unlike Magnes's enactment of the fall of the mighty, Lachmann, by contrast, was destined to play the part of the anti-hero, who only posthumously emerges as a *true* hero. Whatever analysis one might apply to the personae whose interaction loomed large in our tale, we can hardly escape the tragic feeling conveyed by the tale as a whole. Indeed, it is a sad story, but it is of the kind which arouses our compassion in a special way. It makes us empathize with those who were forced to pay a price far beyond their actual guilt, if guilty they were.

Can "The Lachmann Problem" be viewed as tragedy? Yes and no. Tragedy, as we know, underwent many changes since Aristotle first tried to define the genre, yet conflict, transformation and, above all, asymmetry between guilt and consequence remain among its major ingredients. Since Euripides first challenged their conduct, tragedy has relinquished its capricious, irresponsible gods (whose blunt disregard for humans passed unrebuked by the classic dramatists), turning the essence of *each* individual into a battleground where right and wrong waver. Though tragedy entrusted destiny to the hands of Man, it was unable to give its heroes full control over the consequences of their behavior, for the world of humans is an interconnected world, in which individuals also suffer the consequences of each other's actions. Thus, regardless of choice, Fate still "lurks at the cross-roads." Like life itself, tragedy contains blind spots between God's justice and Man's will.

There is no shortage of playwrights who, while mirroring life, saw fit to compare Life to a stage. The stage highlights the roles played by individuals in relationship to each other within a given frame, i.e., it contextualizes their behavior. The characters derive their delineation from a process of interaction which compels each actor to assess and re-assess his own actions, anticipating consequences which he can never be sure will materialize. The inability to control *un*anticipated consequences, Shakespeare tells us, is due to the fact that "Life's but a walking shadow" causing the individual to act like "a poor player, that struts and frets his hour upon the stage, and then is heard no more."[126] That Shakespeare should choose Macbeth, of all people, to tell us that life "is a tale told by an idiot, full of sound and fury, signifying nothing" is itself most telling. It is so precisely because Shakespeare counted on our knowing that Macbeth *had* a share in his downfall, and yet...

It cannot be denied that in a man-made world people are responsible for both misery and delight. Logical though it sounds, the statement provides little insight into societal behavior, let alone guidance for individual conduct. Paul, the venerated apostle, who trusted God more than Man, saw fit to qualify his assertion "whatsoever a man soweth, that shall he also reap" by adding "let us not be weary in well-doing: for in due season we shall reap, if we faint not. So then, as we have opportunity, let us work that which is good toward all men."[127] Having presented men with a seemingly reasonable choice, Paul's addendum, in fact, deprives the individual of his ability to judge, in humanly conceived terms, the consequences of his action, even were he to follow Paul's advice. Man's actions, moreover, may not assure his well-being, even "in due season," unless contemplated from the start with the well-being of "all men" in mind. Given his attributes, the Almighty should have no difficulties with the ambiguities Paul expects ordinary mortals to overcome. Yet Paul's innocent exhortation leaves a great deal of guesswork not only for the skeptic, but for the pious as well. However, whereas the pious relegate the greater part of the riddle to God, trusting His judgement and benevolence, the rest expect History to unravel some of the puzzle, albeit in retrospect.

History, as we all know, is construction based on a selection of details importing signification. It is obvious, especially nowadays, that such constructions are never value free. However the historian may try, he can never completely divorce himself from his own time and his personal leanings. Since viewing the past in light of the present is inescapable, the unveiling of the past was invariably accompanied by constraints. Those who wished to minimize the distortion of the past were expected to provide

---

126 See Shakespeare, *Macbeth*, act v, scene iv.
127 See The Epistle of Paul to the Galatians (chap. 6, 7–10).

evidence that had a bearing on their claims and, above all, to resurrect, as much as possible, the *context* in which their tale transpired. Naturally, these operations are related to each other in intricate ways, leaving a great deal of leeway for speculation and persuasion. Nonetheless, such constraints lay bare the many factors that guide historians towards the conclusions they reach. More important, they enable other historians to take issue with both – the conclusions, as well as the factors on which they are based – in their own attempts to amend the pictures that were painted.

The past is constantly "in the making." Man shapes and reshapes life in a continuous drama in which the known and unknown interact in mysterious ways, leaving much room for contemplation. Historical narrative does not, as a rule, use the language of drama. Though it abounds in dramatic moments, it highlights only those moments that carry some significance for a general map of events. Indeed, on a world map it seems futile to designate the location of each and every town, however exciting those places might be. More limited maps, however, include that which more encompassing ones omit. On the historical map of music, Robert Lachmann was associated with a significant turning point in the study of music, as we knew all along. Yet "The Lachmann Problem" transcends the borders of that specific map, for it is, unto itself, a Tale beyond a tale!

APPENDICES

DOCUMENTS, LETTERS AND LECTURES OF
ROBERT LACHMANN

Appendix I

Personal and Professional Documents from Germany

Document 1

    Auf Grund von § 3 des Gesetzes zur Wiederherstellung des Berufsbeamtentums vom 7.April 1933 werden Sie hiermit in den Ruhestand versetzt.

    Wegen der Regelung Jhrer Bezüge wird der Herr Generaldirektor der Preußischen Staatsbibliothek weitere Verfügung treffen.

    Berlin den 19.September 1933.

        Der Preußische Minister
    für Wissenschaft, Kunst und Volksbildung

        Jn Vertretung
        [signature]

An

Herrn Bibliotheksrat Dr.Robert Lachmann

    in

    <u>B e r l i n NW 87</u>

    Altonaer Str.4.

<u>A IV</u>   Lachmann   3 a

<u>B 2 a</u>

Appendix I

Document 2

Der bisherige Bibliothekar an der Preußischen Staatsbibliothek in Berlin Dr. L a c h m a n n wird hiermit zum Bibliotheksrat an dieser Bibliothek ernannt.

Berlin, den 28. November 1930.

Namens des Preußischen Staatsministeriums

Der Minister für Wissenschaft, Kunst und

Volksbildung

Jn Vertretung

[signature: Lammery]

Bestallung

für den bisherigen Bibliothekar
an der Preußischen Staatsbibliothek in Berlin Dr. L a c h m a n n
als Bibliotheksrat an dieser
Bibliothek.

– U I Nr. 42442.1 –

Document 3

Der Generaldirektor
der
Preußischen Staatsbibliothek

Berlin NW7, den 25. September 1933
Unter den Linden 38

Tageb. II Nr. 1489/33.

⸺   Auf Grund der beigefügten Entscheidung des Herrn Ministe für Wissenschaft, Kunst und Volksbildung vom 19.September 19 - A IV Lachmann 3a - werden Sie gemäß § 3 des Gesetzes zur Wiederherstellung des Berufsbeamtentums vom 7.April 1933 zum 1.Januar 1934 in den Ruhestand versetzt.

    In der Angelegenheit Ihrer Bezüge erhalten Sie demnächst weitere Nachricht.

[Signature: D. Krüss]

Herrn Bibliotheksrat
Dr. L a c h m a n n

Appendix I

Document 4

Der Generaldirektor
der
Preußischen Staatsbibliothek

Tageb. II Nr. 2219/33

Berlin NW7, den 10. Dezember 1933
Unter den Linden 38

Auf Ihre Eingabe vom 21.d.Mts teile ich Ihnen ergebenst mit, daß die Pr.Bau- und Finanzdirektion in Berlin veranlaßt worden ist, Ihnen vom 1.Januar 1934 an ein Ruhegehalt von jährlich 3230,08 RM, in Worten: Dreitausendzweihundertdreißig RM 08 Rpf, durch ihre Hauptkasse zu zahlen.

Der Berechnung des Ruhegehalts sind bei einer ruhegehaltsfähigen Dienstzeit von 17 Jahren 215 Tagen 49/100 des Grundgehalts von 5800 RM und des Wohnungsgeldzuschusses mit dem Durchschnittssatz von 792 RM zugrunde gelegt worden.

D.Krüß.

Document 5

Muster 17 zu § 88 W.-O.

Berechtigungsschein
zum einjährig-freiwilligen Dienste.

Der *Abiturient Robert Wilhelm Lachmann*, geboren am 28ten *November* 1892 zu *Berlin*, Kreis .... Regierungsbezirk .... Bundesstaat .... erhält

nach Prüfung seiner persönlichen Verhältnisse und seiner wissenschaftlichen Befähigung hiermit die Berechtigung, als Einjährig-Freiwilliger zu dienen.

Behufs Zurückstellung von der Aushebung hat sich Inhaber beim Beginne desjenigen Kalenderjahres, in welchem er das 20. Lebensjahr vollendet, sofern er nicht bereits vorher zum aktiven Dienst eingetreten ist, bei der Ersatzkommission seines Gestellungsortes schriftlich oder mündlich zu melden.

Bei der Meldung zum Diensteintritt ist dieser Schein und ein obrigkeitliches Zeugnis über die sittliche Führung seit Erteilung der Berechtigung vorzuzeigen.

Wer den Zeitraum der gewährten Zurückstellung verstreichen läßt, ohne sich zum Diensteintritte zu melden, oder nach Annahme zum Dienst sich rechtzeitig zum Dienstantritte zu stellen, verliert die Berechtigung zum einjährig-freiwilligen Dienste.

Die Einreichung eines Gesuchs um weitere Zurückstellung entbindet nicht von der Verpflichtung der Meldung zum Diensteintritte vor Ablauf der Zurückstellung.

Berlin, den 10ten *Oktober* 1911.

Prüfungskommission für Einjährig-Freiwillige.

Nr. L. 207
Original kostenfrei. Duplikat 50 Pf.

Kanzlei-Formular Nr. 1.

Appendix I

Document 6

Geschäftsnummer:

8 6 Gen. V 1/R 397

Bescheinigung.

Der Dr. Robert Lachmann

wohnhaft in Berlin

geboren am 28. November 1892 in Berlin

hat am

mit Wirkung zum 30. November 1929 — seinen —

~~ihren~~ Austritt aus der ~~katholischen~~ Jüdischen Gemeinde ~~Kirche~~

erklärt. **Austrittstag der** 31. Oktober 1929.

Berlin C2, den 31. Oktober 1929.
Neue Friedrichstr. 12/17

Das Amtsgericht Berlin-Mitte.

Abteilung 86

Justizinspektor
als Rechtspfleger.

A.G.I.
Vordruck Nr. 57. Bescheinigung über den Austritt aus der Kirche.
Gesetz vom 30. November 1920 (Pr. Gesetzsammlung von 1921, S. 119).
Buchdruckerei Reinhold Kühn A.G., Berlin SW 68

Document 7: The Full List of Subscribers to the Journal

- 1 -

Joseph A c h r o n
    2631 Beachwood Drive
        Hollywood, Calif. U.S.A.

Üniversite
    A n k a r a
        Turkey

Dr. Henryk A p t e
    Ul. Bracka 7
        Krakow. Poland

Türk tarîhi tatkikcem'iyeti başkanliği
    A n k a r a
        Turkey

Üniversite Türkologi institüsü direktörlüğü
    A n k a r a
        Turkey

Verlag des A n t h r o p o s
    St. Gabriel
        Post Moedling. Niederoesterreich

Musiki muallim mektebi direktörlüğü
    A n k a r a
        Turkey

Dr. A. A. B a k e
    Santiniketan
        Bengal. Brit. India

Biblioteca de Catalunya
    Palau de la Generalitat
        B a r c e l o n a. Spain

Mrs. B a r d i n
    Beham's House
        West Carmel, Haifa. Palestine

Phillips B a r r y
    5 Craigie Circle
        Cambridge, Mass. U.S.A.

Béla B a r t ó k
    Csalán ut 27
        Budapest. Hungary

Appendix I

- 2 -

Koninklijk Bataviaasch Genootschap
van Kunsten en Wetenschappen
   Koningsplain West 12
      B a t a v i a C. Java. Dutch Indies.

Professor Dr. Gustav B e c k i n g
   Ovocný Arh. 5
      Prague. I. Czechoslovakia

Bay Halil B e d i
Musiki muallim mektebi
   Ankara. Turkey.

Professor Victor B e l a i e v
   Novinsky Boulevard 31, Lodg. 4
      Moscow 69. U.S.S.R. Russia

Mrs. Laura C. B o u l t o n
   Field Museum of Natural History
      Chicago, Ill. U.S.A.

J. S. B r a n d t s B u y s
   Wiragolnan wétan
      Jogjakarta. Java. Dutch East Indies

Professor G. B r e a z u l
   Str. Principesa Ileana 32
      Bucureşti VI. România

Dr. Manfred B u kof z e r
   Rosentalstr. 5
      Basel. Switzerland

Edwin G. B u r r o w s
   Bishop Museum
      Honolulu. Hawaiian Island

Dr. Rudolf C a h n-S p e y e r
   Viale Milton 17
      Firenze. Italia

Institut de Musique Orientale
   Avenue de la Reine Nazli
      L e C a i r e. Egypte

Miss Gladys C h a m b e r l a i n
   121 East 58th Street
      New York City. U.S.A.

- 3 -

Alexis C h o t t i n
   Inspecteur des Arts Indigenes
   Les Oudaïas.
       Rabat. French Marocco

Dr. Elsie C l e w s P a r s o n s
   Harrison, New York
      U.S.A.

A.K. C o o m a r a s w a m y
   Museum of Fine Arts
     Boston. Mass. U.S.A.

Henry C o w e l l
   Menlo Park
     California. U.S.A.

Mrs. Louise M. B. D y e r
   1 Rue Scheffer
     Paris. France

Dr. Alfred E i n s t e i n
   Monte Oriolo
     Firenze. Italia

E s t o n i a n Academy of Music
   Tallinn (Reval)
     Estonia

Dr. Henry George F a r m e r
   Dâr el-Salâm.
    Stirling Drive
      Bearsdon. Dumbartonshire. Scotland

Professor Dr. Karl Gustav F e l l e r e r
   Fribourg University. Switzerland

Professor Dr. Rudolf v. F i c k e r
   Schackstr. 4
     Munich. Germany

Mrs. Eliza M. C. F l o w e r
   168 East 63rd Street
     New York City. U.S.A.

A.H. F o x S t r a n g w a y s
   13 Princes Gardens
     West Acton. London, W. 3. England

Amedée G a s t o u é
    Rue Gambetta 25
        Chamart (Seine). France

Professor Dr. Rudolf G e r b e r
    Giessen
        Moltkestr. 26. Germany

Dr. Becket G i b b s
    99 Claremont Avenue
        New York City, N.Y. U.S.A.

Julius G o l d
    Bellaire Apartments
    1101 Green Street
        San Francisco, Calif. U.S.A.

Percy G r a i n g e r
    7 Cromwell Place
        White Plains, N.Y. U.S.A.

Otto H a a s
    Antiquarian Bookseller
    49 a, Belsize Park Gardens
        London, N.W. 3. England

Mrs. Mary H a a s S w a d e s h
    Room 250 I.H.R. 333 Cedar Street
        New Haven, Conn. U.S.A.

M. M. H a b i b
    Ministry of Education, Music Section
        Cairo. Egypt

Miss Eleanor H a g u e
    640 Hillside Terrace
        Pasadena. Calif. U.S.A.

S. G. H a m m e l
    209 West 14th Street
        New York City N.Y. U.S.A.

Professor Dr. Jacques H a n s c h i n
    Basel
        Oberwilerstr. 35. Switzerland

Dr. R. E. M. H a r d i n g
    4 King's Parade
        Cambridge. England

- 5 -

J.P. Harrington
    General Delivery
        San Juan Capistrano. Calif. U.S.A.

Professor Glen Haydon
    Department of Music   North Carolina
        Chapel Hill, North Carolina. U.S.A.

Dr. Mahmoud El-Hefny
    Director, Department of Music,
        Ministry of Education
            Cairo. Egypt

J. Herscher-Clément
    55 Rue Rennequin
        Paris. France

Professor M. J. Herskovits
    Northwestern University
    320 Harris Hall
        Evanston, Ill. U.S.A.

Dr. George Herzog
    Department of Anthropology
    Columbia University
        New York. U.S.A.

Mrs. M.W. Hinman
    353 West 57th Street
        New York City N.Y. U.S.A.

Max Hinrichsen
    c/o Novello
        Wardour Str.
            London. England

Paul Hirsch
    Frankfurt a. M.
        Neue Mainzerstr. 57. Germany

T. Hopkins Evans
    140 Edge Lane
        Liverpool 7. England

M. Humbert-Sauvageot
    5 Rue Jean Bart
        Paris 6^e. France

- 6 -

Java-Instituut
  Solo
       Java. Dutch East Indies

Istanbul konservatuari direktörlügü
  Istanbul
       Turkey

Dr. Karl Gustav I z i k o w i t z
  Museum
       Goeteborg. Sweden

Miss Adele T. K a t z
  277 West End Avenue
       New York City N.Y. U.S.A.

Mrs. Raina K a z a r o w a
  Veliko Tarnowostr. 12
       Sofia IV. Bulgaria

K e g a n, P a u l & Co.
  38, Great Russel Str.
       London, W.C.1. England

Dr. C h u n g S i k K e h
  Union Christian College
       Pyeng Yang. Korea

Miss Bernice M. K i n g
  1015 South Cedar Lake Road
       Minneapolis, Minn. U.S.A.

Staats-und Universitäts- Bibliothek
  K o e n i g s b e r g i. Pr.
       Mitteltragheim 22. Germany

Professor Dr. Fuad K ö p r ü l ü
  Akbíyík
       Istanbul. Turkey

Dr. Philaret K o l e s s a
  Lwów (Lemberg)
       Ul. Poninskiego 6. Poland

Dr. M. K o l i n s k i
  108 Rue Goffart
       Bruxelles. Belgium

- 7 -

Thorvald K o r n e r u p
   Holger Danskesvej 82
      Copenhagen. Denmark

Professor Dr. Ilmari K r o h n
   Helsinki
      Temppelikatu 15. Finland

Dr. Jaap K u n s t
   Hobbemalaan 53
      Bilthoven. Holland

Professor Dr. Ernst K u r t h
   Musikwissenschaftliches Institut der Universitaet
      Bern. Switzerland

F.C. L a t h r o p
   53 Pineapple Street
      Brooklyn. N.Y. U.S.A.

Mr. L. L a v e n è r e
   Caixa postal 66
      Jaragua. Alagoas. Brazil

Miss Dorothy L a w t o n
   121 East 58th Street
      New York City. N.Y. U.S.A.

Professor Dr. D.N. L e h m e r
   2736 Regent Street
      Berkeley, Calif. U.S.A.

Dr. Cajus L e p a
   Scuala Normala "D. Tichindeal"
      Arad. România

Miss Irene Le w i s o h n
   133 West 11th Street
      New York City. N.Y. U.S.A.

Miss Elma L o i n e s
   3 Pierrepont Place
      Brooklyn. N.Y. U.S.A.

Royal Asiatic Society
   of Great Britain and Ireland
   74 Grosvenor Street.
      London W. 1.

– 8 –

The Royal Empire Society
   Northumberland Avenue
      L o n d o n W.C. 2. Emgland

Dr. E. M a h l e r
   Tuellingerstr. 56
     Basle. Switzerland

Robert W. M a r k s
   Murray Boulevard at Tradd Street
     Charleston. South Carolina. U.S.A.

Miss Clara W. M a y e r
   66 West 12th Street
     New York City. N.Y. U.S.A.

M e s u d C e m i l Bey
   P.T.T. Istanbul radyosu
     Turkey

W.H. M o n t a g u-P o l l o c k
   British Legation
     Belgrad. Yugoslavia

Thomas M u n r o
   Curator of Education
     The Cleveland Museum of Art
     Cleveland, Ohio, U.S.A.
       Station E.

The Editor,
   N a t u r e (Macmillan & Co. Ltd.)
   St. Martin Street.
     London, W.C.2. England

Chanoine Prof. J. van N u f f e l
   Wilsonlaan 72
     Mechelen. Belgium

Dr. Otto O r t m a nn
   Peabody Conservatory of Music
     Baltimore. Maryland. U.S.A.

Dr. Helene P a l a z z o
   Via Palestro 95
     Roma (21) Italia

Musée d'Ethnographie
   Palais du Trocadéro
      Paris 16e. France

Musée Guimet
   6 Place d'Jéna
      Paris 16e. France

Musée de la Parole
   (M. Dévigne)
     19 Rue des Bernardins
      Paris. France

Rev. H.A. Popley
   National Council, Y.M.C.A.
   5 Russel Street
      Calcutta. India

Mark Potter
   414 West 118th Street
      New York City. N.Y. U.S.A.

Dr. Julian von Pulikowski
   Warsaw
      ul. Wilcza 26a. m.4. Poland

Mrs. Dorothy Quackenbush
   Killam's Point
      Branford, Conn. U.S.A.

Bibliothèque générale
   et Archives du Protectorat
   Avenue Biarnay
      Rabat. Maroc

Bay Mahmud Ragıb
   Musiki muallim mektebi
      Ankara. Turkey

Harold Reeves
   210 Shaftesbury Avenue
      London, W.C. 2. England

Werner Reinhart
   Winterthur
      Rychenberg. Switzerland

Appendix I

- 10 -

Mrs. A.M. R e i s
   50 East 86th Street
      New York City. N.Y.   U.S.A.

R e v i s t a   S e f a r d i t a
   c/o Dr. George E. Sachs
      Casa de las Españas
        Columbia University
          435 West 117th Street
             New York City. N.Y.   U.S.A.

Prosper R i c a r d
   Chef du Service des Arts indigènes
     Medersa des Oudaïa
        Rabat.   French Maroc

Mustafa Bey R i d a
   Directeur de L' Institut de Musique arabe
     Avenue de la Reine Nazli
        Le Caire. Egypte

Professor Dr. Helmut R i t t e r
   Istanbul-Bebek
     Yalilar Caddesi 16.   Turkey

Miss Helen H. R o b e r t s
  Box 56
    High Watch
      Tryon, N.C.   U.S.A.

Dr. Herbert R o s e n b e r g
   Classensgade 34^v
     Copenhagen.   Denmark

Jules R o u a n e t
   Ermitage du Rebiga
     Miramar-Supérieur par St. Eugène
       Alger.   Algeria

P. Theodor R u e h l   S.V.D.
   Catholic University
     Peiping.   China

William R u s s e l
   182 Claremont Avenue, Apt. 52
     New York City.   N.Y.   U.S.A.

- 11 -

Professor Dr. Kurt S a c h s
   New York University
      New York City. N.Y. U.S.A.

Bay Hüseyin S a d e d d i n A r e l
   Yenibahçe sokağe 3
      Şişli-Istanbul. Turkey

H. S a d e t t i n, Avucat
   Latif Han
      Galata. Istanbul. Turkey

M. S a l a h el-D i n
   Ministry of Education
   Music Section
      Cairo. Egypt

Adolfo S a l a z a r
   Madrid
      Goya, 89. Spain

Madame Olga S a m a r o f f S t o k o w s k y
   1170 Fifth Avenue
      New York City. N.Y. U.S.A.

Professor P. S a m b a m o o r t h y
   2/15 Harrington Road
      Chetput, Madras. India

Dr. Alfred S a r a s i n
   Lange Gasse 80
      Basle. Switzerland

Andre S c h a e f f n e r
   Musée de l'Homme
   Palais du Trocadéro
      Paris 16e. France

Dr. Hermann S c h e r c h e n
   Musikkollegium
      Winterthur. Switzerland

Joseph S c h i l l i n g er
   2 West 67th Street (Apartment 10 F.)
      New York City. N.Y. U.S.A.

Percy A. S c h o l e s
   Chamby
      Montreux. Switzerland

Professor Carl E. S e a s h o r e
   University of Jowa
      Jowa City, Jowa. U.S.A.

Charles S e e g e r
   New School for Social Research
   66 West 12th Street
      New York City. N.Y. U.S.A.

Tibor S e r l y
   c/o Dr. George Herzog
     249 Institute of Human Relations
   333 Cedar Street
      New Haven. Conn. U.S.A.

Dr. Harold S p i v a c k e
   Chief, Division of Music
     Library of Congress
      Washington. U.S.A.

Mrs. W. D. S t r e e t
   4 Ridgeview Avenue
      White Plains, New York. U.S.A.

Professor A.M. T o z z e r
   7 Bryant Street
      Cambridge. Mass. U.S?A.

Professor J.B. T r e n d
   10. New Quebec Street
      London, W.1. England

Mrs. T u r t l e
   Friend's School
      Broumana. Libanon

Douglas V a r l e y Esq.
   c/o The Royal Empire Society
     Northumberland Avenue
      London W.C.2 England

V a s s a r College
   Poughkeepsie
      New York. U.S.A.

- 13 -

Chistos V r i o nii d e s
 P.O.B. 871
  Babylon, Long Island
   New York. U.S.A.

Mrs. E.P. W a l t o n
 25 Washington Square
   New York City. N.Y. U.S.A.

Professor Dr. Egon W e l l e s z
 1 Cadogan Gardens
  Sloane Street
   London. England

Professor Dr. Max W e r t h e i m e r
 New School for Social Research
  66 West 12th Street
   New York. U.S.A.

Miss Mary W h e e l w r i g h t
 c/o C.C. Wheelwright
  344 Atlantic Avenue
   Boston. Mass. U.S.A.

 Jane L. W i n n e
 2065 Lanihuli Drive
   Honolulu Hawaiian Island

Library of the School of Music
 Y a l e University
  New Haven, Conn. U.S.A.

Joseph Y a s s e r
 7 West 83rd Street
   New York City N.Y. U.S.A.

Dr. Y u e n R e n C h a o
 National Research Institute of Social Sciences
 1 Chi Ming Szu Road
   Nanking. China

M. de Z a y a s
  "Rivoiranche"
   Le Monestier de Clermont
     Isère, France

Appendix I

Document 8

Staatliche Museen
Staatliches Museum für Völkerkunde

J.⸗Nr. E. ....
Bei Beantwortung
diese Nr. angeben.

Berlin SW 11, Stresemannstraße 110

den 22. Januar 1935.

<u>Bescheinigung</u>

Das Phonogramm-Archiv des Museums für Völkerkunde verdankt Herrn Dr. Robert Lachmann neben japanischen, persischen und türkischen Aufnahmen seine grösste und best klassifizierte Sammlung nordafrikanischer Musik (etwa 450 Aufnahmen). Im Rahmen der wissenschaftlichen Veröffentlichungen unseres Archivs hat Herr Dr. Lachmann folgende Beiträge gegeben.
1. Die Musik in den tunesischen Städten. Arch. f. Musikw. V, 1923. 2. Musik und Tonschrift des No. Kongr. d. deutschen Musikges. 1925. 3. Ostturkestanische Gesänge in Le Coq, Von Land und Leuten on Ostturkestan 1928. 4. Musik des Orients 1929. 5. Die Weise vom Löwen und des pythischen Nomos 1929. 6. Musik der aussereuropäischen Natur-und Kulturvölker 1930. 7. Asiatische Parallelen zur Berbermusik 1933.

Die geplante Errichtung eines Phonogramm-Archivs in Jerusalem läge auch in unserem Interesse 1. weil wir dadurch unsere Sammlung im alleinigen Austauschverfahren vergrössern können, ohne dadurch Devisen in irgeneiner Form beanspruchen zu müssen, 2. weil Dr. Lachmann ein sehr erprobter Sachverständiger ist.

Heil Hitler!

Dr. Marius Schneider.
Leiter des Phonogramm-Archivs.

Appendix II

"Liebe Eltern" – Robert Lachmann's Letters to his Parents (March 5 – May 1, 1932)

The following group of letters were written by Lachmann to his parents from his last extended expedition to Egypt. These letters, in their own way, constitute a multi-layered historical source. To start with, they represent a genre which is practically extinct nowadays, having been replaced by other means of communication, with styles of their own. They echo, however, a world beyond that of the genre in which they were written, for they refer in interesting ways to the immediate social and professional networks which Lachmann was part of. In retrospect, we discern some of the false calm that preceded the storm.

The letters contain professional observations about the 1932 Cairo Conference (in which, as we know, he performed an important role), short sketches of some of his colleagues, and colorful descriptions of the social habitats of the people whose music he set out to record.

The fact that these letters were addressed to his parents also permits a glimpse into the close ties and attentiveness that characterized enlightened German Jewish families. Above all, these delightful letters, written with a light but steady hand, convey the spirit of Robert Lachmann – the scholar and the man – more vividly than a detailed analysis can provide.

"Liebe Eltern" – Lachmann's Letters to His Parents[1]
(March 5-May 1, 1932)

March 5, 1932

My dearest parents,

My telegram from Genoa and the cards from Genoa (for Agnes) will have reached you long ago. The train journey passed very pleasantly. My partner

---

1 Translated from the German.

to the compartment was an engineer who, for business purposes, traveled with instruments and, at the Swiss border, promptly had difficulties with the customs. By the way, he also arranged for each of us to have his own sleeper compartment.

In Zürich I was welcomed by Hornbostel and Prof. Handschin who, together with his wife, had received me so kindly last summer in Zürich. We had lunch together in the station restaurant, but had to be in somewhat of a hurry, and I was just in time for my train (which had stopped for 40 minutes only).

Up to that moment we had had brilliant sunshine. On the way to the Gotthard Pass it got colder and the sky became overcast, and at the southern side of the pass, the train traveled through a dense snowstorm that kept going until Milano and further until Genoa. Genoa was in deep snow and the train arrived with a delay of – hear, hear – 40 minutes, that is, at about 3/4 to 1 at night. The hotel bus had already left and as I could not get hold of a taxi, I found a truck which, together with my baggage, brought me to the hotel recommended by Cook's and situated at the main square (Piazza de Ferrari). By the way, during the entire journey I had no trouble with my baggage, only in Genoa, when I was about to pass the gate, I was stopped because I allegedly had too much hand luggage. At this point I pulled out the letter from the Foreign Office I fought so hard to obtain, with the effect that the official became unsure of himself and said to his assistant: "He is a foreigner, he has a letter," and let me pass.

Next morning (Wednesday) I tried to change my money, first at the Banca Commerziale Italiana. There I was told that they did not take German money as, according to an emergency regulation, they could not get rid of it again. However, at the Credito Italiano I got it changed. Then I drove to the steamer, all that still through snow and ice.

The enormous fares of this shipping line are not justified. At least on this ship, admittedly an older one, there is no warm water in the cabins, and in other aspects, too, it does not compare favorably with the French ships with which I usually travel. The food, though, is "colossal."

In first class, the ship was so empty that I could at once exchange my (double-bed, but single-occupant) cabin for a much better located one. As it moreover turned out, the three German couples which were on board were traveling only as far as Syracuse, so that from there on the place became still emptier.

In Genoa, the ship spent hours to unload cotton and sailed only at about 8 o'clock (instead of 3 o'clock in the afternoon), a delay that was made up for by shortening the stay at Naples. When I woke up on Thursday morning, one could see the coast between Rome and Naples, the weather had cleared and, in the afternoon, when I used the stay in Naples for a short walk through the nearest alleys, we already had something like June weather. Upon departure, the gulf spread magnificently in the evening sun and above the Vesuvius floated the obligatory smoke cloud, creating a weirdly threatening impression.

Friday morning, upon waking up, I just caught a glimpse of the Etna, projecting as a white cone and, this time, quite cloudless. Then, as second stop, came Syracuse, surrounded by the sea on three sides, with its densely crowded, almost white houses, and with a stone wall abruptly dropping in to the surf. A magnificent view!

From this point on, the ship began to roll. At first, I stayed on the deck, but later on I preferred the horizontal position in which I remained until the main meal (at 8 o'clock on the evening). I felt the whole day somewhat giddy, but without getting sick, as is always the case with me in such situations. During the night, too, the ship was unstable, and since I had dozed all day long, I slept only intermittently. By the way, the drug Vasano has proved to be quite helpful.

Today the sea is much quieter than it was yesterday and I hope it will stay like that to the end.

For entertainment there is provided a band: piano, violin and cello. An Englishman who introduced himself to me and appears to understand a lot about music himself, rightly said: "the world's worst trio." This trio also accompanied the nightly cinema performances. I saw all of them, although they were of a dreadfully old vintage and, on top of all, were screened silently, even if they were sound films. In spite of all that, they constituted nice entertainment, during which one curiously enough totally forgets about the ship's movements.

Next letter from Cairo.

Be embraced,
Your Robert

Cairo, March 8, 1932

My dearest parents,

The last day on board did not produce anything remarkable. On Sunday the 6th, the ship arrived quite on time at Alexandria. The landing stage was hardly set up, when there appeared first a messenger with a telegram from El-Hefny who apologized for not having come to Alexandria, he would welcome me in Cairo. (He would have had to stay over night in Alexandria to receive me here; it is a 3-hour train ride.) Secondly, there arrived two men from Alexandria who were sent by the Ministry of Culture to receive me, and expressed their welcome. A picture, taken by a newspaper reporter, is enclosed. Then, they packed me into a car and we drove at first to Cook's, where I was informed that one of the three boxes with cylinders broke on the way. (Right now I was in Cairo in Cook's office and tomorrow I will be at the custom house, to inspect the damage.) After that they drove me to the school, or rather to the best known and most distinguished school in Alexandria. On the way one could have a glimpse of the beautifully designed seashore road. A visit of the school was arranged. Besides myself, another congress participant had just arrived, the collaborator of Baron d'Erlanger[2]; the Baron himself was ill and could not come. Language instruction is given by an Englishman and a Frenchman, both of which, being state employees, wear the red tarbush. After that, we drove to the railway station and boarded the Cairo train. The heat made itself rather strongly felt. Together with the Tunisian, whom I knew from my visit with the Baron, there came also a medical student who wanted to see Egypt during his vacation, and an American, the sole interest of whom were his expenses. The train travels across fertile, flat land; many villages, now and then canals or an arm of the Nile.

In Cairo I was warmly greeted by El-Hefny. Also present at the station were his brother-in-law and the President of the Institute which hosts the Congress. El-Hefny had rented for me a room in a German pension which,

---

2 French authority on Arab music. He made an intensive study of Arabian music history, translating many major theoretical tracts. The Arab Congress (Cairo, 1932) was convened at his suggestion.

however, I did not like (no running water), and so I arrived at this hotel which has only Arabic service. It is located close to the Institute, and the room is very cheap: 75 Mk a month.

Day One (Monday). The morning was devoted to the necessary visits. First of all, I signed my name in the King's Visitors Book, then, under the auspices of El-Hefny, I visited the Minister of Culture, his deputy and some other people of the Ministry, furthermore also the German Ambassador and the German Consul – all formalities about which there is nothing to tell. El-Hefny has an apparently good and relatively independent position: he is in charge of music affairs, that is, mainly music schooling and education.

Altogether, I have naturally seen a whole whirlwind of figures moving past. Very pleasant was the first evening: with El-Hefny, his brother-in-law, the collaborator of the Baron and a Syrian musician, first in an Arab restaurant, then in a café near the Azhar University in the Arab part of the city. Yesterday I also received your letter, little women, with the enclosed letter from Constantinople. Temperature yesterday evening at 9: 23°C. Yesterday I had dinner at El-Hefny's and, at that opportunity, greeted his wife who has had a serious illness, but looks very well now. The three little girls were also introduced.

I am now translating the title of the picture: "Dr. Lachmann (in the middle) upon leaving the ship in Alexandria, on his way to the Congress for Arabian Music. He is flanked by two Professors of the Ras el-Tin School, who came to welcome him." The newspaper is called Al Ahram (= the Pyramids).

More next time
Best love
Robert

The picture below mine is that of the collaborator of the Baron d'Erlanger.

P.S. As it is too difficult to distinguish between important and unimportant letters, I beg you to forward all of them, as you did before. As I learn from the letter, the post office has already been instructed to that effect.

March 11, 1932

Dear people,

Today only a short, summary report. First of all about the boxes with the cylinders. Fortunately only 24 of the 200 were broken, so that it is not necessary to order a new shipment. Altogether, I have wasted a terrible amount of time, sitting about in rooms and restaurants, and deliberating with El-Hefny on the program of the Congress. The money matter is progressing for the time being, inasmuch as installments of 50 Egyptian pounds were suggested, granted by the Ministry, but not yet disbursed. The final sum of 200 Egyptian pounds holds of course good. Everything is dragged out, amidst coffee drinking, mutual politenesses etc., exactly what I wanted to avoid. This, however, is not only due to the local oriental lethargy (with the French in Tunisia, it is true, things moved much faster), but one has to take into account that El-Hefny has to carry the entire load of the Congress preparations himself. After the Congress, the plan is for me to travel with him to the country. From what has happened so far, I, in any case, have drawn the conclusion that this expedition must be prepared long in advance, to prevent delays over days.

I have received a letter from the *Notgemeinschaft* according to which the professional committee has agreed to 800 Mk (instead of 1000), with the final decision being due in the second half of March. If that will be the situation, it is certainly gratifying. By the way, life is very inexpensive here. As I have already mentioned, I pay for the (very pleasant) room no more than 75 Mk. Food in the restaurant, as expected, costs me much less than I would have to pay anywhere for full pension. It is funny that, as soon as one orders a glass of beer, one is served, gratis, a number of small dishes with meat, vegetables, salads and, in addition, bread.

Yesterday arrived Dr. Farmer from Glasgow. In spite of his thorough knowledge of written Arabic, to which mine is altogether incomparable, he speaks only English and is as a matter of fact dependent on me. Fox Strangways' gloomy prophecies notwithstanding, we get along very well and, accompanied by El-Hefny's brother-in-law and Baron d'Erlanger's secretary, we spent the whole day together. First we drove to that part of the city which borders on the Nile and stayed a while on the banks of the river which is somewhat wider than the Seine. At the bank there moored boats with their characteristic curved masts, with the natives unloading their cargo while singing. Beyond the river one sees far into the land, as far as the desert and the pyramids, which even from the distance make a powerful impression. The visit to the pyramids themselves I am postponing until the others will have arrived. Afterwards we walked under the burning summer sun, against wind and terrible dust through the old part of Cairo, a semi-dilapidated part of the City, and visited a Coptic (Christian) church. After lunch we went to the high-lying Citadel. Immediately above it there is located a huge mosque. One also has a beautiful overview of Cairo, the surroundings and, again, the pyramids. Stop! Before that, the main thing: we attended the ceremony, taking place every Friday, of the so-called Whirling Dervishes, a ceremony that, having been forbidden in its homeland, Turkey, can be seen only here. We knew one of the Dervishes, the flutist, and got a particularly good place. There was a huge throng of foreigners and local people. The ceremony takes place in a domed hall, opens with, and is accompanied by, music. It essentially consists in that the members of the Order gyrate in a wider and in a narrower circle like planets about themselves and also about the hall. The impression is enhanced by the fact that they all wear long, caftan-like robes, and that these robes begin to flutter and, during the gyration, flare open, like dancers' skirts. Besides, after some gyrations, the arms, which at first were held against the chest in a crossed position, are then stretched out and lifted above the shoulders. Due to the incessant gyrations which, particularly in the inner circle, are very fast, the participants naturally enter a trance, and it is quite remarkable how they succeed to nevertheless keep their distance, and when they interrupt the dance – the ceremony commences three times – to stand still at once.[3] At the end, we and some other guests were received by the head of the Order (who, during the ceremony, sits motionless at the edge of the outer circle, while his deputy walks about between the inner and outer circle) in a adjacent building – with the customary coffee. The only jarring note was that among the instruments of the band playing

---

3   This colorful description of the Whirling Dervishes is one of the finest descriptions of the subject. Note that Lachmann incorporates this description in a letter to his parents!

on a gallery, the native violin had been replaced by a European one.

After that, and after the visit to the Citadel, we took a walk through the bazaars which constitute the oriental section proper of Cairo, otherwise European in its buildings. It offers the same colorful aspects, the same picturesque corners as does Tunis.

After this comprehensive bout of sightseeing, each of us went his own way.

Incidentally, I have received the registered letter with the Congress program, much thanks!

On the way we met several Moroccans who were on a pilgrimage to Mecca and asked me who would be elected President in Germany!

Embraces,
Robert

March 16, 1932

My dearest parents,

I intended to write an exhaustive letter, but am again able to spare a few minutes only. Since my last letter I have, firstly, received several letters with detailed news from the little women – many thanks! Secondly, the Congress has started working full steam. On Sunday arrived Mesud from Constantinople. His joy at meeting me was touching and he sends you his best regards. He also brought along his wife and, together, we visited the local zoo. On Sunday noon the Germans arrived. Hornbostel waxed quite enthusiastic about the journey and, on his first encounter with Cairo, went from one rapture into another. I have never seen him like that, Wolf, on the other hand, did not quite feel at home.

By Monday afternoon the members were practically all at hand and an official tea party took place in our honor in the garden of the Music Institute, in the presence of the minister and the deputy minister, and we were once again photographed. To my great joy, an old Tunisian friend of mine arrived, too, the Kaid of Mahdia, with whom I stayed once for three days.

The meetings began on Tuesday morning. I was elected Chairman of the commission which was to select suitable musicians and pieces for the gramophone recordings and to supervise the recording sessions. This involves much work and takes a lot of time, but is the most interesting part of all. Yesterday we listened to a group from Mesopotamia with a vocalist that caused the entire commission to time and again break into storms of applause. This was one of my deepest musical experiences.

The other Germans stay at the Metropolitan, where they pay per day for food (which they can't eat up) as much as I in 4–5 days. I am glad I don't have to stick with them continuously.

The outcome of the election is quite favorable, I assume?

Embracing you,
Robert

March 20, 1932

My dearest parents,

The last week was rather labor-intensive. About the Opening Tea I think I have written to you. This was followed by morning and afternoon meetings, in which the musicians were auditioned and pieces suitable for recording selected. I must also be present at the recordings that take place in a house opposite the Institute, to see that everything goes smoothly. In the evenings there are concerts to give also the other Congress participants an opportunity to listen.

In my commission (the recording commission) everything evolves satisfactorily. Hornbostel and the famous Hungarian composer Bela Bartok are also members, the rest mostly French. Relations are highly amicable. Hornbostel, his sterling qualities notwithstanding is very slow and (outside his field) sometimes somewhat childish. The Directors of the Congress appear to be very satisfied with the work of, in particular, this Commission.

Many thanks for the little women's letter and the newspaper with the report about Helfritz. Rest assured: as far as order is concerned, Egypt is to Arabia like Switzerland to Montenegro.

I am sending you pictures from the Opening Tea, taken from a newspaper.

A lot of Congress participants were in Heliopolis yesterday to listen to the Greek-Orthodox Service especially arranged for us. We also used this opportunity to take a walk along the edge of the desert and witnessed the sunset with its glorious colors.

Today in the afternoon I am going to see the pyramids in Giza. Life is rather pleasant.

Be embraced
Robert

Picture top right: Moi, Hornbostel, half behind him: Heinitz, Hindemith, Wolf, Mrs. Hindemith, Farmer, Messoud, the Minister of Education, Wellesz and Mrs. Wellesz.

Picture on the left, third from above: in the center (with map) Abdelwahhab, the Tunisian Kaid with whom I stayed in 1929.

March 23, 1932

My dearest parents,

We are now in the middle of the Congress, in top gear. In the next few days I shall complete the report of my Commission and present it to the plenum at the beginning of next week. French has asserted itself as the principal language (apart from Arabic).

On Monday the Germans and Austrians were invited at the German ambassador. Some other people were also there. Lunch was excellent, but the high point was reached when a German baron and Hornbostel for quite a while exchanged compliments in French, because each assumed the other to be a foreigner.

Yesterday we had a demonstration of a magic rite. Quite a number of women (some with children) were brought to the Institute and showed how amidst incantations, crashing drum rolls and the wafting of incense, demons could be exorcised from sick people. As the sick acted two young girls who, violently flexing their bodies, danced around the incense vessel and from time to time dropped to the floor in exhaustion, upon which the female chief magician blew water onto their faces and into their ears. During one of the dances, one of the "possessed" held out a fez to the onlookers, soliciting money contributions. Seeing that, Hindemith said: "With this rite I am familiar."

This morning we must attend the Coptic religious service; it starts exactly on time, good bye.

Embracing you,
Robert

March 29, 1932

My dearest parents,

The last days were full of events. On Saturday I finished the "preparatory work"; in fact this concluded the essential part of the Congress as far as I was concerned. With the formulation of the report on the work of my Commission, which had to be written in French, I had charged one of the French members, Monsieur Stern (!). Unfortunately, the actual writing had to be done in such a hurry that it turned out rather muddled. Thus on Good Friday afternoon I went with the secretary to a tea garden (behind the Aquarium) and revised the entire stuff, surrounded by a wonderful silence and enjoying the magnificent, sunny weather.

Easter Sunday we were invited by the Minister of Education to travel to Giza to view the excavations of the new, fourth pyramid discovered by the Egyptians. We were picked up in the afternoon from the Institute by two cheese trucks. I sneaked away from the excavations which I had already seen on the previous Sunday under expert guidance and, instead, visited with a Frenchman (Chottin) the interior of the Cheops pyramid. It was an eerily grandiose experience. After one has reached the entrance by climbing a few meters of outside stairs hewn into the stone blocks, one reaches the center of the pyramid via sloping shafts which are partly so low that one has to walk in a stooped position. Each visitor has a guide who makes sure that one does everything as should be. The passage ways are sparingly illuminated electrically, the rather steep ascents and descents in the interior being made possible by iron railings and wooden planks with cleats (like the gangways leading onto ships). In the center is the "King's Chamber," a huge room made of very few, tightly fitting, polished granite blocks; immediately below, accessible through a low, horizontal shaft, the "Queen's Chamber." Breathing is facilitated by air shafts included in the original design. The structure is 4700 years old; the impression is overwhelming.

After that we again joined the others for the official Tea that took place on a verandah of the Mena House Hotel. I was seated at the Minister's table (as Chairman of the Commission). It was all rather formal and decorous; a lot of Pashas, etc. The two guests on my side failed to show up and I conversed across the table with the Baron Carra de Vaux, a member of the Congress and an acquaintance of Mr. d'Erlanger. Poor Wolf had been forgotten in the seating arrangement and was furious.

The next morning the official part of the Congress was opened by a long speech, in Arabic, of the Minister of Education. Carra de Vaux and my friend, the Tunisian Kaid, responded. The first official meeting in the afternoon was that of my Commission, due to which fact I had the Chairmanship of the Congress (which, naturally, I regarded as an extraordinary honor). The report was read out in Arabic by El-Hefny, in French by the secretary of the Commission, and met with acclaim. It was unanimously accepted by the members of the Congress. It largely consisted of instructions concerning methods for future collections and recordings and also included the Commission's proposal to let El-Hefny and myself make a trial trip. This is finally the beginning of the realization of my plan. The proposal was today conveyed to the Minister and, I hope, will be responded to soon.

Later I had a conversation with Wolf concerning the extent of my vacation. He showed himself to be very fair: it is only at Whitsuntide that I must be back in Berlin. That was yesterday.

Today was the second meeting, over which presided the Chairman of another Commission. I am thus an "ancien président." As I plan to return via Syria and, time permitting, intend to add a few recordings there, I got in touch today with another member of my Commission, the "directeur des beaux arts" of Morocco. Sitting on the terrace of the famous Shepherd's Hotel, we had a look at the map of Syria, and he will give me a letter to the French High Commissioner.

The rest of the afternoon we (i.e., a few Congress members) spent in Heliopolis at the home of an immensely rich Copt. He served a large Tea and we listened to parts of the Coptic church music, performed by two (!) priests and the church singers. It was a repetition of the church music we had earlier heard in the Coptic church in Old Cairo. In the church, the impression was obviously stronger, but the singers were excellent also in the salon.

Mesud Djemil reaped great applause with his drum performance.

I must conclude. Many thanks for the last letter.

Embracing you,
Robert

Tomorrow some Germans, amongst them also myself, are invited to a soirée with the French ambassador.

I have just received word from the *Notgemeinschaft* that the 800 Mk have been allocated. Am very glad!

April 2, 1932

My dearest parents,

The news from you is rather meager. I assume, however, that tomorrow or the day after the post will bring some more. In the meantime, the official Congress, too, is almost over. After my meeting which, as I reported, passed without any objections, often rather agitated discussions took place in other Commissions, which mostly dealt with the introduction of the piano. The controversial issues were eventually passed on to an Academy yet to be founded.

On Wednesday evening there was a Soirée at the French Embassy which resides in a very beautiful house furnished in the Arabic style. It was a glittering affair; the Tunisians, Moroccans and Algerians who participated in the Congress as musicians, provided the music. On Thursday morning there was a reception with the King; enclosed is a relevant newspaper notice. Received were the Chairmen of the Commissions and several representatives of the countries. Upon entering, he shook hands with each guest, then everybody sat down to his left and his right and sitting, the King gave a short address in French, saying that he hoped in a few years to renew the Congress, if in a more modest composition. As oldest participant, a Jesuit father from Beyrouth responded, after which, again with a hand shake, we were permitted to leave.

In the evening, a number of Congress participants, amongst them Hornbostel and Wolf, left for Luxor. On Monday, Hornbostel goes home, with only one hour's stopover here. Wolf probably leaves for Jerusalem.

On Friday afternoon we had a steamboat excursion to the reservoir dam. We had magnificent weather, a ship especially for the Congress, and a Tea (with the Minister of Education) on the lawn of a beautiful garden.

Today I have penned down some remarks for tomorrow's meeting on "General Questions." In the afternoon is the official concluding meeting, and in the evening: Gala Opera with the King, for which occasion Sachs will deliver a speech.

Starting on Monday, I will intensely go about the preparations for my trip to the country.

The weather continues to be beautiful, not at all too hot, and the air is gentle, indeed delightful. In the country, all of this will be felt to an enhanced degree.

From Mr. Ricard of Morocco I have received a very warmly formulated letter of recommendation addressed to the Governor of Syria for my possible stay there.

Embracing you,
Robert

April 8, 1932

My dearest parents,

I cannot but begin with the Soirée at the Opera, which concluded the Congress. All the Congress musicians appeared, also Messoud, who earned rich applause. He left next morning with his wife and sends best regards. I shall possibly see him in Constantinople on my return trip. In the intermission, when I was sitting with Hornbostel in the foyer, the Director of the King's Foreign Department approached me to talk about my trip with El-Hefny. He promised to take care of the preparations. Next morning most of the Congress participants departed. Only Wolf, who is about to travel to Jerusalem, to friends of Mrs. Lesser, was still here. Together with him, I took a car trip to the step pyramid in Saqqara. The next day, together with a Copt, I visited the Patriarch of the Coptic Church, to obtain permission to prepare phonograph recordings of the chants of his Church – in which I succeeded. He looked like the Patriarch in the theater, 80 years old, with a long, white beard. He presented me with a rosary.

The day after, I had a farewell lunch at the Shepherd's Hotel with Abdulwahhab, the Tunisian Kaid.

To shorten the period of waiting for the expedition with El-Hefny to be realized, I decided to do some recording in the Delta in the meantime. A friend of El-Hefny's an official in the Ministry of Agriculture, took me along to Tanta, the major city of the Delta. Fortunately, they have here a pretty, new hotel. I was at once introduced to a lot of people. The agricultural inspector invited me to an extended lunch. El-Hefny's friend is busy organizing cooperatives, to which end he visits villages and took me along to three of them in which, without delay, through the good offices of the village mayors, musical performances were presented. I was therefore able to make quite a number of interesting recordings. Today (Saturday) afternoon, I was taken through the entire course of a wedding. The entire village (Sanadid) gathered in front of the village mayor's house, singing and playing until eight in the evening.

On Thursday evening, the evening of my arrival, I visited the "red-light district" accompanied by a police officer, to sample some music. It was interesting, but did not yield much. In the villages, in comparison, one feels truly transposed to antiquity, and I am therefore very satisfied with my stay here. The finale of today's visit to the village was highly romantic. As I set out to leave, the crescent and Venus lucently beckoned from the sky; the musicians with their wind instruments and drums played a farewell song, and the entire population, including women and children, walked me to the car.

Embracing you,
Robert

April 13, 1932

My dearest parents,

Tanta has in the meantime become civilized to such a degree that I can write in ink. Your last letters have been forwarded to me from Cairo – many thanks! I was very much amused to learn that Altmann's bellyaching on the radio – probably delivered in the usual lachrymose intonation – has revolted you to such a degree.

Here it is very beautiful, primarily after work and, after the noise of Cairo, rather restful. The music which I am listening to in the villages is completely different, but just because of that, very interesting for me. About the beautiful afternoon with the village mayor, when the entire village gathered together, I already wrote you. A sequence to this, which has taken place in the meantime, is less elating, but very characteristic. Taking up the offer of the village mayor to receive me again any time, I traveled the other day again to that village, taking along an acquaintance of mine, a pharmacist from Tanta. The village mayor was absent and I thought it very strange that, in his absence, it turned out to be impossible to listen not only to women, but, altogether, to musicians. After a while, a few boys came and told us that the mayor had arrived, which was, however, denied soon after. I passed the time by taking a walk through the prettily located village. When I returned, it was confirmed that the mayor had not returned and, indeed, would probably not return before night. Thus, nolens volens, we had to return. Explanation: upon my first visit with the mayor,

I had given him 60 Piasters as a remuneration for the musicians. This money he has in all probability kept for himself. That is the reason why I could not be allowed to see the musicians again!

Tomorrow I will presumably hear some music in another village. In any case, by the end of the week I shall be able to report on my future plans.

People are very kind to me here, especially the Inspector of the Ministry of Agriculture, one of the few educated people in Egypt who, at the same time, impresses one as being an outdoor type. He is also very anxious to make sure I will be given to hear whatever I like. Unfortunately, the village in which the above incident took place belongs to a different administrative district, otherwise it would not have happened.

Please tell Kurt and Lotte that I very much enjoyed their letter. Naturally I have no time to write a letter, but will soon begin to again toss off postcards.

Newspapers here have copiously reported about Hindenburg's reelection and are already releasing reports about the imminent elections in Prussia. What will they bring us?

Embraces and best greetings,
Robert

Tanta, April 15, 1932

My dearest parents,

I am sending you another few lines prior to my departure for Cairo, since I do not know whether I will find there enough time for a longer letter. From my present stay I am quite satisfied; I believe to have listened to the essential things. This I owe first of all to the kindness of the agricultural inspector (Aarif Bey) whom I have mentioned earlier. During the last days here he has acquainted me with a wealthy farmer who has twice taken me along to his village (Difra) and has invited all available singers and musicians to his home, thus enabling me to make recordings in all leisureliness. His four boys (12–3 years) were also introduced to me; in gratitude I brought them heaps of sweets. I even managed twice to see his wife, a fat, heavily painted person busying herself in the kitchen: the first time, when I was introduced to her, and the second time, when she thanked me for the presents. What I mainly heard were women's songs which, naturally, I was particularly interested in. The difficulty in recording songs with women resides in the fact that quite in the middle, and quite unprovokedly, they break out giggling. Still, I am satisfied with the yield.

Yesterday evening I received a telegram from El-Hefny informing me that the Egyptian government had granted me 50 Egyptian pounds for my study trips in the country. While this is very gratifying as such, I shall be able to get to the bottom of this decision only in Cairo. To be sure, this appears to be the answer to the proposal, accepted and forwarded by the Congress, according to which I was to undertake a study trip with El-Hefny, in order to teach him the methods of collection and recording. Yet the above answer can be seen as a refusal of the Congress proposal, as at least in the telegram there is no mention made of El-Hefny's participation. It is possible that he has hit on this way out by compensating me with an after all quite considerable sum, and has succeeded in getting his way with his authorities. He was never very enthusiastic about the idea of the trip, nor, apparently, was his wife. His preferred occupation is sitting at the desk. It is, however, also possible that now, after the Congress has already swallowed so much time, he could get no more leave of absence. As to myself, I am naturally equally glad to travel alone, especially when I find on the location as much cooperation as I did here. After I spent more than one week on the Delta, the Siwa oasis is too far away; also it appears to be too expensive. I will thus have to be satisfied with the Kharga oasis which can be reached by train, will in any case visit Luxor and stay a while in Fayoum (three hours from Cairo). Whether I will be still able to make a detour to Syria is a further question. I will inform you of everything in good time. My address remains Capsis House.

Before I forget, I shall add that Wednesday last week, before my departure for this location, I visited the Egyptian Museum in Cairo. Although I don't understand anything about archeology, this visit, together with the interior of the Cheops pyramid, was my most impressive experience here. To begin with, there are the statues from the fourth dynasty

– that is, statues 4600–4700 years old – which are unsurpassed in lifelikeness. Everything, however, pales when compared to the impression made by the discoveries from the tomb of Tutankhamen, which take up a substantial part of the museum. There is first of all the golden coffin of the Pharaoh, contained in a painted wooden coffin. The other objects, carriages, furniture, vases with pictorial representations, etc., defy description as far as splendor and exquisite taste are concerned. Every single item could itself serve as a showpiece for any room, and there are so many of them that I could not find enough time to view all of them. As this Pharaoh, the wonderful head of which is preserved in a portrait-like execution and as a mask, died at the age of 20 years, one can imagine the contents of tombs of kings that had reigned for 40–60 years. Nearly all of these tombs, however, were plundered by ancient grave robbers.

Finally, I also saw the jewelry and gold treasures of the museum, amongst which, too, the most ancient ones mostly surpass in artistry and taste everything of later date. Some anticipate Swedish filigree work.

Let that be all.

Regards to everybody.

Embraces and cordial greetings,
Robert

Cairo, April 17, 1932

My dearest parents,

Since I sent you a longer letter from Tanta as recently as Friday, the present one is only by way of short greetings. As planned, I returned to Cairo and have used the whole time on preparations for my further travels. Yesterday and today I was at noon with El-Hefny. He appears to be very satisfied with the solution, put through by him, of the affair – i.e., that I would travel alone, but at government expense, and will provide me with official letters of recommendation for the places I will go to. The plan is as follows: 1) Kharga oasis, 2) Fayum. First of all, I will go for a short visit to Luxor, for which purpose I have bought a white linen hat. This – that is, going to

Luxor – is a comfortable, but costly affair: 1st Class, Sleeper. My train leaves in half an hour.

Embracing you,
Robert

Luxor, April 21, 1932

My dear parents,

My enthusiasm about Upper Egypt I have fired off in a large quantity of picture postcards. Now still some more details. Connection to Luxor is very comfortable: sleeper, arrival at half past seven in the morning. On Monday I visited the antiquities most worthwhile seeing. First of all the Kings' tombs (which include also the tomb of Tutankhamen). To get there, one must cross the Nile by boat and travel from there by car to the hills of the Libyan desert. It is into these totally barren hills that the tombs have been sunk. On the way back through the Nile valley, one visits the Ramesseum, the ruins of a temple structure and the two Colossi of Memnon, one of which, in the past, has produced the famous sounds. Adjacent to the Colossi there is located a water bucket wheel (Sakiya) which I photographed. It is very impressive: in the noon heat, the creaking wheel, driven by a bullock trotting round and round in a circle. The bullock is urged on by a small boy by certain incessant shouts; with all this chimes in the babble of the delivered water, glistening in the sun.

In the afternoon I visited the large temple of Karnak. In between I paid a visit to the German consular agent, an ancient Copt with a highly assiduous son. He showed me his guest book and, upon first opening, I saw: "Paul Lachmann, Consul of Mexico, and wife, 1908." Very funny, isn't it? I explained to him the purpose of my journey and he at once invited me for supper, to let me make the acquaintance of all the relevant people. These people, whom I then met at an opulent supper, truly did their best, so that I had several opportunities to make recordings, especially of tunes sung by the crew on ships.

Today I received a telegram from El-Hefny, informing me that in the

Kharga oasis, my next station, as well as in Fayum, my impending arrival has been officially acknowledged. I can thus look forward to further developments with a tranquil mind.

Embracing you,
Robert

Kharga, April 24, 1932

My dearest parents,

I recently wrote from Luxor that this was probably the high point of my journey. But now my stay there has been surpassed by far. Since yesterday I am here in the Kharga oasis, and my journey to this place, as well as my stay here, are of an indescribable beauty.

I left Luxor shortly before the hotel was shut down. All the furniture except for the most essential had already been removed, so that staying there on the last day was somewhat ghostly. For all that, the owners, South Germans, were very kind and obliging. I departed from Luxor on Friday noon together with a French lady who came from Damascus, where her son-in-law holds an administrative job. Quite by chance he happens to deal with Bedouin affairs, which for me are naturally of particular interest. He could possibly be of help to me in Syria, but I am afraid time is getting too short and I will have to limit myself to Egypt this time. In any case, she promised to ask her son-in-law for some information for me.

After a northwards journey of 4 1/2 hours, I mounted in Wasla (Oasis Junction), a little railway station, a small motor trolley which I had to order and rent especially, as according to regular schedule, there was only one train to Kharga per week, and that at a time not suitable for me. In about a quarter of an hour we passed through half the Nile valley and, at sunset, arrived at a road house near the village Qara, which is located at the edge of the desert. A road house is a kind of a hotel of the smallest size. I was served an excellent supper. Apart from me, there were present only the caretaker serving also as cook, and the stationmaster, both Egyptians. With the latter I took a walk; he believed I was a physician and could examine his sick child. The transition to the night was magnificent, the colors at sunset, and then the starry sky with the rising moon, are indescribable. I went to bed early, because next morning I had to get up at half past four, with the motor trolley starting at half past five. A narrow-gage track leads 200 km. through the desert. At first a slight ascent through a bald, hilly land, then about 120 km. across the almost plain desert. A debris-strewn soil, as far as the eye reaches. The monotony was so overwhelming that I almost fell asleep several times. Along the track is strung a telegraph wire; at large intervals there are provided protective huts for the workers who must maintain the track and who greeted us as we passed. The fact that I traveled alone brought with it the convenience that I could stop the trolley from time to time, to take pictures. Towards the end of the journey which took five hours, one passes again through mountainous land, downwards, and then through a plain strewn with sand instead of debris, towards the oasis. Close to the terminal there is another road house where I stay now as the only guest and which, with all the simplicity of its structure, is managed like a first-class hotel as far as service and kitchen are concerned. The owner is an Egyptian who also owns the small road house in Qara. The local one has six beds. In the guest book were entered the names of many prominent people, e.g., Prof. Eduard Meyer.

From the terminal I was picked up by a government car. The governor (who, by the way, had gone to Dakhla and is not back yet) has, following orders from Cairo, left instructions to assist me. After I had changed, I went to the Government House, where I provided details concerning the purpose of my stay. In the afternoon I took a walk through the oasis, together with my host, saw the spring which supplies the entire district with water, as well as the village, the streets of which are largely arranged below ground or, rather, totally covered; it looks like a maze. Another part consists of houses built in palm gardens. When I returned home, a large part of the notables had gathered. I drank tea with them, and then began the singing and recording which are continuing in day-time today. Some old women who at first were rather shy and sang out of a separate room, produced a few interesting items.

Now, the work having been done, I am sitting in front of the house, under the starry sky, in wonderful quietude and the clear desert air. It is still so warm that I am wearing only a shirt and trousers. What I shall do in the next days has not yet been decided. In the second half of the week I will probably go to Fayum, for which I have also official letters of recommendation.

Embracing you,
Robert

During the recordings the room is always full of people – an event in their monotonous lives here.

Fayoum, April 29, 1932

My dearest parents,

To my great joy, I found today a large pack of letters (15–20), and learn from them that you are well. In the Kharga oasis I naturally received no letters, as they have a train only once every 8 days. For this reason, on my way to Kharga, of which you have in the meantime received my report, as well as on my way back, I had to use the motor trolley, which cost a lot of money. Well, Hornbostel has set you worrying about my health. I had indeed a small bout of indigestion but, I believe, because of the weather rather than because of food, with which I am very cautious. Yet it has been overcome, as you can see from my traveling the length and breadth of the country.

The last days in Kharga were very productive, yielding a great many recordings of women, men and children. The Deputy Governor was present every evening. Once he disappeared into one of the hotel rooms, to say there the prescribed evening prayers, which could also be heard from the outside. Take an example from this, poor old father. Incidentally, all recordings take place before a huge audience; as I already mentioned in my Delta letter, the music, but first of all, the recording attracts big and small. In the late morning of the last day in Kharga (Tuesday) I made a round-trip with the government car, first to the ruin of a temple built under

Persian rule(!), then to a churchyard of an early Christian community with partly well preserved murals on the church walls. After that, I returned to the village and visited the physician who had studied in Vienna and wanted to air his German. He showed me the hospital (the verandahs all protected with fly netting) and his garden with two gazelles. As all these visits were carried out in the car, I was fortunately only little aware of the immense heat which, at about noon, was 43°C! In the afternoon I stayed in the road house because of the recordings. A wind started to blow which kept on for the entire next day and considerably prolonged my return trip with the motor trolley. I returned in the morning at half past four (accompanied by the railroad inspector who, by chance, had come here for an official visit) through the desert. The impression was as stark and monotonous as on my way here. Still in the dark, the driver had to clear the sand blown onto the track, and thus I missed the Luxor-Cairo train at half past nine in the morning. I rested in the Qara road house and traveled then throughout the night, arriving in the morning at half past seven. During this night travel I found myself in a comical situation. Since I had heard nothing about the elections in Prussia, I tried the entire evening to get hold of an English or French newspaper, but without success. Finally, I picked out the main facts from Arabic newspapers letter by letter. Here, too, it is impossible to obtain a European newspaper. I can well imagine that you were stunned by the election results, but I nevertheless hope that one will be able to tack along.

Here, too, I had a letter of recommendation from the government to the provincial authorities. More valuable, however, was a private recommendation from an acquaintance of El-Hefny's to his cousin, a wealthy farmer living here in a village on the edge of the desert (Fayoum is as a matter of fact also an oasis). Yesterday I undertook a car trip through the region. The villages lie in an amply irrigated, fertile plain quite picturesquely in the middle of wheat-, cotton-, etc. fields. I visited two pyramids of which one was easily climbed and offered a panoramic view. This morning I went to see the farmer (after I had received the pack of letters). The drive across the land was magnificent; it is much cooler here, about the same as with us on a rather warm summer day. The reception was truly surprising: an excellent lunch and the most eager readiness to show me everything musical that the province could offer. After the meal (including water and perfume lavation), I did a few recordings with Bedouin, again drawing a great crowd.

I intend to stay in this beautiful region for another couple of days, then return to Cairo, prepare my departure and eventually try, at the Suez Canal, to record some eastern Bedouin, of which undertaking I am, however, not quite sure. In any case, I will write at most one more letter, as on Monday the 9th I am supposed to embark in Alexandria.

Apropos Hornbostel: his enthusiasm with regard to Egypt is very childish, as is his character altogether. People appear to him so tranquil and friendly, simply because he does not understand them or deal with them. Given a longer stay, he, too, would perceive that the unpleasantnesses which he believes to escape when living here, would return with a vengeance, and that there are even fewer pleasant people here than with us. Wolf is the opposite: dissatisfied with everything.

Embracing you,
Robert

Fayoum, May 1, 1932

My dearest parents,

In my letter from the day before yesterday I forgot to ask you not to forward the post to Egypt any longer, but to keep it for me.

There is no news; yesterday I again went to the country, having magnificent weather and doing recordings with the Bedouin. The farmer from the day before yesterday was again of great help.

Best regards to everybody.

Embracing you,
Robert

Appendix III

"Oriental Music": A Series of Twelve Talks on the Palestine Broadcasting Station (1936–1837) by Lachmann

To accommodate a large segment of the population, The Palestine Broadcasting Station had been broadcasting Oriental music regularly. However, as far as Lachmann was concerned, this was done with little regard for the true heritage of those the station was trying to please. Yet the listeners themselves, like the broadcasting station, were unappreciative of their untarnished musical heritage, however genuine, having become accustomed to popular Arabic music transmitted from the urban centers of the surrounding countries. Lachmann, naturally, wished to change their misguided attitude. He was also eager to enlighten those to whom Oriental music made no sense whatsoever, lacking the rudimentary tools needed to appreciate it *as* music, albeit of a kind different than their own. Lachmann, moreover, was set on driving home the idea that this music, no less than European music, merited careful study.

In the following radio lectures (delivered between November 1936 and April 1937) Lachmann tried to accomplish these several tasks at one and the same time. They may be viewed as a carefully designed introductory course, crafted by a great master who aimed to promote the status of Oriental Music, not only in the eyes of Europeans, but of Orientals as well. More broadly, it is an elegant exposé of the assumptions and logic that guided those who promoted the comparative study of musical traditions, stressing its importance. It shows how similarities among musical practices of ostensibly different societies are expected to yield answers to a variety of questions – some of a historical nature and others related to the idiosyncrasies that differentiate closely related societies. Thus, living musical traditions, primarily those sheltered from the West, are seen to contain possible vestiges of extinct civilizations, clues to the origins of musical practices, and intimations concerning culture contacts.

In addition, of course, it offers insight into the variety of functions that music serves and the variety of meanings that a given musical tradition imparts to those who uphold it. Eager to drive home the importance of his scholarly field, as well as to illustrate its present-day implications, Lachmann takes his listeners by the hand, guiding them gently through questions he himself raises in order to reveal the means and ways in which they might be answered. Only a person at home in both worlds, as Lachmann was, could have conveyed his manifold message with the kind of lucidity and elegance that characterize the following radio talks. They remind one of the occasional good fortune of undergraduates at certain distinguished universities when the most celebrated scientist in the discipline – a senior scholar who also remembers how to teach – is persuaded to offer the freshman course.

I
18 November, 1936

On first hearing a genuine piece of Oriental music, Europeans are invariably struck by the enormous difference which exists between this music and their own. Unfortunately, they generally interpret their first impression to the disadvantage of what they have heard. They often deny that it deserves to be called music at all or they claim that, at any rate, it must be music of an inferior kind, music on a low stage of development as against European.

These statements form a strange contrast with the Orientals' own ideas about their music. Music and song, with them, takes as high a place as with Europeans or, perhaps, an even more elevated one. This is true with regard to all the civilized nations of the East. Can we suppose that all of them, the Japanese, the Hindus, the Arabs, and so on, should deceive themselves as to the value of their music? Shall we believe that the same nations who have so wonderfully succeeded in art, in literature, in architecture, should have sadly failed in music, – failed just where they imagine they have succeeded best?

On the other hand, it seems strange that Europeans, while they readily and even enthusiastically admit the high value of other manifestations of the Eastern mind, should, on the whole, be unanimous in rejecting Eastern music. Music, as is commonly believed, has a more direct and spontaneous appeal than art and literature. One should, therefore, expect that foreign music should be appreciated more spontaneously than foreign art and literature. As this is obviously not the case as regards European hearers of Eastern music it seems logical to infer that something must be wrong with Eastern music.

But you can easily imagine that I refuse to draw this conclusion. I shall rather try and start from the other end. Let us suppose for the moment that the Eastern nations are justified in exalting their music. This would mean that Europeans when they disparage it simply have not understood it. Now, one of our popular notions about music is, as I said before, that music comes to us naturally and that we need not make any effort in order to understand it. We shall have to overthrow this cherished belief; we shall have to abandon the idea that music is an international language, clearly expressing grief and joy to every listener irrespective of race and country. We shall rather have to take an opposite view. Just because music comes from those regions of the human mind which are not controlled by language or analysis, it is hard to know as a foreigner what it expresses. So we have to ask ourselves whether, in spite of this, it may be possible to gain access to the music of foreign nations, and by what means.

But before going into this it may be worth while considering a few typical European attitudes towards Eastern music. One of them may be called the artistic attitude. Many European composers, in past and present, have taken a fancy to Eastern music, to its atmosphere, to some tunes or fragments of tunes. Their impressions, sometimes quite vague, have inspired compositions some of which have attained great repute. But all these products of an erotic style in European music are interesting as part of their composers' work rather than as reproductions of Eastern music. Couperin's Les Chinois may have sounded very Chinese, and Beethoven's Turkish March very Turkish, in their contemporaries' ears. But today we have come to know that these pieces have no resemblance with their alleged originals and even the more general erotic impression that they must have conveyed has faded away in the course of time.

It is particularly the French who tend towards spicing their music with a foreign flavour; think of Saint-Saëns' Suite Algérienne or of Bizet's Carmen. To most of us, Spanish music is known only through Carmen; but then, Spaniards insist that the music in Carmen is not Spanish at all. It is but natural that the creative musician in catching up scraps of foreign music should at once transform them into something else, something essentially his own. The very qualities which distinguish him as a composer make him unfit for helping us towards a better understanding of foreign music.

A different attitude towards Eastern music is taken by those whom I would refer to as reformers. If Oriental music is less developed than European, why not improve upon it and raise it to a higher degree of perfection? As a matter of fact, this has been tried over and over again. Harmony, e.g., is either lacking in Eastern music altogether, or only exists in a rudimentary state while, in European music, it has come to be an indispensable element, and is used as a principal means of expression. Many people, therefore, have undertaken to provide Eastern music with chords and so to add that lustre to it which they felt to be missing.

Another offence found in Eastern music regards its scale. Very frequently the musical intervals of the voice as well as of the instruments deviate from the European scale. In all these cases, Eastern intonation strikes the European ear as faulty. This difficulty as well has attracted the active mind of the reformer. He simply replaces the original instruments of the East by others on which the European scale is fixed once for all and he so arrives at forcing European tuning on Eastern melody. The most suitable instrument for both these purposes, for harmonizing Eastern music and for re-tuning it, is the piano; and really, during the last century and the first decades of the present one, with the rise of European romantic interest in matters Oriental, a growing number of Eastern or would-be Eastern tunes and songs have been published to the accompaniment of the piano or the harmonium.

These attempts at reforming Eastern music have an interesting parallel in the tendencies of a certain class of Oriental musicians. With them, too, the questions of harmony and of European tuning are predominant. However little they may have done till now towards building up a new kind of Eastern music, they have set their minds on having the piano as its representative piece of furniture. It is, however, worth mentioning that the only official body which, up to now, has given an opinion as to these attempts, the Egyptian Ministry of Education, has rejected the piano as unsuitable for the performance of Eastern music, and has strictly excluded it from musical education.

We cannot predict the future results of the various efforts and influences which contribute towards Europeanizing Oriental music. But the introduction of European harmony and tuning into present day Oriental music, if it is meant to raise it to a higher standard, certainly misses its aim. It is curious to note in what way the character of Oriental tunes is changed by imposing harmony and the European scale upon them. Above all, the application of European chords does not necessarily stress the main points of the melody, but may, on the contrary, detract our attention from them, and thus confuse rather than guide us when we try to understand its natural flow. An Eastern melody may, e.g., have the note D as its tonic. The accompaniment would, in this case, according to European rules of composition, have to strike a D-minor chord. But the notes F and A which belong to this chord may not be prominent, or may not even as much as occur in the melody. The accompaniment, therefore, would, instead of supporting the melody as it invariably does in European music, be at cross purposes with it. But even when the tune and the accompaniment do not actually contradict each other, Eastern melody is in no need of accompaniment. While in European music harmony is essential because it is conceived along with melody, the salient notes in Eastern tunes need not be stressed by chords; they are established in the course of the tune itself by purely melodical and not by harmonical devices.

This is an important point not only with respect to traditional Eastern music. It also concerns Europeans who try and compose unaccompanied tunes – for which there is a growing demand in this country at present. It will not do to compose unaccompanied tunes on an harmonic basis. If played or sung without an accompaniment they will always sound imperfect; the accompaniment, in such cases, is not superfluous, but is only suppressed. Instead of this, one should rather turn to traditional Eastern music as a model; there, we find everything that it is necessary to know about the construction of unaccompanied melody as distinguished from European harmonic music.

As to the piano, it is easy to see why it is inadequate as a medium of Oriental music. Firstly, there is the question of scale. In many parts of the East, the notes of the scale do not coincide with those to be found on the keyboard; and in the Near East as well as in India, the number of notes in use exceeds those offered by the piano. So, to accept the piano for Eastern music, in many cases means to merge neighbouring notes which the Orientals have been careful to keep apart, following, evidently, the demands of their ear and their musical sense. Nor is the piano capable of rendering all those delicate shades of tone which Oriental musicians manage to produce on their own instruments, especially on plucked strings.

No – we certainly do not bring Eastern music any nearer to our understanding by tampering with it. Nor does it benefit from it in any other way; instead of the real thing, we obtain a hybrid production, typical neither of East nor West, and shallow like ditchwater.

If, on the other hand, we take it as it is, leaving all European prejudice behind, we may hope to penetrate to its core. In no other country, perhaps, the need for a sound understanding of it and the opportunity of studying it answer each other so well as they do in Palestine. For the European, here, it is of vital interest to know the mind of his Oriental neighbour; well, music and singing, as being the most spontaneous outcome of it, will be his surest guide provided he listens to it with sympathy instead of disdain.

The opportunities, in this country, of hearing traditional music are most varied. I shall try, during this series, to give you examples of at least some outstanding kinds of it, and to mention, in every case, a few points that need to be understood. I hope that in this way you will become acquainted with the main aspects of the present day music of the Near East and with the principles underlying it.

But this will not be all. It is almost impossible to discuss Eastern music without being led into the past. In fact, this is one of its highest claims to our interest; through the mouth of a present day musician we may hear tunes which have charmed audiences of a thousand years and more ago. Thus, the study of the music as found here and now may throw some light on what has been said about music by ancient and medieval authors, and would otherwise remain obscure; and it may revive the mute scenes of music which have come down to us as the work of ancient painters and sculptors. Present day Bedouins, in playing the fiddle, follow rules established by musicians at the court of the early Abbasid Khalifs; negroes of the Sudan can correct our notions about how the lyre of ancient Egypt was handled; and who knows how much may possibly be learnt from Oriental Jews of today about the singing at the ancient temple in Jerusalem?

II
2 December, 1936

The three Yemenite Jews who will presently illustrate this talk with examples from their liturgical cantillation are sitting opposite me waiting for their turn and one cannot help reflecting on the strange contrast between these men who have been brought up in medieval ways of behaviour and thought and their present surroundings – a modern broadcasting room with its technical outfit. What, above all, may be in their minds as to the object of their recital? If they were told that they were being expected to perform what we call a concert of sacred music they would hardly understand; nor are they likely to realise the interest attached to it from the point of view of musical history.

As an introduction to the Oriental outlook on music and song I would mention an incident which occurred a few years ago. A friend of mine, when preparing for a research tour to Yemen, sought the advice of a number of persons who were considered to be authorities on the conditions in that country and on the manners and customs of its inhabitants. Among other things he mentioned his intention to carry a phonograph with him in order to record specimens of Yemenite music. The answer to this invariably was that music, in Yemen, was strictly prohibited and that it would, therefore, be useless to search for it and even dangerous to be found searching for it. Fortunately he did not act on this expert advice, and had the satisfaction of recording and bringing home a unique collection of Bedouin and other songs from that remote part of the world.

It is quite true that in Yemen as well as in other parts of the East a ban on music exists. This ban, however, does not affect everything that Europeans are used to call music. It only extends to certain branches of it, namely those which, from the point of view of Muslim orthodoxy, are discredited because of their connection with immoral pleasures.

In this respect, the three great religions which originated in the Near East have a great deal in common. Each of them has a long record of pamphlets on the harmfulness of music and theologians have over and again denounced musical instruments as prompting evil instincts and dissipation. I have myself, in connection with my work, come up against a situation which arose from this orthodox attitude. When I visited one of the Jewish communities on the isle of Djerba in order to study their Synagogue song they pointed out to me that I would not be permitted to make phonograph records. I first thought that the sacred nature of the cantillation was held to be incompatible with its reproduction by a machine. But what they really objected to was not the mechanical reproduction of sacred song, but the horn which was prefixed to my old-fashioned recording machine and which, in their opinion, gave it the character of a musical instrument. It was most difficult to overcome their scruples as they had never before tolerated musical instruments within their town.

In Europe, the moral prejudice against professional musicians remained alive until little more than a century ago – remember the treatment Mozart suffered at the hands of his archbishop at Salzburg. The old struggle against the evil influence of music was revived but recently when Argentine dances and, later on, jazz obsessed people's heads and bodies.

Still, the European nations, in a long and complicated historical process, evolved a new outlook on music. The various branches of music, however different their function in life and their effect on the hearers, came to be considered as parts of one thing, that is to say, of music in the widest sense of the word. We cannot stop to discuss whether or to what extent this development was due to the influence of ancient Greek thought and the Greeks' keenly artistic feeling. Even the Greek word music to which there is no equivalent in other languages may have contributed a great deal towards impressing upon us those qualities which are common to all the different branches of music. But the recognition of the unity of music would not have been brought about except for a material change in musical practice. Above all, the medieval church, endeavouring to make the power of secular music serviceable to religious ideals, came to accept musical instruments and the scales of secular music. Thus, the difference between the various branches of music gradually diminished.

With the Orientals, on the other hand, the different kinds of music have, on the whole, remained separate. Dance music, e.g., to them, is essentially different from the recitation of heroic poetry; and liturgical cantillation, again, stands by itself. They do not use a general term to obliterate the difference; and the instruments employed in one of the different kinds of music are generally particular to it and not liable to be transferred to another. A prohibition, therefore, of certain kinds of music or of musical instruments does not affect music as a whole; they do not think of music as a whole.

So we have to regard the various groups in Oriental music as separate just as the Orientals themselves do, and have to judge each of them by its own standards and principles. Europeans are only too apt to miss this point; they apply the standards of any one kind of Oriental music to another or even the standards of European music to Oriental, and wonder why they do not fit. It does not occur to them that they might as well find fault with a pen-and-ink drawing for its lack of colour or with a water colour painting for its lack of neat outline. As a matter of fact, different kinds of music in the East do not only vary as to their moral effects or their function in life, but also in their musical system.

All this must be kept in mind when approaching the subject of Oriental liturgical cantillation. It is hardly an exaggeration to say that religious cantillation, in the East, is not a branch of music which happens to be connected with liturgy, but rather a part of liturgy which happens to be chant or akin to chant.

Oriental Synagogue song supplies a characteristic instance of this type of music – if it is to be called music. Its distinction from secular music, either purely instrumental or sung to the accompaniment of instruments, is self-evident. Fixed intervals and scales, being a natural and visible result of the handling of musical instruments, are alien to it; the unaccompanied voice yields no standard intervals. Synagogue song, therefore, is not originally grouped according to a system of scales and whenever a

Synagogue singer claims that his cantillation is based on some scale we may be sure that this is a modernization due to the influence of secular urban music.

In the cantillation of the Synagogue the word is all-important. The text dictates the course of the voice; the melodic element serves to enhance its impressiveness by reducing the fluctuations of speech to a definite number of melodic phrases and cadences. Nor is the cantillation regulated by any system of musical metre. There is no strict time as we find it marked, in other kinds of music, by drums or plucked strings. In this respect, too, the text dominates; the musical time-values are in the service of syntax and rhetoric.

The cantillation is divided into groups which correspond to the different books of the Bible and other parts of the liturgy. Each of these parts has its particular set of melodic phrases and cadences which, used in the succession required by the text, constitute a melodic mode (in Hebrew, niggūn). Here, again, the preeminence of the text is worth remarking upon; the different melodic modes take their names from the books of the Bible and the other parts of the liturgy. Thus, the cantors distinguish a Pentateuch-, a Prophets'-, a Psalms'-, an Esther-mode and so on.

You will now hear some specimens of this cantillation. The melodic element of Synagogue song varies considerably from one community to another. On the present occasion, the Yemenite tradition has been chosen; it may claim a more than ordinary interest because of the early seclusion of the Yemenite Jewish community. This and the frugal conditions of their life have their counterpart in the simple and archaic style of their cantillation.

The first item is from the Song of the Sea (šīrāt ha-yam). Although forming part of the second book of the Pentateuch, this song, owing to its special character, is recited in a mode reserved to certain outstanding parts of the Pentateuch while the rest is in the ordinary Pentateuch mode.

  (Recitation)

You are now going to hear the end of the book of Esther which is recited in a mode of its own. The last verse is repeated by the community who, of course, transform the cantor's free rhythm into strict time.

  (Recitation)

As a third and last specimen of Yemenite Synagogue cantillation the beginning of the book of Proverbs (mišlē) will follow. Its mode is the same as that of the Song of Songs.
 (Recitation)
The non-liturgical songs of the Yemenite Jews which, again…[1]

III
16 December, 1936

It is, perhaps, indiscreet to talk about the preparations of a performance to those who expect merely to hear and, possibly, appreciate the results. But the present case deserves to be an exception as throwing some light on the nature of the music to be performed, i.e., the chanting of Oriental Christian liturgy. Indeed, it has been difficult to provide illustrations from this chanting. We should not be complaining about this. Anybody who takes a deeper interest in this kind of music will in any case have to go and hear it in its legitimate place, the church, instead of contenting himself with the isolated specimens presented here tonight which, at best, can be no more than an incentive to further study. On the contrary, the attitude taken up by the Church authorities should command our respect. Their hesitation as to whether their liturgy should be performed at all outside its own sphere and, if so, what parts of it would be permissible for the present purpose shows that they are far from considering their chant as a mere musical entertainment; for them, as I pointed out in my previous talk, it is primarily and essentially part of their liturgy. You therefore have to consider the present programme of Coptic chant as a compromise resulting from an endeavour to present its main distinctions without surrendering, to a secular audience, the parts held to be most sacred.

 A chief point of attraction in the chant of the different Christian Churches lies in its diversity. This is due to a main feature inherent in Christianity, namely, its missionary character. In proportion as Christianity spread over

---

1 The end of this talk is missing; it was nowhere to be found in the "Lachmann Files."

a variety of peoples these came to colour its liturgy with their own special ways of singing. So the liturgy, musically as otherwise, differs from people to people and each variety in itself would merit special investigation.

As to research into the music of the Oriental Churches, little has hitherto been done. We should like to know how much, exactly, they have in common with each other and to what extent their common or their separate tradition is indebted to Ancient Jewish cantillation; and we should, further, like to establish a kind of chronological order between them. But at present, our knowledge of them is too superficial for us to answer any of these questions. Particularly as regards the Coptic and Ethiopian Churches, we are unable to enter upon a discussion of technical detail. I shall, therefore, confine myself to some main points of Coptic chanting.

Gregorian liturgical chant, i.e., the chant of the Latin Church, is divided into eight modes. But this neat grouping of melody into eight categories implying definite scales is the final outcome of centuries of development, and traceable to a system of secular music. Gregorian chant, thus, has adopted a system originally alien to ecclesiastical cantillation. But even this European branch of Christian chant has never wholly succumbed to the secular instrumental conception which tends to dissolve a melody into the isolated notes visible, as a scale, on the instruments on which it is performed – a conception which has ultimately led to using these notes for a free and untraditional invention of melodies.

In the early period of Christianity, liturgical cantillation was not divided on a basis of scale, but of melody types depending, in their turn, on the different parts of the liturgical text. Nor is the division into no more and no less than eight modes an inevitable consequence of liturgical demands. While some Oriental Churches, such as the Byzantine and the Armenian, have eight modes, the Coptic and the Abyssinian Church divide their liturgies in an altogether different way. Each of them distinguishes only three melody types which bear the names of the three Masses to which they are applied; but these Masses and their melody types are not the same in the Coptic and Abyssinian service.

You will hear examples from all the three Coptic melody types. Besides the cantillation of the Mass, each comprises a wealth of hymns which, contrary to the recitation of the mass which is in free rhythm, are chanted in strict time and with the support of percussion instruments – a triangle and a pair of cymbals. The use of these or similar instruments is current in the rituals of many ancient creeds and the Coptic Church may simply have kept it up; still, this preservation of a pagan usage is remarkable considering the insistence of Christian fathers on the total exclusion of musical instruments and even of hand-clapping from the services which must be kept pure of any profane element.

It is sometimes claimed that in the music of the Coptic service Ancient Egyptian music in the times of the Pharaohs survives. This claim is based on the fact that the Copts themselves, or part of them, are descendants of the Ancient Egyptians. But at the present stage of our knowledge it is impossible to decide whether their use of percussion instruments or any other musical element in their service can really be regarded as a vestige of Ancient Egyptian practice.

We now pass on to the musical illustrations which, with the kind permission of His Grace, the Coptic Bishop of Palestine, will be executed by priests of the Coptic Monastery in Jerusalem. The first item is a hymn based on the mode of the Kyrillus Mass which is considered to be the most ancient of the three. Its place in the service is the time when the bishop or another dignitary enters the church on a solemn occasion.

(Recitation)

The following hymn is in honour of Virgin Mary, and is chanted in the middle of the Basilius Mass. This Mass is the most important of the three; it is performed at every ceremony whereas the performance of the two others is left to discretion.

(Recitation)

The last and final recitation is in the Gregorius mode. It is not a hymn, but forms part of the Mass itself. Unlike the hymns it is not accompanied by percussion. It consists of the priest's cantillation and the answer of the community.

(Recitation)

IV
6 January, 1937

Before going into tonight's special subject, the religious song of the Kurdish Jews, it may be useful to say something more definite about the character of liturgical music than on previous occasions. It is not enough to point out that liturgical song is essentially different from secular song. It is necessary to determine, in addition, the various features which make it so different. We can conveniently divide these features into two groups the first of which concerns the spiritual, and the second the technical side of religious song.

The spiritual foundation of religious ceremonies in general goes back to prehistoric conditions of life. In those times the usages of which have been preserved by primitive society, the salient feature of the cult lay in a magical ceremony intended to attract benefit to, and dispel misfortune from, the respective community. The sorcerer or medicine man of the tribe works himself into a trance by means of intoxicants and bodily movements. In this state, the voices of demons speak through him. After that, the community itself also takes an active part in the ceremony in song and dance. We must not imagine that this ceremony, in spite of the low standard of civilization of the tribe concerned is wild and unorganized. From the magical point of view, nothing short of scrupulous precision can achieve the desired effect of the ceremony.

Perhaps the proposition that there should be any connection between those crude acts of superstition and the solemn service of religion may be repellent. But this connection cannot be overlooked by students of the history of civilization and I shall try to illustrate it with a few examples.

The name of shāman which means a medicine man is believed to go back to the same root as the first part of the word Sāma-Veda, the name of the book which contains the text used for chanting the Ancient Indian ritual.

The elaborate curing rituals of a certain American Indian tribe are stated, in an ethnological study, to "involve in a most detailed procedure lasting at times for eight nights. A single mistake in the place, wording, order of the hundreds of songs included would render the whole proceeding invalid." Likewise, the Yemenite and other Oriental Jews believe that mistakes in the cantillation of the liturgy deprive the religious service of its efficacy and even may have disastrous consequences for the culprit and his family. This accounts for the fact that the office of cantor is but reluctantly accepted in Yemenite communities.

In primitive ritual the danger of evil spirits disturbing the force of the spell is obviated by the sound of rattles and clappers. This may throw some light on the use of bells, e.g. in Buddhist and in Christian service. It is interesting to think that the solemn peal of bells valued, nowadays, on aesthetical merits, should originally have served very practical purposes, namely, to keep away evil spirits from funerals, to avert the dangers of lightning and, on the other hand, to make a propitiatory noise on festive occasions such as births.

The demon who is supposed to inhabit the medicine man's body cannot, of course, have a human voice. This explains the strange and, sometimes, incredible tones in which the magic formulae are pronounced and, I believe, opens up a perspective far beyond magic ceremonies. The disguised voice of the medicine man is probably responsible, to a certain extent, for the vocal technique, so obnoxious to Europeans, of Oriental singers generally, a technique which has also extended to secular singing. You will hear particularly significant examples of this disguised voice on a later occasion when Samaritan priests will recite passages from the Bible.

Jewish religious service represents an outstanding instance of the ways in which primitive musical usages have been gradually transformed and raised to a high level. While the shofar has retained the character of magical instruments the reciter's voice has been moulded in accordance with the requirements of the complex and delicate structure of the Scriptural text. The Lord's voice speaks through Moses to the community pronouncing the Ten Commandments. In Kurdish cantillation, this passage is made to stand out from the ordinary mode in which the Pentateuch is recited; it has a melody type of its own which you are now going to hear.

(Recitation)

As to the technical side of cult music, some traits are universal. Above all, the peculiar way of reciting sacred texts cannot be classed under a common heading with the singing of ordinary tunes. Strictly speaking, there are no tunes; the voice travels along lines established by the textual structure; the text determines its point of rest and the places where ornaments are inserted. Therefore, the cantillation sometimes comes near the accents of the speaking voice, and is invariably in free rhythm. Only on certain occasions does the melodic strain acquire some of the autonomous qualities of a set tune. In Jewish cantillation, this is mostly the case at such places where the text changes from its usual prose into a poetical form. The most important example of this is the Song of the Sea in Exodus which is cantillated in another and more lyrical way than the rest of the Pentateuch. In Kurdish tradition, Deborah's song as well follows the melody type of the Song of the Sea, thus standing out from the ordinary Prophets' mode.

(Recitation)

In a similar way as the magic incantation of the medicine man is followed and contrasted by the song of the community, the various liturgies of the civilized world have, over and again, been enriched with hymns. These hymns, mostly sung to metrical texts, supply a welcome relief from the strain of the solo cantillation. Being sung by a chorus they are naturally in strict time; they have regular balanced tunes which are repeated strophically; in short, the prevalence of the word over the melody is here reversed.

In connection with the technicalities of sacred cantillation, short mention, at least, must be made of the curious fact that the textbooks are usually provided with signs of recitation. This is equally true of the Vedic books of Ancient India, further, of the medieval liturgical books of most Christian Churches and, likewise, of the sacred books of the Jews and Muhammedans. These signs have varying forms and functions. None of them are what we should call a musical notation such as the signs, alphabetic or similar to the alphabet, as used for Ancient Greek and for medieval European and Arab tunes; or such as European staff notation. Here, again, it comes into evidence that, in antiquity and in the Middle Ages, religious cantillation was an entirely separate thing as against tunes of a secular and instrumental nature. Secular notation is independent of texts; liturgical signs of recitation cannot do without them.

Among the signs which accompany liturgical texts, two groups have to be distinguished, one of them indicating the structure and the rhetoric of the text, the other – the neums of the Christian Churches and the numeric signs of the Sāman chant – delineating, roughly, the rise and fall and undulations of the voice. The Christian Churches as well as the Vedic liturgy use both forms side by side. The Jewish and the Muhammedan sacred books employ only one form; and there has been, at least with regard to the Jewish signs, a great deal of dispute as to whether this form has to be interpreted as a distinct musical notation or as a guide to the textual structure which, in itself, has evolved certain melodic modulations of the voice. The study of the Jewish accent marks, the ta'amīm, would, I think, profit greatly if an historical connection between them and the Christian signs could be established. But even at the present stage of our knowledge we may safely say that, whereas the neums can be considered as a musical notation, some essential characteristics of such a notation are lacking in the ta'amīm.

It has thus been shown that the various religions, in their liturgical chant, have some main features in common and that some of these can ultimately be traced back to primitive forms of cult. It might be attempted to establish a kind of chronological order between the different kinds of cantillation which now exist throughout the world, according to their more or less developed style. On the other hand, the distinguishing features must not be left out of consideration. There are strong points of difference not only between the chant of the various religions, but also between the chant of the various populations adhering to the same creed. In the case of Christianity, this musical diversity, as I mentioned in a former talk, is due to the large variety of nations which came to be Christianized. But Jewish cantillation, as well, has fallen into a number of separate traditions. The reason for this, obviously, is the dispersion of the Jewish people after the destruction of the Second Temple. It has therefore become a chief question for students of Jewish musical history, which one of these traditions may have kept closest to the original; but it is not yet possible to say the final word about this. Another question, closely linked up with the former one, concerns the different influences which have tainted the original. We know that, in the Near East as well as in Europe, Synagogue song has taken over musical traits of the nations among which the Jews came to live.

These traits are clearly marked as far as hymns are concerned. A Moroccan Jewish sacred song, e.g., cannot be understood without the knowledge of the system of the Arab secular music of that country. As to alien influence on the cantillation of the Bible, however, we must, again, profess our present inability to make definite statements although it is possible to say a great many vague things about Arab or Slav or German impregnation.

Kurdish cantillation, at any rate, has a distinct character of its own which, I think, exactly conforms to other characteristics of the Jews of that region. It certainly lacks the intense strain and religious fervour inherent in Yemenite cantillation. Akin, in some way, to the Babylonian branch of tradition it is distinguished from it by its straightforward delivery and its male robust vigour. The first chapter of the Book of Jonah as recited during the afternoon service of the Day of Atonement may serve as an example of this.

(Recitation)

In conclusion, a passage from Zohar, the chief book of cabbalistic doctrine, will be recited. Among the Kurdish Jews this book can be read in two different modes of which you will now hear the more ancient one.

(Recitation)

V
20 January, 1937

In the present series of talks this is the first one dealing with secular music. Its particular subject is Arab song and recitation accompanied on the Rabāba, one of the two chief instruments in use among Bedouins and peasants, the other being a reedflute.

The Rabāba is a bowed instrument, a primitive fiddle with a rectangular body which consists of a wooden frame covered with parchment. The instrument has only one string made of horse hair. It is held upright like the European violoncello. The player usually sits on the ground in the Oriental fashion and so does the one whom you will hear presently.

To European hearers, the peculiar charm of this kind of recitation is, perhaps, not easily accessible. The true way of approach is, of course, to let ourselves be captured by its genuine spirit and atmosphere. But it may be of help if we also try to understand its connections with similar kinds of music and to fix its place in musical history. For this purpose, we shall pass, for a moment, from this country to Europe and from the present time back to antiquity.

We are inclined to think of the recitation of epic poetry as a custom belonging to a remote past. In this we are right as far as Greece and the Western part of Europe are concerned. We know that the great heroic epics, the Homeric poems, the Anglo Saxon Beowulf, the lay of Hildebrand, were not delivered in ordinary speech, but were recited to the accompaniment of an instrument. In Ancient Greece the recitation was accompanied on a lyre or harp. As to Old English and German epics, we do not even know the precise character of the instrument. Besides, there are other important points of doubt regarding epic recitation. If the poems were not spoken in an ordinary tone of voice, what other kind of recitation was used? Were they sung? And, if so, to what kinds of melody? To sing thousands and ten thousands of lines not even grouped into stanzas means either constantly to introduce new tunes or to repeat one tune over and over again; the one would bewilder the hearers, the other fatigue them. Further: what part was assigned to the instrument? Were the tunes – if there were tunes – played in unison with the singer's voice or was the instrument only used for occasional interludes?

No satisfactory answer to any of these questions has been found in literary sources. Still, modern research in folk-music has shown a way towards forming at least an approximate idea of what epic recitation may have been like centuries and milleniums ago. In recent years, special attention has been given to the recitation of popular epic poems in Montenegro and the neighbouring regions. They, too, like most ancient epic poems, consist of thousands of lines not grouped into stanzas; the normal duration is three quarters of an hour. The poems have a heroic character; they express the mental attitude of feudalism, thus leading us back to conditions of life prior to urban civilization and similar to those in which ancient epic poetry originated. These conditions are, obviously, indispensable for producing poetry of this kind and for keeping it alive. Since modern civilization has begun to penetrate even into this remote corner of Europe the practice of epic recitation is rapidly dying out there, or is undergoing reforms – which practically means the same.

Epic poetry, in Montenegro, is neither sung nor spoken; it is difficult to find the adequate word for the way in which it is delivered. The recitation is distinguished from ordinary speech in the first place by the movement of the voice being restricted to a small number of more or less definite notes, mostly five. Moreover, the voice is highly strained; the reciter makes use of what, on a former occasion, had been called a disguised voice.

You may remember that, on that occasion, the disguised voice was mentioned as one of the characteristics of magical incantation which passed into ritual service and even into secular song. In this as well as in other respects, epic recitation as represented by Balkan singers can be shown to be related to sacred cantillation. Other features common to both are the close dependence of the melodic structure on the text, the strict limitation to a few melodic turns and cadences and, above all, the fact that in both cases a single person, priest or poet, keeps a large audience spellbound.

On the other hand we must be careful not to obliterate the difference between liturgical and epic recitation. The textual difference between liturgical prose and epic metre results, musically, in a contrast between free rhythm and unequal divisions as against a more or less regular sequence of stressed and unstressed notes. Another important distinction lies in the fact that while sacred cantillation is purely vocal epic poems are usually recited to the accompaniment of an instrument.

In Montenegro, the accompanying instrument is the Gusle, a bowed instrument which is distinguished from the Arab Rabāba mainly through the form of its wooden body, an elliptical bowl covered with parchment. The five notes of the recitation are produced on the open string and by the four fingers excluding the thumb. The places where the fingers stop the string are not indicated by frets nor do they yield rational tones and semi-tones. All the notes are used in the course of one recitation; but only four are substantive while the ringfinger always has a subordinate function.

In recent times, efforts are being made to reform this scale by substituting intervals of the diatonic scale for the irrational ones of popular tradition. The effect of this reform shows how closely the traditional scale which, to a modern European ear, sounds out of tune, is bound up with the epic style. The reformed scale distorts the character of the recitation and, as a student of it has rightly remarked, degrades the reciters of heroic feats to village tenors.

The function of the Gusle consists not only in supporting the voice, but also in supplying a prelude and interludes. The prelude is a feature common to all Oriental music working up both the player's and his hearers' minds to the spirit of the recitation to come; we shall have to deal with it at greater length in connection with urban music. The interludes are generally short; they serve to stress the metrical divisions, mostly between one verse and another and, at the same time, to give the reciter breathing space.

Arab literature, from pre-Islamic times onward, does not include epic poems. In spite of this, we are entitled to place the practice of singing to the Rabāba side by side with the epic recitation in Montenegro. The technique and function of the Rabāba coincide, on most points, exactly with those of the Gusle. Before going into details of this practice I want to let you hear a specimen of it. The singer and player, on this occasion, is Bağis Hanna Ma'addi, a peasant from Taiba in the Ramallah district. He will first sing one of the poems which storytellers insert into their narratives. In order to be able to appreciate recitations of this kind it is, of course, indispensable to understand the meaning and context of the poem. These may, in the present case, be summarized as follows.

For eight years a feud was carried on between two Bedouin tribes. One of the two leaders planned to take possession of a place then in the other's hand. The place, represented as a bride, was given liberty to choose between them. The poem expresses the bride's answer in which she fervently favours her actual owner.

(Recitation)

In this form of song, exactly the same notes are used on the Rabāba as those which constitute the scale of the Gusle. The ringfinger, used merely as a passing note on the Gusle, is here left out altogether.

You will now hear another form of recitation which, on certain points, contrasts with the former one. This song as well is connected with a story. A Bedouin chief has married a girl belonging to a hostile tribe. After a happy but short period of married life she dies and he spends every day of

the year following her death in composing poems expressing his poignant grief. This is one of them:
    (Recitation)

Unlike the former recitation the present one is in free rhythm. They also differ as to their scale. The ringfinger, formerly in disuse, has come into prominence and the note of the middlefinger, formerly a substantive note, has now dropped out.

For this alternative use of the middle- and the ringfinger which is the salient point of the present system of Rabāba playing, the Gusle presents no analogy. We have reason to believe that it represents a later stage of the Rabāba practice, and has to be attributed to the influence of an urban system of scale which was practised on the lute before the tenth century and which is known to us chiefly through indications in the Book of Songs, the Kitāb al-aghānī of Abū l-Farag al-Isbahānī. The prominence of the middlefinger would thus be the original stage during which the Rabāba was in total agreement with the Gusle.

Thus some light may have been thrown on Ancient epic recitation through present day practice. It is not proposed that they are identical. Instruments like the Gusle and the Rabāba are certainly not the same as those that were in the hands of Ancient Greek or Western reciters; the fiddle probably came from Central Asia and did not appear in the Near East before the later part of the first millenium after Christ. Yet the way in which epic poems are recited in the Balkans nowadays supplies a possible answer to the question as to how they may have been recited elsewhere in the far past. At any rate we have no other answer to give and no reason to reject the one which offers itself.

The Arab and Balkan practices of recitation are linked up by the striking similarity in the form and handling of the respective instruments, the Rabāba and the Gusle. It is quite possible that there is an historical connection between them. The fiddle may have been brought by wandering tribes from Central Asia as far as the Balkans, and its original practice preserved there whereas the Arabs, after taking it over from them, adapted it to their own purposes. The recitation to the Rabāba, owing to the lyrical character of the poems recited, has to be set apart from epic recitation proper; but it still belongs to the same atmosphere of heroic feats and passions. The mental attitude from which it proceeds as well as the musical system which it preserves make it an invaluable inheritance of the past, all the more so as there is reason to doubt whether it will survive the growing influx of modern civilization.

VI
3 February, 1937

A survey of religious music in the Near East which did not include Samaritan cantillation would omit one of its most remarkable aspects. The importance of this type of religious chant is out of all proportion with the very small number of those who are keeping it alive – members of a community which numbers less than 200 persons. In trying to find out what makes Samaritan sacred music so interesting we shall have to ask what distinguishes it from the music of other Oriental liturgies, Jewish, Christian, and Muhammedan.

The Samaritans claim that their present cantillation of the Pentateuch has been preserved unchanged from antiquity like all the rest of their customs and traditions. With all due reserve towards claims of this kind – which are raised rather too frequently among Oriental nations – we must admit that the Samaritan claim carries a great deal of conviction. The Samaritans are a mixed population consisting of Jews who had remained in Palestine after the main bulk of the Jewish people had been exiled to Babylon, and of colonists who had immigrated from Assyria. Ever since their fatal dispute with the Jews after the Babylonian exile, the Samaritans have kept strictly to themselves. With the exception of a small Jewish group they are the only people who have inhabited the country from that ancient period down to the present day. They were not influenced, to any appreciable extent, by the nations who came to dominate the country after the dispersion of the Jews. Even the Arabs whose language they took over for every day use did not cause any substantial change in their manner of life. They still scrupulously observe the teachings of their only sacred book, the Pentateuch. They still use the ancient Hebrew script, and still perform their ancient religious ceremonies, above all, their offerings on

Mount Gerizim, on the eve of Passover. Their strict seclusion, maintained almost to the point of self-extinction, has made them easily distinguishable from any other group of the population of Palestine; their outward appearance, tall build, bearded faces, priestly deportment, cannot be mistaken.

The same can be said of their chant. You will presently hear three representative performers of it: the High Priest of the community, Taufiq Kohen, his brother Ibrahim Kohen, and Yishaq Amran Kohen, the son of the former High Priest.

When I first heard Samaritan cantillation I was reminded of a certain Englishman's impression of the Japanese Nō, the most ancient form of Japanese drama. There, too, an unbroken tradition is being kept up to the present day by singers and actors who, by birth or adoption, belong to the families of those who originated the play. This Englishman says that his first reaction to the extraordinary way in which the actors used their voices was an almost irresistible desire to burst out laughing. But, having, of course, to suppress this impulse he felt, during the next half hour or so, how the recitation which at first had seemed to be nothing but a challenge to common sense, slowly grew upon him until he sat listening to it in a kind of quiet rapture like the Japanese themselves. This result, he thinks, was due to the unswerving consistency with which the actors pursued their manner of singing, thus creating a sphere of expression with a reality of its own, however unreal it may appear to us.

It is, perhaps, useful to remember this account of Nō chanting when first hearing Samaritan recitation – the more so because there is not sufficient time now to let it exercise its own full effect. You will first hear a fragment of the Song of the Sea from Exodus. But you will find it difficult to follow the recitation of the text. Nearly every word is drawn out to considerable length by means of expletives – a device to be found also in Ancient Indian cantillation.

(Recitation)

You will agree with me in thinking that this style of recitation sounds highly archaic. How can we verify a general statement of this kind? You may remember that, on a former occasion, I drew your attention to various points of relation, spiritual as well as technical, between the highly developed liturgy of civilized nations and the magic ritual of primitive communities. Now, Samaritan cantillation, more than Jewish, Christian, and Muhammedan, is apt to establish this relationship on a musical basis. The sorcerer or medicine man, in shamanic ritual, pronounces magic formulae for the cure of the sick and for bringing about other desired effects. On these occasions, he works himself up into a state of ecstasy; his soul is supposed to leave his body and to communicate with good and evil spirits and, at a certain stage of his trance, he becomes possessed with a demon who takes the place of his soul during its absence. His voice seems to illustrate the whole process. It ranges from a monotonous recitation to uncanny outcries; and at times, it really seems to belong to a demon rather than to a human being.

Among civilized nations, the nearest approach to magic chanting is found in the Japanese Nō drama and in Samaritan cantillation. In the Nō drama, the connection with magic modes of expression is confirmed by the frequent presence of ghosts and demons among the dramatis personae and by the resemblance of certain scenes to magic ceremonies. [But both here and in Samaritan cantillation, the magic style of chanting, if we may use this term, has been purified, not only as regards vocal technique, but also in that it has been subjected to a system.]

In both cases, the system establishes a definite number of melodic phrases or modulations closely linked up with the text. Leaving the Nō chant aside, we find that the Samaritan system assigns the different turns of the voice to different parts of the textual structure. [All those striking characteristics of the cantillation, those shakes, glides, sudden stresses, and sudden lapses into ordinary speech which, at first hearing, seem to be spontaneous are, in reality, made to respond and to lend colour to various stereotyped properties inherent in the syntax, rhetoric, and emotional character of the liturgical text.] Each of these ten properties has its special name, and is marked by a special sign; and the names give us the exact meaning of the musical sounds or groups of sounds which correspond to them. Some of the names, like conjunction and separation, simply point to structural qualities; others, as, e.g., astonishment, supplication, and exasperation, refer to the contents.

This system, evidently, places Samaritan cantillation in the immediate neighbourhood of Jewish cantillation – which, considering their close historical connection, is precisely what we should expect. The Jewish system, as well, establishes a restricted number of melodic phrases, and assigns them to certain points of the text; and the Samaritan recitation signs correspond, of course, to the Jewish accent marks, the ta'amim, which they resemble both by their names and graphically.

The similarity of the two systems can be followed up still further. Just like Jewish cantillation, Samaritan as well discerns a number of melodic modes. In Jewish liturgy, each of the modes or neginoth belongs to a special book, or group of books, of the Bible. The Samaritan scriptural canon includes only the Pentateuch; accordingly, all their eleven modes refer to this one book. Each of them is used on a different occasion, one, e.g., on ordinary Sabbaths, four others at different hours of the Day of Atonement, one for funerals, one on joyous occasions, and so on. The different melodic modes, therefore, represent different moods; but, for a foreign listener, it is difficult, if not impossible, to recognize these moods from the character of the music.

Every liturgical reading is preceded by the recitation of two lines from Moses' song in Deuteronomy; in this recitation, the character of every melodic modes is reduced to a concise formula. You will now hear successively three of these formulae. The first one expresses joy, and precedes the cantillation on festive events such as the celebration of the birth of Moses.

    (Recitation)

The second one expresses mourning, and is used for dirges.

    (Recitation)

The third mode is used for the cantillation referring to the miracles performed by Aaron before Pharaoh; it is considered to be in a cheerful mode.

    (Recitation)

The Samaritan system of eleven modes, like the Jewish system, only applies to liturgical cantillation and neither to sacred nor to secular song. The rhythmic and melodic form of these songs is simpler than that of the cantillation. But here, too, strange accents and glides like those with which the cantillation abounds are woven into the texture and, above all, the general style of recitation is unmistakably the same. As an example you hear a convivial song in Arabic in which a soloist alternates with a chorus. The use of the Arabic language, in this song, makes it particularly clear how far remote it is from genuine Arab song.

(Recitation)

The investigation of Samaritan song and cantillation has not been carried far enough to yield definite results. One point, I think, may be considered as settled. As regards the evolution of sacred cantillation, the Samaritan style represents a stage intermediary between magic incantation among primitive tribes and the comparatively tame expression of religious feelings in Near Eastern service. It is certainly more ancient than the cantillation preserved in any of the Jewish communities.

This does not necessarily mean that Jewish cantillation, at any time, was identical with Samaritan. While they are closely akin, as we have seen, with respect to their musical system, i.e., the grouping of the cantillation into melodic modes and melodic phrases, they are, on the other hand, wide apart as to their melodic substance and as to the way in which it is delivered. As a matter of fact, no kind of song or cantillation throughout the Near East, as far as I know, resembles Samaritan. This leads us to think that Samaritan chant, apart from representing an earlier stage of development than Jewish, may possibly represent, also, a different racial style. But the style of what race? Can we hope to have discovered, in Samaritan cantillation and song, the music, or vestiges of the music, of one of the nations which, in antiquity, dominated the Near East – some nation now extinct unless it survives in the Samaritan community? I prefer stopping here to being drawn on to soft ground.

VII
17 February, 1937

Tonight you will hear some of the main musical items of a Yemenite Jewish wedding. You will thus, by way of example, be enabled to form an idea of the function of music in the life of an Oriental Jewish community. This function cannot easily be overrated. Practically all the important events in Eastern communal life, sacred and secular festivals, as well as events of family life, like birth, marriage, funeral, are permeated with music and song.

This fact is confirmed in every description of the manners and customs of any Oriental people. But most of these descriptions fail to go beyond the bare fact that certain ceremonies and other activities are accompanied by, or even culminate in, music. With few exceptions, we learn nothing from those accounts about the character of the music employed on these occasions; examples of it in staff notation are rare and generally incorrect.

In this respect, the student of Oriental music has an interesting task before him. Going over the principal events in the social life of an Eastern community he can closely attend to the musical features contained in them, and thus add the indispensable element of sound to mute descriptions as given by others. In doing so he will not only render an invaluable service to ethnology, but, at the same time, have a reliable guidance in his own field of research. To make a complete survey of musical forms existing in a social group in the East he can do no better than follow up its manners and customs.

This method, if it were applied to European music of the present day, would yield but scanty results. For about a century, by far the greatest and most important part of the musical production in Central and Western Europe has been conceived independent of special occasions. The legitimate place for this kind of music is the concert hall with its neutral atmosphere where people assemble with the sole object of listening to music and of appreciating its intrinsic qualities. In contrast with this, applied music, i.e., music composed for definite social ends or events, has been pushed into the background.

But it is of little help to insist on the contrast which exists between present day musical practice in East and West. This would easily lead to exaggerations and false generalities. We had better remember that, a few centuries ago, the social functions of European music were not at all unlike those of Eastern. At that time and even more when we go still further back we find that in Europe as well music fell into groups vastly differing from each other according to their function in social life and to their distribution among different social classes. Johann Sebastian Bach's cantatas, to mention one instance, were intended not to figure each as an item in some concert programme irrespective of time and place, but for immediate use at his own church on a particular Sunday. Further: the difference, in style and function, between instrumental and vocal forms of music is not peculiar to the East. The English, with their conservative attitude towards music, still speak of "music and song," thus giving them two separate names.

It would also be a mistake to exaggerate the prevalence, in the East, of applied music, of music for a special situation and incapable of being disconnected from it. The fact that music and song are indispensable features of certain festivals does not necessarily imply that the musical items performed on these occasions are peculiar to them. The frequent use, in Roman Catholic and Protestant service, of secular tunes adapted to religious purposes by simply providing them with a new text has analogies also in the East.

Throughout the East, men's and women's songs are strictly apart from each other. In the domain of music as well as in others, women, with the exception of dancing-girls and other professionals, are kept in seclusion. But even professional female musicians in the urban sphere are allowed only a limited field of activity. I hope that, on a future occasion, I shall be able to let you hear a programme of Oriental Jewish women's songs; at present, we are concerned only with male songs.

Generally speaking, men's songs are less frequently bound up with particular situations of life than women's. This also applies to the wedding songs from which a selection will now be given; the different forms which they represent are not restricted to the wedding. You will hear these songs in the chronological order in which they are recited at the wedding and it will be necessary to point out the precise stage of the festival to which each of them belongs. The present performers are Sa'adiyya Nahum, Yahya Nahari, and Hayyim Mahbub, all of them born in Yemen.

An Oriental wedding, Jewish the same as Arab, extends over a number of days. Most of the ceremonies performed during that time have a magical significance; they serve to protect the young couple from evil spirits. Among these ceremonies those of applying henna to the hands and feet of the bride and the bridegroom are of outstanding importance, and are always accompanied with singing. Both henna-ceremonies are performed at night. The bridegroom, according to Yemenite Jewish custom, is first painted by the morē, the scholar, who takes a predominant part throughout the wedding, then by the singers, and lastly by wedding guests who have to buy this privilege with a small money present. The songs recited on this occasion belong to the form called Našīd; here is one of them.

(Recitation)

On a later day, in the evening, the bridegroom's head is shaved in the presence of his friends and relatives. This, as well, is an occasion for the recitation of songs. The following one which belongs to the form called Hidduya is specially favoured.

(Recitation)

After the act of shaving, the bridegroom is led to the bride's house where the marriage-ceremony takes place. The bridegroom signs the marriage-contract, and afterwards hands it over to the bride whom, on this occasion, he sees for the first time. Before this ceremony the following song is recited.

(Recitation)

After the marriage-ceremony, the bridegroom is taken back to his house. On the following day which is the last one of the wedding he returns with his escort to the bride's house early in the morning. On the way his companions sing a song in praise of the bride which belongs to the form called Zaffa.

(Recitation)

The bride is then conveyed in procession to her future husband's house where the wedding is brought to its close.

The songs that you have been hearing do not by any means exhaust the musical repertoire of the Jewish Yemenite wedding. Above all it must be kept in mind that only the male part of it was represented. My next talk will, I hope, be illustrated by some items from the women's musical programme, and will thus supplement the present one.

A recital of all the musical items occurring in the course of a wedding would acquaint us with some additional forms of secular song. It would very nearly complete the whole series of musical forms extant among Yemenite Jews. In this particular case, therefore, it appears that the method of studying the music of a community in connection with their manners and customs provides us with a full knowledge of their musical production. The same is true of many other cases; so the collaboration of the ethnologist and the musical scholar yields results highly to be welcomed from both points of view.

VIII
3 March, 1937

As suggested during my last talk which dealt with the music at a Yemenite wedding, I propose to give you, tonight, the supplement to it, namely, the women's part in it.

This is the first occasion on which women and women's songs have been introduced into this series of Oriental music and it may remain the only one. It therefore seems to be the proper place to stop for a moment and consider the woman's part in Oriental music, generally.

On the whole, we can discard women as creative musicians. In this, there is hardly a difference between Oriental and European women except for the fact that, in Europe more often than in the East, ambition stirs women to try and assert themselves as composers. I should not like to draw any rash conclusions as to their being excluded from this field of artistic production by the nature of things. But if we can cherish any hopes of future woman composers, these hopes can hardly be built on their achievements, in this direction, during the last and the present centuries when their production – scanty as it was – seemed to proceed from a tendency to compete with men in this field as well as in others, very much remote from music, rather than from a genuine outburst of musical imagination. In the past, anyhow, their musical talents have with rare exceptions, lain elsewhere and I think we can, in our present survey, pass over these exceptions of which the famous Ancient Greek poetess Sappho has remained the most outstanding – although her music has not come down to us.

Far more can be said about women as executants of music, vocal and instrumental. From antiquity onward there has been, in most Eastern countries, a class of professional female musicians. We can see pictures of them with their instruments on reliefs and vases playing, for the most part, stringed instruments or hand-beaten drums, but not, as far as I know, wind instruments. This is confirmed by present day practice. One need only remember the Geishas in modern Japan who have to undergo a full training in vocal and instrumental music, and the Indian nautch-girls with their reputation for music and dancing. In Arab musical history as well, distinguished female musicians have been on record ever since the rise of Islam, and have formed an integral part of noble households, together with their male colleagues. While these women, in the Middle Ages, mostly had the standing of slaves, with the change of social conditions during the 19th century they have come to be independent professionals, the foremost of them keeping bands of male instrumentalists as an accompaniment for their singing.

Women singers, even Umm Kalthoum, the great contemporary Egyptian singer, have their poems and the tunes to which they sing them specially composed for them. The same is true of most of today's prominent mean singers; still, a few of them "melodies," as the Arabs express it, that is to say, they compose their tunes themselves, which, in the old times, they were expected to do as a matter of course, and which women were not. Another difference is that, among the various kinds of urban music, not all are practised by women while none of them are peculiar to them. But the general style of urban melody is the same with male and female professionals.

To find an exclusively female type in Oriental music we have to turn to the domestic sphere of life. Here, the music belonging to men and to women is as strictly separate as their social functions. Women's songs, in this sphere, are as far removed from any other kind of music as is, for instance, sacred cantillation from secular singing, and it is, therefore, possible to enumerate the qualities – positive and negative – which establish it. All through the Near East, women, irrespective of race or creed, sing their domestic songs to the sole accompaniment of hand-clapping or handbeaten drums; among the Berbers of Algeria, women's songs are actually named "hand-clapping," this, evidently, being considered to be the outstanding feature of these songs. The characteristic scales of string- and wind-instruments, therefore, are absent in this class of music. Nor are women's songs subjected to any of the modal systems evolved by these instruments and by the position of the notes on them.

While unimpaired by instrumental influences, women's songs, on the other hand, do not receive their melodic shape from the words as liturgical cantillation does. Although purely vocal like liturgical cantillation they are in character more remote from it than from any other type of vocal music. Above all, they are never in free rhythm, as the practice of hand-clapping and drumming shows. On the contrary, they are invariably built on the simplest rhythmical scheme conceivable. They consist of two sections which may be described as "up and down," "to and fro," or "question and answer." This pendular motion shows them as belonging to that large class of songs which is connected with regular bodily movement, and which is represented in its simplest form by children's songs and nursery rhymes like "Ring-a-ring-a-roses." These nursery rhymes, by the way, in spite of all the usual protestations as to music being an international language, are really the only tunes which seem to be common to all nations, Eastern and Western, civilized and primitive.

Women's songs represent the same type in a more elaborate, but still simple, way. They, too, consist mainly of one melodic line, with a half-close in the middle, and this line is repeated to innumerable verses. Obviously, the words, and especially the sequence of the sentences are more or less immaterial in this class of song. Here it is not the melody which carries the text, but, on the contrary, the text simply helps to keep the tune and its pendular movement going, and is often replaced by mere senseless syllables. The regular movement inherent in this kind of melody may or may not serve to accompany an actual bodily occupation. Some of these songs accompany the rocking of the cradle, the turning of the hand-mill, or games and dances. But even when this is not the case the singers can hardly help swaying their bodies.

This description holds good of practically all the different forms of women's songs in the Near East, and so applies also to their wedding songs. There is one curious exception for which I cannot account, but which I would mention for the sake of completeness. Berber women of Algeria sing one song, in the middle of their Henna ceremony which entirely deviates from the usual type both in its melody and by being in free rhythm. I never came up against any song of this kind either in Arab or in Jewish surroundings.

Arab and Jewish women's songs are closely related to each other and this relation is stressed by the fact that Jewish women, as well, sing in Arabic without exception. Shall we suppose that this approximation to the Arab style has narrowed down the range of Ancient Jewish women's songs? Certainly, if you have fed your expectations of what Jewish women's songs might be, on Miriam's or on Deborah's song, you will be disappointed in the modest little tunes that you are going to hear. But then it is unfair to conjure up musical feats which mark climaxes in Scriptural history, as models for everyday use. And, on the whole, what we hear of women's music in biblical times does not contradict the observations that we can make with regard to their Oriental descendants. Miriam, in Exodus, after all, only takes up the men's words and her companions accompany her song with percussion, just as is done today.

Parallel to the men's wedding songs that you heard last time, the women, too, have songs peculiar to the Henna ceremony and the other stage of the wedding. First you will hear one of the songs sung while the henna is applied to the bride's hand and feet.

(Recitation)

The second song is performed during the act of cutting the bride's front locks. This is on the day preceding the night on which the marriage contract is read and the blessing pronounced.

(Recitation)

Apart from songs like those that you have just heard and which have their definite place in the respective ceremonies there is another group including songs which may be sung at any time of the wedding, and serve to entertain the bride and her companions during the long hours which separate the various ceremonies. These songs, in contrast to those of the first group, accompany dances. They are also distinguished from the first group musically. Instead of slow beats at equal distances, the drum here accompanies the tunes with vivid patterned figures. You will now, in conclusion, hear a series of such songs.

(Recitation)

IX
16 March, 1937

Arab urban music is often alluded to as <u>the</u> music of the Arabs. Henry George Farmer's History of Arabian Music, e.g., the only comprehensive work on the subject, deals exclusively with urban music; in the same way, the Congress of Arabian Music held in Cairo in 1932 took hardly any notice of other kinds besides urban. This seems to imply that, in Arab music, the urban kind is held to be the only one worth discussing. Now, this is obviously wrong, for two reasons. In the first place, Arab rural music, the music of the Bedouins and the peasants, can claim to occupy a considerable part of the entire field of Arab music. Secondly, urban music in Arab countries is representative of the Arab spirit in music only with some reservations. If, on one hand, it undoubtedly is one of several kinds of music practised among Arabs, on the other hand it also belongs to a large class of music of which other varieties are Turkish, Persian, and even Indian. As a racial expression, therefore, it is less entitled to being called Arab music than the rural kinds of song.

It would be too much to say, however, that urban music, in contradistinction to rural, is international as far as the Near and the Middle East are concerned, and that rural is not. Arab urban music is clearly distinguishable, especially by its delivery, from Persian, Turkish, and Indian although their musical system is more or less the same. Nor can it be maintained that Arab rural music is incapable of being accepted by, or of absorbing influence from, people not belonging to the Arab race.

The difference between Arab urban and rural music lies elsewhere. They belong to different social groups which, at the same time, represent different stages of civilization. This is clearly reflected in their structure and design. Rural music is simple and straightforward; it ranges over a small number of notes; it uses a comparatively small number of melodic phrases and rhythmical devices, and only a small number of instruments. Naturally, music of this description would not be subjected to theory and analysis. There are systems of scales both in the practice of the fiddle (rababa) and of the reed-flute; but these systems can be shown to have originated in the urban sphere. Rural music is entirely a thing of oral practice, so much so that not even the names of prominent singers (who, at the same time, are poets) are recorded in writing.

Arab urban music, on the other hand, has developed an increasing number of notes, of melodic modes, and of rhythms, a variety of complex vocal and instrumental forms, and diverse and elaborate musical instruments. This corresponds to its different social standing. It has been, as it still is, among the chief entertainments of the higher classes since the rise of Islam and before. Many of the Khalifs, during the most splendid periods of Islamic rule, were ardent music lovers and the courts of Damascus, of Baghdad, and of Moorish Spain were centres of musical competition. Evidently, the musical taste of this society and the music created to suit this taste was as different from that of nomads as a Moorish palace is from a tent, although each of them may be perfect in its own way.

Owing to the literary and scientific renaissance in medieval Arab civilization urban music became an object of interest with scholars. Through chroniclers we are informed, sometimes in minute detail, as to the lives and personalities of many medieval urban musicians, their particular musical talents, and even the extraordinary fees which some of them received from patrons of their art. What is even more valuable for present students of the subject than these records of musical personalities and of the position of music at court and in town is the large number of writings, from the 9th century onward, dealing with the musical system underlying urban music and with its spiritual background. Considering that the music itself has not been preserved any more than Bedouin music, these writings are the only evidence from which to form an idea as to its characteristics in the past and from which to judge to what extent present day urban music may have retained them.

The theory and philosophy of Arab urban music, like most other branches of medieval learning, was derived from Ancient Greek and Hellenistic thought. According to ancient ideas, music is not an isolated product of the human mind, but is closely connected with the elementary forces of the universe of which it is considered to be one. Thus, a system of cosmic harmony was established in an attempt to determine the precise mutual relations between these forces, the relations, e.g., between sounds, colours, human temperaments, times of the day, seasons of the year, and celestial bodies. It is easy to see that this system is nothing but a more coherent and more rational expression of the belief, prevailing in primitive societies, that magic forces govern both the universe and human fate. And in the same way as the influence of those irrational magic beliefs can be recognized in ritual music, so can the influence of the cosmological system as worked out at a higher stage of civilization be shown to pervade secular urban music.

The cosmological system, in being handed down from antiquity to the Middle Ages, and in passing from one country to another, has undergone changes which it would be impossible to follow up here. There are characteristic differences between Chinese, Indian, and Hellenistic tradition; the Hellenistic came to be the basis for medieval writings both in Europe and the Near East. A few examples may illustrate the system. In China, the five principal notes were identified with five planets, with the four seasons and the whole year, the four cardinal points and the centre, and so forth. The seven notes of the Ancient Greek scale were coordinated with five planets to which the sun and the moon were added, and, hence, with the seven days of the week which bear their names. The starting note of the Dorian mode, e.g., corresponds to the planet Mars, that of the Hypolydian to Venus; this accounts for Plato recommending the former as promoting manly virtues and a warlike spirit and condemning the latter for its erotic and wanton character.

There are other and cruder instances, both in ancient and medieval writings, of the belief that music, as represented by its different notes, rhythms, and melodic modes, can act upon public and private life as well as on external nature, much in the same way as the stars do according to astrological doctrines. It was essential for musicians to know the magic forces inherent in music. A certain tune played or sung at an inappropriate time and in adverse circumstances was held to shake the harmony of the universe whereas music employed in the proper way was relied upon as bringing about all kinds of favourable effects such as curing the sick, fertilizing barren soil or taming wild animals, a feat with which Orpheus was credited.

A great number of these beliefs survive among Arab urban musicians of the present day. The different modes or melody types of this music are still supposed not only to correspond to different humours, but also to belong to different days and hours. The system of melody types is first mentioned in the 11th century. It embraces a great many melodic modes each of which is defined by its scale and by a number of typified melodic phrases peculiar to it. On a later occasion we shall have to go more deeply into the nature of these melody types; a melody type (in Arabic, maqām) is a musical category which has no exact equivalent in European music. The character of each of them is best represented by the instrumental solos in free rhythm which preface, as it were, recitals of urban music. Only a small selection can be played tonight; but it includes some of the most important melody types. They will be performed on the 'Ud, the Arab lute (the ancestor of the European) by Mr. Ezra Aharon from Baghdad whose playing is typical of the 'Iraqian style of urban music.

The first item is a prelude (in Arabic, taqsīm) in the mode of Hijāz the name of which suggests that it originated in that country. The mode is considered to express cheerfulness; its appropriate time is Thursday night.

(Recitation)

The second prelude is in the mode of Saba. The name signifies a soft North Wind greatly appreciated in the Arabian desert. This melody type has a sad character; it is played at dawn, but is not connected with any particular day.

(Recitation)

The third and last melody type in tonight's performance is Sika. This name, unlike the preceding ones, is Persian, and thus points to the fact that Persian musicians contributed greatly towards creating the system of melody types. The mode itself is quite common among Arabs. Sika means the third degree, i.e., the third note of the Arab fundamental scale which lies between European mi and mi^b, and is the tonic of the mode. It is considered to be moderate in character, but is apt to lend itself to various moods. Its allotted time is Monday night.

(Recitation)

According to orthodox believers in the magic significance of the melody types, it has certainly been a mistake to perform these three at the same time of the day, and two of them on a different day from those to which they are attributed. I hope you will not be afraid of harmful consequences arising from this transgression of time-honoured rules. There are musicians in the Near East even nowadays who would refuse to break these rules. One of them told me that he once omitted to respect the character of a certain melody type which ought to have been performed in the open, by performing it indoors. This offence, he added, was promptly punished; three days after it had been committed, burglars broke into his house and robbed him of all his property.

After having dealt with the cosmological and magical aspect of Arab urban music a number of other points concerning it will have to be raised; they will be the subject of my next talk.

X
31 March, 1937

Last time, we were concerned with the spiritual background of Arab urban music. It was shown that the doctrine of cosmic harmony as handed down from antiquity is still present in the musicians' minds even nowadays and that superhuman forces are still held to be largely responsible for the effects that music can produce.

We now pass on to the music itself. However little Europeans may know about it, they generally have some vague notion of its being in quartertones. This hardly seems attractive, and is not even accurate. So it may be worth while saying a few words about the real function of those quartertones.

The scale system of Arab urban music has been taken over from Ancient Greek theory. Like every scale system among Ancient and Oriental nations it is based on numerical relations as applied to string instruments and pipes, and is not based, as people often believe, on observations of intervals as executed by the human voice. It would lead too far to elaborate this point now. In support of it, it may only be said that in the whole domain of purely vocal music, and especially in liturgical cantillation there exists no original system of scales and no musical notation establishing standard notes and intervals; where there is any notation at all, it only gives vague indications as to the rise and fall of the voice.

The different scale systems of Ancient and Oriental urban music are all demonstrated on a specially favoured instrument. In Arab theory, this instrument is the 'Ud which, together with its name, also passed into European musical practice where it is known, in English, as lute.

The first Arab treatise on music which has come down to us dates from the 9th century. It establishes a system of twelve notes within the octave, that is to say, the same number of notes as that represented, in later times, by the white and black keys of the European piano. In European theory, this series of twelve notes is called a chromatic scale. But it is not really a scale. In Arab music as well as in European, scales consist, at most, of seven notes and the set of twelve notes merely provides a supply from which to choose seven note scales of varying structures.

While in European music the system of twelve notes has remained the final stage of development down to the present day, Arab theory, soon after its start, increased the number of notes available and, from the 10th century onward, recognized seventeen notes within the octave until about two centuries ago when the number of notes was again increased, and the present system of twenty-four notes was established. With regard to this modern system, we can indeed speak of quartertones, the octave now being divided into double the number of sections than the European chromatic scale.

But in alluding to the Arab system as including, successively, twelve to twenty-four notes we must always remember that the actual scales consist of no more than seven degrees. Why, then, you might ask, should the number of notes available have been raised? The answer is that Arab urban music aims at a finer differentiation of melodic steps than European and that, in order to achieve this, it required to have an increasing supply of notes at its disposal. So some of the steps used in Arab melody are unknown in European music; one of them, e.g., is about midway in size between the tone and the semitone, another midway between the major and the minor third, and so forth. But the quartertone itself as a musical interval does not occur any more than in European music.

Arab urban melody, thus, possesses niceties of intonation absent from European. On the other hand, it lacks, and has always lacked, that system of harmony which European music has gradually evolved and which, with its consonant and dissonant chords, has come to be one of its chief means of expression.

There is another and equally important point on which the musical conception of the Near East differs from European. The classification of melodies, in Arab urban music, does not rest solely on their difference in scale. Beyond its own scale, every melodic category or mode has its own melodic turns and phrases; and it is this traditional melodic material which ultimately determines the character of the respective mode. This means that musicians are not at liberty to invent any kinds of tunes in a given scale. They must use the melodic material that they have received from their masters and it is difficult to say how much freedom they are allowed in handling this material.

The melodic character of each mode (in Arabic: maqām) can be recognized, more clearly than in any other form of song, in the introduction which precedes every recital and of which several examples were played in my last talk. In contrast with these introductions which may be sung as well as played, all the pieces following it are in strict time. The melodic connection between them and the introduction is of supreme importance for the understanding of the melodic mode or maqām. All these pieces draw upon the melodic material as exposed in the introduction, but they sometimes transform it in such a manner that, at a first hearing, the relation is but dimly perceived by outsiders.

In the following example, a vocal and instrumental introduction is immediately followed by a song in strict time. In this example, I think, it is easy to notice that the melodic material is common to both.

(I must apologise for the fact that, in illustration of tonight's talk, I am compelled to use records instead of collaborating with musicians, and that some of the records are a little worn. But the particular types of music that I want to show you are not practised in this country.)

(Record: Odeon 93324)

The melody in strict time is accompanied, as you have heard, by a drum. This practice of drumming, a typical feature of the music of the Near East and India, does not merely serve to mark the time. The beats of the drum have quite a different function from those in military marches;

they constitute a rhythmical phrase repeated throughout and thus forming a steady background as against the fluctuations of the melody. In Arab urban music, a number of such rhythmical types or patterns are distinguished. This as well as the grouping of melodies into melody types or maqāmāt is characteristic of the Oriental mind fixing on concrete configurations of melody and rhythm rather than on abstract tabulations of scales and time-values.

The melodical as well as the rhythmical types in Arab urban music are traditional; but the tradition has not remained, if ever it was, uniform. Above all, there is a strong difference between an Eastern and a Western style, the latter extending from Tripoli westward to Tunis, Algeria, and Morocco. Each of the two styles, the Eastern and the Western, again falls into several groups. The Eastern style may be reserved for future discussion; we are now concerned with the West.

In Western North Africa we should expect to find one common tradition. The names of the melody types and the texts of the musical repertoire are mostly the same. Moreover, musicians of all the three countries, from Tunis to Morocco, claim to have preserved the musical inheritance of Moorish Spain. But in reality, there are three traditions instead of one as you may judge for yourselves. The introduction and song which you heard before is a good specimen of the Tunisian style; the next example is from Algeria.

(Record: Odeon 93571)

The Moroccan style, again, is obviously different. Its peculiar character may be due to the fact that the population in Morocco, more than in the two other countries, has retained its Berber qualities. A large proportion of the country has not even accepted the Arabic language; so it is quite possible that the Berber element may have influenced the tradition of urban music in Morocco.

(Record: Baidaphon 093364)

The question as to which of the three Western styles may be nearest to the Original Moorish music, the music of Andalus, has to remain open until further investigations. These investigations will have to extend also to the remnants of Moorish song in Spain. As a matter of fact, a certain manner of song practised in Southern Spain, the Flamenco, no doubt bears traces of the Moorish past. It is in free rhythm like the preludes of Arab urban music and its melodic style is Arab and not Spanish. But, as compared to North African urban music, the Flamenco conveys a picture of distortion and decay. The rhapsodic vocal part does not, like the introductions that you have heard, deliberately expose the outlines of a melody type; it has retained the mannerisms, and lost the meaning and function, of those introductions. It has, moreover, been placed in a most unsuitable setting consisting of a few typical chords on the Spanish guitar. I will close the present talk with an example of this curious hybrid kind of music.

(Record: Gramófono 262608)

XI
14 April, 1937

When I was dealing with Moorish music, i.e., Arab urban music in Western North Africa I hinted at the possible influence that Berber song may have exercised on it, especially in Morocco. This influence would account for the general difference between an Eastern and a Western style which is so strongly marked in the practice of urban music in the Near East.

We are now going to study the Eastern group extending from Egypt to Persia, and even to India. Here, the musical style is far less uniform than in the West. This is due to the fact that, in these parts, the nations which have contributed to the system and practice of what we call Arab urban music are highly dissimilar in race and customs, and are connected with each other only through their common adherence to Islam and their common political fortunes in certain periods of the past.

The musical elements common to these nations may therefore be expected to lie in the theory and system of music rather than in melody and rhythm and least of all in musical delivery. The system of music as being purely a product of the intellect is hardly restricted by racial and national boundaries. As to musical practice, it is generally believed that tunes are fully characteristic of the nations in which they originate. But this is hardly more than half true. There is, of course, an obvious difference between the melodies of nations vastly differing in race and civilization as, e.g., the English and the Turks. On the other hand, it is a well-known fact that we can easily embarrass even a trained musician by playing a tune and asking him to decide to which of two European countries it belongs. Which elements in Chopin's music are French and which are Polish? Which, in Handel's later compositions, English and which, German? Or which, in Mendelssohn's, German, and which, Jewish? Questions similar to and as puzzling as these arise as to the music of the different nations in the Near East.

We do very little towards characterizing a melody by taking down its main steps and time-values in staff-notation from direct hearing. We may try this method, e.g., on an Arab song and then have the written tune sung by a European. Let us suppose that his rendering of our notation will be scrupulously correct; still, it will sound hopelessly wrong as compared to the Arab's own rendering.

The unmistakable genuine colour of a tune is due to subtler elements of it than to the mere sequence of notes. A foreign tune may, e.g., be in common time and its rhythm, therefore, may sound quite familiar to us; but the stresses, in the original rendering, will be distributed in a way slightly different from our own, or there may be an almost imperceptible difference in the relative length of the four time-units as against that to which we are used. In the same way, the tune may proceed in musical intervals roughly identical with those of our own tunes; but the transition from one note to another may be slightly smoother than with us, or the contrary; or the final note of a phrase may be broken off abruptly instead of dying away, or the reverse. These and other delicate shades in the delivery of a tune make all the difference in its effect. They are not the result either of training or of aesthetic judgment. They proceed from unconscious physiological impulses and cannot, therefore, be imitated. These traits, then, and not the bare facts which we can ascertain about the scale and the melodic outline of a tune are characteristic of the deepest elements at work in music.

These general remarks are intended to direct your attention towards the difference between the following examples chosen from the Eastern group of Arab urban music.

They are all based on the same musical system. This system of melody types or maqāmāt can be traced back as far as the 10th century. From the outset, it contained both Arab and Persian elements as borne out by the names of the melody types, the Hijāzī mode figuring side by side with the 'Irāqī and Isfahan modes. The theorists were of various origin; al-Fārābī, e.g., the most eminent among them, was a Turcoman by birth.

The present musical system, therefore, cannot be claimed as the exclusive property of any one of the nations concerned; they have all contributed towards it. But this does not apply to the music itself. Egyptian music, during the last century, and especially instrumental music, has been largely influenced by Turkish. But besides this, traditional Arab forms of song have maintained themselves. The following example is representative of one of these forms. The musical mode of the song is Sika, with the note mi as its tonic; its rhythmical pattern, al-Nawaht, consists of seven time-units. The singer, Sheikh Said as-Safti, was held in high esteem as a conservative interpreter of this style.

(Odeon, 0.5168b)

The next item is an example of the Turkish urban style of instrumental music. It is played on the tanbur, a long-necked lute which, like the short-necked 'Ud, goes back to the Middle Ages and even, under its correct name of pandura, to antiquity. The tanbur is specially favoured by the Turks, but hardly ever used by Arabs. The melody is played on the highest string only; the other strings are used for occasional chords.

I believe that Turkish music, in comparison with Arab, tends towards smoothness, delicacy of tone, and the display of emotion. It has a preference for quick triplets and for expressive pauses stressed by chords. Both these traits are unusual in, or absent from the Arab style which might be described as restrained, but, at the same time, as highly strung.

The piece belongs to the melody type Shet arabau; its form is known as Saz Samai. The performer is Djemil Bey who, in his time, was the best tanbur player in Turkey.

(Orfeon 10524)

The Persians have largely contributed to the urban music of the Near East as regards both theory and practice. Among the musicians at the splendid courts of the early Arab dynasties, many singers and players of rank were of Persian origin, above all Ishaq al-Mausili, the famous court musician of the Abbasid Khalifs, Harun ar-Rashīd, Al-Ma'mūn, and their successors.

Present day Persian music has scarcely been investigated as yet. The following item, a typical example of its style, may serve to show that it would be worth while being studied. It is characterized by curious fluctuations of the voice and by an equally curious instrumental drone and its impressioned delivery produces an unfailing effect on Oriental listeners.

(Odeon 0.5168a)

It is doubtful whether a specimen of Indian music may be legitimately included in this group. Indian music, certainly, is a unity clearly distinguishable from the music of the Near East. It has scales and rhythmic patterns of its own. Its melodies seem to come from a far distance, an impression which is enhanced by the unsubstantial sound of sympathetic strings attached to Indian viols and zithers.

On the other hand, Indian music is connected with that of the Near East by a number of common features. It has taken over from it some instruments with their Persian names and at least one musical form, the Ghazal. But above all it is divided into melody types like Arab urban music. One might say against this that the grouping of melodies into melody types can be traced back, in Indian music, to times prior to the rise of Islām. But the present Indian system of melody-types or rāgas is very probably due to Muhammedan influence in the 12th and 13th centuries. Arab urban music, in its Persian variety, would thus have influenced Indian music with regard to its system and other external features without, however, affecting its melodic substance or its peculiar mode of expression.

The present specimen of North Indian song is in the Rāga Malkus which is supposed to express love and laughter, and to belong to the hours from midnight to the early morning – exactly in the same way as Arab musicians claim a certain emotional character and a special hour of the day for each of their melody types or maqāmāt.

(Odeon 95113)

XII
28 April, 1937

After some excursions to other countries of the Near East, I am now coming back once more to song and music as practised in Palestine. On former occasions, you heard the traditional songs performed at Yemenite Jewish weddings. This time, a number of songs from an Arab peasant wedding will be recited. I would lay particular stress on the fact that it is not the purpose of the recital to present to you extraordinary feats of professional skill on the part of musicians and singers, but rather to give you an idea of what is ordinarily heard at a village wedding in central Palestine. The vocal parts will be performed by Mhammed Abu Msellem and others[1] and the flute will be played by Ahmed Smīr.[2]

In order to appreciate the songs and dance tunes of an Arab villagers' wedding it is necessary to know the circumstances surrounding them. A wedding, with them as with rural populations all over the world, consists of a long chain of events and ceremonies each of which has its fixed place and time. It is a public feast; the whole village and even the neighbouring villages share in the rejoicings of the families concerned.

The musical programme of the wedding consists both of men's and women's songs; but at the present recital we must content ourselves with the men's part. The first section of it takes place on an evening after the marriage has been definitely agreed upon and after the bridegroom's family has brought new clothes for the marriage. This part of the musical programme precedes the marriage by one day or a number days and, in the latter case, is repeated every night until the marriage.

At dusk the bridegroom lights a wood fire on an open space, mostly in front of the guesthouse, and different groups of villagers successively assemble for dance and song. The first who come are boys about 8 to 15 years of age. Their singing is a sign for a second group to appear; these

---

1   Mhammed 'Abd ar-Rahīm Abu Msellem, of the Beni Murra tribe, from 'Ain Yabrūd, Ramallah district; 'Abd al-Fattah as-Sahāda, of the Beni Mālik tribe, from Qatanna near Jerusalem.
2   From Qatanna.

are young men up to the age of 25. Lastly, after the evening prayer, they are joined by older men and notables.

The performers of the dance range themselves in one line in front of the fire or in two lines with the fire between them, everybody keeping tightly to his neighbours. The closeness of the line is a particularly striking feature in Arab dances of this kind; both peasants and Bedouins, on these occasions, although they have a wide space at their disposal, behave as if not an inch could be spared to right or left. While dancing and singing they stretch their arms forward and clap their hands; hence, this form of song is called sahga which means clapping.

The dance consists of stamping on the ground with a certain kind of rhythmical steps. The two rows of performers alternately advance towards, and retreat from, the fire. But the way in which the dance is performed is variable in character and pace. The young men violently rush forward and backward; they work themselves up into a passion and it sometimes occurs that instead of retreating they stop at the fire with their knees bent and challenge those opposite by throwing their headgear at their feet, similarly as medieval knights threw down their gauntlet. This impetuous form of the dance, with corresponding words, takes its name from the word hamäsa which means bravery and a war-like spirit. You will hear a song in a similar style later on.

The dance in which the older men partake has a moderate character; the dancers move on the spot and the song is slower. Here is an example of it.

    (Recitation)

After the various stages of this dance, refreshments as coffee, milk, tea, or cinnamon (qirfa) are served. Then, all the performers, old and young, form one row, everybody, again, keeping close to his neighbours. A singer walks along the row and sings verses everyone of which is answered by them with a burden, as, e.g., yā halālī yā mālī or yā halābak yā halābu. This song is immediately followed by what is called a dahhiyya, consisting of almost breathless repetitions of this word. Then the performance breaks off.

    (Recitation)

The women, all through the evening, attend from a distance, from time to time spurring the dancers and singers with their well-known penetrating trills.

On the marriage day, there are, again, various occasions for dancing and singing. About the middle of the day, the bridegroom takes a bath and then dresses in his wedding clothes. This ceremony is preceded, accompanied, and followed by various songs. When he reappears in his new dress the women besprinkle him with salt, barley, and perfume to protect him from the evil eye and sing in order to bless his bath. The young men, before and after the bath, recite songs belonging to a kind called zaffa; these, too, like the young men's songs in front of the fire at night, have an impetuous character.

(Recitation)

The bridegroom then rides or walks to a place outside the village and the young men follow him in procession. He rests in the shade, under a tree, and watches horsemen performing games, and riflemen aiming at a target, in his honour. At this time, the programme of music and dancing reaches another climax by the performance of a debka.

The word debka refers to treading and stamping, various kind of accentuated steps being a main feature of the dance. It is not performed in rows, but in a circle, one man behind another, and a piper and a singer in the middle. The instrument may be a śubbäba, a reed-flute with six holes in front and one at the back and without a mouthpiece, or a double clarinet, in Arabic migwiz (but Palestinian peasants also call it a nayya), or an arghūl, a kind of clarinet with a long drone pipe attached alongside of it. In the present example it will be a śubbäba or reed-flute. Various songs may be sung on this occasion, such as 'ala del'ūna or others.

(Recitation)

An hour or half an hour before sunset, the bridegroom is conducted back to the village, either to the guesthouse or to the house of a villager who acts as...[1]

---

[1] Page 5 of lecture XII is missing and was nowhere to be found in the "Lachmann Files."

...was to let you hear as many and as various specimens of unadulaterated Oriental music as possible and to try and show you ways towards understanding them and towards understanding, through them, Oriental music generally.

You have been hearing specimens of very different kinds of music: religious and secular, urban and rural, vocal and instrumental, male and female songs, lyrical recitation and choral entertainment songs. It has been one of my chief endeavours to show that these kinds differing in their social functions also have musical systems and forms of their own. Remember, e.g., the difference between religious cantillation, male songs and female songs in Oriental Jewish communities and the difference between the urban and the rural style in Arab music. The melodic steps in sacred cantillation are fundamentally different from the scales used on a viol in accompaniment of epic or lyric recitation, and both of them from the scales of urban music.

Another distinction had to be made with regard to national and racial styles in music. Urban music in the Near East differs owing to its Berber element in North Africa and to the predominance of Arab, Turkish, and Persian elements respectively, in the Eastern group. But this division is not superior to the division according to the social functions of music. Religious cantillation, e.g., as performed in one nation, may have more features in common with that of another nation than it has with other groups of music belonging to the same nation.

These principles of division, the national style and the social function of music, have both to be considered in determining the precise character of a song or a piece of music. Nor must we forget that they do not present themselves as clearly separate; historical developments have blended them in various ways. In urban music and in liturgical cantillation, international relations are more active, and national characteristics, therefore, less obvious, than in rural music. Further, urban music, again and again, has influenced liturgical cantillation and the music of more primitive classes of society. This is specially interesting as permitting us to recognize different historical strata in cantillation and in rural forms of song.

The immense variety of Oriental music resulting from its various racial, social, and historical conditions has been illustrated, in these talks, almost exclusively by singers and musicians belonging to communities in this country. This is all the more worth remarking since it has not been possible to include specimens of all the kinds extant. Unfortunately, there are influences at work towards destroying this diversity and towards Europeanizing Oriental music. European influence should not be considered as similar to those processes which, as I mentioned, have brought about changes in Eastern music in the past. It is not stimulating like them, but destructive. Nor can this influence be welcomed, as some are inclined to think, as part of modern technical progress. A motor tourist will certainly be delighted at finding, even in remote corners of the East, standardized parts to fit his damaged car. But there is no reason to delight in hearing, in the same remote corners, dance tunes of fashionable European bars echoed by a gramophone or played on a shepherd's flute. The only effect of modern standardization on music is to deprive it of its characteristic power of expression and to turn it into a tedious noise. This process may be inevitable; still, we should, instead of promoting it, try to counteract it by encouraging genuine local music. Its practice is, as the illustrations of this talk may have shown, still fully alive in this country. To further it, means, at the same time, to further the development of more ambitious kinds which, throughout history, have relied on folk-music as their true and natural basis.

Appendix IV

Four Lectures on Eastern Music delivered at the International Association of University Women Palestine Branch

The four lectures on Eastern Music differ considerably from Lachmann's twelve radio talks. While they, too, may be viewed as a fine introductory course on the subject which they address, i.e., Eastern Music, they go far beyond their professed intent. In these lectures Lachmann tried, above all, to debunk the long-held notion about music as a universal language of mood and feeling, spontaneously understood irrespective of background. Music, Lachmann tells us, is an integral part of culture; like other expressive languages, it manifests cultural differences and cultural predilections. Hence, what may be spontaneously understood in one culture may not at all be understood by another. The decoding of musical expressions rests, as it were, on cultural *prerequisites*, whether acquired through socialization and practice or through deliberate and careful study. The study of music, at any rate, must take into account the cultural outlooks of its bearers, for they are the ones who ultimately circumscribe and confine its meaning.

Lachmann's cultural-anthropological approach to the study of music no longer strikes us as novel. Much has been written on the subject since it was first seriously entertained by those who initiated the scientific study of non-European music. Lachmann's exposition, however, remains quite unique, for it is precisely the already convinced that stand to learn from it the most. The lucid and persuasive way in which he approaches the subject, not to mention the substantive observations he makes about major musical-cultural differences, is both interesting and illuminating. It is remarkable how he succeeds, at one and the same time, to delineate functional differences, regional commonalties, and to specify the characteristics whereby Eastern music differs from that of the West.

As in the radio talks, one cannot help but admire Lachmann's wide-ranging scholarship and erudition. Beyond driving home the ideas he wished to convey, he also wished to acquaint his audience with substantive materials which would have been altogether unfamiliar. He manages to do this in a smooth, "by the way" manner, turning the entire learning process into a pleasant eye-opening experience. Above all, these lectures allow us yet another view of Lachmann's mind at work – not only what he thinks, but how he thinks – which cannot be overlooked even by those who may wish to introduce corrections, here and there, to his use of some of the materials. After all, musicology has not stood still.

I

There is a wide-spread saying according to which music, as against speech, is an international language, mutually understood and appreciated by all. To be more precise, music is claimed to be the international language of moods and of feeling. In speaking, we can only address ourselves to those who have learnt the meaning of our words; but everybody will spontaneously understand our griefs and joys if conveyed in terms of music.

On the whole, this is a wrong opinion. We shall see later on that it does apply to some special kinds of music, as children's songs; but then, the same is true to a certain extent with regard to children's language, at least to the most rudimentary words. So, if music, in particular cases, is indeed an international mode of expression, the same can be claimed for speech.

On the other hand, in the same way, as languages can be groups in different families and subdivisions, this must also be said of music. The divisions between languages do not coincide with those of music; but this does not mean that, with regard to music, no divisions can be made at all. Contrary to a very general opinion this is not even true of European music. English or German people may have a special liking for Spanish or Italian song as conveying the vitality of Southern nations and as reminding them, by its clear-cut tunefulness, of the more obvious beauty of Southern landscape as compared to Northern. But do they really understand them as well and in the same sense as they do their own songs? And is it not rather its being unfamiliar what attracts them? – I think we all feel that the tunes which we have heard, and learned to sing, in our childhood and with which we have grown up, have an appeal to us which they will not yield spontaneously to strangers, – an appeal which we should be unable to explain to them. Certainly, we must suppose that the same applies to other nations; they, too, have grown up with tunes which will not, or very rarely, disclose all their secrets of expression to others. This leads up to something that may appear paradoxical to you: we can, to a very high degree, arrive at understanding what is said in a foreign language; but we can hardly arrive at really understanding foreign music. The reason for this is evident. Language chiefly addresses itself to our intellect; words can, to a certain degree, be defined and translated. Music is a more direct mode of expression. But while its directness, its spontaneity, as we have seen, is generally considered as its chief claim to be an international language, it is precisely this quality which separates the musical expression of one people from that of another. Instead of saying, therefore, that music need not be translated, we ought rather to say that it cannot be translated.

Music as well as language is difficult for us to understand not only when it belongs to foreign nations and civilizations, but also in proportion to its age. This seems to be disproved by the recent general tendency towards reviving European music of the times prior to Bach and Handel, the music of the Renaissance and even of the Middle Ages. But what does this revival really mean? In the first place, to the broad masses of listeners it means nothing. On several occasions I heard German and English lute music of the sixteenth century from a broadcasting station. A number of people were present, average people with an average liking for music. After three minutes, at most, they all agreed to switch it off; the music, obviously, had no spontaneous appeal to them. The revival, then, concerns those only who are willing to go out of their way for it. They may, and, as a matter of fact, some do come to like ancient music. But here, again, we must ask ourselves if liking that music does not mean something quite different from understanding it. People will tell you that it is its strangeness, its remoteness, its "quaintness" which attracts them, a quality which was certainly not the one which impressed itself on the contemporaries of that music. It may safely be said that most of those who admire old music, have no access to those of its qualities which were appreciated in its own time, these qualities, that is, which express the spirit of the age.

(I must add here that doubts I have expressed with regard to a real understanding of old music by modern hearers, are not to discredit the efforts which are being made towards reviving it. The occupation of modern scholars with the music of the Middle Ages and the Renaissance has become more important for its side issues than for its original purpose. It has produced wholesome effects on the development of present day music. It is largely responsible for the tendency towards simplicity and rigidity of form which grew in reaction to the gorgeous display of colour which is typical of the music of the pre-war period.)

It is hardly necessary to prove that non-European music is not generally understood or even liked by Europeans. This can be observed in this country at any moment. The other day, a radio transmission of the voice of the most cherished Egyptian singer, Umm Kalthoum, was heard in Jaffa Road (Jerusalem) from an Arab restaurant. Yet a British soldier, when passing, calmly remarked to his company: "Come on, it is mere noise." This is a typical expression of European public opinion on Oriental music. Sometimes endeavours are made to justify and elaborate this opinion. A young man who is devoting his life to the study of a particular branch of medieval Hebrew poetry (which, in its time, was not recited, but sung) insisted that anyone who said he liked Oriental singing must be pretending. It was quite plausible, he went on to say, that one nation, or group of nations, should be more highly endowed by nature with certain talents or achievements than all the rest, and this applied to the self-evident European superiority in music.

But this healthy European disdain of Oriental music is equalled by the Oriental dislike of European music. Father Amiot, a missionary in China in the second part of the 18th century, to whom we owe the first careful study of non-European music, has a passage in the introduction to his "Musique des Chinois tant anciens que modernes" which, in this connection, it seems worth quoting in full:

"Je savoie passablement la musique, je jouois de la flûte traversiere & du clavecin; j'employais tous ces petits talens pour me faire accueillir.

Dans les différents occasions que j'eus d'en faire usage pendant les premières années de mon séjour à Pekin, je n'oubliai rien pour tâcher de convaincre ceux qui m'écoutoient, que notre musique l'emportait de beaucoup sur celle du pays. Au surplus, c'étoient des personnes instruites, en état de comparer et de juger; des personnes du premier rang qui, honorant les missionnaires françois de leur bienveillance, venoient souvent dans leur maison pour s'entretenir avec eux de quelques objets concernant les sciences ou les arts cultivés en Chine.

Les Sauvages, les Cyclopes – pièces de clavecin et de caractere du célebre Rameau –, les plus belles sonates, les airs de flute les plus mélocieux et les plus brillans du Receuil de Blavet, rien de tout cela ne faisait l'impression sur les Chinois. Je ne voyois sur leurs physionomies qu'un air froid et distrait qui m'annonçoit que je ne les avais rien moins qu'émus. Je leur demandai un jour comment ils trouvoient notre musique, et les priai de me dire naturellement ce qu'ils en pensoient. Ils me réponsirent le plus poliment qu'il leur fit possible, que 'nos airs n'étant point faits pour leurs oreilles, ni leurs oreilles pour nos airs, il n'étoit pas surprenant qu'ils n'en sentissent pas les beautés, comme ils sentoient celles des leures. Les airs de notre musique', ajouta un docteur, du nombre de ceux qu'on appelle Han-lin, et qui étoit pour lors de service auprès de Sa Majesté, 'les airs de notre musique passent de l'oreille jusqu'au coeur, et du coeur jusqu'à l'âme. Nous les sentons, nous les comprenons: ceux que vous venez de jouer ne font pas sur nous cet effet...."

Similarly, the educated Arabs everywhere are almost unanimous in their negative attitude towards the music of Europe which they have such ample opportunities of hearing. It will have struck you that you hardly ever see an Arab among the audiences of the frequent recitals of European music in this town. This exactly corresponds to the almost entire absence of Europeans from Arab moving pictures, from the crowded performances, e.g., in which the famous Egyptian singer Abdelwahab appears, or from the concerts given almost daily near Damascus Gate.

Sometimes Arabs do visit a European recital. An Arab acquaintance of mind told me that he was once invited to hear a famous player on the violin or piano. After the first piece, all he desired was to leave the place; just as Arab music to the British soldier, so European music, to him, was "mere noise."

We must not be deceived by symptoms which seem to point to the contrary. Arabs and Indians, most of them students sent to Europe by rich parents, can often be seen in opera houses and, more often, in dancing places, there. They will assure you that they like European music. But when you inquire into it more closely, as I sometimes did, it appears that they have not noticed even the most elementary facts about it. One of them, e.g., professed that he specially admired "Lohengrin" and "Aida". Some tunes from these operas had caught his ear, but he did not know that the tunes were throughout supported by harmony. He had perceived it dimly, but had not attached any importance to it.

Another instance: I received a book of four part songs for review from some missionary centre in West Africa. The author was a negro who had been taught European music. There was nothing brilliant or remarkable about the compositions: negro tunes had been altered in such a way as to fit with the most trivial chords of the European system. But one thing stood out: almost all the songs were written in keys abounding with sharps or flats; some of the very simple tunes had five flats, others had four sharps, &c.

In both these cases, for the Egyptians as well as for the negro, the main source of attraction, obviously, was not in the essence of European music, but in some concomitants of it. The negro was proud of exhibiting his command of staff notation (which, in itself, is a mysterious thing to his compatriots), even with its most intricate signs. Would it be too bold to compare this with the habit, among Japanese with perfectly good eyesight, of wearing gold-rimmed spectacles? Or would it be too bold to assume that, for the Egyptians, it is the social side of operas and dancings, with its dressing up and its elegance, that affords them the main pleasure? While purely musical performances without any side issues did not attract them any more than the Orientals in this country.

These examples are not give for mere fun. They are to illustrate the irresistible fascination that European civilization exercises on outsiders. But obviously, this fascination does not emanate from the true qualities of European music which, as we have seen, are not even recognised by Orientals; music is simply accepted as part of a civilization which, to them, means a display of uncanny technical achievements: gramophone, broadcast, and, more generally, aeroplanes, machineguns, &c. You see that an inquiry into the influence of Western music on Eastern would lead us straight into politics and I shall therefore refrain from pursuing it.

Personally I am convinced that Western music would not occupy Eastern minds to any appreciable degree unless there were the vision of Western power behind it. This means that if, in future, Eastern music should be penetrated increasingly by Western influence, it would be mainly due to causes outside the musical sphere. This would by no means be a unique case in the history of music. History is full of instances proving that important musical changes have been brought about by factors which, on their surface, do not seem to have anything to do with music. Remember, e.g., that the nature of European music, has undergone a complete revolution through the advent of Christianity.

If, in spite of the present dislike of European music among the vast majority of the Orientals, Eastern music should gradually be turned, as it were, into a musical dominion of Europe, this would not be the first instance of the kind. A similar process has taken place, and has come near its final stage, with regard to the music of the Slav nations. We can trace the gradual increase of Western influence on them throughout the last few centuries. The change that Slav music has undergone during that time can be judged from the existence, in folk song, of certain tunes and kinds of music which survive to the present day, and form a strange contrast with more recent and more domesticated kinds. In Rumania, e.g., there are two types of melody for the recitation of lyric and epic poetry; both types are called Hora. The older one greatly deviates from the European scale and is in free rhythm; it is also found in Ukraine (Dumy) and still further away. The younger one is in strict time and in scales which present no difficulties to Western hearers; this type includes what we usually understand by folktunes. This change is evidently due to Western influence. In this hybrid state, now, Rumanian and Slav folksong, generally, has attained that peculiar flavour which makes it so strangely attractive to Western ears. A similar flavour also keeps the works of Slav composers apart from the bulk of European music. Although, since about the middle of the 19th century, these composers are fully equipped with the harmonic, instrumental and formal devices which had been developed in the West, the best of them, through the traditional difference of their musical ear and conception, have added new charms to the musical language adopted from the West.

I dare not predict whether similar results are to be expected from the future development of Oriental music or of any part of it. My intention in referring to Slav music simply was to point out what <u>may</u> happen to music when it succumbs to Western influence. So I am not going to make any forecast, but shall come back to our former subject which is not what may or may not become of Eastern music, but what it actually is like and how it came to be as it is.

The first condition for approaching this question is, of course, not to have, or to overcome, that dislike of Eastern music which, as mentioned before, is so frequent and almost general among European hearers. On the other hand, liking it is not sufficient for understanding it; as I have pointed out with regard to our attitude towards old European music, liking a certain kind of music is quite compatible with misunderstanding it. With regard to this I would refer you to the beginning of the admirable book on "The Music of Hindostan" by Mr. Fox Strangeways, the musical critic of the Observer. He says: "People who have lived in India have often asked, with various inflections of the voice, 'Do you like' – or, 'Do you really like Indian music?' The more one thinks what the answer to this should be, the more it seems to resolve itself into another – 'Do you really understand it?' – to which there can, of course, be no final answer. Indeed, it would be difficult with regard to our own music to reply satisfactorily to the question, or to do more than put down a few of the points that need to be understood."

Going on now to mention "a few of the points that need to be understood", it may be useful to begin with a general comparison between European and Eastern music.

II

European music, although it can be shown to have inherited quite a number of features from the East, has come to be fundamentally different from the music of all the rest of the world. Mainly two things have brought about this difference: the growth of harmony and the development of staff notation. It is true that neither harmony nor the invention of written music is peculiar to Europe. Harmony or part singing, apart from European influence, is found in many parts of the world and, which is specially remarkable, just among primitive tribes, as African negroes, Malakkans, and South Sea islanders; and their unsophisticated forms of polyphony have a great deal in common with the earliest European forms. Further: various kinds of notation have been invented throughout the great Eastern civilizations; but they have never been, nor are they, used by musicians for singing and playing. We may conclude from this that neither harmony nor notation in itself would have produced the unique evolution of European music; it was brought about by that curious interrelation between them, by the mutual support which they gave each other.

The European system of harmony demands that, in singing and playing, the different parts, although each of them may pursue its own way, should be in constant connection with each other. Any melodic step taken by any one of the parts in disregard of the others, can destroy the harmonic scheme which underlies them all. This means, or rather it came to mean in the course of time, that the harmonic scheme rather than the melodic course is the all-important feature in musical composition. This gradual change of musical conception led up to the memorable sentence, pronounced by the famous French composer and theorist, Rameau, that "melody is born of harmony".

What secures the European musician against taking any wrong melodic steps, i.e., steps endangering the harmonic process, is staff-notation. The more complicated the harmonic texture became the more indispensable it was to be able to rely on written music. In fact, there is no other way to make complicated musical textures known except by writing them down. It is due to this development that people had to think and speak of an authoritative version of a musical composition: every rendering of it had to go back to a piece of writing, and oral tradition, therefore, came to be superseded by visual tradition.

As long as we are exclusively concerned with European music we hardly notice how strange this change from an oral conception to a visual really is. From our childhood we see that whoever performs music first takes out a book or manuscript, puts it on a stand, and tries, more or less successfully, to sing or play exactly what he sees written in front of him. Deviating from it means striking a wrong note; no subterfuge is possible especially when part of the audience, as has become usual in classical concerts, have the written music in their hands, follow the recital by means of that, and can point to mistakes with their fingers. In the East, as we shall see later on, the performer, in singing or playing a traditional melody, is allowed a certain amount of freedom; it is a test of his skill and mastership whether he can make a certain moderate use of it and if he does he can be sure of his hearers delighting in it. In European recitals of the present day, no performer (with the characteristic exception of a jazz player) would, or could dare to follow sudden flights of his own imagination. He must be faithful to the letter or rather to the note; and the field for individual interpretation has been narrowed down to niceties of expression, such as modifications of tempo, accentuation, intensity, unless even they are marked by the composer.

All this appears as perfectly natural to us or, at least, to those of us who have not come into touch with any music except European. They think of a melody in the way as staff-notation has fixed it, i.e., as a sequence of separate dots groups by bars and double bars and, sometimes, by slurs. And this analytical representation of music applies to all the different kinds of music, without differentiating between different instruments or even between vocal or instrumental execution.

Non-European music, even if it had nothing else to convey to us, would still be interesting as showing that the modern European conception of music which rests on its special historical development, has no right to claim universality, but that music is capable of other aspects.

Non-European musicians do not fix their compositions by writing. They cannot, therefore, even if they had such an idea, wait for a future appreciation of what they sing or play. Their music must have an immediate appeal to their community, or else it is doomed.

Further: when you ask a primitive or an Oriental singer to repeat a song, you will, in many cases, notice deviations: the two successive renderings, in your opinion, will not be alike, although, in his opinion, they are identical. This is an important point. You cannot explain it away by saying that the respective singer has no musical ear. The truth of the matter is that both parties are right. When you say that the two or more renderings of the tune are not identical you mean that they do not correspond to each other note by note. But you now know that for the Oriental or the primitive singer notation does not exist; a request, therefore, to repeat a melody note by note would have no meaning for him. He has different ideas about the identity of a tune. In speaking of modern European interpretation I mentioned that, in the course of development, the freedom of interpretation has gradually been restricted to niceties of expression while everything fixed by notation is not liable to changes. For non-Europeans, whose melodic freedom is not tied down either by harmony or by notation, a melody does not consist of a series of immovable notes, but of a characteristic musical gesture which the voice or instrument has not one, but a number of ways of performing. The renderings of a melody, to them, are identical as long as the character of this gesture is maintained; and the difference of their versions which, to us, changes the substance of the melody, with them is left to the performer's discretion, just as the niceties of expression are in European music. This is certainly not improvisation as European hearers often call it; it is simply the result of a different conception as to what is substantial and what is incidental in a melody; a great deal of what we include in the substance is incidental for them.

This difference of conception became particularly clear to me when an Arab once told me about the experience he had made with a European lady who took lessons in Oriental music with him. He demonstrated the way she sang a melody and the way it really had to be sung. She had memorized a version of it, and conscientiously recited the exact notes of which it consisted. The result was that, in her rendering, the melody fell into disconnected notes grouped by bars and double bars which became almost visible while in his own renderings the melody was a flowing stream which did not for a moment suggest that it might be dissolved into separate atoms. European musicians at their best may create a similar impression; I think that Casals, e.g., does, and that this is the cause of the spell which his playing exercises. But then, a European can only arrive at this by the double process of first studying the notes of the written music and then making a synthesis of them which makes us forget the analytical process the music had gone through in being written.

Europeans have often marvelled at Oriental musicians some of whom keep a store of more than 500 melodies in their memory. It is, indeed, marvellous, but perhaps not quite so much as we think. In the first place, oral tradition is in itself a safeguard against forgetfulness whereas our memory automatically weakens in proportion as we get used to rely on writing. But their memory is not only helped by their (oral) methods, but by certain qualities inherent in their music.

This specially refers to the developed music of highly civilized Eastern countries. Primitive songs and folktunes are handed on in the same way as in Europe; they are simple enough to be picked up without any training. On the other hand, the classical style of music from Japan to the Near East is far from simple. Compositions in this style cannot be executed satisfactorily except by professionals who receive a regular and, in some countries, a severe training. A musical education in Japan, e.g., is supposed to last seven years although it does not include any theoretical training; the time is spent on getting acquainted with a large repertoire of increasingly difficult compositions. An education in Arab classical music, as well, is a matter of several years' training. A Tunisian singer with whom I studied Andalus music, i.e., the music which is considered to go back to Moorish Spain, told me that pupils used to learn the tunes along with the words in the following way: The teacher sang the first phrase of about a bar's length and the pupil repeated it, until he rendered it to the satisfaction of the teacher. Then the teacher repeated this phrase, but added the next one to it and this longer piece was again repeated by the pupil and so on until he had reached the end.

It belongs to the technique of composition throughout these countries that every piece, vocal and instrumental, is interspersed with typified motives. The nature of these motives and the manner in which they are used vary a great deal from one country or group of countries to another; we shall have to come back to this later on. At present, it is sufficient to mention the existence of these typified motives and the fact that their use is a leading principle in Eastern composition. This principle is most important for keeping up oral tradition. It is true that in Europe, too, one can find a great many typified phrases. But one might say that in the course of time European composers have been endeavouring more and more to avoid them in favour of an original and individual mode of expression and that their occurrence in Europe has become more and more the result of an unconscious process. A European composer may be said to use typified phrases in spite of himself while Eastern practice, on the contrary, insists on using them.

This may be sufficient to give you a preliminary idea of the main points of difference between non-European, i.e., Eastern and primitive music on one hand and European on the other.

These points, if I may repeat them, are the wide and immediate appeal of non-European music which is due to its tradition being exclusively oral; secondly, the difference of conception with regard to the identity of a given melody; and thirdly, the existence of, and insistence on, typified phrases or motives in non-European music. But non-European music is, of course, not one thing. When we contrast it with European music, but only then, we are led to think of it as a unity. On closer inspection and leaving European music apart as far as we can, it comprises a great variety of systems and modes of expression. In dealing with these, the usual way is to proceed geographically: to group primitive music roughly according to continents as the music of the American Indians, of the African negroes, of the tribes of the large islands of South-Eastern Asia, of Australia and the South-Sea Islands, &c., and to divide the music of more civilized nations according to countries. This would be a vast programme to which it would be impossible to do justice on the present occasion. Besides, it would not bring out some features with sufficient clearness which I particularly wish to point out. I shall therefore choose another and less orthodox way. First of all, primitive music in its details has to drop out; it can only be referred to by occasional hints. Secondly, we shall put off our inquiry into the music of the different Eastern countries until later, and begin by discussing three musical forms or tendencies which are not restricted to any special region or any special race.

1. As to the first group, I shall, before describing it, let you hear examples of it.[1] You will have recognized that this type of song is very similar to

1 Here a few discs of Ramadan songs sung by a group of boys and recorded in Jerusalem were played. These discs can be had on application to the Archive of Oriental Music, Hebrew University. They are Nos. 58, a, b, and 59a of the collection (£P 0.20 each).

European children's songs. It is used in Germany, e.g., for a large number of nursery rhymes, and for children's games. In some parts of Germany, children walk in procession, carrying paper-lanterns in their hands and singing this tune with many repetitions in early autumn. This is strikingly like the habit, among Muslim children, of walking from house to house on Ramadan evenings, and singing the songs that you have just heard; and they, too, carry a lantern. The same tune has also been found among American Indians and among primitive tribes of Ceylon, and I am sure that, if attention were given to it, it could be traced in many other parts of the world as well.

We now come to the difficult question as to how this distribution can be explained. With the same kind of question the student of ethnology is faced on many occasions: Is a certain phenomenon which we find scattered over different parts of the world, the property of any one of these places and has it spread from there, or can it be supposed to have been invented or to have arisen several times independently? In our particular case one might perhaps say that the custom of carrying lanterns in connection with a special tune must go back to a definite time and place of origin, but I am at present unable to point to any such definite time or place. As to the tune itself, the problem is quite different. It is a very simple tune and may, from our point of view, come into anyone's mind any moment. But then, of course, we must not rely on our own judgment of what is simple in music; tunes which may sound quite unsophisticated to us may have had an advanced character in the far past. It has been claimed by the author of a history of German music that this tune has to be regarded as the nucleus of Teutonic melody. But by what means should the tune have travelled from ancient Germany to South America or to Ceylon? If we accept that it originated in one place and that its occurrence elsewhere is due to historical influence, it is certainly not the North of Europe where it came from. This would be contrary to all our notions of early migrations of peoples or cultural goods. But it is premature to try and solve the question of the origin of this tune; further investigations will be needed for a definite solution.

You may be wondering why I should spend so much time on a thing which may seem most trivial to you. But it was done on purpose. Children's songs like those you have heard now, are typical examples of one of the main tendencies in music. This tendency may be described like this: a perfect equilibrium, in rhythm and tune, between tension and relaxation, closely connected with some regular bodily motion whereas the words matter much less. You will recognize that this description covers a multitude of song types: lullabies sung by mothers while they rock the cradle with a regular up- and downward movement of a foot; occupation songs as those of women turning a handmill or pounding seeds in a mortar: songs for this purpose and with exactly the same tune as the children's have been recorded from South American Indians; boatmen's songs on the Nile and elsewhere which likewise follow regular bodily movements; refrains sung by a community in response to a priest's or another protagonist's solo; songs sung to primitive dances; and many others. It would be interesting to follow up this tendency to more highly developed forms of music, some of which are obviously derived from the same recurrent change between tension and relaxation, or question and answer. Most of these kinds of song address themselves to an audience; they grow out of the common spirit of a group and everybody present is supposed to join in.

2. We now go on to the opposite tendency; example of this, too, can be freely chosen from many different parts of the world. In contrast to the former one, the word, here, is all-important. The text dictates the course of the voice; the cantillation aims at giving the words impressiveness by reducing the cadences of the speaking voice to a few typical forms; it is only at the close and half-close of sentences that it amounts to anything that we should call melody and even this more independent treatment of the voice is in the service of syntax and rhetoric. There is no independent musical rhythm; it is the rhythm of the language which dictates the musical time-values. The prototype of this kind of musical production, if we may give it this name, is the incantation which is recited by the medicine-man of primitive tribes when magical rites and ceremonies are performed. It is clear that the words which are spoken on these occasions cannot be uttered with ordinary accents. According to the belief which underlies these ceremonies it is not the shāman or medicine-man himself who speaks, but the demon by whom he is possessed, and it is a matter of course that the

superhuman spell which he is supposed to perform, in curing diseases, in influencing crops, in driving away the evil spirits lingering about at a funeral – that the magical formula which is to achieve all this cannot be pronounced except in a superhuman tone of voice. A necessary quality, therefore, of these incantations is that the voice should be disguised. This is done by giving it an extraordinary sound-colour, and by providing the recitation of the words with formidable trills, glides and accents. I am sorry I cannot give you an example of this from a primitive tribe, but you will hear a recitation now which is closely related to it and shows all its characteristics.[2]

The main point about this is, as I said, that the strained recitation arises from the ecstasy which the magical and, on a later stage of development, the sacred text demands. The more this ecstasy becomes domesticated or civilized, the more the characteristic style of the recitation is smoothed down. In this smoother manner we find it in the Jewish and Christian liturgies and in the Vedic ritual of India. (It is worth mentioning that the Sanskrit word for chanting Vedic texts, Sāman, may be connected with shāman, the medicine man.) The magical origin of the ceremonies has left unmistakable vestiges, not only in the treatment of the vocal part, but also in other features: think of the Jewish shofar and of the bells of the Catholic service.

But the recitative tendency, represented at its purest by the incantations of the primitive medicine man, has not remained within the limits of liturgy. It has had far-reaching effects on musical history. Out of the spirit of magical beliefs and of an ecstatic state of mind grew ancient tragedy and its musical belongings. Ancient Greek tragedy originated from the cult of the god Dionysus which was connected with the ecstatic ritual of the vintage. The music and chants belonging to it have not come down to us. But there is a similar kind of drama which has been faithfully preserved to the present day; it was created from elements closely akin to those of Greek tragedy, and resembles it in many details. This is the early Japanese Nō-drama which received its present form in the 15th century.

[2] Here a disc containing a Samaritan cantillation from Exodus was played (No 28b of the collection of the Archive of Oriental Music, Hebrew University, Jerusalem; cf. former note).

The Nō-drama was not a spontaneous growth. Ecstatic rituals as the festival of the rice gathering, legends and historical events, and Buddhist ideas and ceremonies have merged in it. Its peculiar dramatic form was imported from China where, however, it has not survived. But China cannot have been its place of origin either; we have to look for it further west. In the Japanese Nō there are two principal dramatis personae, a hero (who may be a woman, but is represented by a man, as all the others), and a second person. Both may have one or two satellites; besides there is a chorus. The principal characters wear masks; the stage has no decorations. Several plays are acted on one day; they are separated by comical interludes. Every one of these features and a number of others link up the Japanese Nō with Greek tragedy; and the occurrence of them all in both kinds of drama leads us to think of an historical connection with a probability bordering on certainty. This connection may have been provided by India where a rich dramatic production arose at a period intermediate between the Greek and the Chinese drama. The Japanese drama, therefore, enables us to form at least an idea of what the recitation of the Greek drama may have been like. At the same time, the close resemblance of its chanting with liturgical cantillation bears witness of its ritualistic and magical origin.[3]

A third instance of the recitative style is supplied by the recital of epic poems. In Montenegro, the heroic feats of the forefathers are chanted to the accompaniment of the Cusle, a primitive fiddle, to the present day, and a corresponding practice exists among the Bedouins. Both the voice and the accompaniment are restricted to three or four notes each of which has its special function in differentiating the rhetorical accents of the text. Short interludes supply the bard with breathing space and the frugal use of the voice with its ever recurring climax and anticlimax serve to carry on long narratives far better than could be done by a rich display of melody.[4] Here, again, present day practice leads us back to antiquity: we have to suppose that the great epic poems in the heroic days of Greece, the Odyssey

---

3   Here, a record of Japanese Nō chanting was played.
4   Here, a Palestinian Arab chanted a Bedouin romance to his own accompaniment on the Rabāba.

and the Iliad, and of Northern Europe, as Beowulf and the Hildebrandslied, although their own tradition has perished long ago, were executed in a similar manner.

The recitative style which is characteristic of liturgical cantillations, of certain parts of ancient tragedy and its offsprings, and of epic recitation, is in direct contrast with the first mentioned one, not only musically, but also in its social aspect. While the former one is practised by a community or an anonymous member of it, the recitative chant is addressed to a community by an outstanding personality, as the priest, the dramatic hero, or the bard, respectively.

3. A third and last group includes what may be called lyrical singing. This is neither an utterance of common spirit, nor is it addressed to it; it is the expression of an individual left to himself. Its form is not dictated by regular motion and it therefore lacks the balance of social songs; nor is it directed by magical or sacred words or rhetoric of any kind; the words, in this style of singing, may be of no importance, or be missing altogether.

Instances of this style are the wordless jubilations in the Gregorian chant so well described by St. Augustin[5] and the warbles of Bedouins during their solitary rides, with one of their hands pressed to their cheek.[6]

These three tendencies in singing do not always appear separately. In later stages of development they may be combined to form a unity. In the Gregorian service all the three styles are represented; and, similarly, they co-exist in European opera where the recitative is followed by the lyrical outburst of the aria with its wealth of grace and ornament and where both are contrasted with the balanced structure of the chorus.

III

Till now, no allusion has been made to music systems, to the structure of scales and rhythms. The discussion of these questions is now due. The

---

5 "He who jubilates utters no words, but conveys a heart melted with joy," Yc. (Migne, Patrologia Latina, 37, 1272).
6 Here, a disc containing an Arab song was played (No. 69 of the collection of the Archive of Oriental Music, Hebrew University, Jerusalem).

general lover of music usually has some notion of Eastern music being connected with quarter-tones and polyrhythm, and shrinks from approaching a subject which seems to him to involve intricate calculations, rows and columns of incomprehensible figures and fractions without conveying any musical meaning to him. I wish to stress from the beginning that I am not going to perplex you with arithmetic. What I wish to point out is that the questions of scale and rhythm are not merely a piece of lifeless theory remote from musical practice, but that they contribute an important part to the understanding of Eastern musical conception and of Eastern thought, generally.

Even an untrained ear notices that in many cases the intonation of Eastern songs deviates from the scales provided by the European musical system and instruments. The easiest way of accounting for this is to say that Eastern singers sing wrong notes – an opinion which one can hear often enough and which adds to the disdain in which Eastern music is held by many. But we can easily convince ourselves of the fact that deviations from our scale do not only occur in Eastern singing, but also in the tuning of Eastern instruments (on which good players can and do bestow every possible care), and in the scales established by Eastern theories. This is sufficient proof that the difference between European and non-European intervals is not due to mistakes, but that non-European intonation has standards of its own. What are these standards?

We are often told that our European system of intervals conforms to natural laws; this opinion is also expressed in speaking of "just" tuning with regard to the numeric values of our untempered diatonic scale. We need not go into this now; by the way, the statement is not correct: the intervals of our scale are not dictated by nature. What we are concerned with is not the relation between the demands of our ear and the physical or the arithmetical qualities of tones and intervals, but the question what tones or intervals the human ear chooses or prefers uninfluenced, as far as possible, by outward phenomena or by theories. To obtain an answer to this question we cannot, of course, rely on the judgment of civilized nations or individuals. They all believe that what they have been accustomed to is natural; their judgment of just intonation, instead of revealing the natural state of things, reflects the convention existing in their particular country and age, and this convention is the result of an historical development.

Can we go back to the beginning of all historical development, i.e., to an age where no convention has yet been established? We can, at any rate, go back to the practice of primitive tribes, and state what we find there with regard to the intonation of the voice and the tuning of instruments. One of the facts to be observed is that there is a vast difference between the intervals of an unaccompanied voice and those of musical instruments. We first deal with singing. There are tribes which do not know any musical instruments; here, at last, the voice, being uninfluenced by the sounds of instruments, will behave in what we may fairly assume to be a natural manner. The result of inquiries made into this early stage of development is that the intervals used are far less definite than those fixed on any instrument. There are two kinds of intervals: large ones amounting, roughly, to a fourth or fifth; and narrow ones amounting to anything from an approximate semitone to an equally approximate minor or major third. All these intervals may vary a great deal even when used in repetitions of the same tune and executed by the same singer. The reason for this is obvious. While on instruments precise tones and intervals can be laid down, the voice has in itself no means of doing this; there is no standard measure at which it can aim.

The two kinds of intervals have different and, in fact, contrasting functions. The voice travels from a starting note to neighbouring ones; one of them establishes itself as a kind of tonic, that means, as a point where the tension of the phrase relaxes, and where the voice feels at rest. The melodic process, therefore, consists of tension and relaxation in proportion as the voice departs from, or returns to, the established tonic. The tension increases as the distance from the tonic grows, and relaxes with the return to the tonic. But this process is only one of two elements in the making of melody. Its building material is enriched by a second element. If the voice departs from the tonic beyond a certain distance above or below, it arrives at a region where the tension is distinctly felt not to increase any more, but, on the contrary, to give way to a relaxation similar to that which is felt on returning to the tonic. This curious sensation is explained by the physiological fact that the relation between different notes of the entire tone-range is not characterized only by their distance, but also by an altogether separate quality which is called tonality. When the voice, e.g., passes from one note to its octave by a number of steps, the distance continually grows; still, when the voice arrives at the octave, this note is felt to be more similar to, or, as one might say, more consonant with, the original note than any of the intermediate ones. Now, the octave is not an important interval in primitive melody, which, usually, has a narrower range. But a similar experience applies to the fifth and the fourth. When the voice reaches an approximate fourth, for which it generally needs two or three steps, the tension as produced and increased by these successive steps is all of a sudden diminished, or even subsides as soon as the region of the fourth, i.e., the region of a note similar to the tonic, is reached.

I cannot illustrate these fundamental facts here by examples of primitive singing. It must be sufficient to sum them up. Uninfluenced singing does not conform to a scale in the accepted sense; it makes use of a number of vaguely defined notes one of which is felt as a tonic while, among the others, one part is felt to be dissimilar to it and, therefore, produces tension while the other part is similar to, or consonant with it and, therefore, produces the same or a similar effect of relief as the return to the tonic itself.

You will remember that the question of tension and relaxation had been raised on a previous occasion. It had been stated that social songs (children's, occupation, and entertainment songs) were characterized by a constant and regular oscillation between tension and relaxation, corresponding to the pendular body motion which often accompanies them. Accordingly, in these songs, there is a constant and regular recurrence of the tonic or its equivalents. In ritual and epic recitation there is no such balance. The voice moves on neighbouring notes and the return to rest may be withheld for some time without our being certain when it will finally take place. This is in agreement with the high tension which is felt in listening to these recitations. Individual lyrical outbursts, lastly, may or may not show a predominance of the tonic and the notes similar to it. As a rule, here too, as in the previous group, the relaxation afforded by the tonic or its consonant notes is withheld through prolonged melodic phrases: the singer chanting his highly strung feelings wants some time to discharge them.

A musical system as we understand it cannot originate except by the intervention of musical instruments. This does not mean that the use of instruments in itself establishes a scale. This, rather, depends on the nature of the instruments and on how they are handled. There are instruments, especially those used for signals and in magical ceremonies, which are not elaborated so as to produce the sounds of a melody, but which are simply used for producing those sounds which they yield naturally. Instances of this are the Jewish shofar, and the Tibetan tuba, an instrument of enormous length (2 metres and more), the lower end of which rests on the ground.[7] This disc gives an example of a Tibetan Buddhist ceremony where several instruments, a trumpet made of a bone of a deceased lama, bells, &c coincide, but do not harmonize with the tuba. The tuba in this record is made to enounce its first upper partial and the second one which is between a fifth and a sixth higher. The latter note is produced with great effort; the player can never be sure of producing it at a given moment. It is self-evident that an instrument like this does not inspire or encourage the establishment of a scale.

There is another interesting point about the music of this ceremony. There is no agreement among the instruments, but there is no agreement either between any of the instruments and the cantillation recited at the same time. (This cantillation, to the words of a Buddhist formula, is inaudible on the disc.) This curious practice of singing and playing side by side, without being in touch musically, which is not restricted to Tibetan ceremonies, has not found due attention. It survives, e.g., as you may remember, in the Nō, where the flute and the voice parts form a frightfully discordant counterpoint. We are greatly tempted to call all this tin-kettle concerts, and leave it at that. But does it not mean that concerted music, i.e., music as executed by various instruments and voices in agreement with each other, is by no means a matter of course as we generally suppose? I think that, here too, we are used to regard our own conventions as natural instead of considering them as a result of a gradual development. It is quite possible that the disconnection between instruments and voices in Tibetan rituals and elsewhere represent an early stage of development

---

[7] Here a record of the music of a Tibetan ceremony was played.

and that a great deal of experience and training was necessary before the different organs of sound could be made to converge in the way which we accept as the only natural one.

It is one of the most important questions in musical history by what means and from what outlook people came to construct instruments producing a fixed order of sounds instead of simply making use of their own sounds which the instruments yielded of their own.

Fortunately, this question has been solved through investigations during the last few decades. It may seem strange to you that the explanation is not primarily based on considerations of a musical nature, but that we have to turn elsewhere for it. The fundamental fact has been the establishment of standard measures. This was the achievement of a very ancient civilization; the earliest testimonies of it are available in ancient Egypt, in the Sumerian culture, and in ancient China; but we need not trouble about its exact place of origin now. What is necessary to know is that standard measures and weights are not a matter of course nor do they rest on a natural basis; the European metre, e.g., has been fixed by dividing the equator into 40 million parts. All other standards are equally arbitrary. But this is just what makes them interesting; it is evident that if we find a certain precise and arbitrary standard used in different parts of the world we may safely conclude that there must be an historical connection between the respective civilizations. As a matter of fact, all the ancient standard lengths are either identical or in simple numerical relations with each other (as 10 to 12) and these standard measures while they have been superseded in most of those civilized countries where they were officially in force as in ancient Egypt, Babylonia, and China can now be found in remote parts of the world where they are conscientiously preserved by primitive tribes who have no idea of their original meaning.

These standard measures were applied to the length, breadth, and height of temples and other sacred buildings, to agricultural fields, important tools, and, last not least, to musical instruments. This practice was due to the cosmological belief which permeated all ancient civilization. For the security and stability of life, for the maintenance of order, it was thought essential that everything human should be subjected to the same law of harmony and concord that governs the celestial spheres: the "harmony of the spheres" must find its semblance on earth.

The application of these ideas to music primarily consisted in standardizing the measures of musical instruments. The length of pipes, lutes, and other instruments was chosen according to the acknowledged standard foot or one of its derivatives. This has been proved by two kinds of evidence:

1. the explicit testimony of written documents, mainly of China;

2. measurements of musical instruments, chiefly pipes, as found in Ancient Egyptian tombs and in many other places.

As to the importance attributed to the measurement of musical instruments, the history of China offers an uninterrupted chain of evidence. The dimensions of the pipe producing the fundamental note were standard measures; accordingly, the fundamental note itself was a standard pitch (as the note of 435 vibrations is with us). These standards were used for the tuning of the two Imperial orchestras employed for civil and military ceremonies. The control of these measures and tunings was in the hands of the Ministry of weights and measures. At every change of dynasty, the correctness of the measures and pitches was carefully reconsidered; the down fall of the preceding dynasty was ascribed to the pitch having been either strident or hollow; and in the 10th century two special commissions were appointed to recover the original pitch and thus to settle the question once for all – which they failed to do.

On the whole, the standardization of the dimensions of instruments and the application of cosmological principles to them resulted in two separate ways of constructing scales.

1. Starting from the fundamental note the Chinese arrived at a series of 12 notes by constructing pipes which, alternately, amounted to two thirds and four thirds of the length of the preceding one. This proceeding exclusively employed figures and proportions of cosmological significance; the resulting pitches were considered to be alternately male and female and the Chinese said that each of them "engendered" the following one. The result is a chain of fifths, but, owing to the sound production of pipes, the fifths arrived at metrically are not just acoustically – which, however, was not considered to matter.

2. Starting from the standard foot as embodied by a pipe, the Egyptians

arrived at a series of notes by dividing the foot into inches according to one of the recognized systems (decimal, duodecimal) and by marking the divisions by fingerholes. The method does not result in a scale consisting of just intervals; but the metrical result sometimes coincides with the numeric values of just intervals. So, e.g., when a standard measure is divided into 24 parts and when the pipe representing it has a fingerhole at the 6th division, the relation of 24 to 16, i.e., 3 to 2, is that of a fifth. But here again the acoustical result is not a just fifth – and, again, this did not matter.

These two principles, the generation of metrical fifths, and the division of a certain length into equal sections, at once reminds us of the two tendencies which we have found to dominate unaccompanied song, and named consonance and distance. In the same way as a tendency in singing exists towards establishing the consonant relations of the fourth and of the fifth, the proceeding from one pipe to another by alternate fifths and fourths results in a scale built up on the principle of consonance. And the other tendency of the voice towards simply marking distances by melodic steps reappears in the method of dividing a given length into equal sections.

These two contrasting principles are represented by two different groups of instruments. The first one, standing for consonance, is represented by instruments consisting of a series of sound organs each of which produces only one sound. These instruments, although very different in material, are all tuned in chains of fifths and fourths: every note "engenders" the next one. To mention a few instruments of outstanding importance: harps, lyres; panpipes; zithers or psalteries; xylophones.

The second group consists of instruments representing the principle of proceeding by distance. A single organ of sound is divided into sections of equal length each of which marks an interval of a scale. Instruments belonging to this group are: flutes, hautbois, clarinets, all of them provided with fingerholes; lutes with a long neck and similar instruments provided with frets or bridges.

These two main principles have been blended in later stages of civilization, and, gradually, manners of tuning were devised which served to satisfy the growing demands of the musical ear. But it is important to remember that the rise and first stages of the development of the scale is not due to aesthetical considerations, but is part of a cosmological conception which included music as one of the essential forces of the universe.

The study of the principles and development of rhythm is far less involved. European rhythm has not arrived at a stage of development superior to that of other nations or even of certain primitive tribes. On the contrary, it is generally granted that non-European rhythm is superior to it both in variety and delicacy.

One main division is between free rhythm and strict time; this has already been dealt with in connection with the balanced and the recitative style. Here, too, there are instruments representing the two styles: wind instruments and especially fiddles easily lend themselves to free rhythm while drums and plucked strings, by the regular bodily motion they demand on the part of the player, naturally tend towards strict time.

As to music in strict time, the practice of accompanying tunes with percussion is almost universal outside Europe. But there are two methods: one consists of simply beating time; this needs no illustration. The other consists of employing drums or other percussion instruments as parts equal to the melodic instruments. This results in the famous rhythmical polyphony of non-European music of which you will now hear an example.[8]

The two principles of marking time and of supplying an additional rhythmic part do not coexist, generally; in most parts of the world, one or the other is preferred or practised exclusively. But this belongs to the question of the different musical character of the different Eastern nations or groups of nations, which will be the subject of the next and last lecture of the series.

IV

We have been concerned with unravelling the chief tendencies in Eastern music and have, for this purpose, been dealing with early and simple forms

---

8   Here a disc executed by Tunisians was played containing a duo between an hautbois and a drum.

of it. It is clear that these forms are more likely to reveal the primary forces and elements in music than the forms found among highly civilized nations where these forces have come to blend with each other in a great number of ways. Now that a foundation has been laid it seems to be high time to speak of the kinds of music which have been built upon it. But I cannot resist this last opportunity of reminding you once more of the results hitherto obtained.

We have come to distinguish a purely vocal style without fixed intervals and scales, and a later one which is based on standardized instrumental intervals and scales and where the voice goes together with the instruments.

The purely vocal style includes three tendencies which are found almost throughout the world. Neither of them, therefore, is typical of any individual nation or group of nations. They are rather distinguished by the different occasions on which they are used.

The first tendency is towards balanced melodic structures in strict time and with consonance prevailing. It is generally connected with regular bodily motions and the songs belonging to it mostly have a countless number of stanzas sung to the same melody. This applies to children's songs, cradle songs, and songs sung by communities or groups, such as occupation songs, songs in accompaniment of dances, &c.

The second group consists of recitations of words. The rhythm of the cantillation is free musically, but directed by the syntax and rhetoric of the text. Here, the voice does not aim at consonant intervals, but rather keeps within a limited range of notes. These cantillations are, of course, reserved to soloists. Originally, they were used for magical ceremonies; from there, they passed into religious services, and into epic and dramatic recitation.

There is a third tendency which we have called lyrical. It neither rises from a group or community like the first one, nor does it address. It is an expression of exuberant sentiment. Songs belonging to it abound in ornament; they neither obey the rights of bodily motion nor that of a given text. As instances, I mentioned the jubilation of the Roman liturgy and the melodic outbursts of Bedouins during their rides through deserted country.

The invention of rational tunings and scales arose, as I pointed out last time, from cosmological ideas which were developed in some cultural centre, probably in Central Asia. Two kinds of instruments can be distinguished:

1. instruments consisting of series of pipes or lamellas or open strings, each yielding only one note. The notes usually form chains of fifths starting from a standard pitch. The instruments representative of this principle are: panpipes; xylophones and metallophones, harps and lyres.

2. instruments consisting of mainly one pipe or string divided into sections by fingerholes or frets, respectively. The primary method of arrangement was to choose the whole length according to a standard measure and to divide it into equal sections. Instruments representative of this principle are: flutes, clarinets and hautbois, and the pandura, a longnecked lute whose name, in Arab writings, was transformed into tanbūr.

In later stages of development, these two principles were combined in the construction and tuning of stringed instruments. In addition to this, new methods of dividing the length of strings were worked out. So the Chinese zither as well as the Indian Vīnā which may be either a zither or a lute, and the Arab 'Ūd, a short-necked lute, are all tuned in fifths, but the divisions of the strings are made according to different arithmetical devices.

The number of notes supplied by these instruments varies. The early Arab lute, e.g., has twelve like our piano; later on, five more were added and, at present, twenty-four are recognized. The Indian Vīnā has twenty-two notes within the octave. But, of course, not all these notes appear in one tune. Just as, in European music, not all the twelve notes of the octave are used for one melody, they too only provide possibilities for playing tunes at different pitches or composed of different intervals. This leads us to the question of scales.

A scale is an upward or downward series of notes used in a melody or in a group of melodies. Every scale, therefore, is a selection from the supply of notes which the instruments provide. The number and size of the steps used in different kinds of melody vary a great deal. Accordingly, there are numerous scales differing by the number and size of their steps.

In all the civilized nations of the East, systems of scales have been elaborated and it is often difficult to decide which of the scales were important in musical practice and which were results of speculation. Sometimes, however, writers expressly distinguish between the scales which exist and those which ought to exist in addition to them. Chinese theory in the 10th century, e.g., established 84 scales while only 18 were used in classical music and 3 in popular music.

These systems are interesting as showing the tendency towards speculation so deeply rooted in the Eastern mind. (As far back as in ancient Babylonia the gods were catalogued and in Indian treatises on dancing, every gesture found its place in an elaborate system.) For the present purpose, we need not go into the niceties of scale-tabulation; it may be sufficient to point out some features of musical interest.

Roughly speaking, the nations of East Asia, including the South East, use five-tone scales; in Near Eastern music seven-tone scales predominate; and Indian music with its five-, six-, and seven-tone scales has always kept an intermediate position. This in itself divides the Asiatic nations into three vast musical groups. You shall now hear a few specimens of the first group, first of all a record of Chinese theatrical music.[9]

This, as you will have noticed, is not the classical style of music which survives in the Japanese Nō plays. It sounds rather trivial, but it may serve to show some characteristics of Chinese music. Firstly, the scale used here is the simplest kind of a five-tone scale, i.e., the structure which we find on the piano in touching the black keys only, and which provides no intervals smaller than a tone. The melody is in strict common time.

The next example is in exact contrast to this. It is a Japanese song.[10] Here, too, the scale consists of no more than five notes. But the typical scale of Chinese tunes is composed of tones and minor thirds while the Japanese prefer combinations of semitones and major thirds. To us, the Chinese scale sounds consonant and relaxed, the Japanese scale, with its semitones, highly strung. This impression is enhanced by the respective kinds of rhythm. In Japanese songs (and nowhere else), the voice and the accompanying instrument, when singing and playing the same melody, do not produce the same note at the same time but one follows the other at a short distance. The rhythmic structure may be quite simple, but the rhythm never sounds straightforward owing to this curious and unexplained practice.

---

9 Here a disc containing an accompanied song from a Chinese drama was played.
10 Here a record of a Japanese song was played.

The two contrasting five-tone scales which make it easy for us to distinguish Chinese and Japanese music even if there were no other distinction, are found side by side in the music of Java and Bali. On these islands a strange kind of orchestral playing has been developed. The orchestras mainly consist of series of gongs, metallophones and xylophones, and two solo instruments, a fiddle introduced by the Muhammedans, and a flute. The soft and merging tints of these orchestras recall the technique of colouring called batik, which comes from the same part of the world. The sound of these orchestras is, perhaps, the only feature in Eastern music which has a general and spontaneous appeal to European hearers.

The main instruments, gongs, metallophones, and xylophones, have only five or seven notes in the octave and their tuning, like that of the piano, is fixed. Owing to this, the two kinds of scales cannot by played by the same orchestra. One orchestra is tuned in a five-tone scale without semitones; it is called Slendro. The other one consists of instruments with seven notes; most selections from these notes result in five-tone scales with one or two semitones. This tuning is called Pelog.

You first hear a song accompanied by a slendro orchestra. A curious fact about slendro tuning is that the five-tone scale in this tuning is in equal temperament. Every one of the five notes has the same distance from its neighbour; the scale, therefore, consists of five intervals of about 5 quartertones each. This makes them all sound out of tune for a European ear; the major sixth and the minor seventh are merged into one "neutral" note, and so are the major tone and the minor third.[11] The pelog tuning which is not tempered and which contains semitones can be easily distinguished from this.[12]

Perhaps you have been wondering at the prominent part I have, in explaining these examples, attributed to matters of scale. You may have remembered that, on a former occasion, I made statements which do not seem to be in agreement with this. As a matter of fact, I did say that European staff notation had brought about an analytical conception of

---

11 Here a record of a Javanese song in "Slendro" was played.
12 Here a record of a Javanese song in "Pelog" was played.

melody while Eastern musicians recited melodic strains rather than successions of individual notes. But do not scales present disconnected notes in the same way as staff notation? and must they not, therefore, bring about a similarly abstract conception of melody? To a certain extent, this cannot be denied; the invention of instrumental scales, i.e., the arrangement of notes in upward or downward order, is a product of a comparatively late stage of civilization.

On the other hand, there is a feature common to all Oriental music which counteracts the analytical influence of instrumental scales. Nowhere are the notes of the scales used for any arbitrary combination which they may yield, theoretically. A few only of the countless possibilities of making different tunes out of the notes at disposal occur in reality. Every nation has a certain restricted number of melodic types, motives or phrases, which reappear in many variations over and over again. Melodic invention, in each one of these nations, is fixed to these types and the musicians are careful not to trespass beyond them. This stability of types which also extends to rhythm is the backbone of oral tradition.

The Oriental nations differ in their ways of establishing these types. There is no time for an individual study of their methods. It must be sufficient to show one instance of how they work. We may choose, for this purpose, the melodic system of India and the Near East.

India as well as all the countries in which Islam predominates, distinguishes a varying number of melody types. The technical term for a melody type is Rāga in India and Maqām in the Near East. A melody type includes a scale as well as a kind of melodic raw material. Every single melody, in this system, must be shaped out of this raw material or else it is considered to blunder against the laws of composition. It is difficult to describe the characteristics of any such melody type; a real knowledge of the system can only be obtained by attending to practice.

The best way towards understanding a melody type is offered by the custom, prevailing among Oriental musicians, of opening up a recital by a prelude in free rhythm. This prelude exhibits the raw material of a melody type in the various registers of the scale. The prelude is followed by a series of songs and instrumental pieces in strict time. All these pieces develop phrases or motives taken from the same melody type and so they all point back to some part of the prelude. As soon as you become conscious of the qualities of the melody type you can recognize the relation existing between the prelude and all the melodies which follow it. This recognition is perhaps one of the main pleasures to be derived from Indian or Arab classical music. You will now hear a prelude representing one of the Arab melody types followed by a piece in strict time.[13]

From the Oriental point of view, every melody type not only has a particular scale and particular phrasing, but also a particular power of expression. This, once more, leads us back to the interrelation between music and magic ideas which we have been discussing in connection with sacred cantillation, and with the fixation, at a later stage of development, of instrumental measures and scales. The dimensions and divisions of instruments were established so as to harmonize with the universe. Accordingly, every one of the sounds of an instrument was supposed to correspond to a certain cosmic force or phenomenon. The musical notes were considered as being in accordance with the stars and the signs of the zodiac, with the elements, the seasons, the days of the week, the colours, the human temperaments, &c. The sound, e.g., corresponding to the planet Mars, is red, hot, and warlike; the sound corresponding to the planet Venus expresses love; the sound corresponding to Saturn forebodes evil. From antiquity to the Middle Ages, this cosmological conception was applied to music in many different ways. It was also applied – as a matter of course – to the Indian and Arab system of melody types. The system of maqāmāt, as the Arab melody types are called, originated in the 11th century. Playing in a certain Maqām at the appropriate season, weekday, and hour, was expected to cure illness and to influence nature in much the same way as certain ritual cantillations. The same superstition led people to think that a Maqām, if played at an inappropriate time, could bring misfortune to those who played, and to those who listened to it.

The scales of Indian and especially of Arab melody are different from those of Chinese, Japanese, and Javanese music. There are Indian melody types with five-tone scales and we have reason to believe that these are the most ancient scales in Indian music. Arab urban music, almost

---

13 Here an instrumental prelude and a piece in strict time were played by local musicians.

throughout, has seven notes within the octave. Most of these seven notes can be lowered or heightened in certain melody-types; many of the scales in use, therefore, only differ by a slight shade of intonation. This is the true significance of the so-called system of quartertones. Quartertones are never, as it is sometimes thought, used in succession; the 24 notes of the octave provided for on some Arab instruments only exist for selecting different kinds of seven-tone scales from them: instead of a tone and a semitone, e.g., two steps of a three-quarter tone each, may occur; or a certain melody type has a three-quarter tone and a five-quarter tone in succession instead of a semitone and an augmented second.

As regards rhythm, there is a general distinction similar to that between the scales. The recital of Eastern tunes is accompanied by drums or other percussion instruments. The practice is almost universal; but there are two main kinds of drumming. Just as the East and the West of Asia contrast with regard to scales, so they do in their use of percussion. In the East, drumming generally means beating time, i.e. stressing the strong accents of the bar as, e.g., the first time-unit of a bar. Arabs and Indians, on the other hand, use percussion as independent parts of the rhythmical texture, and so arrive at what has been called "rhythmical polyphony." The effects of this practice are perplexing to European ears; but most of them are brought about by very simple rhythmical devices. The most frequent one is to alternate between two and three beats of equal distance in a section of six time-units, i.e., in terms of European music, to alternate between 6/8 and 3/4 time. But this device is not only applied to bars of 6 time-units, but also to others as, e.g., common time. In common time, the same device results in a structure of 3 + 3 + 2 of the drum as against 4 x 2 of the melody, or vice versa, and the different instruments may exchange their rhythmical "parts." This is difficult as long as you only listen to it; it becomes far clearer as soon as you can watch the drummer's hands.

The two contrasting kinds of practice require contrasting kinds of technique. The Far East prefers gongs and large drums beaten with sticks, the Near East small drums and tambourines beaten with the hands and fingers. It is evident that the latter technique unlike the former one lends itself to a delicate shaping of the drum "part."

This is no more than a rough sketch of how some main characteristics of Eastern music have come into being. It would be tempting to make a detailed study of every one of the nations concerned. But there is no time for it now; so I prefer raising a question which is connected with the preceding subject and which can claim a particular interest here. It is the question of Oriental Jewish music.

The cantillation of the Jewish sacred books and prayers has been dealt with, or at least alluded to, in connection with other Oriental recitations, of which it is an outstanding example, When, after the destruction of the Second Temple, the Jews were dispersed, the tradition of chanting the sacred texts could not remain unchanged. There are differences not only between the Eastern and the European traditions, but also among the Oriental communities themselves. A great number of specimens from most of these traditions have been collected and published by A. Z. Idelsohn, the pioneer in the scientific study of Jewish music, in his Thesaurus of Hebrew melodies.

The problem as to which of these various traditions may have kept closest to the original has not yet been solved definitely. Idelsohn has shown that the communities of the East and especially those which have been remotest from the influence of other nations, like the Yemenite and the Babylonian Jews, are in possession of versions which coincide with those of the Gregorian chant. They must, therefore, date back to a period preceding the separation of the Jewish and Christian liturgy. None of the Jewish communities in Europe can claim an equally ancient tradition.

On the other hand, changes in the cantillation are not restricted to those groups which settled in different parts of Europe. The Oriental communities, too, were affected by the musical styles of the nations among whom they came to live. Thus, Synagogue song among the Jewish communities in Western North Africa is obviously influenced by the style of the urban music prevailing among the Muhammedans of these countries, a style which originated in the Moorish period of Spain and which, accordingly, is called "Andalus."

Still, Synagogue cantillation, in spite of the fact that it became tinged with non-Jewish secular music, held its own throughout the East to the present day. It never accepted the Arab system of melody-types. But in the Middle Ages, types of Jewish song arose which were, and are, closely akin, in spirit and in system, to those of their Arab neighbours. These songs, like the hymns of the Christian church, were introduced into the service for the sake of greater variety. In contrast with the cantillations they are in strict time, and mostly belong to the groups established by the Arab systems of melody-types and rhythms. The poems sung in this manner are called piyyutim, and are themselves imitations of a certain class of Arab poetry. Like classical Arab songs the piyyutim are preceded by chants in free rhythm which indicate their melody type. Innumerable songs of this kind have been preserved in Oriental Jewish communities.[14]

The tunes of these songs, certainly, are as closely related to those of urban Arab music as the tunes of two neighbouring and kindred nations can be. It remains an object of future studies whether there are any essential distinctions and what those distinctions are. In merely listening to them one has the impression that after all there is a difference. But a close analysis is required to find out whether this is due to a difference in the structure or rather in the delivery of the tunes.

In conclusion, I should like to say a few words about the present situation of Jewish music. We have seen that Oriental Jewish song, sacred and secular, expresses musical tendencies common to many other nations of the East in its own way. The music of these nations, in our days, is undergoing a severe crisis; European influence threatens to destroy traditions which had been handed on securely for many centuries. Oriental Jewish music seems to be inextricably involved in this crisis. In the Middle Ages, as I pointed out with reference to the piyyutim, it had largely adapted itself to Arab music. This, we can imagine, was done with little difficulty as it was a kind of musical family affair – both nations ultimately drawing from the source of a common tradition. One might conclude, therefore, that, if the Arabs succumb to the growing fascination of European music, Oriental Jewish song is doomed as well.

But owing to a strange historical coincidence there is another possible way. Jewish communities in Europe were, through centuries, penetrated with the music of the countries in which they lived. This, of course, meant

---

14 Here a record of a Moroccan *piyyut* with its introduction in free rhythm was played (Archive of Oriental Music, No. 104a).

a far more severe break with their oriental musical tradition than any influence exercised on Eastern Jewish communities by the Arabs. The result is evident from the share of Jewish composers in European music, particularly from the 19th century to this day. There may be a common Jewish denominator in the music of Mendelssohn, Meyerbeer, Offenbach, Mahler, Schönberg, &c; but as yet, nobody has succeeded in pointing it out. Most of those who try to discover it move in a circle. They start from the biographical fact that a certain composer is a Jew, and argue from this that those traits in his music which distinguish it from the compositions of his non-Jewish contemporaries must be Jewish. But the distinctions between non-Jewish compositions are often greater than those between any of them and the work of a Jewish contemporary of theirs. All the above-named Jewish musicians, owing to their ways of expression, have their legitimate places in the development of European music. The proposition that their contribution to it is specifically Jewish is certainly most interesting; but it would require new methods – methods, as it were, of musical anthropology – to prove or disprove it.

Recent and present immigration into Palestine has greatly actuated the question of Jewish music. There are musicians who go on as before; others are sensitive of an entire change of atmosphere, and are aiming at an adequate expression of it. I do not wish to enter upon a critical review of the many attempts made in this direction by European Jews. It is obvious that they cannot, simply by coming here, shake off their Western or Slav musical education, and willfully establish a national style. Above all, nothing is gained by picking up some "Oriental" music themes and working them out in the usual European manner.

But I wish to draw your attention to a new kind of music just about to rise. A change in musical style is, as a matter of course, chiefly envisaged by those who come from Europe; to the Oriental Jews who come to Palestine from other Eastern countries, the change of surroundings is less momentous. Accordingly, they hardly partake in the new musical movement. It is all the more interesting to watch any kind of activity on their part towards a new style and I am glad to be able to introduce to you a musician who does try to face the new situation. Mr. Harun Ezra Aharon is a musician from Baghdad trained in Arab urban music from his childhood and a master on its chief instrument, the lute. After having settled in Jerusalem he became aware of the possibility of giving a new impulse to Eastern music by making use of modern Hebrew poetry. His proceeding, in a way, reminds us of the earlier practice of singing Hebrew piyyutim in a style resembling Arab urban songs. He, too, uses the style of his Arab contemporaries. The composition which he is going to perform is a "monologue," a form recently developed in Egypt. Contrary to older forms, each stanza is supplied here with its own music and coherence is not arrived at by a refrain or ritornell, but merely by a certain conformity of melodic invention.

Still, this composition and others from the same source show us a new direction. The spirit of the texts – the present one is a poem of Bialik's – is not of the kind with which an Oriental musician is familiar. Nor has Mr. Ezra dealt with it musically as if it belonged to the class of poetry familiar to him. You will certainly recognize that he has aimed at a new style; although there are allusions to the Arab melody-types, a deliberate effort has been made to do justice to the meaning and atmosphere of the poem in an individual way.[15]

I cannot attempt to predict the future of Jewish music. Perhaps the composition you have been hearing now or the style which it inaugurates has a germ of development in it. Will it grow among Oriental Jews only? or will its appeal reach the minds of European composers as well? It would be a strange coincidence if, exactly at the time when Eastern music, generally, is giving way to Western, Jewish music should go the reverse way, and recover independence through a return to the East.

---

15 Here, Mr. Ezra sang Bialik's "Bein nahar prath we-nahar hidekel" to the accompaniment of lute, a psaltery, and a violin.

Musical Examples Recorded by Lachmann and Incorporated in his Radio Lectures "Oriental Music" (Supplement to Appendix III)[1]

Program II: Yemenite Cantillation
1. Exodus: Song of the Sea (D 354)[2]
2. Book of Ester (D 355)
3. Proverbs: "Song of Songs" Mode (D 356)

Program III: Coptic Chant
4. Kyrillus Mass (D382)
5. Basilius Mass (D 391)
6. Gregorius Mass (D 393)

Program IV: Kurdish Jewish Cantillation
7. Exodus: The Ten Commandments (D 413)
8. Judges: The Song of Deborah. "Song of the Sea" Mode (D 409)
9. Book of Jonah – *Yom Kippur* (D 410)
10. A Passage from the Zohar – "*Patach Eliahu ha-Navi*" (D 411)

Program V: Arab Bedouin Songs
11. Rhythmic Epic Song with *Rabāba* (D 451)
12. Free Recitation of a Tale (D 452)

Program VI: Samaritan Cantillation and Secular Song
13. Exodus: Song of the Sea (D 529)
14. Melodic Formulae for: (a) Festivals, (b) Mourning, (c) Miracles (D522)
15. Secular Song in Arabic (D 540)

---

1 I would like to use this opportunity to thank Mr. Shai Drori – restoration and mastering engineer – for producing the attached disc so that the music can be heard despite the background noises, and Mr. Avi Nahmias – head of the sound laboratory of The National Sound Archive – for helping me locate the original examples in "The Lachmann Collection."

2 The numbers in brackets preceded by D are the original numbers in "The Lachmann Collection" of the National Sound Archives in Jerusalem.

Program VII: Yemenite Jewish Wedding Songs – Men
16. Song for the Henna Ceremony of the Bridegroom (D 588)
17. Song for the Shaving Ceremony (D 585)
18. Song for the Signing of the Marriage Contract (D 586)
19. Song in Praise of the Bride (D 587)

Program VIII: Yemenite Jewish Wedding Songs – Women
20–23. A Sequence of Dance Songs in Arabic (D 606; D 607; D 609; D 603)

Program IX: Arab Urban Music – "Preludes" Improvised on the *Ud* (by Ezra Aharon[3]) in Three Different *Maqamat*
24. *hijaz* (D 623)
25. *saba* (D 624)
26. *sika* (D 625)

Program XII: Songs from an Arab Village Wedding in Central Palestine
27. Song for the Bathe Ceremony of the Groom (D 696)
28. "*Ala dal'una – dabke*" – Circle Dance with Singer and *Shabbabah* (D 697)
29. Song for the Arrival of the Groom at the Bride's House (D 698)

Lachmann's Voice
30. D 1 (2)

---

3   Mr. Ezra Aharon was a famous musician in Baghdad prior to his arrival in Palestine.

בעטיפה: הצילום של הצלם פליקס בונפיס
באדיבות המוזיאון הישראלי לצילום,
בגן התעשייה תל-חי. מאוסף המוזיאון

©
כל הזכויות שמורות
להוצאת ספרים ע"ש י"ל מאגנס
האוניברסיטה העברית
ירושלים תשס"ד

אין לשכפל, להעתיק, לצלם, להקליט, לתרגם,
לאחסן במאגר מידע, לשדר או לקלוט
בכל דרך או בכל אמצעי אלקטרוני, אופטי, מכני
או אחר כל חלק שהוא מהחומר שבספר זה.
שימוש מסחרי מכל סוג שהוא בחומר הכלול בספר זה
אסור בהחלט אלא ברשות מפורשת בכתב מהמו"ל.

ISSN 0334–3758

נדפס בישראל
סדר, עימוד, לוחות והדפסה: ארט פלוס, ירושלים

רות כ"ץ

"בעיית לכמן"
פרק עלום במוסיקולוגיה השוואתית

כולל מכתבים והרצאות של רוברט לכמן
שטרם פורסמו

הוצאת ספרים ע"ש י"ל מאגנס, האוניברסיטה העברית, ירושלים

האוניברסיטה העברית בירושלים • הפקולטה למדעי הרוח
המרכז לחקר המוסיקה היהודית
בשיתוף עם בית הספרים הלאומי והאוניברסיטאי

הוועדה האקדמית
יו״ר: משה אידל
יורם בילו, רות הכהן, דון הרן, גלית חזן־רוקם,
יום טוב עסיס, יורם צפריר, אליהו שלייפר
מנהל: אדווין סרוסי

יובל • סדרת מונוגרפיות
יב